SMART TECHNOLOGY FOR AGING, DISABILITY, AND INDEPENDENCE

SMART TECHNOLOGY FOR AGING, DISABILITY, AND INDEPENDENCE
The State of the Science

Editor

WILLIAM C. MANN

WILEY-INTERSCIENCE

A JOHN WILEY & SONS, INC., PUBLICATION

Published by John Wiley & Sons, Inc., Hoboken, New Jersey.
Published simultaneously in Canada.

For general information on our other products and services please contact our Customer
Care Department within the U.S. at 877-762-2974, outside the U.S. at 317-572-3993 or
fax 317-572-4002.

Wiley also publishes its books in a variety of electronic formats. Some content that appears in
print, however, may not be available in electronic format.

Library of Congress Cataloging-in-Publication Data:
Smart technology for aging, disability and independence : the state of the
science / William C. Mann, editor.
    p. cm.
  Includes bibliographical references.
  ISBN-13 978-0-471-69694-0 (cloth)
  ISBN-10 0-471-69694-3 (cloth)
  1. Self-help devices for people with disabilities. 2. Assistive computer
technology. 3. Technology and older people. I. Mann, William C. (William
Charles)
  HV1569.5.S63   2005
  681'.761—dc22   2004027115

10 9 8 7 6 5 4 3 2 1

To my wife, Gwen
And my children, Stephanie and Jennifer
Who provide love and purpose

To my sister
Lynda
For her spirit and strength

CONTENTS

PREFACE   xi

CONTRIBUTORS   xiii

CHAPTER 1   *AGING, DISABILITY, AND INDEPENDENCE: TRENDS AND*
   PERSPECTIVES   **1**

1.1   Introduction   1
1.2   Key Terms: Technology, Aging, Disability, and Independence   1
1.3   Demographics of Aging and Disability   3
1.4   A Model for Viewing Research and Development in Technology, Aging, Disability,
   and Independence   7
1.5   Addressing Impairment (Motor and Movement, Vision, Hearing, and Cognition),
   Pain, and Fatigue   8
1.6   Personal Assistance   12
1.7   Consumer Perspective   13
   References   27

PART 1   *SMART TECHNOLOGY FOR AGING, DISABIITY,*
   AND INDEPENDENCE

CHAPTER 2   *HOME AUTOMATION AND SMART HOMES TO SUPPORT*
   INDEPENDENCE   **33**

2.1   Introduction   33
2.2   Vision of the Near Future: A Day in Mrs. Smith's Smart Home   38
2.3   The Underlying Technology of the Smart House   42
2.4   Overview of the State of the Science in Smart Homes and Smart Home
   Components and Related Issues   48
2.5   Smart House Construction—An Architect's Perspective   56
   References   65

CHAPTER 3   *ROBOTICS*   **67**

3.1   Introduction   67
3.2   Personal and Assistive Robotics   75
3.3   Other Issues Related to Robotics   100
3.4   Summary   105
   References   105

CHAPTER 4   *OTHER DEVICES AND HIGH-TECHNOLOGY SOLUTIONS*   **111**

4.1   Introduction   111
4.2   Smart Technology for People with Vision Impairment   111

4.3 Smart Technology for People with Hearing Impairment 125
4.4 Smart Technology for People with Mobility and Movement Impairments 134
4.5 Devices for Cognitive Impairment 147
4.6 Other Devices 153
4.7 Conclusion 155
    References 156

CHAPTER 5 *TELEHEALTH* 161

5.1 Introduction 161
5.2 State of Science: Today's Telehealth Devices 170
5.3 Caregiver Issues 202
5.4 Legal and Financial Issues 204
5.5 Current Limitations and the Future 210
    References 212

PART II *RELATED ASPECTS OF AGING, DISABILITY, AND INDEPENDENCE*

CHAPTER 6 *BASIC ASSISTIVE TECHNOLOGY* 221

6.1 Introduction 221
6.2 Low-Technology Devices and Impairment 221
6.3 Funding for Assistive Technology in the United States 238
6.4 Resources for Assistive Technology 240
    References 244

CHAPTER 7 *ELDER DRIVERS AND TECHNOLOGY* 247

7.1 Introduction 247
7.2 Elders and Driving 250
7.3 Older Driver Interventions and Technology 259
7.4 Summary 275
    References 276

CHAPTER 8 *TRANSPORTATION AND COMMUNITY MOBILITY* 285

8.1 Introduction 285
8.2 Public Transit and Disability 289
8.3 Pedestrian Infrastructure: Roadway and Access Improvements 299
8.4 Use of Low- and High-Tech Mobility Devices to Increase Community Mobility 301
8.5 Summary 303
    References 304

CHAPTER 9 *HOME MODIFICATIONS AND UNIVERSAL DESIGN* 307

9.1 Introduction 307
9.2 Home Modifications 308
9.3 Universal Design 318

9.4 Other Environmental Considerations **340**
9.5 Long-Term Care Facilities Environment **341**
9.6 Conclusion **345**
     References **345**

CHAPTER 10 *INJURY PREVENTION AND HEALTH PROMOTION* **351**

10.1 Introduction **351**
10.2 Falls **352**
10.3 Medication Errors **357**
10.4 Fire **360**
10.5 Poisoning **363**
10.6 Nutritional Health **367**
10.7 Conclusion **368**
      References **368**

INDEX **373**

PREFACE

This book focuses on strategies for promoting independence and quality of life for people as they age, with a major focus on emerging technologies. We have drawn from the December 2003 *International Conference on Aging, Disability, and Independence*, the professional literature, and product descriptions to provide an overview of today's assistive technology to support independence. We also report on research and development underway for the next generation of assistive technology and smart environments.

This book is the first in a two-volume set. The second book, edited by Dr. Sumi Helal, will provide a more technical discussion of the topic. Our audience for this first less technical book includes health-care providers, older persons who might benefit from the technology, and caregivers of people with disabilities.

The first chapter of this book provides the groundwork by providing definitions of terms, along with a look at the changing demographics in the United States and throughout the world. Chapters 2 through 4 are grouped as Part I: Smart Technology for Aging, Disability, and Independence. In Part I we discuss smart homes, robotics, telehealth, and other devices and high-technology solutions to promote independence. Chapters 5 through 10 form Part II, which includes some focus on technology, but covers other very critical areas in relation to maintaining independence as we age. These areas include use of basic assistive technology, driving, transportation, community mobility, and home modifications and universal design.

The book is edited by William C. Mann, who directs the Rehabilitation Engineering Research Center on Technology for Successful Aging at the University of Florida (UF). Nine UF Rehabilitation Science Ph.D. students participated in writing this book, each authoring or co-authoring chapters. Bradley R. Milton, the architect who designed the UF Gator-Tech Smart House, contributed to Chapter 2 with an architect's perspective on smart houses, and he faced the challenges of designing a smart house that also serves as a research lab.

Sincere appreciation is expressed to the sponsors and participants of the 2003 International Conference on Aging, Disability, and Independence (http://icadi.phhp.ufl.edu/2003/), the consumers who shared their perspective on technology, and those who granted us permission to use their pictures, tables, and figures; we also thank Elena Casson, who provided organizational and editorial assistance with this book.

William C. Mann

CONTRIBUTORS

Patrícia C. Belchior, OT
University of Florida
Ph.D. Program in Rehabilitation Science
PO Box 100164
Gainesville, FL 32610-0164

Roxanna M. Bendixen, MHS, OTR/L
University of Florida
Ph.D. Program in Rehabilitation Science
PO Box 100164
Gainesville, FL 32610-0164

Rick Davenport, MHS, OTR/L
University of Florida
Ph.D. Program in Rehabilitation Science
PO Box 100164
Gainesville, FL 32610-0164

Jessica L. Johnson, M.A., OTR/L
University of Florida
Ph.D. Program in Rehabilitation Science
PO Box 100164
Gainesville, FL 32610-0164

Michael D. Justiss, MOT, OTR/L
University of Florida
Ph.D. Program in Rehabilitation Science
PO Box 100164
Gainesville, FL 32610-0164

Shin-yi Lin, M.S., OT
University of Florida
Ph.D. Program in Rehabilitation Science
PO Box 100164
Gainesville, FL 32610-0164

William C. Mann, PhD
Professor and Chair, Department of Occupational Therapy
Director, Rehabilitation Engineering Research Center on Technology and Aging
University of Florida
PO Box 100164
Gainesville, FL 32610-0164

Dennis P. McCarthy, MEd, OTR/L
University of Florida
Ph.D. Program in Rehabilitation Science
PO Box 100164
Gainesville, FL 32610-0164

Bradley R. Milton, AIA
Partner, RDG Planning & Design
900 Farnam on the Mall
Suite 100
Omaha, Nebraska 68102-5089

Cristina Posse, MHS, OT
University of Florida
Ph.D. Program in Rehabilitation Science
PO Box 100164
Gainesville, FL 32610-0164

Megan R. Witte, OTR/L
University of Florida
Ph.D. Program in Rehabilitation Science
PO Box 100164
Gainesville, FL 32610-0164

CHAPTER 1

AGING, DISABILITY, AND INDEPENDENCE: TRENDS AND PERSPECTIVES

William C. Mann

1.1 INTRODUCTION

This book focuses on strategies for promoting independence and quality of life for people as they age, with a major focus on emerging technologies. We have drawn from the December 2003 International Conference on Aging, Disability, and Independence (ICADI), the professional literature, and product descriptions to provide an overview of the state of today's assistive devices to support independence. We also provide a glimpse into research and development of the next generation of assistive devices.

We begin this chapter with definitions of the key terms: technology, aging, disability, and independence. This is followed by a compelling argument for the need to promote independence for people as they age. We discuss population trends that clearly demonstrate the increasing numbers of people who are considered old, along with their independence-related needs. We follow this with a model for viewing disability and independence, and we discuss each of the types of impairment that can be addressed with compensatory strategies such as assistive technology and environmental interventions. We also discuss personal assistance, along with its relationship to assistive technology. In developing technology and modifying the environment, those who know best about what is most appropriate are the intended users: the "consumers." We conclude this chapter with a major section on "consumer perspective."

1.2 KEY TERMS: TECHNOLOGY, AGING, DISABILITY, AND INDEPENDENCE

Technology   In this book we discuss technology that can support people as they age. The terms *assistive device, assistive technology*, and *assistive technology device* are all used interchangeably. The term *assistive technology device* was first defined in federal legislation in the United States in the Technology-Related Assistance for Individuals with Disabilities Act of 1988 as *any item, piece of equipment, or product system—whether acquired commercially, modified, or customized—that is used to increase, maintain, or improve functional capabilities or individuals with disabilities.*[1]

Some approaches that can support people as they age relate more to fixed aspects of our built environment. In a sense this is a form of technology, but we use the term *environmental interventions* to refer to home modifications, from simple removal of throw rugs to adding a ramp or lift to a home. Environmental interventions also include modifications in yards, driveways, sidewalks, and (in apartment buildings) elevators. In the community, environmental interventions include adaptations in such places as public transportation systems, stores, places of worship, and theaters. To maintain independence, elders require an approach that considers the built environment as well as assistive devices.

Aging There are many definitions for "the elderly" or "older persons." Some are tied to eligibility requirements for programs like Social Security. Some definitions include people as young as age 50 (membership in the American Association of Retired Persons), while others reach up to age 70 (past mandatory retirement age for professors in the United States). Most definitions suggest age 60 or 65 as the entry point for becoming an "older person." In this book, we cite studies that most often use age 65 as the entry point for becoming an "elder" or "older person." In much of our own research, also reported in this book, we have used age 60 as the youngest age for inclusion criteria for study participants.

Disability Disability has been defined in several laws in the United States. The Social Security Administration defines disability in terms of long-term inability to work. The American with Disabilities Act states that a person with a disability is an individual who has a physical or mental impairment that substantially limits one or more major life activities; has a record of such an impairment; or is regarded as having such an impairment. Note that the terms impairment and disability become interchangeable in this definition. Later in this chapter, we discuss a model for viewing disease, impairment, and disability. In this model, and as we use the term in this book, disability refers to the inability to perform tasks and maintain life roles. An older person with impairments may not be disabled if he or she can find ways to compensate for the impairment, such as the use of technology and environmental interventions. Frailty is another term often used in discussing certain groups of older people, especially the very old. While often used but not clearly defined in the past, more recently, the term has been discussed in the medical literature.[2]

Independence Independence is an important concept for what we hope to accomplish in our use of technology and environmental interventions. We define independence as the ability to complete basic daily tasks without personal assistance. Basic daily tasks are often divided into two groups: activities of daily living (ADLs) (eating, grooming, dressing, toileting, walking, and bathing) and instrumental activities of daily living (IADLs) (managing one's house, managing one's money, shopping, getting to places outside the home, using a telephone). We add to ADLs and IADLs one more important set of activities for older persons: leisure activities. One's perception of their quality of life is related to their independence in ADLs, IADLs, and leisure.

1.3   DEMOGRAPHICS OF AGING AND DISABILITY

Each year there are more older people living in the world, and the percentage of total population represented by older people is increasing. Table 1.1 illustrates the percentage of people over age 65 in the world's 25 oldest countries in the year 2000. Italy ranks first, with 18.1% of its population represented by people over age 65. A similar analysis by continent, breaking down the older population into those over 65, over 75, and over 80 years of age, is presented in Table 1.2. The oldest-old—those over age 80—have the highest rate of dependency in basic everyday tasks.

TABLE 1.1   Percentage of Population over age 65 in 25 Oldest Countries

Country	Percent over 65
Italy	18.1
Greece	17.3
Sweden	17.3
Japan	17.0
Spain	16.9
Belgium	16.8
Bulgaria	16.5
Germany	16.2
France	16.0
United Kingdom	15.7
Portugal	15.4
Austria	15.4
Norway	15.2
Switzerland	15.1
Croatia	15.0
Latvia	15.0
Finland	14.9
Denmark	14.9
Serbia	14.8
Hungary	14.6
Estonia	14.5
Slovenia	14.1
Luxembourg	14.0
Ukraine	13.9
Czech Republic	13.9

Source: U.S. Census Bureau, 2000.

TABLE 1.2 Percent of Population over 65, 75, and 80 years of age in 2000 to 2030

Region	Year	65 years and over	75 years and over	80 years and over
Europe	2000	15.5	6.6	3.3
	2015	18.7	8.8	5.2
	2030	24.3	11.8	7.1
North America	2000	12.6	6.0	3.3
	2015	14.9	6.4	3.9
	2030	20.3	9.4	5.4
Oceania	2000	10.2	4.4	2.3
	2015	12.4	5.2	3.1
	2030	16.3	7.5	4.4
Asia	2000	6.0	1.9	0.8
	2015	7.8	2.8	1.4
	2030	12.0	4.6	2.2
Latin America / Caribbean	2000	5.5	1.9	0.9
	2015	7.5	2.8	1.5
	2030	11.6	4.6	2.4
Near East / North Africa	2000	4.3	1.4	0.6
	2015	5.3	1.9	0.9
	2030	8.1	2.8	1.3
Sub-Saharan Africa	2000	2.9	0.8	0.3
	2015	3.2	1.0	0.4
	2030	3.7	1.3	0.6

Source: U.S. Census Bureau, 2000a.

Figure 1.1 illustrates that 31.2% of those over age 80, and 49.5% of those over age 85 require assistance with everyday activities.

The Administration on Aging of the United States Department of Health and Human Services published a report based on Census 2000 data.[3] In 2000, approximately one out of eight people in the United States were over age 65, about 12.4% of the population. This was an increase of almost 4 million older Americans in one decade. This represents a 12% increase in older Americans. Over the next 20 years, the rate of increase will escalate to 34%, as the baby boomers enter the ranks of seniors. Looking back to 1900, the percentage of the population represented by older Americans has tripled, while the actual number has increased from 3.1 million to over 35 million—more than a tenfold increase.

It is also important to note that the older population as a group is getting older. People are living longer. In 2000, U.S. life expectancy at age 65 was 84.2 years for females and 81.3 years for males. While the 65- to 74-year-old group increased 8 times over the past 100 years, the 75- to 84-year-old group increased 16 times, and those over age 85 increased 34 times. And for those living to age 100, there were 50,545 in 2000, a 35% increase just in one decade: In 1990 there were 37,306

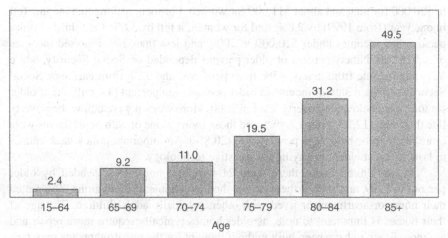

Figure 1.1 Percent of people needing help with everyday activities by age (1991).

Americans over age 100. This trend is projected to continue, with the oldest-old representing the fastest growing segment of our population. This is very relevant for our work in finding ways to promote independence, as it is the oldest-old who have the most difficulty in completing basic daily tasks independently.

The ratio of the number of older women to older men is also increasing. In 2000, there were 1.43 women for every man over age 65. However, for people over age 85, there were 2.45 women for every man. This is directly relevant to the need for finding ways to assist older people in maintaining independence, as women have higher rates of disability than men. With increasing numbers of older people and with more women than men, there will be many more people requiring assistance with basic daily tasks of living.

The number of older people living alone is also increasing. In 2000, approximately 30% of all noninstitutionalized elders lived alone, 40% of older women and 17% of older men. As age advances, the percentage of the age group living alone increases. Half of women over age 75 live alone. Households with more than one person can share the daily tasks of living, and each person in the household can handle those tasks that meet their abilities. When only one person is living in a household, sharing tasks is not possible. This is another compelling reason to develop technologies to assist people in maintaining independence as they age.

The percentage of older Americans living in nursing homes was 4.5% in 2000, representing 1.56 million people. The percentage of the older population living in nursing homes rises sharply with age: from 1.1% of those age 65–74, to 18.2% of those over age 85. Most people prefer to live at home, and the cost of nursing home care is very high. In 2004 in the United States, the cost of a day in a nursing home was on average approximately $115.00 per day, or $42,000 per year.[4] Again, this underlines the need to develop approaches to helping older persons maintain independent living in their homes.

Income of older persons is declining in the United States, and this is similar to income trends in most other countries. Overall in 2000, median income was close to $20,000 for men and about $11,000 for women. For men, real median income fell in one year (from 1999) by 2.8%; and for women, it fell by 3.6%. One-third of older persons had incomes under $10,000 in 2000, and less than 25% reported incomes over $25,000. Ninety percent of older persons depended on Social Security, while 62% had income from assets, 43% from pensions, and 22% from earnings. Social Security provided 38% of income of older persons. Ten percent (3.4 million) of older persons were below the poverty level in 2000. More women were below the poverty line than men (12.2% versus 7.5%), and those living alone or with nonrelatives were more likely to be below the poverty line (20.8%). An important policy issue relates to how to assist elders in paying for assistive technology.

In the United States there were 21.4 million households headed by older persons in 1999, and 80% of these owned their own home; the remaining 20% rented their home or apartment or lived with others, typically adult children. The age of their homes is important to note, as older homes typically require more repair and are more likely to have been built without thought for the impairments we may face as we age. Half of all homes were built before 1962.

About 4.2 million older Americans (12.8% of the older population) worked in 2000. Of these, 2.4 million were men (17.5% of older men) and 1.8 were women (9.4% of older women). This is a sharp decrease from 1900, when approximately 67% of older men were employed.

As we age, we face age-associated diseases and conditions as well as general decline in function because of the aging process itself. While this book focuses on independence, we recognize that disability is related to disease and trauma. Rather than focusing on specific diseases or trauma, we address applications of technology that can help a person maintain independence even with severe, potentially disabling chronic conditions. In the next section of this chapter we review a model for viewing technology interventions, developed by the National Center on Medical Rehabilitation Research (NCMRR) of the National Institutes on Health (NIH). This is followed by a more detailed discussion of four major impairment categories: movement, vision, hearing, and cognition. We also address fatigue and pain, common symptoms experienced by older persons and which influence independence.

Figure 1.1 illustrates that the older we are, the more likely we are to need help with basic daily tasks: Almost half of those over 85 require assistance with at least one basic activity of daily living. Twenty-six percent of people over age 65 self-reported their health as fair or poor in 1999. Most people over 65 have one or more chronic conditions that can influence ability to engage in activities. The chronic conditions with the highest prevalence include arthritis (49% of older persons have arthritis), hypertension (36%); hearing impairment (30%), heart disease (27%); cataracts (17%), and orthopedic conditions (18%). Older people have more days of hospitalization than younger people (1.6 days on average versus 0.4 days). Older persons also have more contacts with doctors than younger persons, an average of 6.8 contacts in a year versus 3.5 for younger persons. Health costs represent a significant proportion of older persons' out-of-pocket expenditures, an average of 11% (versus an average for the total population of 5%).

1.4 A MODEL FOR VIEWING RESEARCH AND DEVELOPMENT IN TECHNOLOGY, AGING, DISABILITY, AND INDEPENDENCE

The NCMRR defines medical rehabilitation as *the study of mechanisms, modalities, and devices that improve, restore, or replace lost, underdeveloped, or deteriorating function.*[5] The NCMRR model includes five terms that help define the level of research and development or of clinical intervention: (1) pathophysiology, (2) impairment, (3) functional limitation, (4) disability, and (5) societal limitations (Figure 1.2). These terms are discussed below.

Pathophysiology refers to aberrations in normal physiological processes within our bodies, and research at this level is on cellular structure and events following disease, injury, or genetic abnormality. Most research and development at this level is focused on cure and recovery processes, rather than on compensatory applications and ways of maintaining independence as we age.

Impairment relates to the organ (e.g., eyes) or organ system (e.g., cardiovascular) level. We use the categories of hearing, vision, cognitive, and motor and movement impairment throughout this book.

Functional limitation is defined as *restriction or lack of ability to perform an action in the manner or within the range consistent with the purpose of an organ or organ system.* We use the term *impairment* more often than *functional limitation*, as we have established our compensatory intervention model based on organ/organ system rather than on specific action.

Disability is defined as *a limitation in performing tasks, activities, and roles to levels expected within physical and social contexts.* A person may have difficulty dressing (task), but this could be due to cognitive impairment, vision impairment, or motor impairment, each of which would require a different compensatory strategy. Technology directed at impairment is also likely to reduce disability. If a person uses a hearing aid, it is not simply to improve hearing, but to provide the mechanism for participating in conversations, for attending meetings, and for listening to music.

Pathophysiology—Diseases/Trauma—Cellular Level

Impairment—Organ Level

Functional Limitation—Action Level (moving, seeing, hearing)

Disability—Task-Role Level

Societal Limitations—Barriers resultant from attitudes and policy

---

Figure 1.2 Model for viewing research and development and interventions in technology and aging, based on terminology from NCMRR.

Societal limitations is the highest level in the NCMRR model, and it refers to barriers resultant from social policy or general societal attitudes. Technology is less often developed to address societal limitations, although it can be employed to do so. All televisions sold in the United States are now required to include a technology that provides closed captioning for people who are hard of hearing or deaf. Alternatively, access to technology applications can be limited by our policy (laws) and attitudes. In the United States, reimbursement under Medicare, Medicaid, and private insurance is very limited for many types of technology that could promote independence, health, and quality of life, while several European countries and Australia have much more liberal policies regarding provision of assistive technologies. Societal attitudes regarding aging also can encourage a more dependent status for older persons.

We have selected the National Institutes of Health NCMRR Model for organizing the approaches toward promoting independence that are addressed in this book. An alternate model is represented by the World Health Organization's *International Classification of Functioning, Disability, and Health* (ICF) (http://www.who.int/icf/icftemplate.cfm). The NIH Model is very similar to the earlier World Health Organization's *International Classification of Impairment, Disability and Handicap*. The latest ICF Model has removed many of the more negative terms, and it presents the major concepts with positive terms: (a) functioning versus impairment and (b) social impairment and environment versus handicap. The domains of the ICF are health domains and health-related domains. *These domains are described from the perspective of the body, the individual, and society in two basic lists: (1) Body Functions and Structures and (2) Activities and Participation. As a classification, ICF systematically groups different domains for a person in a given health condition (e.g., what a person with a disease or disorder does do or can do). Functioning is an umbrella term encompassing all body functions, activities, and participation; similarly, disability serves as an umbrella term for impairments, activity limitations, or participation restrictions. ICF also lists environmental factors that interact with all these constructs. In this way, it enables the user to record useful profiles of individuals.*[6] The ICF Model is meant to serve as a unifying language for functional status, health, disability, social impairment, and environment factors.

1.5 ADDRESSING IMPAIRMENT (MOTOR AND MOVEMENT, VISION, HEARING, AND COGNITION), PAIN, AND FATIQUE

Motor and Movement Impairment

Movement involves the musculoskeletal system and the central and peripheral nervous systems. We move our arms, do fine tasks with our hands, walk, bend, and turn our heads. These movements are used in getting to places and completing tasks. Movement impairment can result from injury or diseases to the musculoskeletal system (e.g., hip fracture, arthritis) and can make it difficult or impossible to use our hands, walk, or move our trunk and neck. Table 1.3 highlights the prevalence of specific types of movement difficulties. Clearly, as we get very old (over 85 in Table 1.3), a much larger proportion of people have difficulty with basic movements and everyday tasks.

Arrangement   There are many assistive devices that can compensate for movement impairment, most largely mechanical in form such as canes, walkers, and wheelchairs. More recently there have been advances in wheelchairs, with several teams developing what are called "smart wheelchairs," designed to prevent collisions: One follows a track laid along the floor, while another uses infrared sensors to detect obstacles at different distances. We discuss these in some detail in Chapter 4.

TABLE 1.3   Functional Limitations of Persons 65 Years and Over by Age and Type of Living

Functional Limitation	Persons 65 years and over	65 to 74 years	75 to 84 years	85 years and over	Living alone	Living with others
Total 65 years and over:	30,748	18,397	9,920	2,430	9,634	21,214
Percent with difficulty[a]						
Walking	14.3	9.2	18.8	34.9	18.1	12.6
Getting outside	15.9	8.7	22.3	44.8	20.7	13.8
Bathing or showering	9.4	5.6	11.3	30.6	11.2	8.7
Transferring[b]	9.0	5.9	11.6	21.9	10.8	8.2
Dressing	3.9	3.8	7.0	16.1	6.3	5.6
Using toilet	2.6	2.0	5.7	14.2	4.8	3.9
Eating	2.1	1.3	3.1	4.1	2.2	2.0
Preparing meals	8.6	4.5	11.7	27.6	9.1	8.4
Managing money	7.1	2.8	10.3	26.2	8.4	6.5
Using the telephone	7.1	3.8	9.7	21.4	7.1	7.1
Doing light housework	11.4	6.6	15.5	30.8	13.6	10.4
Percent of total receiving help[c]						
Walking	5.9	3.3	8.2	16.8	4.9	6.4
Getting outside	13.2	6.3	18.8	42.3	17.2	11.4
Bathing or showering	5.9	3.3	7.0	20.9	5.0	6.3
Transferring[b]	3.9	2.5	4.8	11.0	2.7	4.5
Dressing	3.9	2.3	5.0	11.1	2.7	4.4
Using toilet	2.6	1.3	3.9	7.8	1.9	2.9
Eating	1.1	0.5	1.9	2.5	0.8	1.2
Preparing meals	7.5	3.6	10.5	25.4	7.0	7.8
Managing money	6.4	2.5	9.1	24.6	7.4	5.9
Doing light housework	8.9	4.8	12.1	27.3	9.6	8.7

[a] Difficulty due to a physical or mental health condition.
[b] Getting in or out of a bed or chair.
[c] Receiving help due to a physical or mental health condition with the specified difficulty.

Source: U.S. Bureau of the Census. 1991 Survey of Income and Program Participation. Functional Limitations and Disability File, wave 3, unpublished tabulations.

At the "societal limitations level," mobility has been enhanced through curb cuts where streets meet sidewalks, as well as through ramps and lifts on the outside and inside of public buildings. In the United States, legislation such as the Architectural Barriers Act (1968) and the Americans with Disabilities Act (1990) ensure that people with disabilities have access to public buildings.

Research and development in the area of technology, aging, and independence for people with motor and movement impairment will address better ways to move about, as well as assistance with tasks that require our arms and hands. More development of helpful, personal robotic devices is needed—robotic devices that can complete tasks, fetch objects, and assist in walking (sensing fatigue and unsteadiness and providing more support or the opportunity to sit and rest).

Vision Impairment

Most elders with vision impairment are not totally blind, but rather have partial or low vision. Today eye disease is being diagnosed and treated much earlier than in the past, and this has led to a greater proportion of older persons with low vision. Approximately 8.6% of Americans over age 18 experience problems with vision, even with corrective measures. Older persons have a much higher incidence. By 2020, there will be approximately 54 million blind persons over age 60 worldwide. The severity of vision loss and the resulting limitations vary with age of onset, support systems available, and coping strategies.

There are a number of low-technology products to assist people with vision impairment, eyeglasses being the most common. Other devices include magnifiers, larger-size products (such as large clocks, thermostats, television remote controls, and game boards), and alerting devices such as the EZ Fill, which makes it possible for a visually impaired person to add hot or cold liquid to a container—a buzzer sounds to alert the user when the liquid is poured to 1-inch from the top. There are a number of talking products—such as talking thermometers, watches, and clocks. These products are discussed in more detail in Chapter 9.

There also are a number of more high-tech assistive products for people with vision impairment. These include video magnifiers, such as (1) the pocket-sized Pico http://www.telesensory.com/products2-1-16.html, which offers full color and negative modes with magnification up to 5×, and (2) the somewhat larger but still portable MiniViewer, which provides (a) magnification from 5× to 15× in both color and black-on-white or (b) inverse white-on-black, which is easier for some people with vision impairment to read. Desk-sized electronic magnifiers include such products as the Aladan Pro 75 and the Smartview 1000. There is a significant level of research and development in high-technology devices for people with low vision and people who are blind. We cover this in Chapter 4.

At the "societal limitations" level in the NCMRR model, we have seen legislation in the United States that requires that audible traffic signals, where appropriate, be included in new transportation plans and projects [Sec. 1202(g)(2)].[7] Accessible pedestrian signals (APS) provide audible and/or vibrotactile information coinciding with visual pedestrian signals to inform blind pedestrians when the WALK interval begins.

Hearing Impairment   In the United States, 33% of people over age 65 have hearing impairment, and this will increase, because there are more people age 45 to 64 with hearing loss than those 65 and older. Loss of hearing is so gradual that many older persons accept the loss as a normal process of aging and do not seek assistance. Hearing loss impacts negatively on communication and can result in isolation and depression. Hearing loss can also impact on safety and health in other ways as well, such as failing to hear a fire alarm or not being able to clearly understand a pharmacist's directions for taking medications.

Low-tech assistive devices for hearing loss include vibrating alarm clocks and smoke detectors, flashing-light doorbells, and a variety of sound amplification products. Some of the sound amplification products could be considered high tech, such as advanced assistive listening devices, which like hearing aids can be digitally adjusted for individual users. In the high-tech realm, development of smart phones with voice-to-text translation could provide a universal communication tool for people who are hard of hearing or deaf. Low-tech hearing devices are discussed in more detail in Chapter 9, and high-tech devices are covered in Chapter 10.

Cognitive Impairment   Approximately 10% of people over age 65 have cognitive impairments that impact on their ability to complete everyday tasks independently. Alzheimer's disease results in a progressive decline in cognitive performance, and it is the most common cause of significant cognitive impairment in people over 65. Stroke is the second most frequently occurring cause of cognitive impairment. With impaired cognitive function, a person may experience confusion, disorientation, limited attention, memory impairment, and decreased ability for learning. A person's activities of daily living are influenced by impaired cognition. A person with Alzheimer's disease will decline in ability to meet safety, self-care, household, leisure, social interaction, and vocational needs. Eventually, the person will lose the ability to perform basic activities of daily living, including eating, dressing, toileting, grooming, bathing, and locomotion.

An emerging area of research is focused on assisting persons with cognitive impairment in their daily activities through the use of computerized devices. In some cases, devices being developed are in the form of a prompting system to guide elders with cognitive impairment through basic daily tasks. Related studies suggest that even individuals with severe cognitive impairment might benefit from a prompting device/system. As a group, people with cognitive impairment have traditionally used the fewest number of assistive devices—even if they had other types of impairments. We must develop smart devices and smart systems that make it easier for a person with a cognitive impairment to participate in even the most basic daily tasks. Development of robotic assistants for people with cognitive impairment should also be a goal. We address these devices and systems in the following chapters.

Pain   Pain is a very common experience of older adults: Close to 85% of elders have conditions such as arthritis, peripheral vascular disease, and degenerative neurological conditions that can cause pain.[8] The percentage of elders who actually experience pain has been estimated to be in a range between 2% and 40% of the population.[9] Location of pain varies, but one study found that headaches are most common, impacting 78% of all people in the United States within one year; back-ache ranks second, with 56% of people impacted, followed by muscle pain 53%, joint pain 51%, and stomach pain 46%.[10] The percentage of people experiencing pain increases with age. Trauma from accidents, especially those that result in fractures, is another major cause of pain.[11] Pain is most commonly diagnosed through self-report.[12]

Approximately 18% of older people in the United States take medication for pain, with more than half taking it for over 6 months.[13] Typically, a medication intervention is begun with acetaminophen; if this does not work, nonsteroidal anti-inflammatory drugs are prescribed. Pain, especially joint pain, appears also to be a contributor to disability.[14] Pain also appears to be associated with late-life depression,[15] which in turn can impact functional status. Pain may be difficult to diagnose for a person with cognitive impairment, if they are not able to communicate their experience with pain. In these cases, one must rely on facial expressions, alterations of movement, and reports by others who are close to the elder. Development of technology to detect pain in nonverbal cognitively impaired elders would be a major advance.

Fatigue   Fatigue can impact independence, making it difficult or impossible to get to places beyond the home, to participate in favored leisure activities, and to complete ADLs. Fatigue is a common symptom of many diseases. For people with cancer, fatigue can be a major activity-limiting factor. A recent study demonstrated an association between fatigue and pain, mood, and sleep, with pain being the most highly associated. In this study, pain accounted for the largest amount of variance in fatigue, but mood modified this relationship. The authors stressed the importance of assessing pain when someone reports fatigue.[16]

1.6   PERSONAL ASSISTANCE

In varying degrees, we all rely on others for many things. However, when it becomes difficult or impossible for us to independently complete ADLs and/or IADLs, either a technology intervention is needed or personal assistance is required—often it is a combination of both. Our basic assumption is that it is best to maximize independence through technology and environmental interventions, recognizing that some degree of personal assistance may also be required. As a person's abilities decline, then both the technology and the amount of personal assistance must be adjusted.

Many older persons rely on their spouse for personal assistance. Often they may both have impairments, but have complementary abilities that allow them to be "independent couples." Others rely on adult children, other family, friends, and neighbors. We refer to these groups as "informal caregivers." When assistance from informal caregivers is insufficient, formal, paid caregivers are needed.

When a spouse or adult child provides caregiving for an older person, they may themselves be older and facing impairments. Assistive devices and home modifications that promote independence can assist both the elder with a disability and the caregiver. Assistive devices, such as lifts, may be essential for tasks that require strength or endurance beyond the capability of the caregiver.

1.7 CONSUMER PERSPECTIVE

Consumer Perceptive: The AARP Report

The ICADI Consumer Perspective Track featured a keynote presentation by Dr. John C. Rother of the American Association of Retired Persons (AARP). Dr. Rother summarized the AARP recently published report, *Beyond 50: A Report to the Nation on Independent Living and Disability*, which drew heavily on the views of older persons themselves. Key findings from this study are presented in this section. The report provides new analyses of the federally sponsored Medical Expenditure Panel Survey and the National Long-Term Care Surveys and an AARP survey conducted by Harris Interactive. This section is drawn from the Executive Summary of this AARP report.[17]

(1) Persons 50 and older with disabilities, particularly those age 50–64, strongly prefer independent living in their own homes to other alternatives. They also want more direct control over what long-term supportive services they receive and when they receive them.

Loss of independence and loss of mobility are what people with disabilities 50 and older say they fear the most as they look to the future. They also say having more control over decisions about the services and help they receive would cause a major improvement in their current lives. For example, a large majority of people with disabilities would prefer to manage any publicly funded in-home services themselves, rather than have an agency do so. In addition, a majority would prefer cash payments for such home care services over services provided directly by agencies.

(2) Many persons with disabilities, especially those with severe disabilities, have unmet needs for long-term supportive services and assistive equipment in their homes and communities. Some of these needs would be relatively simple to meet; others, such as providing more personal assistance services, would require significant resources and our collective will.

Only about half of persons 50 and older with disabilities report receiving any regular help with daily activities from one or more people. The vast majority of such help is the unpaid assistance of family or other informal caregivers. In addition, only one out of three uses any community-based service. Because there is no organized "system" for delivering services, many individuals do not know about sources of support or how to find them, or if they are eligible for any publicly funded services.

Our data indicate there are high levels of unmet need among persons 50 and older with disabilities:

* *Almost one-quarter report needing more help than they receive now with basic daily activities, such as bathing, cooking, or shopping.*
* *One-half said they were not able to do something they needed or wanted to do in the past month because of their disability. These needs were very basic, such as doing household chores, getting some exercise, or getting out of the house.*

- *More than one-third of homeowners would like to make home modifications that would make their lives easier, such as installing grab bars in the bathroom, but have not done so, largely because of cost.*

(3) On average, people with disabilities 50 and older give their community a grade of B–/C+ as a place to live for people with disabilities. While some community features receive good marks, others are rated poorly by persons with disabilities, particularly public transportation. In addition, many older residents of federally subsidized housing are at risk of needing more supportive housing environments with services.

Barely one-third of respondents currently give their communities a "B" or higher rating for having dependable and accessible public transportation. Getting safely to places they want to go is the second most important concern persons with disabilities have about their communities. Among persons 65 and older with disabilities, the perception that crime is a serious problem in their neighborhoods nearly doubled, from 4.5 percent to 8.2 percent between 1984 and 1999.

Residents in federally subsidized housing for older persons share many of the characteristics of those at high risk of needing long-term supportive services. Subsidized housing residents are overwhelmingly female, report more disabilities than older persons who do not live in subsidized housing, and are less likely to have someone to whom they can turn if they become sick or disabled.

(4) Family support remains strong, but the impact of such trends as greater longevity, more women in the labor force, and greater geographic dispersion is now hitting home. Either in person or "at a distance," families are finding themselves with new roles as caregivers to aging parents, spouses or siblings, aging children with developmental disabilities, and other relatives and friends. Caregivers age 50 and older often experience considerable stress as a result of their caregiving roles.

Strong social support from families and friends can protect against functional decline and help individuals cope with functional decline if it occurs. While contact between persons 65 and older with disabilities and their families and friends remains strong, it has declined since the mid-1980s.

Larger social trends are affecting the composition of families and their roles as caregivers, including the growing number of women in the workforce who must juggle work and caregiving responsibilities. Among 50- to 64-year-old caregivers, 60 percent are working full- or part-time. In addition, significant economic sacrifices during peak earning years are common among caregivers 50 and older who have been in the workforce.

Parents caring for aging children with cognitive and developmental disabilities represent a growing group in the older caregiver population. This trend reflects the emergence of two-generation families in which parents among the older or oldest age groups are caring for children who are in their 50s and 60s.

A preference for family assistance for help with everyday tasks is even stronger among persons 50 and older with disabilities than among persons 50 and older in the general population. This preference declines somewhat when 24-hour care is needed.

(5) Inadequate health insurance is at the top of the list of problems experienced by persons with disabilities 50 and older, including those with Medicare coverage. In addition to gaps in coverage, such as the lack of coverage for prescription drugs, problems range from inappropriate care for chronic conditions to lack of coordination between medical care and long-term supportive services for persons with disabilities.

People with disabilities say better medical insurance is the number one change that would be a major improvement in their lives. In addition, one out of three persons with disabilities reports specific needs, such as for particular therapies or equipment, not covered by health insurance. Problems include delivery as well as coverage issues: The overlap between chronic conditions and disabilities increases with advancing age, but little coordination exists between medical care and long-term supportive services. Finally, the trends concerning access to and satisfaction with health care among people 50 and older with disabilities over the last four years are in a negative direction. Concerns about recent trends extend to programs that have historically played a positive role in the health care of people with disabilities. Persons 50–64 with disabilities rely much more heavily on Medicaid than do those without disabilities, but Medicaid budgets are being cut in many states due to budget crises.

(6) Despite some improvements, the quality of long-term supportive services is a persistent problem in all settings. A focus on consumers' quality of life is rare. In addition, there is an unprecedented shortage of the frontline workers needed to provide long-term supportive services to persons with disabilities, such as personal care attendants and nursing assistants.

While the quality of care in nursing homes has generally improved with the passage of the Nursing Home Reform Act in 1987, problems with quality of care and quality of life persist. Two-thirds of persons 50 and older with firsthand experience with nursing homes believe the government is not doing enough to enforce quality standards. Low staffing levels lead to poor care in nursing homes. According to a recent report sponsored by the Centers for Medicare and Medicaid Services, 91 percent of nursing homes do not provide the minimum number of hours of care by certified nurse assistants needed per resident per day to avoid serious quality-of-care problems.

Difficulty in recruiting and retaining direct service staff, such as nursing assistants and personal care attendants, is growing. According to some estimates, the need for these workers will double over the next decade. Unmet need for registered nurses is also increasing. Reports of quality problems also continue in assisted living facilities, despite efforts to support residents' privacy, choice, and independence. Efforts to promote quality in supportive housing other than assisted living have been sporadic at best.

(7) The costs of long-term supportive services, which individuals typically need at the time their income is most limited, are often unaffordable to individuals with disabilities and their families.

The need for long-term supportive services can be financially catastrophic to individuals with disabilities and their families, even those with substantial income and resources. A recent study estimated that only 27 percent of older persons have sufficient income and assets to be able to withstand a long-term care "shock" totaling $150,000 over three years without impoverishing themselves. Lower- and middle-income Americans with disabilities often find that their options are limited and out-of-pocket costs are burdensome. In the AARP/Harris Interactive survey, persons 50 and older with disabilities with incomes "in the middle" were the income group most likely to say that having a way to pay for long-term supportive services (such as help with bathing or shopping) and equipment would be a major improvement in their lives.

The high costs of a long-term disability remain largely uninsured. Public programs such as Medicaid pay only after individuals have spent down their income and exhausted their assets. Private health and long-term care insurance account for only 11 percent of total long-term care expenditures in the United States. Disability income insurance policies aimed at replacing lost wages usually end by age 65 or earlier.

Long-term care is the single largest component of direct health-related out-of-pocket spending by Medicare beneficiaries, followed by spending on prescription drugs. Moreover, the indirect costs of providing long-term supportive services in the home, borne by unpaid family members and friends of persons with disabilities, are immeasurable.

Consumer Perspectives on Assistive Technology: Low-Technology Devices

The most important factor in providing assistive technology and home modifications for elders is the perspective of the person who will receive these interventions. Elders need to be informed fully about their disability in order to participate in the selection of the most appropriate devices. Service providers need to consider the priorities of elders: What do they want to be doing, and do they really want or feel the need for recommended devices? Have they been fully informed about options for different types of devices? Older people represent a very heterogeneous population, and their use of assistive technology varies in large part based on their perception of need, their interests, the impairments they face, their health, and their social supports.

The National Institute on Disability and Rehabilitation Research (NIDRR) has supported a Rehabilitation Engineering Research Center (RERC) focused on Aging and Disability since 1991. A 10-year (1991–2001) longitudinal study of the RERC-Aging, called the Consumer Assessments Study, has provided an analysis of the use of, and need for, assistive devices and environmental interventions by older persons with disabilities. This study followed a sample of 1103 elders, using interviews and observations in their homes and neighborhoods in western New York and northern Florida. Information gathered included:

- *Basic demographic information* such as age, education, and housing
- *Health status* including number and types of diseases present, use of medications, and use of hospitals and physicians
- *Functional status* including ability to complete activities of daily living (such as bathing) and instrumental activities of daily living (such as shopping for groceries)
- *Psychosocial dimensions* including mental status, depression, self-esteem, and sense of responsibility
- *Social resources* assistance available and caregiver needs
- *Current use of assistive devices* including satisfaction and problems with devices, as well as and ideas for new devices

This section draws on the published reports from the Consumer Assessments study, combining a focus on both assistive technology and environmental interventions.

One of the questions asked by the RERC-Aging Consumer Assessments Study related to activities they could no longer do but they would like to be doing. This question sought to determine if "missed" activities might be possible with an appro-

TABLE 1.4 Activities Most Missed by Elders with Disabilities

Activities	Percent of respondents missing the activity
Doing, watching sports	22%
Driving	18%
Walking	17%
Gardening/housework	15%
Socializing	15%
Traveling	7%
Shopping	6%
Art: Painting, sculpting	6%

priate assistive device.[18] Table 1.4 categorizes and ranks the consumer responses to this question. The most missed activities are primarily leisure activities. These activities reflect one aspect of the "consumer perspective"—what is important to the person who might use an assistive device. There are a large number of assistive devices to assist elders with many of the leisure activities they miss. More are being developed.

A major component of the Consumer Assessments Study (CAS) was to explore the consumer perspective on current use of their assistive devices, including their level of satisfaction and problems they were having with their devices.[19] The CAS found that older people owned a mean of 13 devices. They reported using a very high number (mean of 12) and high percentage (mean of 91%) of the devices they own. Overall, satisfaction with devices used was high at 89%. However, while overall satisfaction was high, satisfaction rate varied significantly among different device types. People with arthritis are satisfied with 89% of the devices they own,[20] people with hearing impairments are satisfied with 70% of the devices they own,[21] and people with cognitive impairments are satisfied with 67% of the devices they own.[22]

The CAS also explored problems elders reported with their assistive devices. Table 1.5 is a simple ranking of devices by number of problems reported, which suggests that there is a lower degree of satisfaction and more problems with canes as a device type than with any other assistive device. However, with the exception of eyeglasses, there are more canes than any other type of assistive device. Table 1.6 is also a ranking of devices, but is based on a ratio of number of device problems to total number of devices reported in use. In Table 1.6, canes drop from the number one rank, while hearing aids move up to be ranked as the most problematic assistive device relative to number of users.

We will explore consumer perspectives for a few of these devices:

Incontinence Products The incidence of incontinence within the CAS participants is high and reflects the importance of this problem for the population of older people with disabilities. Of our sample of 1103 frail elders, 471 (42.7%) had some degree of incontinence (FIM score of 6 or less on the Sphincter Control/Bladder Management item). This is similar to findings from a 6-year study of 2025 women

TABLE 1.5   Rank Order of Specific Device Categories by Percentage of Devices in Category "Not Used" (N = 1056 Subjects)

Device category	Number of devices owned	Number (n) and percent (%) of devices owned that are not used
Canes	916	297 (32.4%)
Walkers	588	180 (30.6%)
Commode chairs	229	62 (27.1%)
Magnifiers	415	110 (26.5%)
Bath bench/chair/stool	478	103 (21.5%)
Grab bars/rails	961	149 (15.5%)
Wheelchairs	386	50 (12.9%)
Hand-held showers	388	47 (12.1%)
Eyeglasses	802	49 (6.1%)
TV/VCR remote control	882	44 (5.0%)

TABLE 1.6   Rank Order of Specific Device Categories by Percentage of Devices in Category "Not Satisfied" (N = 1053 Subjects)

Device category	Number of devices owned	Number (n) and percent (%) of devices owned that are unsatisfactory
Hearing aids	170	80 (47.1%)
Magnifiers	426	155 (36.4%)
Wheelchairs	373	112 (30.0%)
Canes	899	258 (28.7%)
Walkers	570	135 (23.7%)
Eyeglasses	804	153 (19.0%)
Phones	728	88 (12.1%)
Grab bars/rails	932	99 (10.6%)
TV/VCR remote control	899	94 (10.5%)
Bath bench/chair/stool	536	82 (6.7%)

over age 65 residing in rural Iowa: A 36.3% rate of urge incontinence and 40.3% rate of stress incontinence was found at baseline.[23] Increased age is associated with increased urge incontinence. There are a number of related incontinence products used by Consumer Assessments Study participants: Some were designed specifically for incontinence, such as Depends®, while others were designed for other purposes, such as paper towels and sanitary napkins. Incontinence affects more women than men. For the 471 participants with incontinence, 72.5% were female and 27.5% male. Many of the CAS consumer comments relate to insufficient absorbency of the product, high cost of the product, and poor comfort and fit. Several comments were made by consumers about the inadequate quality of the incontinence products covered by Medicaid. Comments from many study participants suggest that if certain more expensive incontinence products were covered by Medicaid, or if they could afford them, they would not have a continuing problem with incontinence. Given the association between incontinence and nursing home placement, along with the high cost of nursing home care, it would seem logical for Medicaid and other third-party payers to cover the more satisfactory incontinence products.

Mobility Devices Consumer concerns with mobility devices—canes, walkers, and wheelchairs—resulted in their ranking high in both numbers of problems reported and in the dissatisfaction rate per number of users. Almost half of all problems encountered with canes related to difficult or risky use resulting in incidents of tripping and getting tangled up, or abandonment because the cane was too heavy or clumsy to use. Several consumers' comments related to discomfort: "After long period of use, causes pain in right thumb," "handle hurts hand," and "grip is uncomfortable." Other comments were related to stigma, such as "embarrassed to use."

As with canes, many consumer comments regarding walkers were categorized as "difficult and/or dangerous to use," pointing to the need for careful professional assessment, prescription, and follow up. A relatively small percentage (4%) of walker owners cited stigma as a problem. In the present study, consumers raised another problem common to many assistive devices: difficulty in transporting the device in the car. Many elders use several assistive devices, yet experience difficulty in transporting them outside the home: getting them down steps, getting them into and out of the car, and using them on surfaces different from those found in the home.

Almost one-third of the Consumer Assessment Study participants used a wheelchair, and 40% of these wheelchair users reported at least one problem with their wheelchair. Problems were grouped into the following categories: "maintenance and repair, such as broken wheels, flat tires, (33% of problems); "fit between user and the chair," such as uncomfortable to sit in, unable to propel self (41%); and "physical characteristics," such as too heavy or too wide (26%). There was a significantly higher percentage of elders with wheelchair problems among those who selected their own wheelchair than among elders whose chair selection involved a health professional.

Two primary reasons for not resolving the wheelchair problems in a timely manner related to the consumer's limited financial resources and their need for more information on maintaining and repairing wheelchairs.[24]

Bathing Products Consumers reported their reasons for dissatisfaction with bathing devices as related to amount of space required for the device in the bathroom, difficulty in washing while using the device, and preference to sit in their bathtub (down in the water), rather than on a bath chair or bath bench.

Washing Devices Consumers provided many negative comments about washing devices, such as long-handled bath brushes and sponges. These comments included (a) difficulty in handling the device (especially in getting to difficult-to-reach parts of the body) and (b) the device's lack of effectiveness in washing thoroughly. Unlike incontinence products, expense was not stated as a problem for washing devices. Perhaps this is a reflection of the difference between (a) a product that is disposable and whose supply must be continuously replenished and (b) washing devices that are either infrequently or never replaced.

Controls on Electronic Devices   Many consumers reported that controls on electronic devices presented a problem for them. While not all hospital beds are powered, those that are have a hand-held control. One study participant had a problem with the control falling on the floor, so she had it taped on the back of the bed. Another consumer reported difficulty with manipulating the controls. With hearing aids, two consumers simply stated the controls were difficult to adjust; another, who had diminished tactile sensation and vision impairment, reported difficulty not only with the controls, but with inserting batteries; yet another consumer had difficulty putting the hearing aid in the ear due to amputation of fingers. Television remote controls and phones are other common devices that can be assistive, yet often have controls that present problems for a number of older persons with disabilities.

Summary of Reasons for Problems with Devices

In a published article from the Consumer Assessments Study, we listed 14 categories, not all mutually exclusive, into which consumer comments regarding dissatisfaction with devices could be grouped.[25] We reproduce this list below with permission of the publisher, IOS Press:

1. *Device does not sufficiently help the person do the intended task(s).* This is a common problem with many of the assistive devices used by older persons with disabilities. In some cases, the device worked well in the past, but the person's condition changed, and the device is no longer adequate. In other cases the device never worked well, often due to the person not having had the opportunity to try the device before securing it, or having secured it without professional guidance. In many cases there are more appropriate devices for the person, but they continue to use the one they have. Examples include incontinence products that lack sufficient absorbency, hearing aids that do not adequately assist the person to hear, canes that do not provide sufficient support, and eyeglasses and magnifiers that lack sufficient power or lighting.

2. *Device does not work equally well in all intended environments or situations.* This is particularly true with mobility devices. Different surfaces render some devices ineffective. For example, it is difficult to self-propel a wheelchair over carpeting for a person who is physically weak and fatigues easily, yet the wheelchair may work well over wooden or tiled floors. Individuals who use carts for shopping have reported that the "street is too bumpy, and the cart will not easily go up stairs." Similarly, reachers may not work well with larger or heavier objects such as cans stored in food cabinets, but work well with magazines or pieces of clothing.

3. *Device calls unwanted attention to the person.* Assistive devices that are most clearly associated with impairment carry the most stigma. Metal frame walkers, mobility canes, and raised toilet seats are examples of devices that are sometimes cited as calling attention to one's impairment. In some cases, the person is embarrassed by having the device in their home, not wanting friends and relatives to see the device. In other cases they do not want to be seen as disabled, for fear they will be an easy target for crime. Many inner-city elders live in neighborhoods that have changed over the years, with crime a significant problem. One man who used a white cane for mobility specifically stated that he did not use his cane in his own neighborhood for this reason.

4. *Device is not affordable.* While some elders know of better device solutions for their needs than the one they use, often they cannot afford the better device. Each age cohort of elders with increasing age is increasingly poorer. Mean income for the oldest-old (over age 85) is below poverty level. Even a relatively inexpensive device, such as a $30 reacher, may literally be outside the reach of many elders, who barely have sufficient funds for food and shelter. For more expensive devices, such as wheelchairs, print enlargement systems, and computers, only a very small percentage of elders can afford the purchase with their own funds. Medicare and Medicaid have typically covered only durable medical equipment, and the vocational agencies target most of their funds to younger persons with employment goals.

5. *Device could be dangerous in some situations.* Mobility devices are often involved in falls, although there has been little study of the nature of involvement. For a person using a cane or walker, surfaces such as packed snow or ice can be very dangerous. Use of walkers in cluttered environments could lead to tripping and falls. Attempts to grasp heavy items from a cabinet with a reacher that cannot handle the load could result in the object falling on the person.

6. *Device causes physical discomfort.* Devices that require gripping, such as canes and certain types of can openers, can be painful for a person with arthritic hands. Incontinence briefs are uncomfortable for some elders, reporting bulkiness and a "bunching up" effect. Bath brushes with hard bristles can irritate sensitive skin. Hospital beds do not have the same "feel" as a regular bed, and several users of hospital beds describe them as uncomfortable. One elder reported that a backrest support cushion required more padding, as the metal frame on the lower sides was uncomfortable. Several elders reported problems with comfort for their lift chairs: Three stated simply that the chair was uncomfortable; another elaborated, stating the "vinyl makes a lot of noise as the chair moves and you stick to the chair."

7. *Device is not well-maintained.* This is a common problem with devices that have parts that wear out, such as the tips of canes or the pads on the legs of bath seats. It is also common with devices such as cordless phones that require replacement of rechargeable batteries. Even simple, inexpensive devices like bath brushes become worn, but may not be replaced.

8. *Device is not easily transported beyond the home.* Transporting devices in cars and public transportation is often very difficult. Getting wheelchairs in and out of cars may be impossible for the elder and difficult for caregivers. For someone still driving and using a mobility device, having easy access to the device may be essential. The RERC-Aging Consumer Advisory Board reported the difficulties they have in traveling with their assistive devices when they stay overnight in hotels. This led to the publication of the *Hotel-Motel Resource Guide to Assistive Device Loan Closets*, targeted at the lodging industry in the United States available from the University of Florida Rehabilitation Engineering Research Center on Technology and Aging.

9. *Device requires more space than is available.* This is a common problem with bath chairs and bath benches. Many bathrooms are small and are used by several family members, most of whom do not use the device. Bath benches that extend beyond the tub can impede movement in the bathroom. Walkers and wheelchairs may not be used inside the home because of difficulty in moving around furniture. Lift chairs are also a problem for elders with limited space.

10. *Storage of the device is difficult.* For elders who own many devices, some of which may be large and only used some of the time, storage is often an issue. For example, a wheelchair that is only used on trips beyond the home requires storage space when not in use.

11. *Person does not know how to use the device.* Training is an important issue with many assistive devices, yet all too often training is not provided. One elder reported that he did not use his back brace because he did not know how to put it on. Setup of the device is also an issue for some devices, requiring expertise that may not have been available when the device was purchased.

12. *Device is difficult to use.* In some cases the device may always have been difficult to use. In other cases, declines in physical or cognitive performance may have rendered a once-satisfactory device difficult to use. Devices with electronic controls are often difficult to manipulate, and it may be difficult to see the settings. Manual hospital beds are difficult for some individuals to crank. One elder reported difficulty in using an electric can opener. Many elders report that their canes are too heavy, making them difficult to use. Another elder with severe low vision reported difficulty using a check-writing guide.

13. *Use of the device requires assistance from another person.* Devices that involve mobility and transfers are often used by elders with another person assisting. While this is not necessarily a problem if there is someone nearby to assist, many elders would prefer to do the task independently. For toileting and bathing, privacy is often an issue.

14. *Device was not installed properly.* This is a common problem with grab bars, reported by Consumer Assessments Study participants as "very wobbly," "loosened at rear and unable to repair," "loosens up occasionally," and "not positioned properly to facilitate transfer out of the tub." Grab bars require

professional guidance in their placement, and they need to be installed by skilled workers.

These categories underline the importance of consumer involvement in the selection of devices, along with the need for current information on the kinds of devices and device features that are available. The large number of device problems also supports the need for, at a minimum, professional consultation prior to selecting devices. In many cases, especially with older persons who face multiple chronic conditions and impairments, beyond consultation there is a need for careful professional assessment, provision of the devices, training, and follow-up. Follow-up should monitor not only changing needs of the individual, but the maintenance of the devices.

Consumer Perspective on Assistive Technology: High-Technology Devices

The University of Florida Rehabilitation Engineering Research Center on Technology and Aging recently completed a survey of adults with disabilities, and older persons with disabilities, looking at "needs and barriers" to technology-related devices. Articles about this study focus on specific electronic device types: computers, smart phones, personal emergency response systems, traditional phones, personal digital assistants, and home monitoring devices.[26,27]

Several studies have demonstrated ways in which computers can benefit older persons: mental stimulation and increased competence and feeling of autonomy[28]; a sense of satisfaction, reduced loneliness, and improved sense of well-being[29]; increased social interaction through email and interactive websites[30]; and improved memory, as well as more comfort with using a computer through playing games on a computer.[31,32] There are many web-based support services for psychosocial support and health-related information for older persons and their caregivers.[33]

The RERC on Technology and Aging contacted 598 older persons with disabilities (over age 60) and 70 adults with disabilities under age 60 to determine their perspective on the needs and barriers related to computer use. Study participants from western New York, southern California, and northern Florida were interviewed either in their home or by phone. We also sought participants from across the United States through a mailed survey, with both computer users and nonusers participating. We found that only a relatively small percentage of computer users were not satisfied with their computer, and most of those who had computers had internet access. Maintaining contact with others was a very important reason for using a computer for both older and younger adults with disabilities. Many computer users reported discomfort and pain when they used their computer, but only a few viewed their impairment(s) as barriers to computer ownership or use. Nonusers of computers stated a high interest in using a computer, with a large number stating that cost was the major barrier for them. The need for assessment and advice on workstation and computer setup seems evident from the large number in both groups reporting discomfort and problems in using the computer.

Consumer Participation and Feedback at ICADI

Unless consumers are included in the research and design process, we may not create the useful assistive technology we imagined. Consumers are those older people with disabilities who buy and use the assistive devices and related services that we develop and on which our research is based. In planning ICADI, we sought consumer involvement and invited 10 consumers to attend ICADI and provide feedback through a focus group held immediately after the Conference. The following section reports the ICADI consumer experience.

The 10 consumer participants attended ICADI sessions and provided feedback on the usefulness of the information, and research direction, discussed in the presentations they attended. They also provided feedback on the experience of attending a professional conference, and how consumer participation could be enhanced at similar conferences, providing excellent strategies for improving the communication between consumers and investigators/presenters.

Consumers described the ICADI research conference as very interesting and important to their lives. The terms that participants used to describe their experiences with the conference were "fantastic, educational, intriguing, positive, optimistic, and supportive." As one participant noted, "sometimes we, people with disabilities, feel like we are alone out there. It was very important to know that we are not alone and that other people are really caring and thinking about how to help us to live better lives." The conference also increased knowledge of options for elderly individuals and people with disabilities.

Evaluating the usefulness of the new information, consumers reported that knowledge provided through the conference created in them positive expectations. They considered it to be one of the most important contributions to their day-to-day activities knowing that ongoing research creates a foundation for future disability-related products and services. One participant commented that she was "overwhelmed with how the young and older researchers are trying to make our lives better." This research knowledge is necessary for maintaining an independent life style and remaining self-sufficient as long as possible. Although some participants felt that most of the new knowledge can not be used immediately in their everyday life, this new information can help them to understand how to cope with their disability-related problems in the near future. Another participant added, "new information is important for long-term planning."

Language and Format of Presentation

The way of presenting information and the format of the presentations themselves were extensively discussed by the focus group participants. Although the research jargon used by some presenters was a barrier for consumers, they agreed that it was not a complete obstacle for learning about some interesting facts. Participants had a somewhat lengthy discussion about the conflicting needs of researchers and consumers, particularly at conferences such as the current one. Consumers recognized the need for researchers at times to spend time talking with other researchers. One participant recommended some consideration of a separate track geared toward consumers and oriented toward "end-user" applications of research.

Consumers were concerned with the lack of presentation handouts. As one of the consumers reported, she had to take a lot of notes trying to document the knowledge that she wanted to share later. (This participant works in a church as a volunteer helping more than 160 people who have disabilities themselves or are involved with their disabled friends and relatives.) Participants decided to recommend to the conference committee that they pay special attention to the availability of printed materials (handouts) accompanying the oral presentations. At the conference itself, they recommended that provisions be made for persons with hearing impairments or diminished eyesight. For example, small print should not be used in PowerPoint presentations.

Consumers also raised a concern that the language and the attitude with regard to persons with disabilities are patronizing in general. Several participants commented on the use of some terms associated with aging and disability (e.g., "frail elderly" or "caregiver"). These terms have mostly negative connotations in the disability community because they "give no credit and no power to the person who is aged or receiving the care." For example, "assistant may be a better word than caregiver." One participant indicated that it was disappointing to be referred to as her husband's "caregiver" rather than his "wife." However, consumers also noted that the ICADI conference showed that there is a dramatic positive change underway. The language and terms used throughout the conference reflected a paradigm change from institutional care to community living and empowerment.

Role of Consumers in a Research Conference

Discussing the question of why it is important for consumers to participate in such conferences, the answer was simply: "how else are researchers going to know what persons with disabilities need if you do not ask them (us)?" Participants suggested that there should be more consumers participating in the research conferences, sharing their problems and giving suggestions and concerns to the research community. Researchers need to know how the results of their studies and their products affect disabled persons themselves. At the same time, one consumer noted that, "there is a hunger among elderly disabled people to know what the research community is doing. There really is a market out there for us—consumers."

Consumers are the practical experts who need to be involved with all stages of the research process. They themselves have more first hand knowledge about the specific problems that surround disability conditions than most other people, including researchers. An important role of consumers participating in the research conference was to see how useful this research is from their perspective. Consumers do not deal with the research protocols; they live in the natural setting and therefore have an experience of implementing research applications in real-life situations.

Factors That Influence Effectiveness of Consumer-Researcher Communication

Consumers' participation in research conferences was considered to be one of the major factors that influenced consumer-researcher communication. It is necessary "to make one's voice be heard by the researchers."

Effective communication between consumers and researchers is closely associated with how scientists themselves perceive the role of people with disabilities in the research process. It is also important to learn how this new role of consumers as rightful research collaborators is perceived by non-disabled people and by society in general.

Having an expanded pre-conference discussion with the participation of both consumers and researchers–presenters might provide consumers with more detailed information on how to identify presentations that fit their needs.

Recommendations for Future Disability Research Conferences

Recommendations for agendas of future conferences centered on the effectiveness of the interactions among consumers, researchers, and disability specialists, as well as the problem of dissemination of the research knowledge.

To enhance and develop the conference agenda, it seems reasonable to organize a pre-conference workshop with the consumers where the focus of the upcoming conference and the most important questions will be discussed from the consumers' point of view. Consumers need to be involved in developing the conference agenda from the very beginning, and then through every stage of the conference preparation.

To provide researchers with important feedback, a consumer track at the conference should include presentations made by consumers. Participation of medical practitioners, who work in the disability field together with the researchers and consumers, may provide an opportunity to discuss critical issues from different angles.

The issue of the dissemination of conference materials among the disability community was most important. "Where do we go from here?" was the question that participant–consumers raised again and again throughout the focus group discussion. One participant mentioned that she would return home and search for places to share the information that she received from this conference at her local level.

Accessibility of the disability-related research to the rest of the disability community is still a problem. As one participant noted, "there are a lot of other consumers who are not aware of events like this and do not have access to this kind of information." A lot of this very exciting research-based knowledge is not known at all to the majority of disabled consumers. Focus group participants provided advice on involving the news media in covering the results of the conference and at the same time expressed their willingness to pass the knowledge which they have learned to the people they know, both consumers and caregivers. As one consumer explained it, "ten years ago I did not know about existing possibilities, and even recently I was not aware of many things and information that is available now; so I intend to pass the information that I have learned during this conference to the people with disabilities and caregivers that I know."

One participant also suggested having a political session at the conference where representatives from various governmental agencies would discuss policies that affect the lives of persons with disabilities.

Participants' Overall Conclusions and Recommendations

- Information presented at the ICADI conference is of a great practical impor-tance. It creates positive expectations and promotes positive attitudes toward independent life styles.

- The research conference on disability, despite its professional orientation, plays an educational role for nonprofessionals (i.e., consumers), helping them to build coping resources necessary for disability maintenance.

- Focus group participants will share information on disability research with their communities—caregivers, support groups, specialized societies, and other persons with disabilities who live in their communities.

- Informal communication between researchers and consumers before and during the conference (e.g., informal workshops) should be encouraged, together with the formal participation of consumers and caregivers in profes-sional events.

- The conference committee should pay special attention to the availability of printed materials (handouts) that accompany oral presentations during the conference.

- News media may play an important role in informing local communities about the planned events, as well as in informing persons with disabilities about the results of the conference.

- Dissemination of the research information to the local communities through their representatives participating in the conference needs to be planned in advance.

- The disability community needs access to the research information collected through the conference. The information should be available in accessible forms such as printed materials with large fonts and a user-friendly web site.

- Results of this focus group should be sent to the participants and their local communities in printed form.

REFERENCES

1. U.S. Department of Education, (1988). Technology Related Assistance for Individuals with Disabil-ities Act of 1988, PL 100–407, Section 3 (1988).

2. Fried, L. P., Ferrucci, L., Darer, J., Williamson, J. D., and Anderson G. (2004). Untangling the Concepts of Disability, Frailty, and Comorbidity: Implications for Improved Targeting and Care. *Journals of Gerontology Series A: Biological Sciences and Medical Sciences*, **59**(3), 255–263.

3. U.S. Department of Health and Human Services, Administration on Aging (2001). A profile of older Americans: 2001.

4. NursingHomeReports.com. *The Cost of Nursing Home Care*, Retrieved on March 24, 2004 from http://www.nursinghomereports.com/paying_for_care/cost_of_care.htm.

5. U.S. Department of Health and Human Services, Public Health Service, National Institutes of Health, National Institute of Child Health and Human Development (March 1993) *Research Plan For The National Center For Medical Rehabilitation*. NIH Publication No.93-3509, p26.

6. International Classification of Functioning, Disability and Health, *ICF Introduction*, p3, Retrieved March 22, 2004 from http://www3.who.int/icf/intros/ICF-Eng-Intro.pdf.

7. U.S. Department of Transportation, *Transportation Equity Act for the 21st Century—TEA-21*, Retrieved December 4, 2004 from http://www.fhwa.dot.gov/tea21/h2400.htm.

8. Gallagher, R. M., Verma, S., and Mossey, J. (2000). Chronic pain. Sources of late-life pain and risk factors for disability. *Geriatrics*, **55**(9), 40–44, 47.

9. Verhaak, P. F., Kerssens, J. J., Dekker, J., et al. (1998). Prevalence of chronic benign pain disorder among adults: a review of the literature. *Pain*, **77**(3), 231–239.

10. Sternbach, R. (1986). Survey of pain in the United States: the Nuprin report. *Clinical Journal of pain*, **2**, 49–53.

11. Walker, J. E., and Howland, J. (1991). Falls and fear of falling among elderly persons living in the community: occupational therapy interventions. *American Journal of Occupational Therapy*, **45**(2), 119–122.

12. Jensen, M. P., and Karoly, P. (1992). Self-report scales and procedures for assessing pain in adults. In: *Handbook of Pain Assessment*, (pp. 107–123) Turk, D. C., and Melzack, R. eds., New York: Guilford Press.

13. American Geriatrics Society (1998). The management of chronic pain in older persons: AGS Panel on Chronic Pain in Older Persons. *Journal of the American Geriatrics Society*, **46**(5), 635–651.

14. Daltroy, L. H., Larson, M. G., Eaton, H. M., et al. (1999). Discrepancies between self-reported and observed physical function in the elderly: the influence of response shift and other factors. *Social Science & Medicine*, **48**(11), 1549–1561.

15. Cohen-Mansfield, J., and Marx, M. S. (1993). Pain and depression in the nursing home: corroborating results. *Journal of Gerontology*, **48**(2), 96–97.

16. Reyes-Gibby, C. C., Mendoza, T. R., Wang, S., Anderson, K. O., and Cleeland, C. S. (2003). Pain and fatigue in community-dwelling adults. *Pain Medicine*, **4**(3), 231–237.

17. Gibson, M. J. (2003). Beyond 50.03: A report to the nation on disability and independent living. Washington, D.C.: AARP.

18. Mann, W. C., Hurren, M. D., Karuza, J., and Bentley, D. W. (1993). Needs of Home-Based Older Visually Impaired Persons for Assistive Devices. *Journal of Visual Impairments and Blindness*, **87**(4), 106–110.

19. Mann, W. C., Hurren, M. D., Karuza, J., and Bentley, D. W. (1993). Needs of Home-Based Older Visually Impaired Persons for Assistive Devices. *Journal of Visual Impairments and Blindness*, **87**(4), 106–110.

20. Mann, W., Hurren, D., and Tomita, M. (1995). Assistive devices used by home-based elderly persons with arthritis. *The American Journal of Occupational Therapy*, **49**(8), 810–820.

21. Mann, W., Hurren, M., and Tomita, M. (1994). Assistive device needs of home-based elderly persons with hearing impairments. *Technology & Disability*, **3**(1), 47–61.

22. Mann, W., Karuza, J., Hurren, D., and Tomita, M. (1992). Assistive devices for home-based elderly persons with cognitive impairments. *Topics in Geriatric Rehabilitation*, **8**(2), 35–52.

23. Nygaard, I. E., and Lemke, J. H. (1996). Urinary incontinence in rural older women: prevalence, incidence and remission. *Journal of American Geriatric Society*, **44**(9), 1049–1054.

24. Mann, W. C., Hurren, D., Charvat, B., and Tomita, M. (1996). Problems with Wheelchairs Experienced by Frail Elders. *Technology & Disability*, **5**(1), 101–111.

25. Mann, W. C., and Tomita, M. (1998). Perspectives on Assistive Devices Among Elderly Persons with Disabilities. *Technology & Disability*, **9**(3), 119–148.

26. Mann, W. C., Helal, A., Davenport, R. D., Justiss, M. D., Tomita, M., and Kemp, B. J. (2004). Use of Cell Phones by Elders with Impairments: Overall Appraisal, Satisfaction, and Suggestions. *Technology and Disability*. In press.

27. Mann, W. C., Belchoir, P., Tomita, M., and Kemp, B. J. (2005). Use of Personal Emergency Response Systems by Older Individuals with disabilities in the United States. *Assistive Technology*. In press.

28. McConatha, D., McConatha, J. T., and Dermingny, R. (1994). The use of interactive computer services to enhance the quality for life for long-term care residents. *Gerontologist*, **34**(4), 553–556.

29. White, H., McConnel, E., Clipp, E., Bynum, L., Teague, C., Navas, L., Craven, S., and Halbrecht, H. (1999). Surfing the net in later life: a review of the literature and pilot study of computer use and quality of life. *Journal of Applied Gerontology*, **18**(1), 358.

30. Gietzelt, D. (2001). Computer an Internet use among a group of Sydney seniors: a pilot study. *Asustralian Academic & Research*, **32**(2), 137–152.
31. Danowski, J., and Sacks, W. (1980). Computer Communication and the Elderly. *Experimental Aging Research*, **6**(2), 125–135.
32. Faris, M., Bates, R., Resnick, H., and Stabler, N. (1994). Evaluation of computer games' impact upon cognitively impaired frail elderly. *Computers in Human Services*, **11**(1&2), 219–228.
33. Gallienne, R., Moore, S., and Brennan, P. (1993). Alzheimer's Caregivers—Psychosocial Support via Computer Networks. *Journal of Gerontological Nursing*, **19**(12), 15–22.

PART 1

SMART TECHNOLOGY FOR AGING, DISABIITY, AND INDEPENDENCE

CHAPTER 2

HOME AUTOMATION AND SMART HOMES TO SUPPORT INDEPENDENCE

William C. Mann and Bradley R. Milton

2.1 INTRODUCTION

Home automation is a concept that has been explored frequently at world's fairs, expositions, and exhibitions. The 1933–1934 Chicago World's Fair featured the "House of Tomorrow," designed with 12 sides, 3 stories, and a wedding-cake shape.[1] It was unique for the time, in both design and technology, which included a built-in dishwasher, electric lights with dimmer switches, central air conditioning, and an electric garage door opener. It used passive solar heating, one of the first homes in the United States to do this. The garage was built to hold the family car and airplane, which futurists predicted each family would one day own. At the 1939 New York World's Fair, television and other now-everyday appliances were predicted to be in all homes of the future. The first TV set was sold in 1938, a year before any programs were broadcast.

At the 1964–1965 World's Fair in New York, several exhibits presented visions of the future. "Futurama," by General Motors, and "Space City" reached by the "Magic Skyway" by Ford suggested that future generations would live in cities consisting of very tall skyscrapers connected by tunneled highways and elevated walkways and highways, with computer-controlled vehicles. Futurama also predicted an underwater city 10,000 feet beneath the sea, where workers mined minerals, drilled for oil and gas, and farmed the sea. The underwater city also featured a resort called the Hotel Atlantis.[2] We now have Jules Undersea Lodge in Key Largo, Florida (http://www.jul.com/), and in Dubai a 220-suite underwater hotel will open in 2006. Named Hydropolis, this Dubai hotel will resemble a giant submarine, and guests will enter through a tunnel to a waterside reception area http://travel.guardian.co.uk/news/story/0,7445,1018216,00.html). Predictions at the 1964 the World's Fair included sending a man to the moon and widespread use of personal computers. Today, we take for granted many of the technological advances featured at these not-so-long-ago events.

Smart Technology for Aging, Disability, and Independence, Edited by William C. Mann
Copyright © 2005 John Wiley & Sons, Inc.

More recently, technological advances have been applied to providing supportive environments and tools to support older people in their homes. We begin this chapter on home automation and smart environments by answering the question, "What is a smart house?" We follow this with the author's vision for smart homes of the near future (5 years from the publication of this book) applied to the needs of people as they age. The vision is based on current research and development on smart home technology, which is described following this view of the future.

What Is a Smart House?

As we age, we face declining abilities from age-related diseases and the aging process itself. Our home can assist or hinder our ability to complete self-care and household activities. In Chapter 9, we discuss ways to modify the structure, furnishings, and lighting of a home to optimize our ability to complete everyday tasks independently. In this chapter we focus on the very latest technology, as well as future technology, that can and will assist us in living independently at home into our very oldest years.

There is growing interest in the concept of "smart houses." We begin this chapter by discussing smart house functions—what is it that a smart house actually does, or offers to its residents? Table 2.1 summarizes the following discussion of smart house functions, organizing these functions into "levels" based on complexity and how long the function has been available; in some cases they are not yet available in product form.

Smart House Level I: Offers Basic Communications   Level I technology is necessary for a smart house, but simply having level I technology does not alone make it a smart house. At Level I, technology relates to communications, providing residents with the means to communicate with and receive communications from others beyond the home. Telephones represent one example of communications technology—one that has been available for over 100 years, providing voice communication with others who have the same technology. Today, especially with mobile phones, they exist almost everywhere.

The telephone is especially important for older persons with disabilities. Almost one-third live alone, and for those with limited mobility, the telephone provides opportunities for socialization. In a study of older adults living in rural areas, frequent loneliness was found to be associated with frequent use of the telephone.[3] The telephone also provides a mechanism for calls for help. Many older adults also use the telephone for shopping, banking, and arranging other personal services.

Today mobile phone manufacturers are merging other technologies into the same "box" with the phone. Consider the Sony-Erickson P900 "superphone," which offers traditional voice communications, internet access for web browsing and email, digital camera (and you can send your pictures with this device to others over the internet), MP3 player (and you can download songs from the internet), and all the functions of a personal digital assistant (such as contact list and scheduler).

Not everyone owns a "superphone" with internet access like the Sony Ericsson P900, but in the United States almost 75% of homes now have internet

TABLE 2.1   Smart House Functions

Level 1: Offers Basic Communications

Offers interactive voice and text communication (phone and email)
Provides link to World Wide Web
Offers TV (full range of stations) & radio (AM and FM)

Level 2: Responds to Simple Control Commands from Within or Outside the Home

Unlock / lock door
Check for doors / windows open or unlocked
Turn on lights
Check for land-mail
Get help (in the case of a fall or other problem)

Level 3: Automates Household Functions

Air temperature, humidity
Lights on/off at predetermined times
House made secure at certain times
Music, TV on/off at certain times

Level 4: Tracks Location in the Home, Tracks Behaviors, and Tracks Health Indicators

Determines activity patterns
Determines sleep patterns
Determines health status (vital signs, blood glucose, weight)

Level 5: Analyzes Data, Makes Decisions, Takes Actions

A. *Issues alerts*
   A1. *To resident*
   - Mail has been delivered
   - Person (name given, or stranger stated) at door announced
   - Water leaks
   - Stove has been left on
   - Door is unlocked
   A2. *To distant care provider*
   - Altered, problematic activity or sleep pattern, or health problem
   A3. *To formal service provider*
   - Health alert
B. *Provides Reports*
   To resident, care provider, and formal service provider on status
C. *Makes changes in automated functions based on learned preferences*
   - Adjusts lights, temperature, music to resident's use patterns—can be overridden
     easily

(Continued)

TABLE 2.1 *Continued*

Level 6: Provides Information, Reminders, and Prompts for Basic Daily Tasks

Notification mail has arrived, someone is at the door, stove was left on
Medication reminder
Hydration reminder
Meal reminder
Task prompting
- Washing, grooming
- Dressing
- Toileting/hygiene
- Exercise
- Meal preparation
- Social contacts (e.g., "call. . . .")
- Household cleaning

Level 7: Answer questions

"Have I . . . (brushed my teeth, taken my medications, put all the ingredients in the dish I am preparing"
Orientation—time, day, month, year, season
What is happening today?
General information (any question that could be searched on Google)

Level 8: Make household arrangements

Schedule maintenance and repair visits
Order medications
Prepare grocery lists and send to grocery for delivery
Prepare meals
Handle house cleaning

access (retrieved 8-5-04-http://www.websiteoptimization.com/bw/0403/, as of February 2004). Internet access is an important communication technology, essential if a home is to be considered "smart." And for optimal use of the internet in a smart house, high-speed access is very important. Over 48 million adult Americans have broadband connections at home, which provides high-speed access (4-19-04-http://www.pewinternet.org/PPF/r/121/report_display.asp retrieved 8-5-04)

Television and radio offer additional communication, although traditionally the communication has been one-way. This is also changing. We have Web-TV, an inexpensive way of turning a TV into a web device. TVs are being sold as components; for example, a flat screen monitor hanging on a wall can display TV or input from a computer. Traditional TV, along with other electronic entertainment, is being designed in smart homes as multimedia centers, offering a range of options for media based entertainment (music, movies, television, pictures) and methods for control.

Smart House Level 2: Responds to Simple Control Commands from Within or Outside the Home   At this level, anything in the house that uses electrical power can be "operated" without having to use a switch or control button attached to, or wired into, the appliance or device. Examples of household items that could be controlled include: door locks with an electronic mechanism to set the bolt; lights; small appliances; thermostats; and mechanically controlled curtains and windows.

Ideally, voice commands would provide the simplest way to issue the commands. Most systems currently sold use a remote control device similar to a TV remote. Many systems also allow distant operation through a phone.

Smart House Level 3: Automates Household Functions

Heating and air-conditioning systems that use a thermostat automate air temperature in the house. Keep in mind that the first thermostat for controlling room temperature was invented in 1885, and the first home air conditioners appeared in 1928. Today, for the most part, we take automation of our air temperature for granted.

It has been possible to automate other aspects of our home such as when lights go on and off, when music or television is turned on, when the security system is set, and when our lawn sprinklers go on and off. Today we have products that offer more flexibility or features in this level of automation. Computer-based smart home products allow more easy setup for the on–off cycle, and different scenarios can be programmed for different periods, such as "weekends at home," "vacation mode traveling," and "work-week mode." In some systems, the preset cycles can be broken or interrupted easily, either in the home or through a phone call.

Smart House Level 4: Tracks Location in the Home, Tracks Behaviors, and Tracks Health Indicators

A number of university and corporate labs are working on development of systems to track where a person is located in their home. If the home "knows" where you are, it can take appropriate actions in that room or area. For example, if the smart house is going to issue a reminder (time to take medications) or alert (someone at the front door), it can provide the reminder or alert in the exact location where the resident is sitting or standing. If the resident falls, an alert can be issued stating just where the person is located in the home.

The smart house can also track behaviors, such as trips to the bathroom, visits to the kitchen and refrigerator, tossing and turning in bed, and time spent sleeping, sitting, or exercising. Tracking health indicators could include taking measurements of vital signs and weight.

Smart House Level 5: Analyzes Data, Makes Decisions, Takes Actions

Knowing typical patterns for the smart home's resident, deviations from this pattern could be indicators of a problem, and the smart house could check with the resident, or a family member, to be sure the person was well. Likewise, if a person was losing too much weight, they could be alerted, or a care provider could be notified.

The smart house is also capable of compiling health status reports for the resident, for a family care provider, or for a formal service provider such as a physician. Tracking key health information related to the resident's condition on a daily basis can lead to quickly identifying deviations from what is normal for that person.

The smart house can also learn the resident's preferences in such areas as lighting, temperature, and music. The smart house will then either directly make adjustments (such as raising the temperature in the home just before the person gets out of bed) or "ask" the resident if they would like the adjustment made.

Smart House Level 6: Provides Information, Reminders, and Prompts for Basic Daily Tasks   The smart house will "know" when mail has been delivered, when someone is at the front door, when the stove has been left on too long, or when the resident has gone too long without a drink of water or has forgotten to take medications. It will prompt the resident that the mail has arrived, to take a drink of water or medications, or that it is time to have dinner.

For someone with more significant cognitive impairment, who has difficulty even with basic daily tasks such as dressing and grooming, the smart house will prompt the person with voice and visual cues through each step in the activity.

Smart House Level 7: Answer Questions   Those of us who regularly use the internet appreciate the ease with which we can get answers to almost any question— typically we use Google or some other internet search engine. For questions that go beyond the resident's individual experience, the smart house, with a voice recognition interface, will accept questions, go to the web to seek the answers, and respond with an answer back to the resident. For more personal questions, such as "Have I taken my medications this morning?" the smart house will search its own database and respond appropriately.

Smart House Level 8: Make Household Arrangements   The smart house will know when the furnace filter needs to be cleaned and when medications should be ordered, and it will handle all details of those transactions. The smart house will track food consumption, seek input from the resident on the menu for the next several days or more, prepare grocery lists, order the groceries, and arrange for deliveries. When an appliance requires repairs, the smart house will recognize the need and arrange for someone to come to the home to make the repair.

2.2   VISION OF THE NEAR FUTURE: A DAY IN MRS. SMITH'S SMART HOME

After the following introductory paragraph, we present an edited version of an article by William Mann and Sumi Helal that appeared in the *Journal of Certified Senior Advisors* in 2003.[4]

The story takes place in the year 2010—that is, 5 years from the publication of the present book. Some of the smart house features described below were available while the book was being written, whereas others were in the research and development stage. In 2010, all are available in product form. The University of Florida Research and Development team, working with several university and corporate partners, created a flexible package called the Gator Tech Smart House system.

Mrs. Smith is an 87-year-old widow who lives alone. She no longer drives because her vision is moderately impaired, and arthritis makes it difficult for her to grasp the steering wheel. She is also a bit forgetful, but still plays cards regularly with a group in her community. Her daughter, Sally, who lives 12 miles away, assists with trips to the grocery store and doctor, while Mrs. Smith's friends and neighbors help with trips to church and the community center where she plays cards. Mrs. Smith had a fall 2 years ago which resulted in a hip fracture, but she recovered well and walks slowly with a cane. Mrs. Smith's son, Tommy, lives 800 miles away, but has kept in close touch by phone and visits at least every 3 months. Sally and Tommy recently assisted Mrs. Smith in a move from her large two-story home of 52 years into a smaller ranch style home set up as a smart house.

Bathroom and Bedroom

When Mrs. Smith gets up in the morning, the time is tracked. If it is significantly earlier or later than normal, the smart house notes this. She goes to the toilet—a smart toilet. In the early 2000s the Japanese company Matsushita Electric Industrial Co. designed a toilet that can determine a person's blood pressure, temperature, and blood sugar. This information can be analyzed by the smart house to determine if there is a need to electronically transmit an alert to Sally or Tommy or Mrs. Smith's family physician, Dr. Jones.

Mrs. Smith completes her other basic activities of daily living (ADLs)—taking a shower, combing her hair, getting dressed. While her "forgetfulness" is not severe, the smart house is ready to help with prompting through these activities, should Mrs. Smith need help in the future. Monitors and speakers in the bathroom and bedroom provide auditory and visual prompts for brushing teeth, combing hair, bathing, and dressing. The smart house "remembers" if these activities have been completed. If Mrs. Smith cannot remember if she brushed her teeth, she can ask the smart house: "Have I brushed my teeth, already?" She will get an appropriate reply. Should she go back to brush her teeth a second time, without having consumed food, the system will politely remind her that she has already brushed her teeth.

Hall

After completing these basic morning ADLs, Mrs. Smith goes to the kitchen to prepare her breakfast. On the way from the bedroom her movement is tracked by a number of sensors. Should she stop and stand in one place, or fall, speakers close to where she is standing will ask her if she requires assistance. She can respond that she has stopped to look at some pictures, and the smart house will "know" she is safe. The movement tracking system is also able to ascertain if she has fallen and will ask her if she needs to have a call placed for emergency assistance. She could respond that she fell but did not hurt herself and is able to get up, and there is no need for a call. Alternatively she could instruct the smart house to place the call. If she does not respond at all, the smart house places calls in this order: first to Sally, but if she does not answer, second to a Personal Emergency Response System (PERS) operator for emergency assistance. The smart house tells either Sally or the PERS operator that Mrs. Smith has fallen and she is not verbally responding to questions. Mrs. Smith does not fall today, but feels much more secure knowing that if she falls, the smart house will find her help. When she fractured her hip two years ago, she lay on the floor 4 hours before her daughter came to the house—her daughter had become concerned because her mother had not answered her morning phone call.

Mailbox

On the way to the kitchen the smart house tells Mrs. Smith that the morning newspaper has been delivered to her mailbox.

Kitchen

The smart house offers a number of features for Mrs. Smith in the kitchen. Like her bedroom and bathroom, the kitchen has flat screen monitors hanging on the wall, along with small speakers unobtrusively placed on the walls. Mrs. Smith can call on the smart house for suggestions for breakfast—providing a menu based on the diet recommended by a nutritionist who works with Dr. Jones. Today she decides she is going to make instant oatmeal, using her smart microwave oven. The smart microwave oven recognizes what Mrs. Smith is preparing from an electronic tag on the package, and it automatically sets up the appropriate time and power. This microwave oven is also able to determine if the food or object is not safe—that is, if it contains a substance that could cause an allergic reaction. Mrs. Smith drinks a glass of orange juice and slices a banana into her oatmeal. The smart house tracks the food that Mrs. Smith is eating for breakfast.

Mrs. Smith takes four medications, one of which she takes in the morning and evening; the other three are taken just in the morning after breakfast. Today a half hour after eating breakfast, she is still enjoying the morning newspaper and has not yet taken her morning medications. The smart house reminds Mrs. Smith that it is time to take her morning medications. She has a medication caddy that is designed to dispense the appropriate medications, at the appropriate time, into a small dish. After she takes her morning medications, the smart medication caddy recognizes that Mrs. Smith's arthritis medication is down to a 4-day supply, so a message is sent to the pharmacy regarding the need for a refill. Mrs. Smith receives a call later in the morning from the pharmacist, asking her if she would like the refill, and, if so, would it be convenient to have it delivered by Joe, the delivery man, in about 1 hour. When Joe arrives, the doorbell rings through the speakers in the kitchen, where Mrs. Smith is still reading the paper. She looks up at the monitor and recognizes Joe. The security camera at the front door is also part of the smart home system. She instructs the smart house to "open the front door," and Joe comes in, greets Mrs. Smith, and places her arthritis medication in her medication caddy. When Joe leaves, the smart house locks the door behind him. The smart house tracks all visitors, so Joe's visit is noted.

Laundry Room

After reading the newspaper, Mrs. Smith decides to wash some clothes. She has a combination washer/dryer—the same machine both washes and dries her clothes, saving her the extra step of transferring the washed clothes to the drier. The smart washer/drier alerts Mrs. Smith that her clothes have completed the wash/dry cycle through the monitor/speaker system in the living room where she is now seated. The automatic tracking system always knows where Mrs. Smith is in the house, and it can send the messages to the speakers and monitors specifically to the room she is in. Should she need it in the future, an advanced option for the smart house is to have speakers and monitors on every wall, so that the verbal and auditory messages come through on the monitor she is facing. Mrs. Smith goes to the laundry room, folds her clothes, and takes them to her dresser and closet. The smart house notes that these tasks have been completed.

Living Room

The living room has an entertainment system that is also integrated into the smart house. This system includes music (CD player and AM/FM tuner), video (VHS, DVD, and cable TV), internet access, and integration with files stored on her computer, including her digital picture collection. Today she sits on her couch and verbally instructs the entertainment system to turn to FM 88.7 and she listens to National Public Radio. With classical music in the background, she reads a novel that Tommy had given her on his last visit. The smart house notes this.

Beyond the House: Getting Out

At noon, Mrs. Smith prepares a light meal. Smart house interaction/involvement is very similar to breakfast. Following lunch, Mrs. Smith's next door neighbor stops by to give her a ride to the community center, where she plays cards for the afternoon, followed by dinner out with her bridge partner. The smart house records her lunch, the visit of her neighbor, the departure time of Mrs. Smith, and her arrival time back at the house.

Mrs. Smith always carries her smart phone with her when she leaves the house. Until the recent significant upgrades in voice recognition technology, the smart phone served as the primary interface for human interaction with the smart house. While traveling outside the home, the smart phone tracks her location and can provide assistance if she requires it, as well as make traditional voice calls. When she returns home, information about her trip outside the home will be sent (using Bluetooth wireless) to her computer. Before Mrs. Smith stopped driving 3 years ago, her smart phone interfaced with her car and, through sensors in her car, was able to alert her if she was driving too slowly or perhaps swaying from lane to lane. It was based upon feedback from this smart phone/car system that she decided it would be best to stop driving.

Back Home for the Evening

Arriving home after dinner, Mrs. Smith is reminded by the smart house to take her evening medication. She then watches the news for an hour, completes her nighttime ADLs, and retires to bed at 9 P.M. The smart house notes all of this. Before she retires to bed, Mrs. Smith asks, "Are all doors and windows locked?" The smart house quickly checks and gives her an accurate security report. Mrs. Smith's bed includes biosensors that track her body temperature, heart rate, breathing rate, and movement while sleeping. The smart house notes these measurements.

Data Analysis and Reports

An important aspect of Mrs. Smith's smart house is its capability to interpret data, including movement patterns. If Mrs. Smith "tosses and turns" every night, then this is not unusual behavior and probably not a reason, at least by itself, to send an alert to Sally or Tommy. On the other hand, if Mrs. Smith typically sleeps calmly but on one night is tossing and turning and is also up from bed several times during the night, then Sally will receive a call. Likewise, if Mrs. Smith were sedentary (she is not) and gets up from bed late, remains in her bathrobe all day, eats little, and stays seated in the living room, then the smart house would alert Sally.

Sally can get a daily, weekly, or monthly report of her mother's health and behavior through a secure internet site. She checked the report of this "day in the smart house" and learned that her mother had slept well, was up at her normal time, had two good meals at home, did the laundry, was out in the afternoon and for dinner (which she knew was appropriate because she plays cards on this day), had taken her medications, and had had a medication delivery. Since her mother moved into the smart house, Sally has felt much less stress and worry—much of the burden of care giving had been lifted. Sally still calls her mother each day, but she no longer feels she is being intrusive with asking many questions—she knows how her mother is doing before she places the call.

When Mrs. Smith visits Dr. Jones, he has available, through the internet, a summary of her vital signs and her sleeping, eating, and activity patterns. The large amount of data is analyzed and summarized for Dr. Jones, who receives a one-page summary with clearly marked alerts for any potential health problems. Should Dr. Jones need more information, he can request more detailed reports. He has had several patients with this smart house technology and has been able to identify early symptoms of depression and dementia and thereby provide appropriate treatment.

2.3. THE UNDERLYING TECHNOLOGY OF THE SMART HOUSE

In the previous section, we discussed components of a smart house in terms of functions, with some mention of the underlying technologies, such as sensors. In this section we discuss the *underlying technologies* of the *Gator Tech Smart House*, which include (1) sensors, (2) computers, (3) software, (4) user input devices, (5) user output devices, (6) mechanical hardware, (7) wireless technology, (8) batteries and other power sources, (9) the internet, (10) indoor location tracking technology, (11) smart appliances, (12) other related technology, and (13) human-based service providers. Each will be described below.

Sensors

There are a large number of sensors that can be used in a smart house. Each determines something about Mrs. Smith or her house. Information from sensors is sent to the data storage or data analysis unit—the computer. Specific sensors can detect temperature, moisture, movement, light, sound, acceleration, odors, and much more. Several types of sensors that are being used, or could be used in a smart house, are described below.

Environmental Sensors   These sensors can be placed around the house, or on under furniture and appliances, or on floors and walls. Power consumption is usually less of an issue than with personal, wearable sensors, but it may not be possible for these sensors to determine who is being monitored when more than one person (or person and pet(s)) are present.

Passive Infrared Sensors   These sensors can track movement. Several investigators have used such sensors to study person-movement within living spaces such as homes, nursing, and hospital rooms.[5]

Fiber-Optic Floor Vibration Sensors   Alwan, Dalal, Kell, and Felder describe the use of these sensors in a lab setting to successfully differentiate step count, cadence, pace, and step duration as well as to successfully differentiate among normal gait, limping, and shuffling gait.[6] Furthermore, the sensors can detect falls. The sensors detect gait at distances over 8 feet and work on carpeted, concrete, and wooden floors. Each sensor costs less than $100 and can transmit data wirelessly. Such sensors could be useful in determining general movement in a home (is the person up and doing well), and they can track progress in walking following knee or hip surgery.

Personal, Wearable Sensors   These sensors can be attached to jewelry such as rings,[7] pendants, and watches,[8] or they may be attached directly to the body. While it is possible to collect more basic physiological data with wearable sensors, they have more limitations than environmental sensors: need for power; possibility of not being worn correctly or at all; need for great durability; may be intrusive and potentially uncomfortable or unsightly.

Kinematic Sensor   A recent study demonstrated that body postures (lying, sitting, standing) could be detected with >99% accuracy using a kinematic sensor attached to a person's chest.[9]

Piezoelectric Sensor   These sensors are worn by the person, with voltage produced by body movement.[10]

Computer

A personal computer with an internet connection provides the "smart" (or intelligence) for the smart house.

Software

Several types of software are needed for the smart house. A database program stores the information from all the sensors and commands from Mrs. Smith. An analysis program "digests" the data and sends reports and alerts. Speech recognition software allows Mrs. Smith to give instructions to the smart house simply by speaking them. Many small programs, called "applets," handle sensor and activity specific needs.

User Input Devices

The major input method for the smart house is through voice commands, which require microphone arrays placed around the house (and the speech recognition software). Mrs. Smith can also control many functions in her home using her smart phone, which was the major input device before speech recognition reached its Year 2010 level of sophistication. Occasionally Mrs. Smith, who is an excellent typist, will use a *"projection keyboard and mouse"* to type emails to her family and friends, but her use of these is being superseded by super-reliable voice input.

User Output Devices

The two major output channels for the smart home are video and audio (e.g., flat screen monitors and speakers). Mrs. Smith receives voice messages from her smart house, supplemented by visual messages (video, images or text) on her flat screen monitors. If Mrs. Smith is out gardening (no monitors available), the message is relayed to her phone screen and she receives audio from her phone speakers.

Mechanical Hardware

Some of the devices in Mrs. Smith's home require a mechanical system. These include the door lock, the automatic window opener/closer, and the automatic shades and drapes opener. These devices have been available for several years, but are now integrated into the smart house and can be controlled with voice input.

Wireless Technology

Wireless technology provides an invisible connection between devices. Earlier-generation smart houses typically relied on X-10 technology that used household AC power lines to transmit messages. These systems were often unreliable, as messages could only be sent one way. For example, if the computer sent a message to turn the lights on at 9 P.M., and one light did not go on because the light bulb burned out, the computer would not know this. The advantage of getting a message back to the computer is that it gives the computer the opportunity to take some action, such as alerting Mrs. Smith or the housekeeper, turning on a different light, or adding light bulbs to the shopping list—perhaps all three.

The most common use of wireless technology is for cell phones. We also have wireless systems for connecting our computers to the internet; wireless keyboards and mouse devices; and wireless sensors. The great advantage of wireless technology is the elimination of the need to have a cable or wire between devices, which permits a very high level of mobility. The major downside is that wireless devices require power, usually batteries, which have a limited life between replacement or recharge.

Cell phones use a type of wireless technology that covers a very wide area. The technology continues to advance, and we hear terms like 2G, 2.5G, 3G, and so on, which refer to the generation of the technology. Most digital cell phones in 2001 used either 2G Second Generation Wireless technology or 2.5G. 2G systems for wireless communications offer digital voice and data at low speeds, with limited data connectivity. Some 2G technologies also have low-speed, WAP (defined in next paragraph) mini browsers for access to the internet. Our digital cell phones (standard wireless phones that convert sound into data bits which are then transmitted via radio or microwaves) use 2G.

2.5G provides faster data speeds than 2G. It offers what is called Packet Radio Services with data speeds of 28 Kbps and in some cases higher. Each generation provided a higher data rate and additional capabilities, and 3G (introduced in 2003) offers data speeds up to 384 kbps. A fourth generation (4G) of technology was in the planning and research stages in 2003.

WAP is an abbreviation for Wireless Application Protocol. Internet communications and advanced telephony services to digital phones and other wireless terminals are provided through WAP. WAP is a worldwide standard that operates on any platform providing services that reformat content of internet communications to fit the display screen of the wireless device. This service also supports web browsing, enabling people to search the internet and send messages from a wireless phone. Through the development of WAP, service providers can implement wireless services through a single standard.

Another form of wireless technology is used for communication among devices in much smaller areas such as a home. There are two major types of "small area" wireless technology: Bluetooth and 802.11. Bluetooth is a low-cost short-range wireless radio link that supports communication among portable devices, enabling exchange of information between devices within a small area. This connection is wireless and therefore is not dependent on the use of connecting cables. This technology is also worldwide, uses low power, and operates with minimal interference. In 2003, Bluetooth Home Networking applications included "The Three-in-One Phone" and "The Universal Remote." "The Three-in-One Phone" is a standard cell phone, a wireless service provider, and a cordless phone for use within the home that uses the wired telephone system for service (without the use of a carrier). All of these options are available through the use of "one telephone, one number" regardless of location. "The Universal Remote" refers to the use of Bluetooth devices (PDA, smart phone, etc.) to inquire about and control other devices and appliances equipped with Bluetooth interfaces. Examples are notifications that the clothes are dry or that the dishwasher needs to be run. For devices that are not equipped with Bluetooth interfaces, control of devices via physical interfaces that communicate through a Bluetooth capable home gateway can be used.

802.11 wireless technology operates very similarly to Bluetooth. In 2003, there were three specifications in the 802.11 "family": 802.11a, 802.11b, and 802.11g. The

802.11g offers wireless transmission over relatively shorter distances at very fast speeds: up to 54 megabits per second (Mbps) compared with the 11 Mbps of the 802.11b standard. 802.11a offers the highest speed of 100 Mbps but covers the shortest distance of all 802.11 family. The 802.11b standard is currently considered the most widely used standard in this family and is often called Wi-Fi.

Power Line Communication Networking

The use of household electric lines to carry the same signals as an Ethernet-cabled or wireless computer network has been shown to be possible.[11] While use of these cables had previously been considered too "noisy" to carry data packets, technology advances have made it possible. Thus, appliances could "communicate" over the same lines that provide them power.

Batteries and Other Power Sources

All electronic devices require some type of power. Many of the sensors in Mrs. Smith's *Gator Tech Smart House* system are in a fixed place and rely on the home's AC power source. Others, such as her smart phone, move with her. In 2003, cell phone batteries lasted about a day, and this varied with amount of use.

The Internet

The internet is an important component in the smart house for two reasons: (1) as a pathway for messages and reports and (2) as a source of information and services to the home.

Indoor Location Tracking Technology

The house can be much smarter and much more useful to Mrs. Smith if her location in the house is known at all times. Similarly for Mrs. Smith, it may be important to know where certain objects are located (e.g., a TV remote or her smart phone). Several indoor location tracking technologies have recently emerged including infrared-based, ultrasonic-based, vision-based, and motion detection and point of presence-based. Some of these technologies require that Mrs. Smith wear some identification elements (e.g., a digital tag).

Smart Appliances

Many appliances are now getting smarter and will be part of the smart house. In Mrs. Smith's smart house, the oven will speak out warning Mrs. Smith of a hot surface when she approaches the stove top, or it will call her on the house speaker phone or her smart phone when her food is cooked and ready to be taken out of the oven. Microwave ovens will program themselves to cook frozen food packets. The home theater system will mute when the phone is ringing.

Ambient Intelligence

This term is now being widely used in research and development settings and by technology companies. The idea is that the technology disappears and user needs are met. It incorporates all of the other components described above, with the added aspect of "intelligence." In a home, a system with ambient intelligence is able to discreetly collect relevant information about the occupants, learn their preferences, anticipate their needs, and control their environment with minimal user effort and ease of interaction for user-issued commands.

Other Related Technology

Mrs. Smith's smart house also uses the following technologies, which are a combination of software and hardware.

Feature Recognition   A camera-type device is used to scan a person's face and match to an existing database to correctly identify the individual. This is an important component of Mrs. Smith's security system. When someone rings the doorbell, the person appears on one of her monitors, but with her declining vision she has the extra protection of the smart house "announcing" the person, if the person's face is in the database.

Object Recognition   Object recognition is used to recognize items that might be moved within a home, such as furniture and small appliances. The new location can be noted and used in tracking a person's use of household items. Object recognition methods are considered too slow to use for person tracking.[12]

GPS: Global Positioning System

This is a component on Mrs. Smith's smart phone that provides her with information on where she is and how to get to where she wants to go. Sally can also locate Mrs. Smith when she is outside the home through this system.

Digital ID

Digital ID is a high-tech version of the barcode reader technology. Digital ID is a technology innovated by 3M that offers a variety of products based on radio-frequency identification (RFID), or the transmission of signals between information stored on a "smart tag" and a "reader." The use of digital identification technology requires neither direct contact with a reader, as does magnetic strip technology, nor a direct line of sight with a reader, as does bar code technology. Smart tags contain memory and a dormant memory emitter. When beamed by a reader, the dormant emitter is charged enough to send the memory contents to the reader. Mrs. Smith's smart microwave oven is able to identify food packets with this technology. Should Mrs. Smith's vision decline to where she can no longer select her clothes, this technology could be used in the smart house for her to get a verbal description of a selected clothes item from her closet.

Human-Based Service Providers

The technology requires support. In Mrs. Smith's smart house, the technology is "almost" bug-free, but a technician visits every 6 months to check battery power and to update system components. Technology will never be a substitute for human interaction. Mrs. Smith has a number of supportive people in her life that assist with transportation, shopping, and leisure activities. She has 24/7 human backup support in the event of an emergency. She has delivery people, medical people, friends, and family. Sally, Tommy, Joe, and Dr. Jones are just a few of the people that technology cannot replace; however, smart house technology can make each of them more effective in assisting Mrs. Smith to remain independent.

2.4   OVERVIEW OF THE STATE OF THE SCIENCE IN SMART HOMES AND SMART HOME COMPONENTS AND RELATED ISSUES

This section begins with a description of commercial smart house ventures—that is, actual housing that has been built using current smart house approaches. This is followed by descriptions of non-university-based and university-based demonstration/model home/labs where prototype smart home components are being developed and or demonstrated. Several individual smart home components are grouped in a section on individual smart home devices and components. User interface research and development is then described, followed by a discussion of research and development on the actual home designing process.

Commercial Ventures Using Smart Home Technology

We discuss three commercial residential smart house projects in this section.

Village at Tinker Creek, Roanoke, Virginia   In April 2003, residents began moving into the first community of smart homes in this country, in Roanoke, Virginia.[13] While not specifically designed for people with disabilities, but providing a high level of control, residents can control lighting, air conditioning and heating, and security system from anywhere they have an internet connection—in the home or away from home. A unique feature of the home is the use of web cameras throughout the house. With these cameras, residents can, for example, check to see if the garage door is closed—many people worry that they may have left the garage door open after driving out. The system will not only provide a real-time view of the garage, but will allow the resident to close the door, even if miles away. Another potential use of this system is for security. It can be set up so that police in a patrol car, following notification of an unapproved entry, could observe an intruder in the house via the web and the cameras—even while they drive to the home. In addition to home monitoring for security and control, residents can track community events and news from the Web. For some people, including older people and people with disabilities, the use of cameras in these homes could seem invasive, especially if they are being monitored for safety reasons. Less invasive approaches to monitoring are described in this chapter.

The homes are being built by Commonwealth Builders. The system used in the home was developed by IBM in partnership with CP Technology in His-Chih, Taiwan, and General Electronics in Shanghai. The gateway for the system, called CP Technology Residential Services Gateway, supports OSGI (Open Services Gateway Initiative), so as new applications are developed, they can easily be added to the system. Some of these applications could be downloaded directly from the internet. Smart appliances could be added to the system, offering such features as automatic notification of repair and maintenance providers. The community of 170 homes, costing about $200,000 each, was established with 20 of these smart houses, and the system was offered as an option for other home buyers at a cost of approximately $3500. IBM envisions the system that will eventually to be able to offer self-reading meters, and it also envisions appliances that alert the homeowner in the event of a potential shutdown or failure.

IT Condominiums, Ringblomman, Stockholm, Sweden   e2Home, partnering with construction (Skanska) and telecom companies, designed and built 59 condominiums in Stockholm.[14] The "smart" condominiums address home management, family management, and condominium administration communication. Home management includes security and safety services such as detection and reporting of fires, water leakage, and intruder alarms. Alerts can be issued on site, through phone messages to the occupant when they are away, or directly to an appropriate service provider (fire company, police). The condominiums use an electrical locking system. Family management includes a common family calendar for scheduling activities of all family members. Family management also offers a platform for food management, including shopping and meal preparation. Applications are controlled by an "appliance terminal" with a touch screen, or a personal computer, typically placed in the kitchen or office. Applications can also be controlled remotely via the internet. At present, the home offers greater user control at home or away, energy efficiency, lower insurance premiums, and improved security.

Netherlands Demonstrations   Van Berlo discussed smart homes in the Netherlands at ICADI.[15] They have established a demonstration project with 55 residents in 20 apartments. Major applications in the smart homes address security, care, and comfort, including: access control using a camera, chip card, electronic lock, caregiver access, and an intruder alarm; an active emergency alarm, a passive alarm, and a smoke alarm; automatic lighting; gas stove and gas detector; water-flow meter to determine inactivity; central switch above the bed, automatic curtain closures, movement detectors for lighting at night. Cost is estimated at a monthly service charge of 15 Euros per month. Setup costs were estimated at 5000 to 8000 Euros per house (3–5% of total house cost). While some residents initially had difficulty with the features of the smart house, all were pleased to have the added safety and security it provided. However, several mentioned that they did not require all the functions the house offered. There were also a significant number of problems with false alarms in the first days of use.

Demonstration/Model Homes—Non-University-Based

In this section, we describe Microsoft's EasyLiving project, Honeywell's Independent LifeStyle System, and the Varmdovik Project in Stockholm, Sweden.

Microsoft's EasyLiving   The EasyLiving project at Microsoft, described in 2001, featured a high-technology living room.[16] The project team worked on developing the software (prototype architecture) and related technology for supporting an intelligent environment that could be used in such places as smart houses. The research team identified key areas of the research and development as (1) perceiving people in context, (2) perceiving objects in context, (3) perceiving people for a user interface, (4) perceiving objects for a user interface, and (5) privacy. The first area, perceiving people in context, avoided use of automatic person recognition, as the team felt this could be intrusive or an invasion of privacy. The user must indicate to the system who he or she is, and the system then responds to preset or learned preferences in its responses (such as selection of music, or level of lighting or temperature). The system tracks where people are located and determines the activities in which they are engaged, so that appropriate assistance can be provided in the appropriate place. The second area, "perceiving objects in context," relates to first recognizing objects, tracking them (where things such as furniture and keys are located, even if moved). The third area relates to having the person serve as the user interface, through such means as gestures, pointing, gazing, or, perhaps most easily, speech. For people with severe speech limitations, gestures, pointing, and gazing would offer excellent possibilities for user control of the system. The fourth area, "perceiving objects for a user interface," relates to such now-common devices as hand-held remote control units, as well as such advanced prototypes as Microsoft's XWand. XWand is a wireless device that includes sensors, in the shape of a wand, and can determine its orientation within a room, allowing it to control most devices in the home. The final area of research in this project focused on privacy, ensuring that no unauthorized person had access to any of the electronic information the house gathered.

Independent LifeStyle Assistant™ (ILSA)   ILSA is an intelligent home automation system designed to enable older adults as well as younger people with disabilities to live independently and safely at home. The system is designed to increase social contact and information exchange between the residents and care providing family members. Miller, Wu, Krichbaum, and Kiff described the design principles for ILSA at ICADI.[17] They include the following: (1) use of nonintrusive components; (2) limiting of interface to telephone and web pad; (3) system should generate data on resident's status rather than require self-report; (4) system should require minimal effort for setup and use. Implementation of these principles resulted in such actions as: (1) removal of LED indicators on motion sensors; (2) avoidance of use of interactive switches; (3) resident is not constantly provided with reports of their status, but the resident can initiate an inquiry; (4) medication reminders are provided only by telephone (no alarms); (5) clients were not called and asked questions, but use of phone and web pad were tracked to determine cognitive status; (6) to change settings such as medication regime and sleep time, clients request assistance from caregivers. Justiss, Mann, Helal, Dasler, and Kiff described at ICADI the outcomes of beta-testing ILSA in the homes of four older persons with disabilities in northern Florida.[18] Kiff and Plocher described the technology issues with ILSA at ICADI.[19] They state: "Significant issues were encountered at each stage of development and deployment. Barriers to the commercial deployment of an ILSA-like system include ease of installation and maintenance, development of adequate monitoring centers, successful integration with third-party providers, and accurate sensing of significant events in the home." ILSA had not yet been commercialized at the time of publication of this book.

Varmdovik Project, Stockholm, Sweden   e2Home, working with JM, built a smart house to be used as a demonstration home and as a model for additional smart homes that will be built and sold in Sweden.[20] One unique aspect of this smart house is the interface, called "Screenfridge," a touch screen built into to the refrigerator, supplied by Electrolux. This smart house includes (a) automation for lighting, (b) control and monitoring of electricity, water use, and air temperature, and (c) control of window coverings.

Oatfield Estates, Milwaukie, Oregon   Oatfield Estates is an assisted living facility, designed to incorporate the latest technology. All resident rooms have a touch-screen computer with a high-speed internet connection. Residents and staff wear a small locator badge clipped to their clothing. This badge has a call button and is also used as a room key. The location of residents and staff is tracked using both infrared and radio frequencies and is recorded by computers. Tracking of the time it takes staff to respond to resident calls helps ensure timely responses. Residents' weight and sleep patterns are monitored using sensors placed under the bedposts. Twelve residents reside in each housing unit, with three staff members. Individual residents pay approximately $4000 per month, and couples pay $5000 (*Business Journal Portland*, 2003).[21]

Research Lab/Demonstration Homes—University-Based

Most smart home research labs are university-based, with the major ones at MIT, Georgia Institute of Technology, the University of Virginia, and the University of Florida. Most are used for demonstrating and testing the specific aspect of technology they are developing. Only two (MIT and University of Florida) conduct experiments where people live in the smart house for some period of time. These labs are described in this section.

University of Florida Smart House Lab   This lab, described in ICADI, builds on the concept of pervasive computing to assist older people with disabilities to live independently.[22] Initially, the lab-home was designed to use the smart phone as a universal interface in the home (1) for the resident to instruct the house to do certain tasks (unlock door, check security, turn on lights, control the entertainment system) and (2) for the house to assist the resident (issue medication reminders; alert the resident that mail has been delivered; track the user's movement throughout the home so that if the user fell, an alert could be issued). The above are examples of more than 15 applications that have been developed and successfully tested in the Smart House Lab. More recent advances are enabling the resident (Matilda, a robotic device) to interact directly with the Smart House through voice commands, and they enable the house to communicate with Matilda through speakers in each room and through flat panel LCD displays in each room. With the ultrasound tracking system, the house knows which monitors and/or speakers to use to communicate with Matilda—the house knows where Matilda is in the house and only uses the monitor and speakers in the room, and on the wall when walls have multiple monitors, where she is seating or moving about. Yet more recent experiments in tracking systems are exploring the use of (a) pressure sensor pads under the carpet and (b) vibration detecting sensors in the floor. Successfully tested Smart House Lab applications are moved to the Gator-Tech Smart House, a free-standing smart home, where older people with disabilities live with and use the applications for further user/application refinement.

University of Virginia Medical Automation Research Center (MARC)   The MARC center has been developing a number of components for the smart house of the future. We discussed their use of optic-fiber vibration sensors earlier. Alwan, Kell, Dalal, Turner, Mack, and Felder described at ICADI an in-home monitoring system they are developing that includes low-cost sensors, data logging, and a communications module with a web-based data management server. The system is able to track and infer activities based on "spatial temporal relationships between sensor firings." Current activity, a log of activity, and trends can be accessed through the internet by care providers. The activity tracking system was successfully tested against user activity logs, which were also automated on a self-report system they developed for a PDA. The system provides a time and date stamp for each entry in the activity log for increasing reliability over paper and pencil self-reporting. Recent work has focused on development and testing of a system for an assisted living facility that would also include real-time alerting for staff. Other work includes a low-cost approach to measuring sleep quality, using a number of sensors for body temperature, sleeping position and movement, and breathing and heart rate. Many of these sensors are embedded in a mattress pad that can sense subject position, body temperature, breathing, pulse, and room light level. Yet another system is being developed that analyzes meal preparation patterns. Activity patterns, such as those involved with preparing a meal, are much more difficult to determine than simple physiological signs like heartbeat and body temperature. This system is able to show consistent patterns of breakfast and dinner preparation. Such a system could be integrated into a smart house to determine if the occupant has varied from the normal meal preparation routine and may not be getting meals due to illness or a more gradual loss of appetite, which could lead to malnutrition.

University of Texas at Arlington MavHome   Cook, Das, Gopalratnam and Roy described the MavHome at ICADI (http://ranger.uta.edu/smarthome/).[23] Their research and development centers on a prototype for a home health monitoring system that will also assist in basic daily activities. MavHome sensors track vital signs, movement patterns, medicine taking schedules, and interaction with devices in the home. MavHone can determine water usage in the home, temperature settings, weight of the resident, movement in the home, prescribed and actual medication schedule, use of food items in the kitchen, and time duration and intensity of exercise.

University of Rochester Center for Future Health   Pentland and Philippe described at ICADI a multi-campus effort to develop a technology-based personal health system.[24] The goal of this effort is to use technology to move from a disease treatment, hospital-based "health system" to home and community-based health promotion. While at this point the system is proposed as a model, developed, and implemented, it would identify diseases early through sensors in the home, provide health management tools for promoting independence in the face of chronic conditions, and provide emergency response services. The system would work both in the home and community.

Georgia Institute of Technology Aware Home   Abowd, Bobick, Essa, Fisk, Mynatt, and Rogers described at ICADI an "Aware Home for Aging in Place."[25] The Aware Home was built to meet the design and functional requirements of a home that someone could live in, and it also has facilities for instruments. Each room has sensors and displays to facilitate interactions between the house and residents. A major focus of work has been on applications for supporting persons with cognitive impairment in daily activities and communications. Sensing equipment includes cameras, microphones, infrared, sonar, and tactile devices. Tracking people throughout the home is done with a range of sensors from RFID to computer vision systems. The Aware Home also has an activity recognition system to track the activities engaged in by residents. Specific applications under development include a blood glucose monitor aid, a memory aid for use in the kitchen, and a unique system called "digital portrait," which assists family members in tracking the status of the resident.

PlaceLab   Intille, Larson, and Tapia described their smart-home-related work at MIT.[26] They have developed a portable kit that includes "tape-on" sensors, which are used to study behaviors in people's homes. At this point the sensors track movement of objects in the home such as furniture and kitchen tools—in one test home they deployed 85 sensors. The authors state that information from the sensors can be used to "help people learn about their own behavior . . . how they use their own homes and how they might redesign them." (p. 10) The system can also track behavior in the home, which in turn can be used to determine when behaviors have changed and whether the resident(s) is experiencing a problem. These same investigators have also developed PlaceLab, "a residential observational facility . . . that will serve as a "living laboratory" to study how people respond to new proactive health technologies." (p. 11)[27] The facility was under construction during ICADI, and it was scheduled to open in 2004. PlaceLab will use low-cost sensors attractively placed in the model home to study people living in the home, thereby focusing on long-term proactive health behaviors.

Adaptive House, University of Colorado The Adaptive House focuses on automation of energy conservation approaches.[28] The research conducted for the Adaptive House is focused on designing a home system that programs itself, based on the lifestyle, needs, and preferences of the residents. The house not only learns their needs, but anticipates them. By observing the residents adjusting the thermostat or turning on certain lights at a certain intensity (for three-way or fully adjustable lights), the intelligence of the home will infer patterns on which it takes actions. The home uses over 75 sensors that monitor air temperature, lighting level, sound, motion, and openings of windows and doors. The learning and prediction capability of the house is based on "neural network" software. With this approach the house can predict when the residents will be home or away, when to start heating or cooling the home to a comfortable temperature, when to lower the water heater when there is a certainty no one will need hot water, and control of lighting—both on and off and intensity, including anticipation of rooms that will be entered so lighting can be set before the person enters. Such a home would not only be more energy-efficient, but would make life more comfortable and easier for its occupants.

Individual Components and Devices within a Smart House, and Related Research

Several research and development teams have focused on individual devices that could be integrated within a smart home. We describe several of them in this section.

Memory Aid for Cooking Tran and Mynatt (2002) report on a prototype memory aid for cooking.[29] The system uses PC cameras located under kitchen cabinets (largely out of sight). The cameras capture hand activities on the stove and kitchen counters. The computers are "hidden" in kitchen counters. Output is provided on an LCD flat panel on one of the kitchen cabinets. A collage of images is presented on the LCD panel as the user cooks. The collage represents the sequence of six previous actions while cooking. As the user completes another action, it is posted on the collage, with the bottom right corner presenting the most recent action. At the point of their report, Tran and Mynatt were using a Wizard of Oz approach to simulate the system. Twelve users (all undergraduate psychology students) tested the system, with an additional five control participants who did not use the system but were given the same recipe (for preparing cookie dough) as the system users. Design challenges were determined. For example, with the system using still images, an image of a person adding a cup of flour does not convey that it is the third or fourth cup—there just isn't enough information. Other systems using video replays have been designed, but the disadvantage is the time it takes to review the video. Another issue not addressed by these investigators relates to the usefulness of such systems for people who are forgetful, such as people in the early stages of Alzheimer's disease. Research on the system with persons with memory impairment would be a logical and important extension of this work.

Carewatch   At ICADI, Rowe addressed the issue of sleep for people with Alzheimer's disease and their caregivers.[30] Studies have shown that almost all people with dementia demonstrate abnormalities in sleep–wake pattern when studied in lab situations. These abnormalities include an increase in the number of awakenings and in the time awake. Over 50% of caregivers are impacted by these sleep disturbances. The aim of Carewatch is to develop and test a prototype system to be used by persons with dementia and their caregivers to (a) prevent unattended exits and nighttime injuries, (b) improve caregiver sleep, (c) reduce worry, and (d) potentially decrease the need for nursing home placement. The Carewatch system includes (1) a control panel that is situated next to the caregiver's bed and (2) sensors for detecting motion, door openings, and pressure in bed. When the system detects activity at night, the caregiver is alerted through text, voice, and alert message alarms. The caregiver immediately receives information on the location of the care recipient.

Philips WWICE (World Wide Information, Communication and Entertainment)   Philips, one of the world's largest electronics companies, is developing a system in which is embedded what they term "ambient intelligence," which encompasses ubiquitous computing (access to any information source, anywhere, anytime), natural interaction (voice control), and intelligence. Major functions of WWICE is for entertainment and communication.

Microsoft Light Control Study   Many aspects of a smart house can be fully automated, only requiring adjustment when the user has exceptional needs. For example, the smart house may be able to predict and set the temperature for the occupants automatically on all days. Yet if the occupants are planning a party with a large number of people and want to "take over" control of the temperature so they can lower it prior to people arriving, they will need the option of issuing commands to the house. What is the optimal, preferred way to issue commands? A group at Microsoft Research studied this for one task—turning lights on and off.[31] They had a study group interact with several (but not all) of eight different switching methods and then rank their choices using a card-sort approach. The switching methods included (1) normal switches, (2) touch lights, (3) hand-clapping-controlled, (4) computer panel (on wall) control, (5) computer tablet (could be moved around the room), (6) speech-operated, (7) speech plus pointing, and (8) automatic sensing, with a computer using intelligence to determine what lighting the person would like. The two speech methods (with and without pointing) were ranked highest. Limitations of the study include a very limited amount of time (a few minutes or less) participants had with each method.

Designing a Smart Home   The future of home design and building is also likely to be very different from now, predicts Kent Larson of MIT's PlaceLab.[32] While today home building is largely a local enterprise, large companies not presently in the business will move in, creating competition and innovation. A home, including its smart components, will be designed by its future occupants (in Mrs. Smith's case, with the help of her adult children) using the internet, where they can easily learn about all the options available and select those that match their needs. While there will be much more technology available, cost will actually decline, as mass production and competition in the housing industry come into play. Evidence that this vision of the future has already begun to materialize is found in the creation of a new company, called e2Home, by Ericsson and Electrolux in December 1999. E2Home conducts research, development, and marketing of technology-related services for networked homes, and it is behind two major high-tech building developments in Sweden: IT Apartments and Varmdovik, described earlier in this chapter.

Borodulkin, Ruser, and Trankler stress the importance of an easy-to-use control system for a smart house.[33] They created a graphical interface using 3D programming tools. They base their system on four principals: (1) The user interface should provide a clear graphical "picture" or representation of the home; (2) the system must be easy to set up; as new components are added or removed, the interface should not need major attention; (3) the users should be able to adapt the interface to their own needs and preferences; (4) the system should allow remote (within and away from home) control of the home.

Funded by the European Union's TIDE program, CUSTODIAN (which is an acronym for Conceptualization for User Involvement in Specification and Tools Offering the Delivery of System Integration Around Home) is a personal computer-based system for designing and validating how well a home automation system will work prior to purchasing and installing it. Basically it is a software program, based on Microsoft Vision that assists in the preparation of a flow diagram. The user can design a smart home network by selecting device icons and placing them on a template. The final system will also prepare an item order list and a cost estimate using currently available products.[34]

For a homeowner to set up their house as a smart house, all of the components in their home must be ready to "communicate with each other" and to interact with the homeowner. What if you have a GE dishwasher, a Frigidare refrigerator, and a Sharp microwave oven? Will they all be able to use the same smart house infrastructure? A consortium of companies is working to ensure that it will be possible, through establishment of the Virtual Private Infrastructure, designed to provide guidelines for secure and unified web-based control of appliances and other devices in the home.[35]

Summary   Homes can be made smart with today's technology. With advances in the underlying technologies and the development of new applications, we can expect that in the next several years we will have homes that provide very supportive environments for older people with disabilities. New products and systems will be introduced that can be added to existing homes and as options for new homes.

2.5   SMART HOUSE CONSTRUCTION— AN ARCHITECT'S PERSPECTIVE

Concept

A smart house, at its simplest, is any home that has some measure of automation built into it, the concept being that a smart house can "think" for itself. The precise point at which a house is no longer a simple house with a few gadgets, but a smart house, is an undefined threshold. The common understanding may be, however, that any house ahead of the automation curve is a smart house.

Mankind hasn't always lived in houses. Caves—probably the first step toward a controlled environment—came right after sleeping under the stars or in trees. As we've learned to control more and more of our environment, and as the means of doing so has become less and less expensive, the "technology" to do so—from doors to fuel cells—has found, and will continue to find, its way into our homes. Indoor plumbing, which had been used in palaces and grand homes as early as 4000 B.C., didn't find its way into the average home until the twentieth century. In fact, in the early 1900s fewer than 20% of the houses in the United States had a flush toilet. In the mid-1700s, electricity was first thought of as a potential controllable power source, but it wasn't until Edison produced a practical incandescent light bulb in the late 1800s that indoor lighting became reality. In 1890, only a quarter of American homes had running water, very few had electricity, and none had central heating as we know it today. So we can see that the technology curve is very steep indeed.

In the Gator-Tech Smart House, plumbing, electricity, and central air conditioning are all taken for granted. The technology that qualifies this as a smart house is a central nervous system that interconnects various appliances and fixtures and allows monitoring of, and responsiveness to, the occupant.

The Smart House Movement

The early smart house movement was largely driven by safety and efficiency concerns—safety in the sense that if power to a lamp is turned off in the wall (at the outlet) instead of at the fixture, there is less of a chance of injury to someone plugging or unplugging the lamp or changing its bulb. In practice, one way to accomplish this would be to put a switch behind every outlet. This would of course yield a plethora of wall switches, with a typical living room requiring dozens of switches; more switches would be needed if you wanted to be able to control the outlets from more than a single location. Another way to resolve this would be to provide sensing outlets that could determine whether a lamp required power or not, by checking at high frequency whether the switch on the lamp was closed or open. At such time as the outlet sensed the switch was closed, it would power the lamp.

A simple stereo system is, in many ways, like the electrical system in a house. A single receiver/amplifier can provide music to several sets of speakers, just as the electrical service to a house can provide electricity to numerous outlets and appliances. Consider, however, an installation where a stereo is located in your den and speakers are located in the den, bedroom, dining, and living rooms. Ideally there would be an independent connection run to each of the rooms. This means that there would be many pairs of wires running from speakers back to the den and the stereo. From the stereo in the den, you could select which room or combination of rooms you wanted music to play in. You would have a fair amount of control. If that den later became a nursery, however, the stereo would have to move. You'd be able to plug it in in any room in the house, but all of the speaker lines would need to be re-run.

We have accommodated electrical systems fairly well in our houses. In fact, building codes actually guarantee a minimum level of electrical accessibility, primarily to limit the number of extension cords used and gain a measure of safety from that limitation. Stereo systems are still a young technology, and there are few houses built with central systems that would allow you to move your stereo around freely within the house. There are a couple of reasons for this: One, stereos and speakers have a simple but direct relationship. Whereas the power supplied to most every outlet in a house is a uniform 110 volts, and that is all you require for the lamp or appliance to function as you wish, the speaker output is dependent upon the stereo not just being on, but being tuned to the right source. Were this not the case, you could simply leave the stereo wherever it was first installed, tuned to your favorite radio station, and install a volume control switch on each speaker. This is essentially what is done with electrical power.

The ability to control a speaker from the speaker requires communication between the speaker and the source. It requires a means of transmitting instructions regarding what to listen to, where to listen, and at what volume. The same wires between amplifier and speaker that provide the signal for the speakers output could be used for communication in the other direction of course—as long as the connection at the amplifier side were modified to accept an incoming signal. Ethernet, a network protocol for interconnection of computers, provides a model of this communicating system. The same wires that provide the data stream to the computer also allow the computer to respond to the data source to identify itself and communicate its state—on, off, ready to receive data, and so on. In a simple point-to-point network, a network of peers, two computers are able to share information with one another, and even to control one another.

The progression from lamp to stereo to computer network is one of evolving communication—from a lamp with no communication abilities, only the ability to accept or inhibit input, and the power supply that can also either send or not send; to the stereo, which can send a variety of signals that are interpreted by the speaker to become a variety of sounds; to the computer, which has full communicative abilities enabling it to be operated either locally or remotely—and is seeing a similar parallel in the smart house realm, but is hampered by the vast array of appliances and communications standards produced today. One of the earliest communications standards available to the homeowner is X10. X10 has fairly well captured the DIY end of the home automation market, and today it offers a third-party controller for many consumer devices, from lighting to draperies and security systems. Because of the flexibility of the X10 system, and its ability to be added on after the fact, it provides a suitable means for one to experiment and for the retrofit of existing systems. The X10 is not a full peer-to-peer communication system, but rather a collection of transmitter and receiver modules that communicate via radio-frequency (RF) signals sent over existing AC house wiring. To extend the X10 system beyond the house wiring system, wireless controllers are available that send either RF or IR (infrared) signals to transceiver modules plugged into the power system that translate the signal into an X10 signal to be transmitted over the house wiring. Interfacing this system with a home computer allows complex commands to be sent that can control a number of devices and can time-sequence their operation in order to provide a substantial array of results.

More recently we have begun to see the development of more advanced interconnectivity between devices within the home, much of it centered on the protocol TCP/IP. TCP/IP has advantages over earlier communications systems in that it has essentially developed from the top down. Deployed first on the largest intercomputer network (then Arpanet), it was quickly accepted by those wanting to participate in the sharing of information available on that network. It has since worked its way down from University and Government computing centers to individual computers, and then out to the consumer. Network Control Protocol/Internet Protocol is today's de facto standard for digital networks. While computers were the first devices to make use of the standard, it is quickly gaining in the telephony field, as Voice-over IP (VOIP) takes advantage of existing computer network infrastructure to provide an advanced means of controlling telephone networks within business organizations.

One of the greatest advantages of TCP/IP is the ability to address devices. TCP/IP over Ethernet allows for a simple hub-and-spoke configuration in which relatively inexpensive devices at the hubs direct signals to the appropriate end devices. The X10 communication protocol sends its signal over all branches of the electrical system, and it will trip every device with the same address. Each device on an Ethernet network is individually addressed, and the addresses can be predetermined or assigned.

On the consumer end, we are now seeing the advent of IP entertainment systems featuring music and video streamed over the internet, captured onto massive data storage devices, and played back on demand. Other devices that operate on TCP/IP include video surveillance cameras, email appliances, a wide range of security devices, and, first among common appliances, the refrigerator. IP devices are also prevalent among commercial audio–visual systems, allowing technicians to diagnose or control them remotely. Some will even send out warning messages when they are in need of service.

The opportunity to quickly and easily connect various appliances (refrigerators!) each with the ability to communicate will revolutionize housing as we know it. For a relatively low additional cost, manufacturers can add features that will distinguish their products from the competition. Regardless of how simple it is to program an oven from the control panel, it will inevitably be simpler from a 17-inch touch screen! Especially when, because every appliance in the house is addressable, you'll inevitably have a screen in every room.

Today, however, with all of the various communications needs and the multiple standards supporting them that we find in a house, the question quickly becomes one of where to run a connection, and which connection(s) to run. While there is currently something of a standard for wiring a smart house (typically a pair of coax and a pair of cat 5 cables), the cost of investing in a structured cabling system can be exorbitant—unless you are certain of every exact location you will need to have wired, and certain that you will not be changing your mind later.

Housing Construction

There are, generally speaking, two types of walls within a building: space-defining walls and structural—or load-bearing—walls. Space-defining walls form the boundary between functions, giving shape to rooms. Bearing walls also define spaces, but the primary reason for their existence is support—of floors, ceilings, and roofs. In early home construction, most walls were bearing walls because of limits on the means to span large distances. Today relatively few walls in a house are bearing walls because it is more efficient to minimize their number—to be able to stand the structure of a house and close it in—than to divide up the enclosed space into the desired rooms.

Wall construction also falls broadly into two categories: generally speaking, either solid (monolithic) or hollow. In most modern construction, solid walls are also bearing walls. They tend to be brick or block exterior walls, where the mass of the wall provides benefits beyond structure, such as thermal mass, appearance, or durability. Similarly, the horizontal elements of construction (floors and ceilings), while generally both structural and defining, are also either hollow or solid. Why does this matter? Because as long as the technology brought into our homes requires a conduit—be it pipe, duct, or wire—there needs to be passage for the conduit.

If we look again at electrical and plumbing systems, these are typically run in the cavities that exist within wall, floor, and ceiling construction; and for a one- or two-story home with basement and attic, that is a very satisfactory solution. Pipes and wires can be run during construction, and access for maintenance or modifications can be had via the basement or attic. If the floor is concrete (slab-on-grade), things such as electrical wiring are run elsewhere (walls, attic). Things that rely on gravity to function, such as waste water lines, are often buried in or below the concrete.

In more complex construction such as office buildings, chases are provided vertically through the building to allow the interconnection and distribution of systems. Superducts may carry forced air over many floors, giant cables carry power, and thousands of glass fiber strands carry data and phone signals. When these systems are distributed throughout a floor, they are most often concealed in a plenum space between the ceiling and the floor above. Penetrations between the two levels allow interconnection where they must feed through the floor and "drops" from the ceiling provide the connection when there is a concealing wall or the appearance of a lone conduit is not an issue.

In the last decade, commercial office installations have seen the growth of raised floor systems. Originally used only in data centers, this product is now being found throughout the office, the idea being that with a raised floor system the entire necessary infrastructure required to support a modern office environment can be provided close at hand, without needing to raise the ceiling or to bore through the floor. Raised floor buildings are seen as the way of the future, but they have yet to overcome economic obstacles in many areas.

Like offices, houses are filled with equipment and appliances that are mobile. But whereas the extent of "connected" equipment in an office is often limited to computer equipment—PCs, printers, telephones—the range of fixtures in a house is greatly expanded and, at the smart house, may include wired medicine cabinets, beds, chairs, and motion sensors. This means that for this smart house it is desirable to have the most flexible distribution system possible.

The Gator Tech Smart House

The smart house is a simple house: one story, slab-on grade (no basement—the concrete floor is poured directly on earth—with an attic over the whole). The plan for the house is based on a typical three-bedroom unit for Oak Hammock Retirement Community—the community where the smart house was built.

For the specific purposes of the Gator Tech smart house (Figure 2.1), a few minor modifications were made. The secondary bedrooms were converted to lab space—that is, workrooms for monitoring the smart house and its occupants. Halls and doorways were widened to allow independent wheelchair access. The central coat and storage closets were combined to form a single larger storage closet to accommodate furniture needed for events but not for day-to-day operations. Similarly, the den and dining room were combined to allow for a larger space that can be used as a conference space, as well as a living area. The master suite was given more direct entry, and the master bath was reconfigured to provide a roll-in shower and a wheelchair-accessible toilet. Doors in the master suite were also changed to pocket sliding doors, so that they could be left open to provide the least obstruction of passage, yet be pulled closed when privacy is desired.

The Gator Tech kitchen is perhaps the most pronounced change from the standard unit. Although the plan configuration remains largely unchanged, the specific distribution of appliances, as well as the appliances used, has been changed somewhat. The smart house kitchen cabinets all feature roll-out shelves in the base cabinets, eliminating the need to reach into them. Under-cabinet lights illuminate the work surfaces along the wall; recessed lights illuminate the island and sink area. Upper cabinets are a combination of standard upper cabinets for storage of lightweight and infrequently used items.

Figure 2.1   Gator Tech smart house.

The island provides a wet-work area with a pot-filler faucet, dual dishwasher, and under-counter refrigerator. The refrigerator and freezer are independent units, each located beneath the counter. Both are drawer units that eliminate stacking of items through the depth of a shelf, both drawers are easily accessible from a wheelchair, and because the drawers have sides, they retain more "cool" when left open. The dishwasher is actually a pair of dishwashers stacked one above the other. Each drawer can be run independently, so there is the option of only using the top if need is limited, along with the possibility of living from one unit while loading the other, thereby limiting the need to put dishes away!

The pot filler faucet allows for filling of a bowl, pot, or pan without the need to lift it from the sink when full. Similarly, the oven is mounted at counter height, with a pull-out counter beneath it, so minimal lifting is required as food preparation moves from sink to counter to oven. A side-opening door on the oven also allows the cook to get closer to the oven, without having to reach over a hot door. The cook top unit used in the smart house is a halogen-fired unit with a ceramic top. Not only does the immediate illumination of the halogen burner give a better indication of the burner in use than either a gas flame (which is difficult to see under some lighting conditions) or a standard electrical coil, but the ceramic top does a good job of limiting the spread of heat on the surface and also cools relatively quickly. In addition to being easy to clean, the cook top has a raised lip that will contain overflow or spills up to one-half gallon, which aids general cleanup and enhances safety. Finally the microwave oven—an indispensable appliance in a modern kitchen—is located at the edge of the kitchen, convenient to both breakfast and dining room.

The floor system most readily distinguishes the Gator Tech smart house from any of the other club homes at Oak Hammock. As mentioned previously, the smart house is built—like all of the club homes—slab-on-grade with wood-framed walls and ceiling. The roof bears on the exterior walls and, for the most part, spans the interior members of the roof trusses, leaving little room for negotiation within the attic.

For the club home to be successful meant that it would have to be flexible enough to support numerous experiments—perhaps hundreds—during its life as a working laboratory. The primary concern was the ability to provide wired connections to the various sensors and equipment that would be deployed and redeployed throughout the house.

Standard residential drywall construction is amazingly resilient. There is little to encumber any desired equipment placement, particularly when running vertically within a wall, because the wall is essentially parallel vertical voids separated by wood studs and skinned by drywall. Drywall is easily modified and repaired with simple and inexpensive tools and supplies. Understanding a few basic construction principals allows the average handy individual to creatively solve the problem of mounting equipment precisely where needed. Ceiling placement of equipment is also relatively easy, because the construction is similar, but in this case the ceilings are skinned on only one side and are filled with insulation. They are also accessible directly from the attic. Walls and ceilings then provide a satisfactory environment for a living working home laboratory. Equipped with drywall compound, scraps of drywall, paint, and a few tools, it will be possible to continue to modify the smart house as required for years with no great effort or expense.

The design of residential construction can overcome much of the difficulty that might be expected in repeatedly running wires out to new equipment while maintaining a homey appearance can be overcome. Because the Gator Tech smart house is slab-on-grade, however, one of the best potential routes for accessing the walls—from an unfinished basement below—was not available. With the heat in Florida, along with limited access through the attic, it too was eliminated as anything but an occasional route for accessing the ceiling itself. The solution came from the office model.

There are a number of raised floor solutions available today that are built for remodel and low cable loads. Most are in use in Europe and Asia, but a few are making inroads in the United States. Unlike the higher raised floor systems (those in the 12 to 24-inch range), low-profile floors are not adjustable in height. They install directly over the floor slab, and they follow the contours of the slab. But to their advantage and in part because they are nonadjustable, they are extremely simple to install and lend themselves to this type of an installation.

To facilitate use of motion sensing equipment, there is also a dropped crown molding throughout the house that is fed by conduit from the space beneath the floor (Figure 2.2). The crown has a recessed shelf that can support small cameras, infrared or radio-frequency sensors, and other equipment.

The raised product chosen for the Gator Tech smart house is a low-profile floor made up of PVC and steel. It has a small module, allowing it to be easily tailored to the intricacies of a residential plan. The PVC makeup is also a plus in an environment as humid as Florida's. By using a raised floor throughout the house, cables

Figure 2.2   Dropped crown molding in the Gator Tech house for cabling and sensors.

can be quickly and easily run from the workrooms to any room in the house, and they can be reconfigured as the need arises (Figure 2.3). Once the cables are in the right position along the wall, they can be run up inside the wall to any height necessary. The floor itself is very stiff, because it is supported almost continuously, with the maximum span being only about 5 inches. In addition to the ability to run connections throughout the house beneath the floor, the floor also provides a means of distributing sensors that track movement through the house or of weighing an individual as they walk over an area of the floor.

Modular carpet applied over the raised floor provides a look that is contemporary, yet based on traditional. The carpet chosen is a neutral Berber, with a nondirectional pattern that lends itself well to this application, and is indeed a product that has recently been brought to the residential market by a major commercial carpet manufacturer. Their intended target market: a generation of urban loft-dwellers.

Like the raised floor and carpet, many of the components used in the house have come from the corporate world. The electronic strike on the front door that allows the door to be unlocked remotely is commonplace in office environments. Sensing controls of lights, along with zoned heating and cooling systems, also have been used in corporate environments for some time. Like so much of technology, those things that become accepted by business find their way into our homes as costs come down, and new benefits and uses are found.

There will be changes made to the construction of housing to accommodate integrated technology and also to accommodate changing technologies. Much of the research currently being done into these changes is far-reaching, and not of practical value for immediate implementation. For now, with minor adaptation in the extreme case of the Gator Tech smart house—where technology may be changing

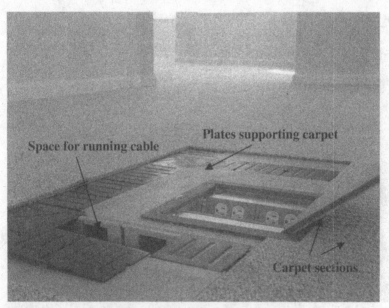

Figure 2.3   Raised floor in Gator Tech house for cabling.

on a monthly basis—current building practices with the simple extension of a raised floor can satisfy the needs of an advanced program.

Whereas the smart house is primarily built on wired technology and that technology is pervasive, houses in the future may see computing environments in which sensors are part and parcel of the materials used in construction—scattered sensor "dust" that respond to a radio signal sweep, carpet that converts fiber motion to energy to power sensors woven into it, paint that uses light as power to mirror the cycle of the day and affect our mood. Until that day, as long as power is wired, communications wiring will play an essential role and will require accommodation in construction. The key to the Gator Tech smart house's success is its flexibility and ability to be adapted. It is already available today to all homes, and as the technology tested at the smart house is proven, it will be able to move directly from the laboratory to our homes.

REFERENCES

1. Into the Future. *A look back at how the last century's visionaries viewed the houses of their tomorrows*, Retrieved April 13, 2004 from http://future.newsday.com/3/hopmain.htm.
2. The North American Integration and Development Center, *Showcasing Technology at the 1964–1965 New York World's Fair.* Retrieved April 13, 2004 from http://naid.sppsr.ucla.edu/ny64fair/map-docs/technology.htm.
3. Kivett, V. R. (1979). Discriminators of loneliness among the rural elderly: Implications for intervention. *The Gerontologist*, **19**, 108–115.
4. Mann, W. C., and Helal, S. (2003). Smart technology: a bright future for independent living. *Journal of Certified Senior Advisors*, **21**, 15–20.
5. Banerjee, S., Steenkeste, F., Couturier, P., Debray, M., and Franco, A. (2003). Telesurveillance of elderly patients by use of passive infra-red sensors in a smart room. *Journal of Telemedicine and Telecare*, **9**, 23–29.
6. Alwan, M., Dalal, S., Kell, S., and Felder, R. (2003). Derivation of basic human gait characteristics from floor vibrations. *2003 Summer Bioengineering Conference*, June 25–29, Sonesta Beach Resort, Key Biscayne, Florida, USA.
7. Rhee, S., Yang, B. H., and Asada, H. (1998). The right sensor: a new ambulatory wearable sensor for twenty-four hour patient monitoring. In Proceedings of the *20ᵗʰ Annual International Conference IEEEE Engineering in Medicine and Biology Society*, Hong Kong, Oct. 1998 pp. 1906–1909.
8. Suunto T6 Information. Retrieved on December 4, 2004 from http://www.suunto.com/t6.
9. Najafi, B., Aminian, K., Paraschiv-Ionescu, A., Loew, F., Bula, C. J., and Robert, P. (2003). Ambulatory system for human motion analysis using a kinematic sensor: monitoring of daily physical activity in the elderly. *IEE Transactions in Biomedical Engineering*, **50**(6), 711–732.
10. Matsuoka, S., Yonezawa, Y., Maki, H., Ogawa, H., Hahn, A. W., Thayer, J. F., and Caldwell, W. M. (2003). A microcomputer-based daily living activity recording system. *Biomedical Science Instrumentation*, **39**, 220–223.
11. Lin, Y. J., Latchman, H. A., and Minkyu, L. (2002). A power line communication network infrastructure for the smart home. *IEEE Wireless Communications*, December, 2002, 104–111.
12. Nelson, R. C., and Green, I. A. (2002, August). *Tracking objects using recognition.* 16th International Conference on Pattern Recognition (ICPR'02), Quebec City, QC, Canada, v2, pp. 1025–1030.
13. Lawson, S. (2003). IBM Builds a Smarter House. *PC World.* Retrieved December 4, 2004 from http://www.pcworld.com/news/article/0,aid,110179,00.asp.
14. E2Home. Retrieved on March 20, 2004 from http://www.e2home.com/new_main.asp.
15. Berlo, A. (2003). Home Networking and Home Automation for Older People. In the Proceedings of the *International Conference on Aging, Disability and Independence*, Washington, DC, USA, December 2003, p. 158.

16. Microsoft Corporation. *EasyLiving.* Retrieved March 28, 2004 from http://research.microsoft.com/easyliving/.

17. Kiff, L., Krichbaum, K., Miller, C., and Wu, P. (2003). Design Philosophies Applied in an Elder Home Monitoring System. In the Proceedings of the *International Conference on Aging, Disability and Independence,* Washington, DC, USA, December 2003, pp. 143–145.

18. Justiss, M., Mann, W., Helal, S., Dasler, P., and Kiff, L. (2003). Partnerships With Industry: Development of an Intelligent Home Automation System. In the Proceedings of the *International Conference on Aging, Disability and Independence,* Washington, DC, USA, December 2003, pp. 174–175.

19. KIff, L., and Plocher, T. (2003). Mobility Monitoring with the Independent LifeStyle Assistant (ILSA) In the Proceedings of the *International Conference on Aging, Disability and Independence,* Washington, DC, USA, December 2003, pp. 170–171.

20. E2Home. Retrieved on March 20, 2004 from http://www.e2home.com/new_main.asp.

21. Moody, R. (2003, February). Oatfield Estates: Assistive Living Community Offers New Options. *The Business Journal.* Retrieved on December 4, 2004 from http://www.bizjournals.com/Portland/stories/2003/02/10/focus2.html.

22. Davenport, R., Helal, S., Mann, W., and Zabadani, H. (2003). Assistive Environments for Elder Care—Integrating Smart Phones with Smart Homes. In the Proceedings of the *International Conference on Aging, Disability and Independence,* Washington, DC, USA, December 2003, pp. 128–129.

23. Cook, D., Das, S., Gopalratnam, K., and Roy, A. (2003). Health Monitoring in an Agent-Based Smart Home. In the Proceedings of the *International Conference on Aging, Disability and Independence,* Washington, DC, USA, December 2003, pp. 154–155.

24. Pentland, A., and Fauchet, P. (2003). Personal Health Systems For The Future. In the Proceedings of the *International Conference on Aging, Disability and Independence,* Washington, DC, USA, December 2003, pp. 176–177.

25. Abowd, G., Bobick, A., Essa, I., Fisk, D., Mynatt, B., and Rogers, W. (2003). Aware Home for Aging in Place. In the Proceedings of the *International Conference on Aging, Disability and Independence,* Washington, DC, USA, December 2003, pp. 122–123.

26. Intille, S., and Larson, K. (2003). Designing and Evaluating Technology for Independent Aging in the Home. In the Proceedings of the *International Conference on Aging, Disability and Independence,* Washington, DC, USA, December 2003, pp. 146–147.

27. Larson, K. (2000). The Home of the Future. *A+U 361.* Retrieved on April 13, 2004 from http://architecture.mit.edu/house_n/web/publications/articles/AU_June1-2000.pdf.

28. Mozer, M. C. The Adaptive House. *University of Colorado Department of Computer Science.* Retrieved on December 4, 2004 from http://www.cs.Colorado.edu/~mozer?house/.

29. Tran, Q. T., and Mynatt, E. D. (2002). What was I cooking? Toward déjà vu displays of everyday memory. *Interruptions in Human-Computer Interactions.* Retrieved on April 1, 2004 from http://interruptions.net/literature/Tran-GIT-GVU-03-33.pdf.

30. Rowe, M. (2003). CareWatch: A Novel Technology of Alzheimer's Caregivers. In the Proceedings of the *International Conference on Aging, Disability and Independence,* Washington, DC, USA, December 2003, pp. 343–344.

31. Brumitt, B., and Cadiz, J. J. (2000). Let there be light! Comparing interfaces for homes of the future. *Microsoft Research Paper.* Retrieved on December 4, 2004 from http://www.research.microsoft.com/research/pubs/view.aspx?tr_id=405.

32. Larson, K. MIT Home of the Future. *Massachusetts Institute of Technology Department of Architecture.* Retrieved on December 4, 2004 at http://architecture.mit.edu/house_n/.

33. Borodulkin, L., Ruser, H., and Trankler, H. R. (2002, May). 3D Virtual "Smart Home" User Interface. VIMS2002 International Symposium on Virtual and Intelligent Measurement Systems, Alyeska, Alaska, USA.

34. Smart Thinking. *Background to the CUSTODIAN Project,* Retrieved April 4, 2004 from http://www.gdewsbury.ukideas.com/custodianbackground.html.

35. Sikora, A., and Brugger, P. (2003). Virtual private infrastructure (VPI) initiative—An industry consortium for unified and secure web control with embedded devices. In Proceedings of *IEEE Conference Emerging Technologies and Factory Automation,* Sept. 2003, pp. 288–291.

CHAPTER 3

ROBOTICS

Rick D. Davenport

3.1 INTRODUCTION

People have been fascinated with the concept of robots for centuries, but it was not until 1962 that the first commercial robot was deployed. Since then, the science of robotics has advanced significantly and takes many forms including: industrial robots that palletize advertising for newspaper companies; medical robots that assist during surgery; police and military robots that assist with bomb disposal and military surveillance; exploration robots that journey into live volcanoes and visit other planets; professional service robots that inspect bridges and nuclear sites; personal robots that vacuum and provide entertainment; and rehabilitation robots that assist with mobility and therapy. The introduction to this chapter reviews the history of robots and current industrial, military, surgical, and personal robots. Section 3.2 addresses the less developed, but more related (to our focus on aging and disability), area of assistive robotics. Important issues surrounding the advancement of robotics are discussed in Section 3.3.

Development of the Terms Robot and Robotics

The concept of "robotics" can be found as early as the 1500s when Hans Bullmann created an android that simulated people playing musical instruments. In 1737, Jacques Vaucanson went beyond this work and created a robot that could play a musical instrument and a mechanical duck that could eat, drink, and paddle in water.[1] In 1920, Karel Capek, a Czech writer, coined the word "robot" in his play entitled "Rossum's Universal Robots." Having witnessed the use of technology against people during World War I, Capek's play included technologically advanced human robots that rebelled against their human creators in an attempt to wipe out the human race.

Isaac Asimov coined the term "robotics" in a 1942 science fiction short story entitled "Runaround." Asimov had a more optimistic view on technology, which can be seen by the introduction of his three laws of robotics: (1) A robot may not injure a human being or, through inaction, allow a human being to come to harm; (2) a robot must obey the orders given it by human beings, except where such orders would conflict with the First Law; (3) a robot must protect its own existence as long

Smart Technology for Aging, Disability, and Independence, Edited by William C. Mann
Copyright © 2005 John Wiley & Sons, Inc.

as such protection does not conflict with the First or Second Law. Although present-day developers are not at the point of developing robots with artificial intelligence depicted in Asimov's 1942 play, researchers and developers are now starting to explore social issues in the design of robots (discussed in the human–robot interaction section of this chapter).

Merriam–Webster defines a robot as a "device that automatically performs complicated often repetitive tasks."[2] The *Oxford English Dictionary* provides a more comprehensive definition of a robot: "a machine (sometimes resembling a human being in appearance) designed to function in place of a living agent, especially one which carries out a variety of tasks automatically or with a minimum of external impulse."[3] With advances in underlying technologies, there has been a shift in robotic research and development from devices reacting to their environment in a limited repetitive fashion (as much of the industrial robots are programmed) to robots with sensing systems and new elaborate independent decision-making abilities.[4]

Industrial Robots

In the mid-1950s, inventor George C. Devol and businessman/engineer Joseph Engleberger designed a reprogrammable industrial robotic manipulator and named it the "Unimate." The first Unimate robot was not sold until 1962 when General Motors purchased it to work in the loading and unloading tasks with heated die-casting machines. Joseph Engleberger later formed the first commercial company, Unimation, which produced industrial robots. Engleberger's many successes in the robotic industry led to his title of "the father of robotics."

From the 1950s until the present time the industrial robotics industry has dominated the robotics market. In 2002, there was one robot for every 10 production workers in Japan, Italy, and Germany's automobile industry, and there were between 770,000 and 1,050,000 operational industrial robot units.[5] Growth in the industrial robotics industry is still strong. Worldwide industrial robot orders increased in the first half of 2003 by 26% compared to the same period in 2002. Yearly average growth is projected at 7.4% through 2006.[5]

With only 770 robots per 10,000 production workers in the United States, the motor vehicle industry lags behind the Japanese motor vehicle industry, which has 1700 robots per 10,000 production workers.[6] However, both the United States and the European Union increased the number of industrial robots by 6% since the middle of the 1990s.[5] The motor vehicle industry accounts for over 50% of the robotics market and is the largest worldwide consumer of robots.[6]

Space Robots

The National Aeronautics and Space Administration (NASA) has developed several innovative robots to assist the space shuttle missions (such as the space shuttle's robotic arm, used for satellite deployment and retrieval), assist with the construction of the international space station, explore the surface of Mars (i.e., 1997

Pathfinder and Sojourner; 2004 Opportunity and Spirit rover); and explore Venus and Saturn (i.e., 1990 Magellan mission to Venus, 2004 Cassini–Huygens mission to Saturn).

Benefits of space exploration are apparent in applications of NASA technology applied to everyday products, such as cordless drills, CT scans, and increased understanding of human physiology.[7] However, some criticism has been directed at the United States government for investing too much on sending robotic rovers to Mars, rather than investing in the development of personal robotics to provide assistance to the aging populations.[8] Although there is not a domestic-robot version equivalent to the Mars Rovers, the NASA prototype Robonaut may have readily transferable technology as a robotic assistant for the elderly.

Robonaut Robonaut resembles a slimmed-down upper half of a human astronaut, with an articulating waist section, a torso with two arms and five-digit hands, and a neck with a helmet (Figure 3.1). Robonaut was specifically designed to use existing tools and control panels that humans use, so that a separate set of tools for Robonaut would not have to be developed.[9] Robonaut has sensors in each glove that provide confirmation of the object grasped. Robonaut also has a sensor platform in its helmet with four articulating cameras and an infrared temperature sensor.[9] In the next 3–4 years, NASA's Robonaut may be ready to assist astronauts with mundane tasks in space such as setting/cleaning up worksites for the astronauts, assisting in performing tasks, and subsequently limiting human exposure to hazardous environments.[10]

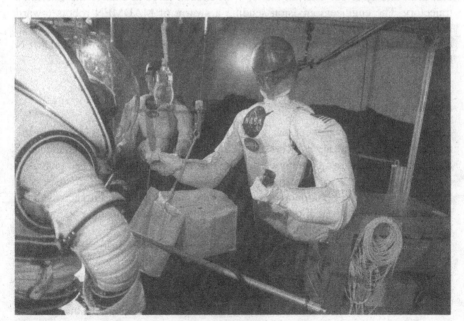

Figure 3.1   Robonaut (picture courtesy of NASA).

In 2003, a collaboration between the Defense Advanced Research Projects Agency (DARPA) and NASA's Johnson Space Center yielded a mobile robot in the form of a Robonaut mounted on top of a Segway mobile base.[11] The Robonaut upper portion weighed 231 pounds and the Segway base weighed 99 pounds. This robot has a maximum speed of 13 feet/second. The Segway base is small in design, allowing Robonauts to operate in human environments (using wheelchair accessible ramps, mobile-Robonaut was able to pass through human-sized doors and work in tight quarters). The mobile-Robonaut worked safely in close quarters with humans by successfully passing objects, following people, tracking people with a flashlight, and automatically adjusting its balance while raising items above its head. All applications were performed in a telepresence mode in which an operator controlled all actions of the Robonaut remotely. Communication between Robonaut and the user was through a virtual reality interface consisting of a helmet, gloves, body sensors, and foot pedals. Plans for future colonization on Mars may entail the use of Robonauts to assist with the preconstruction work prior to human arrival.

MADMEN   Future robotics development may benefit humankind on a global level by destroying asteroids headed for earth. The MADMEN robotic spacecraft is being developed through a grant from the NASA Institute for Advanced Concepts (NIAC). Researchers from SpaceWorks Engineering, Inc. (SEI) have completed a preliminary design of a robot that could defend the planet against near-Earth objects (NEOs).[12] The Modular Asteroid Deflection Mission Ejector Node (MADMEN) spacecraft is envisioned as a one-ton, 36-foot-high robot that would land on the asteroid, drill, and eject-out asteroid matter with enough force to change the asteroid's trajectory. The engineers envision sending a swarm of MADMEN robots toward the NEOs. A second round of funding is needed by NIAC SEI researchers to construct a MADMEN robot. Researchers predict actual testing of the MADMEN by 2014.

Military Robots

The U.S. Defense Department has renewed its interest and increased funding in the robotics field in response to increased military conflicts.[13] Congress mandated that all military vehicles be autonomous by the year 2015. The Pentagon has increased its funding in robotics recognizing that robots could reduce the risk to soldiers in Afghanistan and Iraq.[13] Autonomous vehicles are capable of traveling across unfamiliar terrain to and from a location independently without requiring a teleoperator to control it, thereby reducing risk to soldiers.

Reflecting the increased interest in robotics, the Robotic Institute at Carnegie Mellon University had a 48 percent increase in federal funding since 2000. The Pentagon expects to spend $10 billion on unmanned aerial vehicles by the end of 2010.[13] In 2003 corporate and university funding for robotics was $7.8 million (up 40% since 2000). Researchers in robotics point out that the robotics field has past the initial development stage and the focus is more on the development of robotic applications.

BLEEX   As military applications are developed, there likely will be spin-offs into the private sector. One such military product is the Berkeley Lower Extremity Exoskeleton (BLEEX) which could have applications in assisting elders with maintaining their mobility. The BLEEX project is a robotic exoskeleton for the lower extremities (covered in depth later in this chapter under Mobility Devices).

DARPA Grand Challenge—2004   Further advancement in the areas of robotic sensing, navigating, and independent problem solving were advanced extensively when the Pentagon announced that they would award a $1 million prize to anyone who could build a vehicle that could traverse a desert autonomously. Following the Congressional mandate for autonomous military vehicles, the Defense Advanced Research Projects Agency (DARPA) (which is known for helping develop the internet) issued a challenge to students, researchers, engineers, inventors, and hobbyists to build an autonomous robotic ground vehicle that could traverse a 142-mile course autonomously.[14,15] One of DARPA's goals was to facilitate the development of faster unmanned ground vehicle prototypes. Previous prototypes operated at very slow speeds, and DARPA was looking for a prototype that could travel at an average minimum speed of 15–20 miles an hour. Therefore, one of the requirements of the race was that the autonomous ground vehicle had to complete the 142-mile course in less than 10 hours to receive the $1 million prize.[15]

The difficulty of developing an autonomous ground vehicle field was evident by the end of the Mojave Desert course on March 13, 2004. No team was able to claim victory, and the greatest distance traversed by any of the prototypes was 7 miles. Vehicles were disabled by veering off course and getting lost, brake problems, flipping over, getting tangled in wire, and catching fire. However, Grand Challenge organizers called the event a spirited success. The final DARPA report published on July 30, 2004 concluded that all three of their main goals were met: (1) They were able to increase the number of people exposed to the Department of Defense autonomous vehicle technology field (over 450 televised news specials covered the event and during the weeks surrounding the race, and over 45 million hits were made from 140 countries to the DARPA website); (2) they were able to gain access to this new talent and innovative ideas; and (3) they were able to accelerate the technology development in the United States in the areas of sensors, navigation, control algorithms, vehicle systems, and systems integration.[15]

The next Grand Challenge date has been set for October 1, 2005 and is to be held in the California/Nevada area. The prize has been increased to $2 million. Forty teams will be selected for the qualifying round, with only 20 teams competing for the $2 million prize. DARPA's web site for the 2005 Grand Challenge reports over 550 individuals from 42 states and 7 countries attended the first informational meeting regarding the 2005 challenge.[16]

PackBot   iRobot Corporation has three versions of the PackBot, each of which is unique: the PackBot Scout, PackBot Explorer, and the PackBot EOD (Figure 3.2). The PackBots can reach with a manipulator arm in any direction up to 6.6 feet, detect chemical leaks, conduct explosive ordnance disposal, deliver equipment and medical supplies, and perform reconnaissance. PackBot stands approximately 8 inches high,

Figure 3.2   PackBot Explorer (picture courtesy of iRobot).

weighs about 40 pounds, and is designed to cover all types of terrain including stairs, curbs, rubble or rocks, sand, and mud. Developers at iRobot have plans to add features to PackBot such as the ability to apply bandages or inject medication remotely to injured soldiers. PackBot is battlefield-tested in Afghanistan and Iraq, and the U.S. government spends between $50,000 and $100,000 for each one.[17,18] iRobot Corporation has been named as one of 22 companies to assist in developing future combat systems in a $95 billion program.

Predator   The Predator is an unmanned plane used successfully in Afghanistan to monitor and attack enemy forces. It is awaiting possible funding from the Department of Homeland Security to be used in the United States.[17]

Surgical Robots

The United Nations Economic Commission for Europe 2003 survey of world robotics projected strong growth for medical and service robots.[5] Service robots for professional use includes cleaning (floor, tank, window), medical, demolition, underwater, and surveillance robots. Between 2003 and 2006, over 6000 new installations of robot-assisted surgical robots are projected. The first robot-assisted surgeries were performed in the late 1980s. In 1985 the Puma 560 robot was used to assist in neurosurgical biopsies, and in 1987 a laparoscopic robot assisted in gallbladder removals.[19] The benefits of having robot-assisted surgery include: adding stability while decreasing surgeon fatigue; additional sensor monitoring capabilities, especially in tight spaces; smaller incisions; decreased risk of infection; less postoperative pain, less scarring, and shorter hospital stays.

Today's surgical robots are able to perform transcontinental telesurgery, femur preparation in total hip arthroplasties, mitral valve repair, and endoscopic surgery through voice interface. Surgical robots are expensive: The da Vinci Surgical System, Intuitive Surgical's precision surgical hands that can drill through bone or make precise incisions,[17] costs $1 million. This robotic system was being used by 192 hospitals in 2004, with the cost offset by reduction in patient recovery time and decrease in pain.

Rescue Robots

T-52 Enryu HyperRescueRobot   Tmsuk of Kitakyushu, Japan developed a giant prototype robot that stands at 11.5 feet, weighs 5 tons, and can extend its arms up to 33 feet apart and lift 1100 pounds with each arm.[20] The T-52 Enryu Hyper-RescueRobot has full-range arm movement and can be controlled from an onboard pod or remotely (Figure 3.3). Developers expect to have the HyperRescueRobot in use by the end of 2004. It is designed to move heavy objects following disasters, thereby assisting rescue workers and saving people who are trapped.

Office Robot

Roboceptionist   Researchers at Carnegie Mellon's computer science and drama departments have developed a prototype Roboceptionist that answers the phone, gives directions, and answers simple questions all with a social-ability component.[21] Equipped with motion sensors, Roboceptionist greets visitors as they enter Carnegie Mellon's computer science hall (Figure 3.4). Presently, Roboceptionist's appearance is composed of a business blouse and jacket with an LCD computer monitor that

Figure 3.3   T-52 Enryu HyperRescueRobot (picture courtesy of Tmsuk, Inc.).

Figure 3.4   Roboceptionist (picture courtesy of Carnegie Mellon University).

displays an animated head (positioned above the blouse and jacket). Interaction with Roboceptionist involves using a keyboard and monitor that sits on the desk in front of her. This team is developing a voice interaction interface, and it will replace the LCD animated face with a robotic head.

Inkha   Visitors to King's College London are greeted by a robot receptionist named Inkha.[22] Inkha is short for "interactive neurotic King's head assembly" and is composed of a robotic head mounted on metallic shoulders (Figure 3.5). While the shoulders are frozen in place, the robot's eyes, mouth, head, and neck are capable of moving in response to her environment. Inkha will respond to people by leaning in/when interested and moving away/when sudden movements are detected. A laptop receives input from hidden cameras and sensors and reacts by manipulating nine face and head motors. Inkha can respond to touch screen inquiries and spontaneously doles out colorful remarks such as wanting a cup of tea (when bored) or asking if the visitor got dressed in the dark.

Figure 3.5   Interactive neurotic King's head assembly (Inkha) (picture courtesy of Inkha Ltd.).

3.2   PERSONAL AND ASSISTIVE ROBOTICS

Most of us do not get to see industrial or surgical robots. Our interest is in robots with whom we can interact. Our expectations for personal robots has been reflected over the past 45 years in film and television characters such as the Jetson's robotic maid Rosie (1962); Robot B-9 in Lost in Space (1965); C-3PO and R2-D2 in Star Wars Episode IV (1977); household robot NDR-113, played by Robin Williams in Bicentennial Man (1999); and household robot NS-5 (Sonny) in I, Robot (2004). Hollywood has depicted a future society with an abundant display of personal robots, while, in reality, development has centered on industrial robots. The next section describes robotic devices that can assist older persons and people with disabilities. Some of these robotic devices are available as products, while others are still being developed and/or commercialized.

One of the reasons we do not yet have many personal robots, while the industrial robotics market is rapidly expanding, is due to the complexities of a personal robot.[23] Industrial robots have fixed environments in which they perform, while personal robots must operate in a semiautomous to automous state in changing environments. The ability to adapt to changing environments requires robust sensors, software, and computing power.

Development of personal robots is expected to increase over the next several years.[24] While early-generation assistive robots are expensive and awkward, experts compare the private sector robot industry of today to the personal computer industry of 20 years ago, and they expect an economic boom in the next two decades.[17,24] Manufacturing costs are expected to decrease, and $40,000 robots of today will be reasonably priced in 10–20 years. Innovations in robotic applications, which were once solely driven by industry, will grow dramatically as new applications are developed in the personal robotics area.[24] Predictions suggest that personal robotics will overtake the automobile market in 20 years.[24]

Less expensive robotic components, recent advances in power consumption, and better sensor technology have enabled development of more autonomous robots.[23] Initially, personal robotics were used more to showcase a company's technology. More recently, we are seeing robotic products for the consumer market that can vacuum a room, mow the lawn, and monitor a home's security.[17] More than 50,000 autonomous lawn mowers and vacuum cleaners were sold by the end of 2002, and a tenfold increase is expected by the end of 2006.[5] As robotic technology advances, we will also see a rise in performance, together with a decrease in cost. This already has occurred with industrial robots, where the price for the same performance in 2002 was one-fifth the cost of 1990.[5]

In recognition of their aging population, Japan has taken a leadership role in development of assistive robotics. The proportion of Japan's population represented by elders is similar to how the United States will look in 20 years. In 2002, 12.3% of the United States population was 65 years and older, and by 2025 it will climb to 18.2%.[25,26] In 2002, Japan's 65-year-and-older population was already at 18.5%, and this will increase to 28.7% by 2025.[27] Japan is exploring many options to help alleviate both the shrinking work force and expanding elder population, such as (a) amending immigration policies to allow more foreign workers and (b) investing in humanoid-companion robots to help care for the elder population.[28] Japan's level of investment in robotics is evidenced by the abundant number of robotic devices that are being developed and marketed. Almost every major electronic company and automotive company in Japan has a personal robot in production or in development. Products include Matsushita Electric's robotic bear, Mitsubishi's household robot, Sony's entertainment robot dog, and Honda's humanoid assistant robot. Each of these is discussed in more detail later in this chapter.

Korea is another country with an aging population and a strong commitment to advancing personal assistance robotics. The Korea Advanced Institute of Science and Technology will receive $9 million from the Korean Science and Engineering Foundation to develop home and work robotic systems for the elderly and disabled population.[24] Korea has the goal of developing a "welfare" robotic system in 20 years.

Mobility Devices

PAM-AID (1998)   PAM-AID (Personal Adaptive Mobility Aid) is an early prototype smart walker that was designed by researchers in Dublin, Ireland in 1998 to assist frail and visually impaired individuals with navigation in their environment.[29,30] Set on *manual mode*, the smart walker is able to convert both laser and sonar data into voice feedback (i.e., *object ahead or object above*), which helps verbally guide users with navigation through their environment while still providing voice feedback regarding objects and obstacles they are approaching. When set to *assistive mode*, the smart walker automatically steers away from objects in the path. Users feel a sense of control and can set their pace. The developers purposely did not motorize the smart walker's wheels. Only the steering is motorized. This early prototype smart walker does not require any pre-installation of a map to navigate. It can be used in new unfamiliar settings without additional setup.

PAM-AID (2003)   In 2003 a newer prototype of the smart walker (VA-PAMAID) was evaluated for its safety and performance by the Department of Veterans Affairs in conjunction with Haptica (focused on commercialization of the PAMAID).[31] The newer prototype is 2.94 feet in height, 2.53 feet long, and 2.07 feet wide and weighs 90 pounds (Figure 3.6). The newer VA-PAMAID was similar to the 1998 PAMAID in that it used both laser and ultrasonic sensors to help frail and visually impaired individuals navigate through their environment. *Manual* and *automatic modes* were again included with an additional third mode (*park mode*), which prevents the smart walker from moving by automatically reorienting the front wheels. This provides assistance when a user transfers to and from a chair.

Figure 3.6   VA-PAMAID (picture courtesy of VA Pittsburgh Healthcare System).

The VA-PAMAID can travel 6.8 miles, lasting a little over 6 hours in *automatic mode* with a single charge. It has a maximum effective speed when avoiding obstacles of 3.3 ft/s. It has passed the International Standards Organization (ISO) static stability tipping angles test. However, it was unable to negotiate obstacles over $\frac{1}{2}$ inch high. Primary recommendations included more maneuverability (currently unable to negotiate over rugs or power cords), lighter design (currently 90 pounds), waterproofing the exposed components, and integrating the ability to upload a map of the area so the user could select a location and let the smart walker steer them to the specific location. VA researchers plan future studies with the elderly visually impaired population comparing the VA-PAMAID to low-tech adaptive mobility devices.

Guido (2004)—Latest Version of the PAM-AID   In 2004, Hepatica renamed the smart walker "*Guido*" and has given it a sleeker design, describing the smart walker as "a walking frame that uses robotic technology to help older, visually impaired people regain a degree of independence. . . . It puts the functionality of a guide dog into a robust walker" (Figure 3.7).[32] Like its predecessors, Guido uses both laser and ultrasonic sensors to help users navigate through their environment. However, Guido has additional sensors in the smart walker's handlebars that sense the direction the user would like to go. When set to *automatic mode*, Guido provides mechanized steering away from obstacles. Haptica plans to seek a manufacturing partner to market an updated version of the PAMAID with tentative pricing of $6000 per unit (G. Lacey, personal communication, April 28, 2004).

Koolio   A robotics development team at the University of Florida is developing a prototype traveling autonomous refrigerator robot named Koolio.[33] Presently the

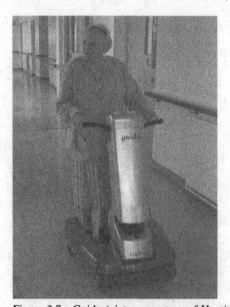

Figure 3.7   Guido (picture courtesy of Haptica Ltd.).

prototype requires logging onto the network to summon Koolio to a location. After delivering refrigerated items, Koolio automatically returns to its docking station.

Exoskeletons

HAL-3   A University of Tsukuba, Japan team is developing a prototype exoskeleton that may replace the need for a cane or walker.[34] The powered assist system named Hybrid Assistive Leg (HAL-3) assists individuals with lower-extremity disabilities ambulate greater distances or maintain a standing position. Weighing over 33 pounds, the HAL-3 is heavy, yet developers report that very little of the weight has to be carried by the person, because most of the weight is transmitted to the floor, bypassing the soles of the feet. HAL-3 can walk at a speed of 2.5 miles per hour without the typical stop and go jerky motions witnessed in earlier models of robotic-assisted ambulation. HAL-3 is an entirely wearable unit composed of three systems: (1) a control system enclosed in a backpack (includes compact-type PC, motor drives, power supply for the PC, EMG processing boards, and sensor interface boards), (2) sensor system (myoelectric sensors attached to hip and knee extensors and flexors, rotary encoders that measure the hip and knee joint angles, and floor reaction force sensors that measure the pressure on the sole and heel of the feet), and (3) the exoskeleton frame (made from aluminum alloy and steel with actuators that provide assistance with torque at the knee and hip joints).

The prototype is designed for individuals with lower-extremity disabilities. The Trading house Mitsui & Co. and 30 other Tokyo corporations plan to set up a joint venture to market the HAL-3 in 2004.[35] Initially, 10 prototype HAL-3s will be leased or sold to hospitals, nursing care facilities, and home care companies with projected cost set at approximately $9000 per unit.

BLEEX   Researchers at the University of California Berkeley Human Engineering and Robotics Laboratory, through funding from the Defense Advanced Research Project Agency (DARPA) developed the Berkeley Lower-Extremity Exoskeleton (BLEEX).[36,37] BLEEX was developed primarily to carry equipment weighing up to 70 pounds in a backpack attached to the exoskeleton over rugged terrain or stairs for long periods of time (Figure 3.8). With this exoskeleton, training is not necessary. The exoskeleton computer constantly calculates how to move the exoskeleton to keep up with the user. The user does not use a joystick, keypad, or pushbutton device to control the exoskeleton. There are over 40 sensors that relay information to the computer, which in turn controls the hydraulic actuators. The user can squat, bend, twist, run up and down slopes, and step over objects while wearing the 100-pound exoskeleton and carrying up to 70 pounds of additional equipment in the backpack. Future models of the exoskeleton will be able to carry up to 120 pounds as well as run and jump with the user.

Wearable Walking Helper   Researchers in Sendai, Japan are developing a prototype exoskeleton that, rather than using biofeedback, uses a control system that provides lower-extremity support at the knee joint based on feedback from the user's posture and joint motions.[38] This device, named the Wearable Walking Helper,

BERKELEY LOWER EXTREMITY EXOSKELETON, 2004

Figure 3.8 Berkeley Lower-Extremity Exoskeleton (BLEEX) (picture courtesy of Professor Kazerooni of University of California of Berkeley).

allows for one degree of freedom and has three potentiometers (at the hip, knee, and ankle joints), dual geared hinges at the knee, and a linear actuator attached to the user's ankle. Researchers had eight healthy adults (age 22–30 years old) stand-up from a 16-inch sitting surface as many times as they could within a 60-second time interval both with and without the Wearable Walking Helper. Results showed that 75% of the participants had increased repetitions while wearing the device, with the highest increase from 33 to 44 repetitions. Twenty-five percent of the participants reported limitations in the fit of the device, with one participant having a decrease of repetitions from 52 to 42 while wearing the Wearable Walking Helper. The device is designed for older persons with lower-extremity weakness.

Power Suit   A common occupational hazard of health care workers is back strain from helping patients during transfers especially in and out of bed. Eliminating this hazard was a primary goal of researcher Keijiro Yamamoto of Kanagawa Institute of Technology in developing the Power Suit (Figure 3.9).[39] The user straps into the 45-pound prototype Power Suit, which assists by sensing muscle activity along the user's arms, back, and legs and simultaneously inflates or deflates air bags via an

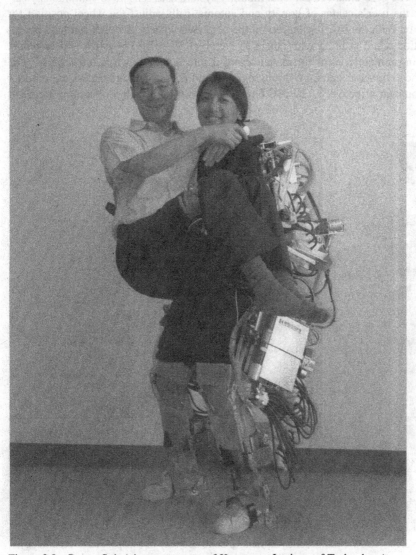

Figure 3.9   Power Suit (picture courtesy of Kanagawa Institute of Technology).

onboard battery powered air pump, which assists with lifting objects.[40,41] The Power Suit effectively assisted in lifting a 95-pound female and a 150-pound man. The present version of the Power Suit will cost $15,000 to $20,000. However, Yamamoto plans to improve on the design to reduce the cost to less than $1700, with the goal of commercializing by 2005.[40,41]

Powered Wheelchairs

iBOT 3000   iBOT 3000 Mobility System created by Independence Technology can elevate the user by raising the powered chair up on the back two wheels (Figure 3.10). The gyro-balanced personal mobility system uses sensors to continuously calculate the user's center of gravity and automatically adjust the wheel position for stability. With the iBOT balanced on the back two wheels, the user can hold a conversation while walking with others at eye level. The iBOT joystick is detachable, allowing remote control for maneuvering it into a vehicle while unoccupied. The iBOT can traverse stairs, go through gravel and deep sand, and access the outdoor environment effectively. The iBOT travels up to 6 mph with a maximum range of

Figure 3.10   iBOT 3000 Mobility System (picture courtesy of Independence Technology, LLC).

12 miles. It is priced at $29,000 and requires a training session and successful completion of a "driver's test" administered by an iBOT Mobility System Clinician.[42]

WL-16 Tmsuk of Kitakyushu with Waseda University in Tokyo has taken a novel approach in powered mobility by shedding the wheels of the powered chair and creating a prototype bipedal robot (WL-16) that can carry a human (<130 pounds) over uneven terrain (Figure 3.11). Presently, the WL-16 can only step up or down a few millimeters, but one of the future concepts of the WL-16 project is to enable individuals in wheelchairs to traverse a flight of stairs. Telescopic legs extending from the bottom of an aluminum chair connect to metal plates (feet) on the floor and move the WL-16 forward, sideways, and backwards. The actuators that control the telescopic legs are able to adjust for possible weight shifts of the person sitting in the chair. Future plans are to add a joystick controller to the unit, which presently is radio-controlled. A working model of the prototype WL-16 is expected by the end of year 2006.

Raptor The Raptor wheelchair robot system has a robotic arm attached at the base of the wheelchair next to the right rear wheel (Figure 3.12). The robotic arm enables the user to lift items (5 pounds max) dropped on the floor, grasp items on the table,

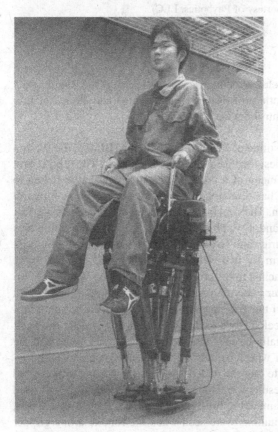

Figure 3.11   WL-16 (picture courtesy of Waseda University).

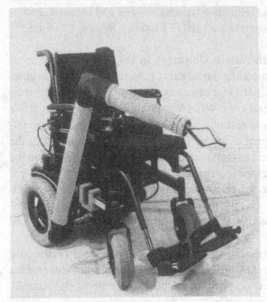

Figure 3.12   The Raptor (picture courtesy of Phybotics, LLC).

control light switches, or depress elevator buttons. The base price of the Raptor starts at $12,500 and includes the robotic arm (Raptor Manipulator) and choice of joystick, keypad, or sip-and-puff control device.[43]

Weston   Developed by Bath Institute of Medical Engineering (BIME), the Weston robot is a prototype robotic arm designed for powered wheelchairs. The robotic arm can be manipulated through the menu of a portable visual screen that is linked to a joystick.[44] The portable screen has directional arrows to move the arm forward/ backward, left/right, and up/down. The robotic arm has a forward reach of 3.2 feet and an upward reach of 4.6 feet, and it weighs 46 pounds.[45] In 2002 four volunteers (two male adults with spinal injuries and two male teenagers with spinal muscular atrophy) evaluated the robotic arm for two weeks in their homes.[44] One volunteer opted to have the robotic arm attached to his power wheelchair. One volunteer used a manual wheelchair, and the other two volunteers normally performed the planned tasks in lounge furniture. Three of the Weston robotic arms were mounted on a separate trolley, which could be wheeled close to the wheelchair to simulate the position the robotic arm would normally be in if attached. One volunteer who had the robotic arm attached to the power wheelchair did not notice any problems with performance or stability, but did state that the added width of the robotic arm created maneuverability issues. Mixed results were found when the robotic arm was used in daily tasks. The volunteers attempted to brush their teeth, eat soup with a spoon, and manipulate a massager. Limitations were seen when the robotic arm's gripper did not have enough dexterity to maintain grasps on smaller items.

KARES II Researchers at the Korea Advanced Institute of Science and Technology (KAIST) are developing a prototype wheel-chair-based robotic arm system, named KAIST Rehabilitation Engineering Service System II (KARES II).[46] The prototype robotic arm system can be mounted on a wheelchair or used as a stand-alone mobile platform. KARES II assists with various daily tasks, such as picking up objects, setting up a meal, wiping, scratching, or shaving the face, turning on/off switches, opening/closing a drawer or door, and changing a CD/tape. Researchers are developing multiple user interfaces to control the robotic arm. The user can manipulate the robotic arm with either their head, shoulder, or with eye movements.

Entertainment and Monitoring Robots

Three of the robots (AIBO, QRIO, ASIMO) discussed in this section are primarily entertainment robots, but future models could include monitoring capabilities.

AIBO Sony's AIBO entertainment robot dog made headlines in June 1999 when 3000 first-generation AIBOs sold out within minutes after being put on the market in Japan.[47] When a second order was taken 5 months later, over 132,000 orders came in from Japan. Each AIBO cost $2500. The AIBO name stems from meaning "companion" in Japanese the words "Artificial Intelligence" and "roBOt." AIBO ERS-7M2 is Sony's latest version of its line of successful entertainment robots (Figure 3.13). AIBO ERS-7M2 weighs 3.5 pounds, its dimensions are 7.1 inches wide, 10.9 inches high, and 12.5 inches deep, and it has a list base price of $1899 per unit.[23,48] AIBO has sensors in its snout, chest, paws, and internal acceleration and vibration sensors. AIBO can continuously run for 1.5 hours, automatically returns to its charging station when the battery level gets below 40%, and takes approximately 2 hours to recharge.

Figure 3.13   AIBO ERS-7M2 (picture courtesy of Sony Corporation).

AIBO has preprogrammed moods/instincts, such as an instinct to move around, search for a ball/bone, play tricks, and to communicate with its owner. Sony reports that AIBO can communicate with its owner efficiently by displaying six distinct feelings (happiness, sadness, fear, dislike, surprise, and anger) through AIBO's 28 LED lights on its head, ears that can move up and down, and sounds played through an internal speaker located in the chest. Owners can also communicate interactively with AIBO via 15 credit-card-size cards. Through visual pattern recognition, when shown a card, AIBO recognizes its instruction, such as "dance" or "take a photo," in a group of people, AIBO can identify an owner(s). AIBO is able to recognize its owner by remembering their facial characteristics, the sound frequency of the their voices and by their petting patterns. Added sensors also enhance communication. AIBO has special tactile touch sensors on its back, head, and chin that help the owner train AIBO in its development process. If the owner wants to encourage AIBO to kick the ball he would give praise when AIBO kicks the ball and AIBO will spend more time practicing kicking the ball. The AIBO Entertainment Player and AIBO MIND 2 Software increases entertainment functionality. Owners can interact with AIBO wirelessly from their PC and control AIBO manually or program AIBO to autonomously monitor the home while at work or on vacation. AIBO can e-mail photos to its owner, record video, or dance with the beat (from digital music files, CDs, or internet radio stations). AIBO can also remind the owner of their schedule and appointments that have been imported from Microsoft Outlook.

Researchers at Japan's Department of Gerontechnology, National Institute for Longevity Sciences wanted to compare the effectiveness of a toy furry dog with that of a robot (an earlier version of Sony's entertainment robot AIBO ~ cost $1000) in *eliciting responses* from elders with dementia.[49] The toy furry dog could wag its tail and sit, while robot AIBO could interact using touch, sight, hearing (responds up to 75 spoken voice commands), and balance. Thirteen elders (average age 84 years old) living in a nursing home and diagnosed with severe dementia were exposed to both the toy furry dog and robot AIBO for 7 days. The results showed both the toy dog and robot AIBO effectively increased the participants' activity. This activity was recorded as the number of times they touched, watched, talked, clapped their hands, and cared for either the toy furry dog or robot AIBO. Participants had to be oriented to the unclothed robot AIBO; but with the toy furry dog, participants automatically knew the toy mimicked a puppy and could easily identify with it. The study strongly suggested that use of a robotic pet could help fill the gap with the shortage of caregivers and helpers. Relief could be seen in providing stimulation to elders (other than the typical turning on the TV or radio) or having a more advanced robot pet that could be programmed to remember names of an Alzheimer's patients grandchildren or help with stimulation/communication with isolated ICU children without having to worry about allergies, biting, and cost of feeding a live animal.[50]

Paro   A robotics team at Japan's National Institute of Advanced Industrial Science and Technology are exploring whether a therapeutic robot pet can elicit similar responses found in traditional pet therapy. The 6.2-pound baby harp seal Paro, is a prototype fitted with air-bag type tactile sensors, light sensors, auditory-microphone sensors, and posture sensors beneath its antibacterial white fur. It is being tested in long-term care facilities in Japan. Approximately 9 million dollars have been spent developing Paro with a commercial model projected to come out in 2004 at a price of approximately $2800.[51] Paro reacts positively to being stroked and reacts negatively to being hit or being ignored. It has a circadian sleep–wake cycle; when it suddenly hears a loud sound, it reacts by looking in the direction of the sound. In a 5-week study at an adult day-care facility, elders who were exposed to Paro three times a week for 20-minute sessions improved mood and communication with nursing staff, and had experienced decreased emotional stress levels.[52] In a 4-week study conducted in an elder health service facility (including subacute, day-care, and long-term care services), urine tests results showed a decrease in stress hormones after elders were exposed to Paro four times a week for 1-hour sessions.[53]

NeCoRo NeCoRo is a robotic cat described as a "communication robot," first marketed in 2001 at a price of $1500.[54] NeCoRo is 10 inches × 6 inches × 12 inches (excluding tail), with synthetic (gray or brown) fur, and weighs 3.5 pounds (Figure 3.14). NeCoRo has over 15 actuators in its body, which move its four legs, tail, eyelids, ears, and mouth. NeCoRo uses replaceable nickel hydrogen batteries and can last for up to 1 hour and 30 minutes on a single charge. It takes 2 hours to recharge its batteries. NeCoRo makes 48 different cat sounds. NeCoRo interacts with its environment through internal sensors, which include: tactile sensors embedded in the head, chin, and back; voice-microphone sensor; internal position sensor; and vision-light sensors. It has its own programmed rhythms for sleep and for cuddling with its owner. When NeCoRo is stroked and cradled, it expresses satisfaction; if hit or shaken, it expresses anger and uneasiness. NeCoRo expresses interest by perking up its ears. When it first wakes up, it stretches its legs. Over time, NeCoRo learns the user's voice and its own name and will respond to its name being called.

Libin and Libin presented a report on NeCoRo at ICADI.[55] The study involved 12 older adults with a mean age of 72 years; 33% had some level of physical or cognitive disability (such as impaired mobility due to a stroke or hip fracture, or initial stage of Alzheimer's disease, or severely impaired vision or hearing). Each of the participants were introduced to the robotic cat and then allowed to interact individually with NeCoRo for a 15-minute session. A video camera was used to monitor reactions and allow for further qualitative analysis after the session was concluded. Sixty-seven percent of the participants found the interactive session with NeCoRo interesting and exciting, and 60% felt that NeCoRo was friendly. Past experiences with real pets did not correlate notably with the older person's perception of NeCoRo. A stronger correlation was found between level of experience with modern technology and attitude toward NeCoRo.[55]

QRIO Sony has developed a non-commercial entertainment robot named QRIO (Figure 3.15).[56] Although QRIO is not for retail sale it can be seen at various events showcasing Sony's robotic development. "QRIO reflects innovation in voice/vision recognition, motion control, and artificial intelligence," says Ms. Dana Kozak, Manager, Sony Corporate Strategic Marketing. Sony has outfitted QRIO with a

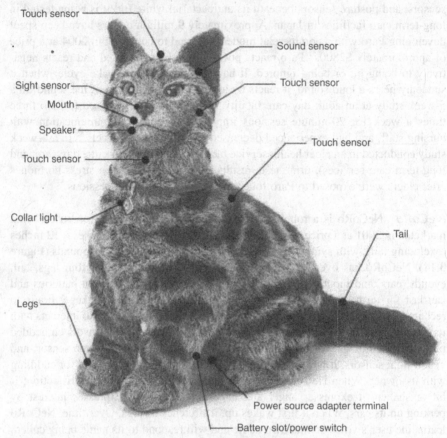

Figure 3.14 NeCoRo (picture courtesy of Institute of Robotic Psychology and Robotherapy).

control method that allows QRIO to adjust its center of gravity to move out of its zone of stability just as humans keep balance with dynamic walking. When pushed, the sensors located in the soles of its feet along with body position sensors relay this to the control system and QRIO takes a step forward (or in whatever direction it was pushed) to keep its balance. If QRIO were to sense it was not going to recover its balance it would instinctively stick out both of its arms, swivel its hips and relax its joints to lessen the impact. Upon falling QRIO is programmed to rotate from whatever position it is in on the floor to a prone position and has the ability to stand back up independently.

With its two cameras, QRIO can memorize a person's face and then address that person individually. With its built-in seven microphones, it can turn its head in the direction of the speaker and pick out the words they say. QRIO can understand tens of thousands of words and has the ability to learn new ones. Built as a partner robot, QRIO is programmed to integrate the things the user likes to talk about and adds conversation input from its own knowledge base. Over time, it memorizes the user's likes and dislikes and uses these preferences in future conversations. It is

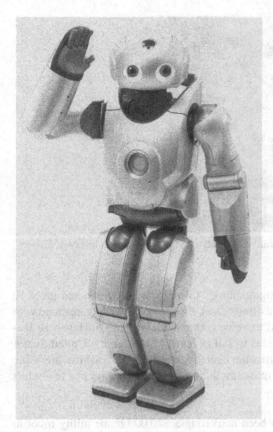

Figure 3.15   Quest for Curiosity (QRIO) (picture courtesy of Sony Corporation).

programmed to signal emotion through its body movements, sounds, and lights. Some of the purely entertainment features involve QRIO's ability to sing, kick a ball through a goal, and dance.

ASIMO   After 16 years of research and development, Honda Motor Company engineers have been working on a prototype robotic humanoid geared toward assisting individuals with various tasks such as turning on/off lights, moving objects, opening and closing doors, and so on.[57] Advanced Step in Innovative Mobility (ASIMO) stands 4 feet high, weighs 115 pounds, has two arms/hands/legs/feet, walks forward and backward, turns, walks up steps, and can walk 1 mile per hour (Figure 3.16).[24] An improvement from its predecessors, ASIMO does not have to pause prior to changing directions. It can maintain a smooth walking pace by adjusting its center of gravity while predicting its next step.[58] ASIMO can maintain balance while walking on uneven surfaces, walking up/down the stairs, or after it is pushed/impacted. However, if ASIMO falls over, it does not have the capability to get back on its feet. The battery on ASIMO can easily be changed. ASIMOs can operate continuously for 30-minutes intervals, with each battery requiring 4 hours

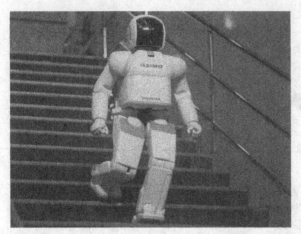

Figure 3.16   Advanced Step in Innovative Mobility (ASIMO) (picture courtesy of Honda Motor Co., Ltd.).

to completely charge. With preprogramming, ASIMO can recognize and greet 10 individuals, shake their hands when offered, and, if someone is waving, respond with a wave back. ASIMO can respond to voice commands (presently in Japanese language only). While there are no plans to sell or lease ASIMO in the United States, it has made an educational tour across the United States in 2004. ASIMOs are being used in Japan as guides in science museums and as welcome greeters in a few select companies.[58]

Banryu   Sanyo and Tmsuk have been marketing a $20,000 home utility robot in Japan since April 2003. Called Banryu, this robot comes with a mobile phone that controls the robot (can also be controlled via wireless LAN). Banryu weighs 80 pounds, resembles a dinosaur, walks on four legs, and can be programmed to monitor the home (automatically recharges after 2 hours of use) and takes real-time images in the home and sends them back to the operator.[59] Sanyo's Banryu robot is equipped with infrared, sonic, temperature, and odor sensors (detects a "burnt scent" which can precede a fire) and is programmed to alert the homeowner if it detects a problem in the home.[60] Banryu, only available in Japan, is also offered on a rental basis.[61]

Wakamaru   Wakamaru is a household robot that is projected to be marketed in 2004 with a price tag of $8300.[62,63] This robot is designed to accompany its owner throughout the day. At night, it stands by at its charging station and responds if requested. Wakamaru is 1.5 feet wide, is a little over 3 feet tall, weighs 66 pounds, and can automatically find a person, follow a person, and go to its own charging station (can operate continuously for 2 hours). You can personalize the Wakamaru by giving it an individual name and by setting the voice to male or female. It can recognize up to 10 faces and address these people by name. Wakamaru uses a dataset of 10,000 words, and will initiate an appropriate topic of conversation spontaneously when it approaches you. When walking with you, it will keep an appropriate amount of distance.

Wakamaru can be remotely controlled via a mobile phone or personal computer connected to the internet. Wakamaru is programmed to find you if (1) conversation or touch is not made with Wakamaru within a selected period of time (especially if you inform it that you are taking a bath or going to the restroom or if you do not notify it that you will be going to bed), and 2) you break your routine with your typical activity pattern. To prevent false alarms, Wakamaru will issue a loud auditory noise to alert the user that it is getting ready to send an alert. The alert will state that the user is nonresponsive and will be sent to a predesignated email address. The periodic checking on the user by Wakamaru is meant to monitor the user for any events that may require immediate attention such as (a) losing consciousness from a fall or stroke, (b) delirium due to dehydration, or (c) medication side effects.

Wakamaru can help manage the user's health by reminding the user when it is time to take medications. It will track the user's activity status by storing the person's location (bedside, kitchen table, couch) along with the activity being performed (sleep, restroom, breakfast) and by asking "Have you slept well, did you enjoy your meal?" and recording the information in a database.

HRP-2 HRP-2 was developed to help Japan with their increasing aging population. HRP-2 stands for the Humanoid Robotics Project (HRP-2) and resembles a life-size plastic toy transformer (Figure 3.17). It is humanoid in appearance with two arms, two legs, and two hands with five digits. HRP-2 stands at five feet in height,

Figure 3.17   Humanoid Robotics Project (HRP-2) (picture courtesy of Kawada Industries, Inc.).

weighs 128 pounds, and can walk up to 1.6 mile per hour.[64] HRP-2 can traverse uneven surfaces and is touted as the first life-size robot with the ability to get up independently from the floor. HRP-2 has incorporated a new cooling system into the leg actuators, which in earlier prototypes tended to overheat.

Cardea Researchers at MIT Computer Science and Artificial Intelligence Laboratory (CSAIL) are developing a humanoid robot (Cardea) that will act as a personal assistant with potential future applications geared toward elder care.[24,65] Cardea moves on a robotic mobility platform (SEGWAY RMP) invented by Dean Kamen. It currently uses cameras (in the eye sockets) and sonar to navigate through the environment. One of the primary objectives of the Cardea project is to help bring the technology from the robot manipulators, which are traditionally located on factory floors, to operate in a personal assistance robot. Traditional robot manipulators are usually not sensitive to objects that block their routine function and have been known to injure people or simply burn out their motors. Cardea uses a series of elastic actuators that are attached to an embedded spring at one end and to the joint axis at the other end. Presently, Cardea has one robotic arm. Future plans include outfitting Cardea with two additional arms (two arms to carry an object and the third to manipulate the environment—such as, opening a door), along with the addition of an expressive human head to facilitate social interaction.

Pearl A team at the University of Pittsburgh and Carnegie Mellon University have created a prototype robotic assistant named Pearl, designed to assist elders in maintaining their independent living. Pearl has a robotic head, LCD computer screen for a chest and a large motorized base. Moving at a pace of 19 inches per second, Pearl can avoid objects in her path (Figure 3.18).[66] Pearl will include an elder reminder system (including medication, hydration, scheduled appointment reminders), a telepresence system (to allow physicians and health-care workers to interact remotely through Pearl with an elder living independently), a monitor and surveillance system (to systematically record trends in activity/health level of elder), a personal helper (to assist with opening/closing the refrigerator, doing the laundry), and a social interaction system (to promote continued contact socially).[67]

Care-O-bot Researchers at Fraunhofer IPA in Stuttgart, Germany have been developing a household assistant robot for the elderly since 1997.[68] The first two prototypes, named Care-O-bot and Care-O-bot I, were mobile platforms in which the user could control home lighting, heating/air conditioning, and security, act as a video phone with physician or family, and help guide the user around obstacles in the home (Figure 3.19). The user could interact with Care-O-bot either through the touch screen or through simple verbal commands such as "go into kitchen"; Care-O-bot navigates through the environment via mounted cameras and sensors.

In designing the third-generation prototype, researchers wanted the Care-O-bot II to assist the elder in manipulation tasks in the home environment (Figure 3.20). They added a hand-held remote control panel (communicates via wireless LAN) and a manipulator arm with a flexible gripper.[69] The manipulator arm is capable of grasp-

Figure 3.18   Pearl (picture courtesy of Carnegie Mellon University).

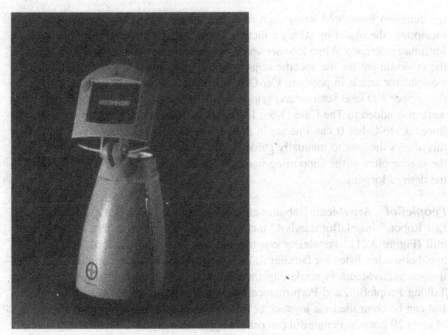

Figure 3.19   Care-O-bot I (picture courtesy of © Fraunhofer IPA).

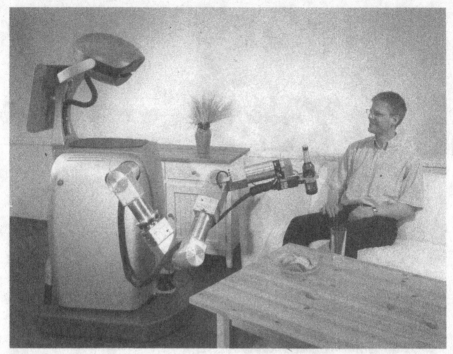

Figure 3.20   Care-O-bot II (picture courtesy of © Fraunhofer IPA).

ing common household items such as coffee mugs, plates, and bottles. The robot memorizes the object by taking a picture of the object and storing it in its database for future reference. When the user sends a request for an object, Care-O-bot II scans the environment for the specific object via the manipulator arm camera. Once the manipulator arm is in position, Car-O-bot II is able to grasp the item by using both the gripper 3-D laser scanner and gripper tactile sensors. Adjustable supporting arms were also added to The Care-O-bot II to provide more support while the elder followed. Care-O-bot II can operate in one of two modes: (1) *Direct control mode*—this allows the user to manually guide the direction of the Care-O-bot via pressure the user applies to the supporting handles. (2) *Target mode*—the user is guided to the desired location.

PeopleBot   ActivMedia Robotics are marketing their PeopleBot as a Human Interface Robot.[70] PeopleBot stands 45 inches tall and resembles the front end of a treadmill (Figure 3.21).[8] PeopleBot can traverse household power cords, play sounds, avoid obstacles, listen for familiar sounds, find and fetch objects, and transmit video images. ActivMedia is marketing three models, which include: Base PeopleBot, Talking PeopleBot, and Performance PeopleBot, priced at $30,000 a unit. People-Bot can be controlled via joystick or run autonomously and can transport payloads of up to 29 pounds. PeopleBot can run for approximately 18–24 hours on three fully charged batteries and requires 2.4 hours to recharge.

Figure 3.21   PeopleBot (picture courtesy of MobileRobots.com).

HIRB Sanyo Electric Company's latest elder care product designed for institutional settings is the Harmony in Roll-lo Bathing (HIRB). It is priced at approximately $50,000. An elder sits in a chair that rolls backward into the back half of a shoulder-high bathtub; the front end of the bathtub closes like a clamshell, leaving only the elder's shoulders and head exposed. The human washing machine then automatically releases soap and begins the wash and soak cycle. HIRB does everything except for shampooing hair and drying, which is done by hand. Residents at one of the first 100 pioneer nursing homes in Japan to purchase Sanyo's new washing machine in 2003 report that they felt better using HIRB because it warmed their whole body and protected their privacy. The nursing home staff report that HIRB reduces the time assisting residents with bathing and also decreases back strain.[71]

Daihen Corp. Patient Transfer System Daihen Corporation is developing a prototype robotic "patient transfer equipment" device (projected to be marketed in 2004) that will assist in transferring patients.[72] A motorized mat slides under the patient, and then it moves the patient on the mat without the patient having to change position or posture.[73]

Robo Nurse According to a report by ANANOVA, China has developed a prototype robo-nurse to help in the event of a future SARS outbreak. Developed by the Chinese Academy of Sciences the robo-nurse can monitor patients, dispense medication/meals, dispose of contaminated trash, and perform other necessary tasks.[74]

HelpMate2 Designed by Joe Engelberger (the father of industrial robotics) and later sold to Pyxis Corporation, HelpMate is a product that assists hospital staff in the delivery of up to 200 pounds of supplies including: prescriptions, lab specimens, medical supplies, x-ray films, and meals.[75] Helpmate is just over 4.6 feet tall, 32 inches long, and 35 inches wide and weighs 600 pounds, with an average speed of 2 feet per second traveling on two drive motor wheels and four casters. It has a storage compartment that is password protected.[76,77] Navigation is accomplished with the use of 20 sensors on Helpmate along with magnetic strips placed in the ceilings and an antenna that can call for an elevator.

When HelpMate was put in use due to a nonfunctional tube system at the University of Mississippi Medical Center (UMMC) in Jackson, Mississippi, he was affectionately named "Rudy" by the staff. Rudy was leased for $3400 a month and operated 16 to 20 hours per day.[76] Rudy is capable of running 24 hours a day (allowing for charging breaks). UMMC found that Rudy was not capable of negotiating the increase in obstacles during the midday traffic and was taken out of use during this time. UMMC reported that they were able to eliminate three full-time equivalent (FTE) positions (whose total cost was higher than Rudy's annual cost of $40,800) while Rudy was in service. Limitations with Rudy related to its having only one security code, Rudy lacked a lock box to carry controlled substances, and there was an increase in monthly maintenance fees with greater distances traveled.[76]

RP-6 InTouch Health is marketing RP-6 (*R*emote *P*resence; 6th generation system) as a robotic communications platform that can project caregivers to another location to provide monitoring, training, and care (Figure 3.22).[78] InTouch Health, a California-based health-care technology firm, is testing whether RP-6 can deliver care from physicians safely to patients in five hospitals across the nation.[79] Although RP-6 is known informally as "rounding-robot," it has been given more personable names such as "Dr. Robot" at Magic Valley Regional Medical Center in Twin Falls, Idaho, "Rosie" at Oakwood Hospital in Dearborn, Michigan, and "Rudy" at University of California Davis Medical Center in Sacramento, California. The five hospitals are using RP-6 for physicians to interact remotely with their patients from their offices or homes.

RP-6 has a robot frame as a body, a computer screen for its head, a video camera for vision, microphone for hearing, and a speaker for a mouth. RP-6 is 5 feet, 6 inches in height, weighs 220 pounds, and can travel up to 2 mph. RP-6 has 24 infrared warning sensors that prevent it from hitting objects in its path. Doctors control RP-6 with wireless broadband technology through the internet from their home or office via a joystick attached to their computer. The head and body of RP-6 can be manipulated separately, thereby allowing physicians to get a better view of the patient's incision. Patients can see and hear their doctor real time through the video screen and speakers. RP-6 is available on a lease basis from InTouch Health

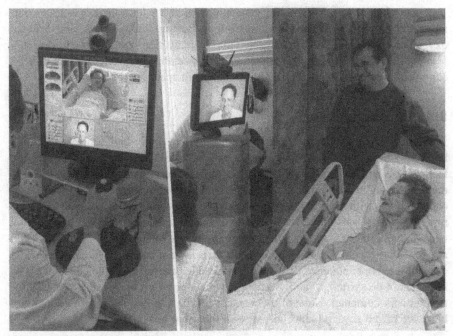

Figure 3.22   *Remote Presence*; 6th generation system (RP-6) (picture courtesy of InTouchHealth.com).

for $3000 a month, which includes computer software, technical support and training.

The argument for this format of technology is that patients prefer to see their own doctor, even if it is through a robot. They prefer the robot approach to an on-call physician who could be a stranger. Physicians like the RP-6 because at 2 A.M., doctors who are at home can make a more informed decision by being able to see an EKG (electrocardiogram) or see the patient. These options are not available when a doctor only has a telephone connection to interact with the patient and hospital staff. Also the RP-6 may reduce medical errors by providing the physician with more information and by putting the patient in contact with the physician who knows them best.

Initial results from a John Hopkins study conducted at the Maryland University Hospital demonstrated that the majority of patients are comfortable with this robot interface with their physician.[80] The study involved 60 postoperative patients with 30 patients randomly selected to receive one visit from the RP-6. The visit involved the physician using the RP-6 to check on the patient's incision site, ask how they were feeling, and answer patient's questions. Two weeks following discharge, the 30 patients were mailed a questionnaire to survey their views on the tele-round from the physician. Results showed that 80% of the patients felt that the tele-round increased their ability to see their doctor; 57% felt comfortable if tele-round visits were part of their future care; and 50% said they preferred a tele-round visit from their own physician to a real-visit from another physician.[80]

Developers state that future generations of RP-6 may include sensors that allow the physician to listen to lung sounds, perform ultrasounds, and analyze oxygen levels in blood.[79] RP-6 may have future applications that involve having RP-6 in rural settings to allow for much-needed specialized consults, or RP-6 to be deployed in combat areas to assist physicians with specialized consults.

Robotic Monitoring

Teddy Matsushita Electrics runs Sincere Kourien, a 106-bed facility retirement home in Osaka, Japan that monitors its patients with robot bears.[81] Although the facility also has sensors throughout the complex, the primary interaction between the resident and technology is through the robot bears. A resident wakes up and typically interacts with the robot bear (Teddy) while the bear monitors patient's response times to verbal questions ("Have you remembered to take your pills? It's the pink ones this morning") via a voice recognition interface, records how long tasks take, and reports to the staff if any item is out of their normal baseline.[82] Family members can call the robot and leave messages that the elder can retrieve when desired.[83] The bear cannot be carried around, because it is connected via wire cable to the facilities network computer. None of the residents of the 106-bed retirement community have verbalized any problems talking with the robot bear.[82]

Robobear As part of a 5-year study in the Japanese city of Ikeda, elderly residents who live alone are given a "robobear."[84] The robobears are programmed to recognize key trigger phases that may indicate a need for further exploration from a health-care provider. Key words are in the form of "I am sick" or "I have run out of medication." Upon processing any key words, the robobear calls the contact center and the elder can talk directly through the robobear to the health-care worker. The robobears are also programmed with leisure activities that encourage singing or simple conversation with the elder.

Tama Tama is a robotic cat designed to be a conversational partner for the elderly.[84] Developed by Matsushita Electric as a "companion" robot for the elderly, Tama is able to recognize its own name by turning its head and blinking, purrs when gently stroked, and will react with an angry hiss when hit. Developers of the product state that Tama can express six basic emotions: anger, surprise, satisfaction, uneasiness, fear, and dislike.[84] Health-care workers at the center can communicate with Tama via cell phone and can program Tama to read the local news, report any medical concerns, and give messages such as "today is karaoke day . . . let's sing a lot" or "today you have an appointment to see the doctor."

Brunnel Active Balance Saddle (BABS) BABS provides Hippotherapy without a horse: The robot was designed by researchers in Poland and Britain to provide children with cerebral palsy similar therapeutic effects to that of riding an actual horse.[85] In 2000, researchers performed a comparative analysis of BABS with walking horses.[85] Orthogonal video cameras were used to measure displacement ranges on both the BABS and walking horses in real time. The range of BABS linear movements were very similar to that of a walking horse, suggesting that BABS may have equal therapeutic benefits for a child with cerebral palsy.

InMotion   Interactive Motion Technologies Inc. (IMT), based in Cambridge Massachusetts, has sold about two dozen upper-limb robotic systems at a cost ranging from $5000 to $70,000.[86] IMT's upper-limb robot system InMotion (versions 1–3) is the successor of the extensively tested MIT-MANUS, which was developed by researchers from Massachusetts Institute of Technology (MIT).[87] The name MANUS is based on MIT's motto, "mens et manus," which means mind and hand. InMotion[2] upper-limb robot system primarily involves the patient's shoulder and elbow motion. InMotion[3] involves the wrist motion, and InMotion[1] involves additional shoulder motions (shoulder abduction, elevation, flexion). The foundation of the InMotion robotic system is that it moves or guides the patient's affected upper extremity through appropriate therapeutic motions repeatedly while analyzing the patient's arm position, velocity, and forces applied.[87] To help keep the patient engaged and motivated in the therapy session, the patient or therapist can select one of six games (such as In-and-Out, Maze, Pick-and-Place, Pong, Slalom, and Squeegee) to be displayed on the computer screen. Developers have plans to utilize InMotion's ability to modify its treatments continually so that it will provide the appropriate amount of difficulty to keep the patient engaged.[86]

In 2004, researchers at Massachusetts Institute of Technology (MIT) conducted a study measuring the effectiveness the InMotion[2] upper-limb robot system with patients with chronic motor impairments.[88] Forty-two adults (19–79 years old) with a diagnosis of single unilateral stroke within the last 1–5 years with chronic stroke-related impairments in shoulder and elbow strength participated. Participants were seated in front of the InMotion[2] robot, and their affected upper extremity was placed in the customized arm support. All subjects engaged in goal-directed shoulder and elbow motions while the computer screen gave them visual feedback. The robotic therapy sessions lasted for 1-hour intervals, three times a week, for a 6-week time period. Results showed that robotic therapy significantly decreased chronic shoulder and elbow motor impairments and decreased shoulder pain levels. In the 4-month follow-up study, motor gains were still evident.[88]

In-home robot   Researchers at the Interaction Lab at the University of Southern California are developing a novel approach to stroke therapy. They are developing a prototype therapeutic robot that does not come into contact with the patient. Their intention is to develop an in-home robot that monitors, guides, and encourages the patient with home therapy.[89] Their aim is to prevent the patient from overusing their functional extremity and ignoring their nonfunctioning extremity. Because it is not feasible to have a therapist monitor the patient throughout the day everyday, the in-home robot will monitor the patient to be sure they complete their rehabilitation program once discharged home. Additionally, developers wish to implement the Constraint Induced Movement therapy (CI therapy) protocol into the robots software platform, thereby replacing the need for a skilled therapist to be in the home for extended hours each week. Specifically, the in-home robot would be programmed to remind the patient to use their weaker arm throughout the day per CI therapy protocol. The in-home robot would utilize their vision-based sensing to follow the patient around their home to be sure that they use their affected arm to evaluate their progress.

Summary

This chapter has presented descriptions of robots in both prototype and product stages. Table 3.1 summarizes information on each of these robots, including name, type, cost, and location.

3.3 OTHER ISSUES RELATED TO ROBOTICS

Human–Robot Interaction

Humans often display feelings for inanimate objects, naming their boat, car, or pet robot. Japanese popular culture frequently displays robots in a friendly manner such as the cartoon character Astro Boy.[90] Astro Boy was a boy robot that had adventures in saving mankind while illustrating how humans and robots can coexist together. Japanese culture also allows for animals and machines to have a soul.[91] This contrasts with uneasiness toward humanoid robots in the West.[91] This uneasiness has been portrayed in many of Hollywood screenplays where humans would have to decide where to draw the line between machine and living being. This conflict can be seen in such movies as Blade Runner (1982), where Harrison Ford's character must hunt down and eliminate Mark 6 Replicant robots who want to live like humans, or Arnold Schwarzenegger's Terminator (1984, 1991, 2003), where robotic machines rise up and conquer the world.

Investigators at Carnegie Mellon University suggest that as technology advances, companies may be able to add personality traits to everyday electronic devices to make interaction with humans a more pleasurable experience.[92] Devices such as copiers may be able to remember your name and your preferences with printing. A coffee dispenser will remember your top three preferences. The new device could have a virtual-robot programmed to say, "Do you want the usual?" or "Is Mr. Smith having you copy things in triplicate again?" Devices that are programmed to tell a joke prior to an interaction may also work for people who have developed apprehension in dealing with technology. A computer that has an operating system with a preinstalled humorous personality may help overcome barriers that people may have developed with technology. An elder may be encouraged to use a computer if it could be adjusted to their preferred interaction level. For example, a user could adjust the computers rate of suggestions. Set at "low," the computer would provide very few suggestions; when adjusted to "high," many hints and suggestions would be given while a task is performed. If a user desired, a computer could be programmed with a fictional personal history and each time the user interacted with the computer, more is learned about the computer's personality. A person may have a stronger desire to interact with a personality-based computer than having to interact with the technical vocabulary of today's basic computers.

TABLE 3.1 Robotic Prototypes and Products

Robot	Type	Estimated present–future cost per unit	Located
Prototype			
Robonaut	Space exploration	—	United States
MADMEN	Asteroid deflection	—	United States
HyperRescueRobot	Rescue	—	Japan
Roboceptionist	Clerical	—	United States
Inkha	Clerical	—	United Kingdom
Koolio	Gopher	—	United States
HAL-3	Exoskeleton	—	Japan
BLEEX	Exoskeleton	—	United States
Walking Helper	Exoskeleton	—	Japan
Power Suit	Exoskeleton	$1,700	Japan
WL-16	Powered wheelchair	—	Japan
Weston	Robotic arm	—	United Kingdom
KARES II	Robotic arm	—	Korea
Paro	Companionship–therapy	$2,800	Japan
QRIO	Entertainment	$12,000–$65,000	Japan
ASIMO	Entertainment	—	Japan
Wakamaru	Monitoring	$8,300	Japan
HRP-2	Humanoid robotic platform	—	Japan
Cardea	Personal assistant	—	United States
Pearl	Personal assistant/mobility aid	—	United States
Care-O-bot II	Personal assistant/mobility aid	—	Germany
Pt. Transfer System	Transfer aid	—	Japan
Robo Nurse	Nurse assistant	—	China
BABS	Hippotherapy	—	United Kingdom
In-home robot	Home therapy	—	United States
Product			
PackBot-Explorer	Reconnaissance	$50,000–$100,000	United States
Da Vinci System	Surgical	$1,000,000	United States
Guido	Smart walker	$6,000	Ireland
iBOT 3000	Powered wheelchair	$29,000	United States
Raptor	Robotic arm	$12,500	United States
AIBO ERS 7M2	Entertainment	$1,900	Japan
Banryu	Monitoring	$20,000	Japan
PeopleBot	Personal assistant	$30,000	United States
HIRB	Human washing machine	$50,000	Japan
HelpMate2	Medical supply transport	Leased $3,400/month	United States
RP-6	Tele-interaction and monitoring	Leased $3,000/month	United States
Teddy	Monitoring	—	Japan
Robobear	Monitoring	—	Japan
NeCoRo	Companionship–therapy	$1,500	Japan
Tama	Companionship–therapy	—	Japan
InMotion	Upper-limb therapy	$5,000–$70,000	United States

When designing robot–human interaction, is it better to have a cheerful humorous robot or serious authoritarian robot to interact with? Researchers at Carnegie Mellon University investigated user compliance of 44 participants (average age 22) with an exercise routine led by a robot.[93] Although participants who interacted with a playful humorous robot were happier, the participants who interacted with the more serious authoritarian robot showed greater compliance with the exercise routine.

Goetz et al.[94] predicted that participants would have a higher compliance with the more cheerful humorous robot if the tasks were more playful (i.e., guessing jellybean flavors), hypothesizing that if the robots demeanor matched the social situation, a higher compliance level would be achieved. Forty-seven college students (average age of 23) were tested with either a jellybean task or an exercise task. Results showed significant compliance when the robots demeanor matched the task (i.e., playful robot elicited more compliance in the jellybean condition and the serious robot elicited more compliance in the exercise condition).

Devices packaged with virtual robots that have adjustable "helpfulness levels" or "humor levels" would add to the overall experience with a device. Also, future-generation virtual robots could automatically adjust personality settings to the user's mood. Researchers at Pennsylvania State University found that computer users commonly assign human attributes to machines and are frequently willing to wait for specific computers in a shared computer environment.[95] Even though we know that computers are inanimate machines, people still speak to their computers as if they were living beings. Having a computer or household device that could read a user's mood and have its virtual robot respond in an appropriate fashion could revolutionize the technological experience. Software that can help determine human emotions via a web cam image has already been developed.[96]

Research on enabling computers to read and respond to emotional levels is a growing field. In January 2004, the European Union (EU) initiated a $10 million program to study emotions as it relates to human–machine interaction.[96] Titled *Human-Machine Interaction Network on Emotions* (Humaine), the program encompasses 11 countries and will focus on issues such as developing theories and models of emotions, signal and signs of emotions, emotion in communication and persuasion, and ethics and good practice.[97] A benefit of a computer that could read emotions and respond appropriately would be in diffusing situations in which users are frustrated and irate with their interaction with the machine. Another benefit may be in developing a computer that will draw users to their computers. A virtual robot would continuously perform psychological evaluations and customize its personality interface with the user to facilitate reaching established goals established by the user. For example, the virtual robot would analyze either (a) the best interface for a user to learn how to use a specific device or (b) the best interface for a user to search the internet.

Should a Robot Look Human?

Researchers at Massachusetts Institute of Technology are developing a prototype robotic head that can move its mouth freely. Researchers at the University of Tokyo report that in 5–10 years robotic skin, composed of metal, rubber, and thousands of embedded organic transistors, will be used in very human-like robots.[24] Accordingly, robotic manufacturers will have the ability to create very human-like robots within the next 5–10 years.

Carnegie Mellon University investigators surveyed 20 individuals to determine their perception of what was "human-like" in robotic design.[98] The survey was based on robotic designs taken from 48 robot images collected from three separate categories: (1) research robots (i.e., Pearl), (2) consumer robots (i.e., ASIMO), and (3) fictional robots (i.e., Transformer). Participants were asked to rate each image on a 1 to 5 point scale from "Not Very Human-Like" to "Very Human-Like." Results showed that the three facial features that increased perception of humanness were the nose, the eyelids, and the mouth. The level of perceived humanness increased with the number of facial features on the robotic head, whereas it decreased as the robotic head became disproportionately wider to the body.

This question of human-like robots has been addressed in science fiction cinema, literature, and television.[24] Researchers report that as robotic assistants become more integrated into our society, the desire to have them look like us will only be natural.[24] However, these same researchers also express hesitation in having a robot look too real, stating that there is a "creep" factor when a robot crosses a line between resembling humans and looking too human.

Although not specifically addressing whether a robot should look human, researchers at the University "La Sapienza," Rome studied adult and elderly Italian subjects through survey design on basic attitudes toward technology and their general views on domestic robotic devices.[99] No differences between generations (adult vs. elder) were found, but familiarity with technology and sociocultural status were factors in attitude toward robotic appearances. The only attribute universally agreed upon was that the robot should be small enough to navigate throughout the home and have direct speech input. Ranges of responses of what the robot should be made from varied from metal to rubber, and the overall color of the robot was from pure metal to vivid colors.

The Future of Robotics

Carnegie Mellon investigators, in a recent *USA Today* article, suggested that robotic development would follow the following timeline[100]:

- 2015—Floor vacuuming robots will be able to schedule cleaning and empty its own dust bins.
- 2020—First-generation robots will be able to prepare breakfast and to set up and clean the table but will have problems with unexpected situations.
- 2030—Second-generation robots will be able to autonomously choose its actions, although choices will be limited.
- 2040—Third-generation robots will be able to have preferences and handle simple conversations.
- 2050—Fourth-generation robots will have the brain power of humans and accomplish abstract thought and reasoning.

Future-generation virtual robots may come standard with all electronic device purchases. The hard-copy manual or CD-ROM disk that is normally packaged with cell phones and PDAs could be replaced with virtual robots. The virtual robots would have holographic interfaces that could demonstrate three-dimensionally how to use various functions. Just as present-day Microsoft operating systems software can visually display steps on a computer screen, futuristic virtual robots could walk a user through the necessary steps in completing all applications. The virtual robot would be able to assess the user's learning preferences and facilitate instructional algorithms best suited for the user. Virtual robots would be good candidates for personality-enhanced software to make interaction with the virtual robots cheerful. Some scientists say that the traditional classroom teacher may be replaced by virtual teachers.[92] Individual teaching styles could be formulated as virtual teachers, working one-on-one with students. Material could be explained from multiple viewpoints, and current information could be continually accessed as the virtual robots are teaching.

What if a person with quadriplegia could control a robotic arm, or a stroke patient could control a keyboard using only their mind? Researchers at Duke University Medical Center are developing an implantable prototype neuroprosthetic device with a wireless interface between the controller and the device.[101] The prototype would be implanted in the brain and could potentially assist patients in controlling a robotic arm, an electric wheelchair, or a keyboard that has text or speech output. Duke researchers have applied for federal approval of a 3- to 5-year study that would involve implanting experimental electrode arrays for long periods in quadriplegic patients. The hope is to find which specific regions of the brain would best control specific tasks.

The Duke work on implanted electrode array control is based on two previous studies. The researchers demonstrated successful brain–machine interface with two rhesus macaque monkeys.[102] Ninety-six to 320 microelectrodes, each with a diameter smaller than a human hair, were implanted into the parietal and frontal lobes of two female monkeys. The monkeys were then taught to (1) grasp a joystick, (2) use a joystick to move a cursor on a video display screen, (3) use a joystick to manipulate a robot arm, and (4) manipulate a cursor and robot arm without the joystick (moved her arm in mid-air). After a few days of moving their arm in mid-air, the monkeys soon realized that they did not have to move their arm at all. The monkeys then kept their arm at their side while manipulating the robot arm by using brain and visual feedback. The brain signals recorded from the monkeys showed that they had incorporated the robotic arm as if it was their own arm.

A second breakthrough was shown when Duke Medical Center researchers conducted a study to evaluate the usability of human brain signals to operate external devices.[101,103] Eleven volunteer patients were identified. All were undergoing surgical procedures involving stimulation of the brain via implantation of microelectrodes to help relieve Parkinson symptoms and tremor disorders. Participants were asked to play a hand-held video game. Prior to the initiation of the hand-held device, electrodes were inserted deep into the participants' subcortical structures to measure the brain signals. The results showed that subcortical brain signals contained enough information to predict hand motions in humans playing a hand-held video device. Thus these subcortical signals could possibly be channeled to control external devices through thought alone. Knowing that subcortical signals may be able to control external devices is an important step in the development of brain–machine interfaces. Neuroprosthetic devices may become the ultimate interface in the future, allowing elders to merely think something and have it happen.

3.4 SUMMARY

The science of robotics has advanced in a relatively short time. Forty-two years after the first commercial robot went to work in the industrial sector, NASA's Mars Rover Spirit had the robotic technologic capability to discover hints of water on Mars. Just as the computer industry has shifted from an industrial sector to the personal realm, over the next 20 years the robotic industry will make a similar shift into the personal sector. Technological advancements in robotics will reduce costs and future technologies will begin to meld together. Exoskeleton, entertainment, monitoring, and clerical robotic technology will all meld into a more efficient personal assistant. Robots will begin to move out of research labs and permeate our society. Although early robotics will not be as robust as Hollywood has predicted, the robotic industry will begin to have a larger visible presence in our society.

REFERENCES

1. BBC News (2001). Timeline: Real robots. Retrieved September 12, 2004, from http://news.bbc.co.uk/1/hi/in_depth/sci_tech/2001/artificial_intelligence/1531432.stm
2. Merriam–Webster (2004). *Merriam-Webster Online*. Retrieved May 25, 2004, from http://www.mw.com/cgi-bin/dictionary?book=Dictionary&va=robot&x=17&y=14
3. Oxford English Dictionary (2004). *Oxford English Dictionary—Online*. Retrieved May 25, 2004, from http://dictionary.oed.com/
4. Kumar, V. (1998). Introduction to robotics. Retrieved May 25, 2004, from http://www.seas.upenn.edu/~meam100/handouts/robotics.pdf
5. UNECE (2003). Press release ECE/STAT/03/Po1, Geneva, 17 October 2003. Retrieved July 21, 2004, from http://www.unece.org/press/pr2003/03robots_index.htm
6. UNECE (2004). Press release ECE/STAT/03/ Po7 Geneva, 17 October 2003. Retrieved August 8, 2004, from http://www.unece.org/press/pr2003/03robots_index.htm
7. Stenger, R. (2003). Who should explore space, man or machine? Retrieved September 29, 2004, from http://www.cnn.com/2003/TECH/space/02/18/sprj.colu.space.future/index.html
8. Enderle, R. (2004). Personal robotics: The technology the US will miss. Retrieved September 12, 2004, from http://www.technewsworld.com/story/33314.html
9. Bluethmann, W., Ambrose, R., Diftler, M., Askew, S., Huber, E., Goza, M., et al. (2003). Robonaut: A robot designed to work with humans in space. *Autonomous Robots* **14**, 179–197.
10. Beutel, A. (2003). Humans, robots work together to test "spacewalk squad" concept. Retrieved May 12, 2004, from http://robonaut.jsc.nasa.gov/press_release1.htm
11. Ambrose, R. O., Savely, R. T., Goza, S. M., Diftler, M. A., Spain, I., Radford, N., et al. (2004). *Mobile manipulation using NASA's robonaut*. Paper presented at the IEEE International Conference on Robotics and Automation, 2004. Proceedings, ICRA '04.
12. Malik, T. (2004). Asteroid eaters: Robots to hunt space rocks. Retrieved September 12, 2004, from http://www.cnn.com/2004/TECH/space/05/19/asteroid.eater/

13. Sheehan, C. (2004). Robotics gains in prestige, in part due to military conflicts. Retrieved September 15, 2004, from http://www.usatoday.com/tech/news/techinnovations/2004-04-08-robotics-surge_x.htm

14. Walton, M. (2004). Robots fail to complete Grand Challenge. Retrieved August 26, 2004, from http://www.cnn.com/2004/TECH/ptech/03/14/darpa.race/

15. Defense Advanced Research Projects Agency. (2004). Grand Challenge 2004 final report. Retrieved August 26, 2004, from http://www.darpa.mil/body/NewsItems/pdf/DGCreport30July2004.pdf

16. DARPA (2004). DARPA Grand Challenge 2005 home page. Retrieved August 26, 2004, from http://www.darpa.mil/grandchallenge/

17. Kanellos, M. (2004). Invasion of the robots. Retrieved July 20, 2004, from http://marketwatchcnet.com.com/2009-1040_3-5171948.html

18. iRobot (2004). Government & industrial robotics. Retrieved August 12, 2004, from http://www.irobot.com/home.cfm

19. Lanfranco, A. R., Castellanos, A. E., Desai, J. P., and Meyers, W. C. (2004). Robotic surgery: A current perspective. *Ann Surgery* **239**(1), 14–21.

20. Betterhumans. (2004). Giant robot to help during disasters: Five ton behemoth can lift one-fifth its weight. Retrieved September 19, 2004, from http://www.betterhumans.com/News/news.aspx?articleID=2004-03-26-3

21. CNN (2004). Technology—Robot secretary gossips, dishes advice, even gets testy. Retrieved May 13, 2004, from http://www.cnn.com/2004/TECH/ptech/02/23/robot.receptionist.ap/index.html

22. Protein Ltd. (2003). Inkha the robot receptionist. Retrieved August 18, 2004, from http://feed.proteinos.com/001744.html

23. Wong, W. (2004). Real-world robotics: An appetite for construction. Retrieved August 26, 2004, from http://www.elecdesign.com/Articles/Index.cfm?ArticleID=8076

24. Valigra, L. (2004). Almost human—Researchers designing robots with more human characteristics. Retrieved May 12, 2004, from http://abcnews.go.com/sections/scitech/US/robots_humans_CSM_040223.html

25. U.S. Census Bureau (2003). Table 13. Resident population projections by race, hispanic origin, and age: 2000 to 2002. Retrieved September 6, 2004, from http://www.census.gov/prod/2004pubs/03statab/pop.pdf

26. U.S. Census Bureau (2003). Table 12. Resident population projections by sex and age: 2005 to 2050. Retrieved August 27, 2004, from http://www.census.gov/prod/2004pubs/03statab/pop.pdf

27. National Institute of population and Social Security Research (2003). Table 2.8. Indicators on future total Population by major age group (3 groups): 2000–2050. Retrieved September 6, 2004, from http://www.ipss.go.jp/index-e.html and http://www.ipss.go.jp/English/psj2003/PSJ2003.pdf

28. Nakamaru, M. (2004). Humanoid-companion robots: The solution to Japan's problems of an aging society and diminishing work force. Retrieved September 6, 2004, from http://www.jasc.org/Delegate/intros/nakamura-megumi_paper.PDF

29. MacNamara, S., and Lacey, G. (2000). A smart walker for the frail visually impaired. Paper presented at the IEEE International Conference on Robotics and Automation, 2000. Proceedings, ICRA '00.

30. Lacey, G., and Dawson-Howe, K. M. (1998). The application of robotics to a mobility aid for the elderly blind. *Robotics and Autonomous Systems* **23**(4), 245–252.

31. Rentschler, A. J., Cooper, R. A., Blasch, B., and Boninger, M. L. (2003). Intelligent walkers for the elderly: Performance and safety testing of VA-PAMAID robotic walker. *Journal of Rehabilitation Research and Development* **40**(5), 423–431.

32. Haptica (2004). The Haptica walker. Retrieved April 27, 2004, from http://www.haptica.com/index.htm

33. Pietrodangelo, B., and Phillipson, K. (2004). Koolio. Retrieved Aug 10, 2004, from http://www.mil.ufl.edu/~brian/Koolio/Koolio.htm

34. Kawamoto, H., Lee, S., Kanbe, S., and Sankai, Y. (2003). Power assist method for HAL-3 using EMG-based feedback controller. Paper presented at the IEEE International Conference on Systems, Man and Cybernetics, 2003.

35. Accessibility.com.au (2003). Japan ready to market "robot suit." Retrieved June 4, 2004, from http://www.accessibility.com.au/news/health/robosuit.htm

36. Berkeley, U. C. (2004). Berkeley Lower Extremity Exoskeleton (BLEEX). Retrieved July 5, 2004, 2004, from http://bleex.me.berkeley.edu/CV/BLEEX-Summary.pdf

37. Berkeley, U. C. (2004). UC Berkeley Researchers developing robotic exoskeleton that can enhance human strength and endurance. Retrieved July 5, 2004, 2004, from http://www.berkeley.edu/news/media/releases/2004/03/03_exo.shtml

38. Nakamura, T., and Kosuge, K. (2003). Model-based walking support system with wearable walking helper. Paper presented at the 12th IEEE International Workshop on Robot and Human Interactive Communication, 2003. Proceedings, ROMAN 2003.

39. Hadfield, P., and Marks, P. (2001). Nurses get bionic "power suit." Retrieved July 20, 2004, from http://www.newscientist.com/news/news.jsp?id=ns99991072

40. Time Magazine (2003). Put some pep in your step. Retrieved July 20, 2004, from http://www.time.com/time/2003/inventions/invpowersuit.html

41. Kunii, I. (2003). A muscle suit you can strap right on. Retrieved July 20, 2004, from http://www.paralinks.net/muscle_suit.html

42. Independence Technology (2004). Retrieved July 12, 2004, 2004, from http://www.independencenow.com/index.html

43. Advanced Rehabilitation Technologies (2004). The Raptor wheelchair robot system. Retrieved September 18, 2004, from http://www.appliedresource.com/RTD/Products/Raptor/

44. Evans, N., Hillman, M., and Orpwood, R. (2002). The role of user evaluation in designing robotics. British Journal of Therapy and Rehabilitation **9**, 485.

45. Hillman, M. (2003). Weston robot essential figures. Retrieved September 18, 2004, from http://staff.bath.ac.uk/mpsmrh/robot/westonspec.htm

46. Bien, Z., Chung, M. J., Chang, P. H., Kwon, D. S., Kim, D. J., Han, J. S., et al. (2004). Integration of a rehabilitation robotic system (KARES II) with human-friendly man-machine interaction units. *Autonomous Robots* **16**(2), 165–191.

47. Williams, M. (2000). More pet robots on the way. Retrieved August 26, 2004, from http://www.cnn.com/2000/TECH/computing/01/26/aibo.robots.idg/

48. Sony Style USA (2004). Entertainment robots: No fleas, no food, no fur? *Meet AIBO*. Retrieved August 26, 2004, from http://sony.com/

49. Tamura, T., Yonemitsu, S., Itoh, A., Oikawa, D., Kawakami, A., Higashi, Y., et al. (2004). Is an entertainment robot useful in the care of elderly people with severe dementia? *Journal of Gerontology A: Biological Science and Medical Science* **59**(1), M83–M85.

50. Kageyama, Y. (2004). In gadget-loving Japan, robots get hugs in therapy sessions. Retrieved July 14, 2004, from http://www.usatoday.com/tech/news/techinnovations/2004-04-11-robot-helpers_x.htm

51. BruneiDirect. (2004, 4-11-2004). Robots seen as companions for elderly. Retrieved April 11, 2004, from http://www.brudirect.com/DailyInfo/News/Archive/Apr04/120404/wn03.htm

52. Wada, K., Shibata, T., Saito, T., and Tanie, K. (2002). Robot assisted activity for elderly people and nurses at a day service center. Paper presented at the IEEE International Conference on Robotics and Automation, 2002. Proceedings, ICRA '02.

53. Wada, K., Shibata, T., Saito, T., and Tanie, K. (2003). Psychological, physiological and social effects to elderly people by robot assisted activity at a health service facility for the aged. Paper presented at the IEEE/ASME International Conference on Advanced Intelligent Mechatronics, 2003. Proceedings, AIM 2003.

54. Omron Corporation (2001). "Is this a real cat?" A robot cat you can bond with like a real pet—NeCoRo is born. Retrieved September 19, 2004, from http://www.omron.com/news/n_161001.html

55. Libin, A., and Libin, E. (2003). Older persons' perception of and communication with a companion robot. Paper presented at the 2003 International Conference on Aging, Disability and Independence.

56. Sony Global (2004). Sony dream robot—QRIO. Retrieved September 18, 2004, from http://www.sony.net/SonyInfo/QRIO/top_nf.html

57. Guide, G. H. T. (2004). Honda's Asimo. Retrieved May 11, 2004, from http://www.gizmohighway.com/robotics/asimo.htm

58. Honda Motor Co. (2004). ASIMO Frequently asked questions. Retrieved August 30, 2004, from http://asimo.honda.com/news_media_center.asp

59. France-Presse, A. (2004). Robot "Rovers" to help care for world's aging population. Retrieved April 11, 2004, from http://www.spacedaily.com/2004/040314031152.7ikux0ft.html

60. SANYO Electric Co. Ltd. (2002). tmsuk and SANYO reveals new and improved "Banryu" home-robot. The first "serious" new-age gadget is to be brought to the market in 2003. Retrieved May 11, 2004, from http://www.global-sanyo.com/news/0211/1106-e.html

61. Martyn, W. (2004). Gadgets for commuters. Retrieved July 14, 2004, from http://yahoo.pcworld.com/yahoo/article/0,aid,115708,00.asp

62. Batista, E. (2003). Wakamaru Bot at Your Service. Retrieved April 11, 2004, from http://www.wired.com/news/print/0,1294,58593,00.html

63. Mitsubishi Heavy Industries Ltd. (2004). Wakamaru. Retrieved July 12, 2004, from http://www.sdia.or.jp/mhikobe-e/products/etc/robot.html

64. Kaneko, K., Kanehiro, F., Kajita, S., Hirukawa, H., Kawasaki, T., Hirata, M., et al. (2004). Humanoid robot HRP-2. Paper presented at the 2004 IEEE International Conference on Robotics and Automation, 2004. Proceedings, ICRA '04.

65. MIT Computer Science and Artificial Intelligence Laboratory (CSAIL) (2004). Project Overview—Cardea. Retrieved May 12, 2004, from http://www.ai.mit.edu/projects/cardea/index.shtml

66. Rotstein, G. (2004). A Pearl for the elderly. Retrieved May 13, 2004, from http://www.post-gazette.com/pg/pp/04095/295927.stm

67. CMU/Pitt Nursebot Project (2004). Nursebot Project—Robotic assistants for the elderly. Retrieved May 13, 2004, from http://www-2.cs.cmu.edu/~nursebot/web/scope.html

68. Fraunhofer, I. P. A. (2003). II Care offered—the next generation. Retrieved July 22, 2004, from http://216.239.39.104/translate_c?hl=en&sl=de&u = http://www.ipa.fhg.de/PresseMedien/Mediendienst/mediendienst_03_2002_2.php&prev=/search%3Fq%3DThe%2BCare-O-Bot%2BII%26hl%3Den%26lr%3D%26ie%3DUTF-8%26sa%3DG and http://www.ipa.fhg.de/PresseMedien/Mediendienst/mediendienst_03_2002_2.php

69. Graf, B., Hans, M., and Schraft, R. (2004). Care-O-bot II—Development of a next generation robotic home assistant. *Autonomous Robots* **16**, 193–205.

70. ActivMedia Robotics (2004). PeopleBot. Retrieved September 19, 2004, from http://www.activrobots.com/ROBOTS/peoplebot.html#descrip

71. Brooke, J. (2004, March 5, 2004). Japan: Japan seeks robotic help in caring for the aged. Retrieved September 29, 2004, from http://www.globalaging.org/elderrights/world/2004/japaninvention.htm

72. Independent Administrative Corporation of Japan External and Organization—JETRO (2003). RTO Robot Technology Osaka. Retrieved May 11, 2004, from http://www.osakacity.org/rto/rto_e.pdf

73. Brand-New Osaka (2004). Robots from Osaka. Retrieved May 11, 2004, from http://www.pref.osaka.jp/koho/brand/no3/ie_robots/

74. Ananova (2004). Robo-nurse could help cope with future SARS outbreaks. Retrieved May 13, 2004, from http://www.ananova.com/news/story/sm_804253.html

75. Hill, A. (2001). Health-care helpers: Service robots free nurses, pharmacists to do more important work. *Robotics World* **19**(1), 28.

76. Keel, C. (2002). Rudy the robot: Automated help with medication delivery. *American Journal of Nursing* **102**(8), 24A.

77. Pyxis Corporation (2004). Pyxis HelpMate SP. Retrieved August 11, 2004, from http://www.pyxis.com/products/newhelpmate.asp#

78. InTouch Health (2004). Advanced technology solutions for healthcare service providers. Retrieved September 19, 2004, from http://www.intouch-health.com/index.html

79. Davis, R. (2004). Robo doc: Medicine by "extension"; Technology is the middle man in patient care. Retrieved September 19, 2004, from http://www.intouch-health.com/USAToday8-4-04.pdf

80. MSNBC News (2004). Robot doctor gets thumbs-up from patients. Retrieved September 19, 2004, from http://msnbc.msn.com/id/4946229/

81. Lytle, M. (2002). Robot care bears for the elderly. Retrieved March 28, 2004, from http://news.bbc.co.uk/1/hi/sci/tech/1829021.stm

82. Lytle, M. (2003). A yen for a hi-tech life. Retrieved July 14, 2004, from http://www.guardian.co.uk/online/story/0,3605,1039233,00.html

83. The Yomiuri Shimbun (2003). Coexistence of humans and robots: Pet robots fill empty space in lives of elderly people. Retrieved July 15, 2004, from http://www.yomiuri.co.jp/dy/special/spe10.htm

84. Duggan, A. (2004). Robo-pet: A human's best friend? Retrieved August 26, 2004, from http://www.iol.co.za/index.php?set_id=1&click_id=116&art_id=iol1084370152882R131

85. Dziuba, A., Sutherland, I., and Bober, T. (2000). *Hippotherapy: Comparison of the BABS simulator with five walking horses.* Retrieved August 19, 2004, from http://www.medphys.soton.ac.uk/ipem2000/

86. Bender, E. (2004). Robo Rehab. Retrieved September 19, 2004, from http://www.technologyreview.com/articles/04/04/wo_bender041404.asp?p=1

87. Interactive Motion Technologies (2004). IMT's Modular Robot System. Retrieved September 19, 2004, from http://www.interactive-motion.com/html/hardware.htm

88. Fasoli, S. E., Krebs, H. I., Stein, J., Frontera, W. R., Hughes, R., and Hogan, N. (2004). Robotic therapy for chronic motor impairments after stroke: Follow-up results. *Archives of Physical Medicine and Rehabilitation* 85(7), 1106–1111.

89. Interaction Lab (2004). Laboratory profile. Retrieved September 19, 2004, from http://www.robotics.usc.edu/interaction/?l=Research:Projects:post_stroke:index

90. Sony Pictures (2004). Astro boy. Retrieved August 26, 2004, from http://www.sonypictures.com/tv/shows/astroboy/about.html

91. McNicol, T. (2003). A robot pet revolution: The new breed of bots both bows and wows: just in time for Christmas, "comfort toys" promise comfort and jog. Cute, yes—but will consumers cuddle up? Retrieved September 29, 2004, from http://www.findarticles.com/p/articles/mi_m0NTN/is_50/ai_111506873

92. Lamb, G. (2004). Robots get friendly. Retrieved September 6, 2004, from http://www.csmonitor.com/2004/0205/p17s01-stct.html

93. Goetz, J., and Kiesler, S. (2002). Cooperation with a robotic assistant. Paper presented at the CHI, Minneapolis, MN.

94. Goetz, J., Kiesler, S., and Powers, A. (2003). Matching robot appearance and behavior to tasks to improve human–robot cooperation. Paper presented at the 12th IEEE International Workshop on Robot and Human Interactive Communication, 2003. Proceedings, ROMAN 2003.

95. Ink, M. (2004). Humans making computers more human. Retrieved September 8, 2004, from http://www.mckenzieink.ca/edge_072204_EmotionalPC.html

96. McKie, R. (2004). Machine rage is dead . . . long live emotional computing. Retrieved September 8, 2004, from http://observer.guardian.co.uk/uk_news/story/0,6903,1189802,00.html

97. Humaine Consortium (2004). The official humaine project presentation. Retrieved September 8, 2004, from http://emotion-research.net/press/humaine_project_presentation.pdf

98. DiSalvo, C., Gemperle, F., Forlizzi, J., and Kiesler, S. (2002). All robots are not created equal: The design and perception of humanoid robot heads. Retrieved September 6, 2004, from http://www.peopleandrobots.org/admin/uploads/DIS02.pdf

99. Giuliani, M. V. (2003). Psychological aspects in the RoboCare Project: Laypeople's view of domestic robots. Retrieved August 8, 2004, from http://icadi.phhp.ufl.edu/2003/proceedings.php

100. Baig, E. (2003). Robot Science puts on a friendly face. Retrieved August 18, 2004, from http://www.usatoday.com/tech/news/techinnovations/2003-04-30-robot-main_x.htm

101. Duke Medical News. (2004). Human studies show feasibility of brain–machine interfaces. Retrieved September 7, 2004, from http://www.dukemednews.org/news/article.php?id=7493

102. Duke Medical News. (2004). Monkeys consciously control a robot arm using only brain signals; Appear to "assimilate" arm as if it were their own. Retrieved September 7, 2004, from http://www.dukemednews.org/news/article.php?id=7493

103. Patil, P. G., Carmena, J. M., Nicolelis, M. A. L., and Turner, D. A. (2004). Ensemble recordings of human subcortical neurons as a source of motor control signals for a brain–machine interface. *Neurosurgery* 55(1), 27–38.

CHAPTER 4

OTHER DEVICES AND HIGH-TECHNOLOGY SOLUTIONS

Shin Yi-Lin

4.1 INTRODUCTION

This chapter discusses high-technology assistive devices, excluding smart home technology, assistive robotics, and telehealth devices, which are covered in Chapters 2, 3, and 5. We have grouped these devices by the primary type of impairment they address: vision, hearing, mobility and movement, and cognition. We begin with discussing smart devices for people with vision impairment.

4.2 SMART TECHNOLOGY FOR PEOPLE WITH VISION IMPAIRMENT

In discussing smart devices for persons with vision impairment, we cover electronic reading devices, personal organizers, mobility devices, and devices for self-care.

Electronic Reading Devices

A closed-circuit television device (CCTV) is a video magnification system that includes a video camera, a video screen, and a control unit for image adjustment. CCTVs are electronic reading devices that provide advanced magnification, illumination, and contrast options for people with low vision, far exceeding what would be possible with a low-tech optical device such as a hand-held magnifier or nonoptical aids such as large-print materials. A major advantage of CCTVs is that the magnifying power and image size can be adjusted; the image can also be manipulated to produce high-contrast output. CCTVs can be configured with television, video monitors, or computer monitors. Some models, such as the Optelec ClearView 700 Series, can display split output on one screen for both printed material and computer output (Table 4.1).

CCTVs are available as desktop or portable devices. Desktop CCTVs are more common, providing a 12- to 19-inch monitor or video display mounted above the camera. Desktop CCTVs have a relatively wide range of features and permit more

---

Smart Technology for Aging, Disability, and Independence, Edited by William C. Mann
Copyright © 2005 John Wiley & Sons, Inc.

TABLE 4.1 Comparison of Print Enlargement Devices

Model	Discovery Plus	Merlin	MaxPanel	Flipper	JORDY
Company:	Inline Clarity	Enhanced Vision	Enhanced Vision	Enhanced Vision	Enhanced Vision
Type:	Desktop	Desktop	Portable	Portable	Portable
Magnification power:	4×–60× (on a 20-inch TV)	4×–50× on 14-inch monitor 6×–72× on 20-inch monitor	6×–9× on 7-inch LCD screen 8×–12× on 10-inch LCD screen	6×–50× (depends on monitor size)	30×
Mono/Color:	Color	Color	Color	Color	Color
Screen size:	NA	14-inch or 20-inch VGA monitors	7-inch or 10-inch TFT	Portable glasses, any TV or monitor	Portable glasses
Weight:	NA	NA	NA	1 lb	NA
Contrast:	Variable contrast control	High-contrast positive and high-contrast negative	High-contrast positive and high-contrast negative	Multiple-contrast options	High-contrast positive and high-contrast negative
Special features:	SVGA computer connection built-in; different colors for text and background (works only with a computer, not a TV)	Voice activation (optional)	Powered by a battery pack, runs up to 5 hours without recharging.	Autofocus	Digital zoom provided
Price:	$2845	$1995	NA	NA	NA

Web site:	http://www.clarityusa.com/	http://www.enhancedvision.com/	http://www.enhancedvision.com/	http://www.enhancedvision.com/
Model	MagniLink X Split	MagniLink S	ClearView 700 Series	SmartView 5000
Company:	Low Vision International	Low Vision International	Optelec	PulseData International
Type:	Desktop	Portable	Desktop	Desktop
Magnification power:	2.7×–46×	9.5×–30× varied by monitor	up to 56×	4×–74× (depends on monitor size)
Mono/Color:	Color	Color	Color	Color
Screen size:	17-inch TFT	Laptop screen	computer monitor	Optional
Weight:	32.5 lbs	NA	NA	28 pounds
Contrast:	High-contrast positive and high-contrast negative	High-contrast positive and high-contrast negative	NA	High-contrast black and white
Special features:	Can be connected to a computer with split function (vertical or horizontal direction)	The camera picture is presented in a Windows application and both size and position of the window can be adjusted	16 alternate background and foreground color options split screen option, line marks, windowing to eliminate distractions	Video output: VGA and TV
Price:	NA	NA	NA	NA
Web site:	http://www.lvi.se/	http://www.lvi.se	http://www.optelec.com/	http://www.pulsedata.com/

Web site:	http://www.enhancedvision.com/
Model	Compact-Portable Electronic Magnifier
Company:	Optelec
Type:	Portable
Magnification power:	4× and 8× modes
Mono/Color:	Color
Screen size:	4-inch LCD
Weight:	10 ounces
Contrast:	Blue/yellow and black/yellow
Special features:	2-hour rechargeable battery
Price:	NA
Web site:	http://www.optelec.com/

customization. Desktop CCTVs are available for both monochrome and color monitors. Contrast enhancement can be either gray scale or color. The foreground and background contrast is adjustable or reversible. The maximum magnification exceeds 60×.

Portable CCTVs are lightweight, smaller unit and have a limited battery life. Portable CCTVs are helpful for people who need to use them in different places within the home or work setting or who need the device while traveling. Portable CCTVs typically have less magnifying power (below 20×) than desktop models. Some portable models allow the camera to be connected to a desktop video monitor or standard TV. Some of the latest models are about the same size as a PDA (personal digital assistant), which makes them truly portable (e.g., PocketViewer by Pulse Data International Ltd., QuickLook Video Magnifier by Freedom Vision). The PocketViewer is 5.6 inches high, 3.4 inches wide, and 1.4 inches thick and weighing 10 ounces (Figure 4.1). The QuickLook Video Magnifier is 6.5 inches high, 3.75 inches wide, and 1 inch thick, weighing 10 ounces (Figure 4.2).

Figure 4.1 PocketViewer. Photo courtesty of Pulse Data International Ltd.

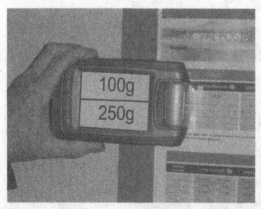

Figure 4.2 QuickLook Video Magnifier. Photo courtesy of Ash Technologies Ltd.

Personal Organizers

There are a number of personal organizers for people with blindness or low vision. An electronic note taker often used by students with visual impairments provides a calendar, address book, and alarm clock for personal organization. Some personal organizers for people with vision impairment have functions much the same as a regular PDA. Accessible PDAs use the same operating system as do main market PDAs, namely, Microsoft Windows CE, which is convenient for people who are familiar with a PC environment. The major differences between an accessible PDA and a regular PDA are input and output. Personal organizers for people with visual impairment use refreshable Braille displays or synthesized speech output, or both. Personal organizers for people with vision impairment operate with either Braille or QWERTY layout keyboard. As a result accessible PDAs are larger than a regular PDA. The most advanced accessible PDAs incorporate the functions of a personal organizer into a mobile phone. In the following paragraphs, we will describe the newer model PDAs, voice organizers, and mobile phones that can serve as personal organization tools.

BrailleNote (Figure 4.3) and VoiceNote (Figure 4.4) are note taker products of Pulse Data International Inc. These note takers incorporate Microsoft Windows CE and allow PC users to create and send/receive the same type of documents and files used by sighted people. BrailleNote and VoiceNote offer word processing, emailing, web browsing, reading ebooks, calendar and scheduler, address book, and

Figure 4.3   BrailleNote QT 32.

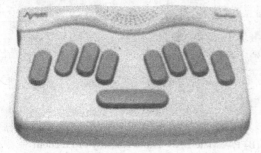

Figure 4.4   VoiceNote. Photo courtesy of Pulse Data International Ltd.

scientific calculator. They have an internal modem for internet and email access. Users can connect it to a computer, printer, or Braille embosser using its PCMCIA slot and infrared, serial, and parallel port. With BrailleNote or VoiceNote connected to a visual display, such as a computer monitor or a PDA, they can be used for real-time Braille translation, or as a screen reader. The PCMCIA card slot or the optional disk drive can also be used for additional storage. Both BrailleNote and VoiceNote have Braille and standard keyboard input. BrailleNote can produce 18- or 32-cell refreshable Braille and synthesized speech output, whereas VoiceNote produces speech output only.

Like BrailleNote and VoiceNote, PACMate by Freedom Scientific (Figure 4.5) also uses Microsoft Windows CE platform as its operation system. The PACMate is based on the Compaq iPaq pocket PC using a screen reader and speech synthesizer software to provide speech. Unlike other note taker products that use the Windows CE platform together with their own proprietary software, PACMate allows downloading and running of applications designed for a pocket PC. The PACMate offers a wide range of ports, including USB, infrared, and Compact Flash,™ that enable a range of peripherals, PCs, and connecting to the internet. Although PACMate has no internal modem or Ethernet capability, PACMate users can purchase their choice of internet access methods (modem, cellular modem, Ethernet, wireless or Bluetooth connection) by using the Compact Flash™ port. PACMate serves as an accessible and portable computer for persons with visual impairment.

In addition to the above-mentioned functions, both PDA products for blind and low-vision individuals can be used with Global Positioning System (GPS) and mapping systems. This feature is described later in this chapter in the section on electronic traveling aids.

Some personal organizers are speech-based, using voice recognition technology for stored data retrieval with flash memory up to 4 MB (90 minutes). The main features of a speech-based organizer are phone book with automatic dialing function, memo pad for to-do list, appointment and schedule management, talking clock and alarm, talking calculator, and voice prompt for keystroke. This device is small in size and lightweight (similar to a cell phone). It also has the capacity to connect to a PC for software updates.

A.   B.

Figure 4.5 PACMate. **(A)** QX series. **(B)** PACMate BNS. Photo courtesy of Freedom Scientific.

In their newest smart phones, the major mobile phone manufacturers now offer functions of a PDA plus a mobile phone. These smart phones can be used for voice communication, text messaging, processing multimedia files, organizing schedules and appointments, accessing the internet, file and data storage, and more. Nokia 9201i is one example of a mainstream smart phone; moreover, by adding software called Talx, it provides synthesied speech output. In addition to speech output, Nokia 9210i can add a Braillino docking station (it can also be used as a Braille note taker) for Braille input and output. Nokia also provides accessibility features for persons who are hard of hearing or deaf.

In addition to accessible mainstream smart phones, the ALVA MPO 5500 is a smart phone that is specially designed for persons with visual impairment. ALVA MPO offers both the features of a mobile phone and a PDA that can be accessed by Braille input and speech output. Currently, ALVA MPO 5500 has the features of a regular cell phone, note taker, text messaging, agenda planner, alarm, and calculator. In the near future, other features such as internet access, GPS, book reader, and MP3 player will be available.

Electronic Travel Aids

The conventional device for assisting people with vision impairment in getting around is the white cane.[1] Some people who are blind use a guide dog. These traditional mobility aids inform mainly on information at the ground level. A white cane user typically needs more than 100 hours of training before actually starting to use it, which is similar the amount of training needed to use a guide dog. The user needs to use the cane to actively scan the relatively small area (within 3 to 6 feet) ahead to detect by contact only obstacles below waist level. Objects above waist level are not discovered with a white cane. The development of a technical solution to mobility and orientation for people with vision impairment has taken two directions. One involves modifying the environment (such as tactile tiles) to provide alternative information and enhance safety. The second approach provides additional aids to traveler with vision impairment. These two solutions are complementary. Technical solutions for travelers with vision impairment provide information about the nearby environment and supplement traditional travel aids such as the white cane and guide dog.

New mobility devices for persons with vision impairment, called electronic travel aids (ETAs), incorporate radar and ultrasonic technologies. ETAs work on similar principles to a radar system. For example, a laser or ultrasonic signal is emitted in a certain direction in the environment. If an object is in the way, the signal is reflected from the object. A matching sensor on the ETAs detects the reflected signal and calculates the distance of the object based on the time difference between the emitting and receiving signals. ETAs produce a warning signal to their users if an object is in the person's path. ETAs can detect objects up to 15 feet away from the user, but ETA users need to actively and continuously scan the environment in the desired direction. Although ETAs provide more information about obstacles in the environment, they do not provide information related to orientation and navigation, such as where a person is located, or what direction one is traveling, or how far the distance is to one's destination. The widely used GPS technology provides a partial solution to orientation and navigation. In the following section, we describe ETAs and GPS systems currently available in the market, along with research on these navigation systems.

LaserCane The LaserCane has three laser beam channels projected from the cane to detect upward, forward, and downward obstacles. When there is an obstacle, it reflects the laser beam, which is then detected by the receiver on the cane. The reflected signal results in the LaserCane producing vibration or sounds to warn the user of the obstruction. Users have the option to inactivate the sounds and use only vibration for warnings. The LaserCane is used similarly to the standard long cane and operates with two AA batteries. An advantage of the LaserCane is that it can detect obstacles in a wide range both horizontally and vertically. LaserCanes can also be used during orientation and mobility training for people with vision impairments. The LaserCane does not work well when the user walks through a high-reflection surface, which results in confusion of the reflective signal received by LaserCane. Problems may also occur with a glass door, which may allow the laser beam to go through without any reflection.

Miniguide The Miniguide (Figure 4.6) is an ultrasonic obstacle detector, offering audio or tactile feedback. It is designed for use with other traditional mobility aids, such as a long cane or guide dog. The Miniguide is not intended as a replacement for these aids, but rather as a secondary aid. The Miniguide works similarly to the LaserCane. It has two sensors, which send and receive signals. If obstacles are sensed, the Miniguide produces sound or vibration to warn its users. The pitch of sound or the frequency of vibration indicates the distance of the obstacle from the user. Miniguide can detect obstacles up to 4 meters away. A single button on the Miniguide can be used for on and off and to select different modes to match user preferences or needs. Long battery life is a major advantage of Miniguide. A small lithium battery is used for the ultrasound sensor, and an AAA battery is used for auditory or vibration output. In low-power mode or normal use, the battery can last for several months. It is also very lightweight and small: 65 mm long by 35 mm wide by 25 mm thick, weighing less than 20 grams.

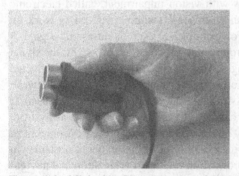

Figure 4.6   Miniguide. Photo courtesy of GDP Research.

Sonic Pathfinder: The Sonic Pathfinder is a head-mounted sonar system for obstacle detection. It is a secondary mobility aid designed to increase safety for people with vision impairment. It can be used outdoors in conjunction with a cane or a guide dog. It is suggested that use of the Sonic Pathfinder be taught by a trained Mobility Instructor. The Sonic Pathfinder gives the user advanced warning of objects that lie within the travel path. Indoor use in a crowded area such as a home environment is not recommended. The sonar system controlled by a microcomputer includes five ultrasonic transducers: three receivers pointing straight, left, and right, along with two transmitters positioned angularly to cover the user's pathway. Echoes from obstacles within the user's pathway are captured by the three receivers. The microcomputer then produces output to either one or both sides of the two earpieces, depending on the position of the object. The Sonic Pathfinder cannot detect the surface texture of the obstacle. The warning signals produced by the Sonic Pathfinder are restricted to the nearest object.

GPS System Added to a PDA   More and more functions are now provided by personal organizers. The newest add-in function is GPS. GPS is a network of satellites originally developed for military navigating purpose. GPS is based on the distance calculation of a signal transmission between a GPS receiver and four GPS satellites. A GPS receiver can locate four or more of these satellites, compute the distance to each, and use this information to deduce its own location on earth with latitude, longitude, and altitude figures. By plugging these data into map files in storage space on a hand-held device, a GPS receiver can tell its user where the person is, along with nearby points of interest. GPS can be used for getting directions, route planning, identifying specific destinations by address, calculation of distances to certain locations or destinations, and locating points of interest such as hotels, banks, hospitals, and so on. As mentioned earlier, PACMate by Freedom Scientific and BrailleNote/VoiceNote by Pulse Data International Inc. both have the capacity to add GPS.

Freedom Scientific adapted an off-the-shelf GPS product: Destinator GPS application to run on their PACMate. The Destinator GPS application is also used by mainstream pocket PC users. By installing the adapted application called StreetTalk, PACMate users are able to use GPS after they purchase the Destinator application and a GPS receiver. The GPS receiver can be connected to the PACMate by using a serial, Compact Flash, or Bluetooth interface. The Bluetooth technology provides wireless capacity within 30 feet of the user. The Destinator application provides maps of the United States, Canada, and Western Europe on CD that can be installed on the PACMate from a desktop computer using ActiveSync. Maps can also be stored on a Compact Flash card, providing more storage space. The price of purchasing StreetTalk, Destinator, and a GPS receiver for PACMate is currently in the range of $579 to $779.

The GPS VoiceNote and BrailleNote use a cell-phone size GPS receiver (Earthmate) connected through a serial port (Figure 4.7). The Earthmate GPS receiver is simple to use with a single switch for on and off. It uses AAA batteries for power. By adding BrailleNote GPS software, an Earthmate GPS receiver, and maps stored on a Compact Flash card, BrailleNote and VoiceNote can guide its users

Figure 4.7 BrailleNote with GPS. Photo courtesy of Pulse Data International Ltd.

to their destination. The price of a BrailleNote GPS package (including BrailleNote GPS software, BrailleNote GPS audio tutorial, U.S. maps, Compact Flash card, nearly 1,000,000 points of interest, and the Delorme Earthmate receiver) is between $1050 and $1350.

Accessible pedestrian signals (APS) APS have been developed and used around the world for more than two decades. The most common forms of APS are push-buttons installed at intersections, buzzers that make bell sounds, and chirp sound signals indicating that it is safe to walk. However, research has demonstrated that depending on the location of the pushbuttons, the volume of the buzzers, and the tone of the sound signals, APS could be confusing to pedestrians with vision impairment.[2-4] The more advanced APS uses a remote infrared communication system to provide more precise and accurate information to pedestrians. The system, called Talking Signs, was designed to provide effective communication between its users and both indoor and outdoor environments. The Talking Signs system consists of permanent installed transmitters and hand-held receivers for users. The transmitters are installed on various landmarks in the environment and send short infrared audio signals to the user's receiver. This system holds a wide range of promising functions to assist people with vision impairment in traveling independently. The transmitter is installed in various facilities, such as traffic lights, public transportation stops, government buildings, and hospitals. The user then simply scans the environment with the hand-held receiver. The user hears information and directions related to the surrounding environment, such as walk/don't walk, street information, bus number, route of the next bus, location of an information desk in government buildings, and entrances to a hospital. The information messages are delivered only to users rather than broadcasting to everyone. The Talking Signs system can be customized for different languages. Another advantage of the system is its potential to combine other accessible devices such as mobile phones and GPS. This kind of system has been used in several states in the United States, Yokohama, Japan, and some European countries.

Using the same concept but different technology, a project related to a personal navigation system for people with blindness and visual impairments called NOPPA (Figure 4.8) was conducted in Finland. The aim of this project was to provide public transportation passenger information and pedestrian guidance for people with vision impairment. This project allowed users to retrieve information from a public service database over the internet for route planning and navigation through GPS. Users could also receive local (within 30 feet) information by using

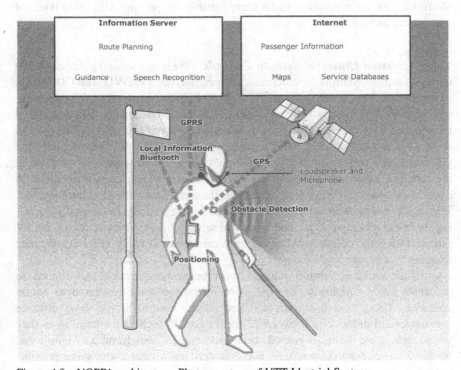

Figure 4.8   NOPPA architecture. Photo courtesy of VTT Idustrial Systems.

Bluetooth wireless technology. Current available technology holds great promise for assisting people with vision impairment in obtaining information and in interacting with the environment.[5]

Devices for Self-Care

If a person experiences vision impairment, his/her ability to carry out activities is impacted, especially instrumental activities of daily living (IADLs).[6-8] In a study regarding adaptations used by people with low vision, major activity limitations perceived by people with low vision were reading, writing, and TV watching.[6] In addition to those activities directly related to seeing, people with low vision reported limitations with using public transportation, managing personal finances, shopping, and socializing. With the assistance of proper assistive devices, people with vision impairment are able to perform most daily activities.[7] Devices substituting visual information with auditory or tactile information are often used to access information. Increasingly, electronic products incorporating voice output can be found in the general marketplace and in special product catalogs. We now have products ranging from appliances like microwave ovens, timer/clock/watches, and room thermometers, to personal health management items such as personal thermometers, scales, blood glucose/pressure meters, pedometers, available in enhanced visual output (large print), and/or voice output or tactile format (Braille). The assistive devices for persons with vision impairment described below address difficulties related to watching TV, handling finances, shopping, and other leisure activities. The accessible features of these products make them suitable for persons with other types of impairment as well.

Voice-Activated Universal Remote Controls   There are several voice-activated universal remote controls for electronic devices, such as TV, DVD, and CD players in the market. These voice activated remote controls use voice recognition technology so users can operate their appliances with voice commands. Voice-activated remotes can recognize and program as many as 50 commands and can be used to control up to eight devices. With a single voice command or a button press, the voice-activated remote can perform multiple task operation sequentially following previous programming. The Accenda voice-activated remote control by Innotech Systems Inc. has a talk-back feature that tells the users what button has been pressed. This model comes with a Menu Key Lockout feature to avoid accidentally operating the menu and setup keys. The menu and setup procedure require use of the TV screen, which for people with vision impairment would likely require assistance from another person.

Voice-activated remote controls must be preprogrammed and trained to recognize voice commands, as well as to match the voice command to button operation. Users hold the voice-activated remote control at the same distance (recommended distance is between 12 inches and 36 inches) for training as they would with actual use. Background noise, including TV sounds, must be eliminated for good voice recognition results. Some models are designed with voice prompts that provide guidance for users throughout the setup and voice training process. Voice-activated remote control can store different sets of commands for each family member, for up to four different voices.

Talking Prescription Readers and Medication Reminders   For many older adults or persons with low vision, reading prescription labels is difficult due to small font size. For elderly persons experiencing multiple chronic conditions, it can be confusing to take different medications, at different times. A device with speech output of the prescription label is now available.

ScripTalk (by Envision America) reads information on a drug label of a medication container: name of the patient, name of the drug, dosage, and side effects (Figure 4.9). When users submit a prescription, the pharmacy prints a smart drug label that includes a microchip and electronic circuit. The smart drug label is printed with a special small-footprint printer and placed on the prescription bottle. Users simply place the smart labeled prescription bottle in front of a ScripTalk reader, and they press a button to activate the scanning and reading process. Using a smart technology called radio-frequency identification (RFID), the ScripTalk reader sends a message to the microchip on the drug label. The drug label transmits the drug information back to the ScripTalk reader, which translates the information into synthesized speech. At the time of writing this book, obtaining or refilling prescriptions using this device was only available through one mail-order pharmacy (http://www.kohlls.com/).

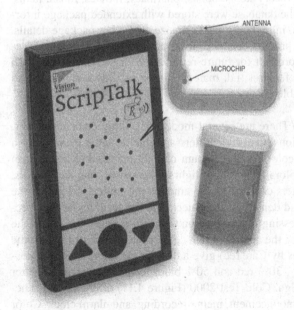

Figure 4.9   ScripTalk talking prescription readers. Photo courtesy of Emvision America.

Figure 4.10   i.d. mate II. Photo courtesy of Envision America.

Talking Bar Code Identifier

A portable bar code scanner, i.d. mate II by Envision America (Figure 4.10), works in the same way as a bar code scanner at a supermarket checkout. Persons with vision impairment can use the omnidirectional scanner on i.d. mate II to scan Universal Production Codes (UPC) on the package of commercial products by easily rotating the scanner around products. The i.d. mate II matches the scanned UPC with a product database stored on a flash memory card and reads the product information using speech synthesis technology. The product database contains information on half a million items such as grocery items, books, pharmacy, movies, music items, and more. Some products in the database were stored with extended package information such as nutrition facts, ingredients, package size, and other package details. If an item is not found in the product database, users are prompted to create voice-recorded information on the product for future retrieval. With the extendable flash memory and voice recording features, i.d. mate II can be used as a digital memo recorder and has an upgradeable database.

Talking Color Identifiers   There are several models of talking color identifiers, and some offer add-on functions. Color identifiers are able to name from under a hundred to several thousand colors by the amount of light reflected to a sensor in the color identifier. Lighter colors reflect more light to the sensor than dark colors. The accuracy of color identifiers depends on the amount and source of light on the detected object, the texture and density of the object, and the accuracy of the spectrometer itself. By simply pressing one or two buttons, color identifiers name the color of the object and describe the quality of that color, such as dark or light. Some models (ColorTest 2000 series by CareTec) give a detailed description of luminosity and color breakdown (e.g., 30% red and 50% blue) for users to make a better match with clothes or art design. ColorTest 2000 (Figure 4.11) offers add-on functions such as time and date announcement, memo recording, and alarm clock. Color identifiers are available in different languages.

Figure 4.11   ColorTest 2000. Photo courtesy of CareTec.

Figure 4.12   Voice-It-all.
Photo courtesy of Maxi-
Aids, Inc.

Money Identifiers   Money identifiers read paper money and speak the denomination of the bills. The technology used in the money identifier is similar to that used in change machines and public transportation automatic ticket booths. Money identifiers are very easy to use by simply inserting a bill in any orientation. The machine automatically turns on and indicates the denomination with voice output or vibration. Money identifiers are available as multifunction machines that include a money identifier, color identifier, and voice recorder (Voice-It-All, Figure 4.12). Money identifiers are available for different currency throughout the world (U.S., Canada, Europe, and universal models).

4.3   SMART TECHNOLOGY FOR PEOPLE WITH HEARING IMPAIRMENT

Hearing loss is one of the most prevalent chronic conditions in the United States, and the prevalence of hearing problems also increases with advanced age.[9] This section discusses hearing aids and assistive listening devices to assist people who have experienced hearing loss.

Hearing Aids

The National Institute on Deafness and Other Communication Disorders states that only one out of five people who could benefit from hearing aids actually has one.[9] Most people do not realize that hearing loss can be addressed with hearing aids. Hearing aids are electronic, battery-operated devices that amplify and change sounds to allow people with hearing impairments to hear better during communication. The amplification function of a hearing aid is made possible with several components: a microphone to pick up sound, an amplification circuitry to increase the loudness of signals, and a speaker to send the amplified sound to ear. All hearing aids include these components, although they differ in size, design, amplifying ability, and other special features.

Styles of Hearing Aids   Hearing aids can be categorized into different styles based on where they are worn.

Body-Worn Hearing Aids   Body-worn (BW) hearing aids are larger devices, with most controls and parts in a case worn on the body. The receiver is in an ear mold in the ear connected to the body-worn case by wire. BW hearing aids are an earlier style of hearing aid, used before the miniaturized electronic components and batteries were developed. Today, BW hearing aids are used only by people who cannot use other hearing devices, who need very high amplification, and who need to avoid acoustic feedback.[10] The large size of this device has the advantage of making batteries easier to replace.

Behind-the-Ear Hearing Aids   Behind-the-ear (BTE) hearing aids sit above and behind the ear with all components contained in a plastic case. The amplified signal is transmitted through a clear tube to a customized ear mold inside the ear. BTE hearing aids are larger than other in-the-ear hearing aids, therefore they allow users to control gain and the MTO switch. The MTO (microphone/telecoil/off) switch is used to select different modes, according to hearing tasks and occasions: The Microphone (M) mode is used for general communication occasions, the telecoil (T) operation mode is used for telephone and induction system use, and the off (O) mode is used for battery saving.[10] These additional functions are more effective for persons with severe to profound hearing loss.[11]

In-the-Ear Hearing Aids   In-the-ear (ITE) hearing aids fill the outer part of the ear with all parts contained in a custom-made shell. ITE hearing aids can be further categorized: (1) ITE aids, (2) partially in-the-canal (ITC) aids, and (3) complete-in-the-canal (CIC) aids.[10] ITE aids are usually equipped with telecoil, where ITC and CIC aids normally have no telecoil inside due to the small size and the possibility of normal telephone use. The small size of the ITC and CIC hearing aids makes battery replacement difficult. The limited battery size also restricts amplification power. However, these two styles of hearing aid sit deeper in the canal, permitting higher signal pressure levels (SPLs).[10] The size of all ITE hearing aids results in greater possibility of feedback due to the close distance between the microphone and speaker. Sophisticated designs for ITE hearing aids are necessary to avoid feedback.[10] The controls of these devices are also difficult to adjust; using a remote control system or automatic volume control helps solve this problem.[10]

Bone-Conduction Hearing Aids   Bone-conduction hearing aids are designed for individuals with conductive hearing loss or occlusion of the ear canal that cannot be treated surgically. The only difference between bone-conduction hearing aids and the above-mentioned hearing aids is the receiver. The bone conduction aids can be BW or BTE style with receivers (vibrators fitted in a headband) that transmit vibration to the skull. The vibration is picked up directly by the cochlea.

Types of Hearing Aid Technology The functionality and adjustability of hearing aids differs depending on the type of signal processing circuitry used. Three types of circuitry technologies are currently used.

Conventional Analog Conventional analog technology is the least expensive type of circuitry, and it allows some adjustability. An audiologist determines particular frequency response, the volume, and other specifications. This type of hearing aid operates on continuous acoustic signals transmitted by a microphone.[12] Although filter and compressing can be applied to the signal, this type of hearing aid amplifies all sounds equally including background noise.[11]

Analog Programmable The second type of circuitry technology is analog programmable. The analog signal from the microphone is controlled digitally by a microchip, which allows customized adjustments to be stored in the digital memory. Gain, frequency response, compression parameters, and electroacoustical parameters can be preprogrammed.[12] Users can select those preset programs based on their need or listening environments by a control button or a remote control. This type of circuitry technology, which can be used on all styles of hearing aids, provides greater accommodations of hearing aids without bulky size and/or large power consumption.

Digital Programmable Digital programmable circuitry technology converts the analog signals into digital signals for process and digital control. The digital signals can further be analyzed by a microchip to determine if the sound is noise or not and make modifications to provide a clearer and undistorted signal (noise cancellation). This digital technology allows shaping of the frequency response. This permits control of acoustic feedback and the signal-to-noise ratio.[12] In addition to acoustic feedback control and noise reduction, the digital circuitry provides greater programmability, better fitting of the hearing aids, and better management of loudness discomfort.[13]

Other important functionality of hearing aids can be built-in to allow accommodation at different settings and situations. Having a built-in telecoil (T-coil) is recommended strongly for hearing aid users. A Telecoil is an induction coil that is made from a metal rod wrapped with copper wire. In an electromagnetic field, a telecoil converts the magnetic energy into electrical energy and transmits it to the hearing aid. Hearing aids then convert the electrical energy to sound. Telecoil induction can be used with telephones and assistive listening systems. Hearing aid users can activate telecoil function with a switch (MTO switch). When switched to the telecoil function, hearing aids pick up only signals trasmitted from the telecoil without other environmental sounds. An M/T mode is also available for users to listen to signals from an induction loop while other environmental sound information can still be heard. Another convenient feature available for hearing aids is direct audio input (DAI). DAI allows direct connection of other devices to the hearing aid, such as a microphone, assistive listening device, computer, or TV. Only BTE hearing aids have the capability of using DAI. Usually, DAI consists of a special "boot" or "shoe" that is physically connected to the hearing aid by wire. Finally, a built-in FM receiver or an FM "boot" for BTE hearings aids is also available for wireless connection to FM assistive listening devices.

Implantable Hearing Devices   Persons with severe to profound sensorineural hearing loss that is caused by damage or abnormality in the inner ear do not benefit from amplifying hearing aids. Some people have outer ear and ear canal problems that make using ear molds impossible or uncomfortable. Implantable hearing devices are considered helpful for these two situations. Similar to hearing aids, ear implants do not restore normal hearing but provide either sound amplification or sound sensation to improve hearing ability. A surgical procedure is needed for ear implants. Now, four types of ear implants are commonly used: bone-anchored hearing aids, middle ear implants, cochlear implants, and auditory brainstem implants.

Bone-Anchored Hearing Aid (BAHA)   A bone-anchored hearing aid consists of a titanium implant, an external abutment, and a detachable external sound processor. The 3 to 4-mm titanium implant is surgically inserted into the skull behind the user's ear. Sounds are picked up by the microphone in the sound processor and then conducted as vibrations through the abutment to the titanium implant. The vibrations are sent to the cochlea in the inner ear without involvement of the ear canal and middle ear. Sound signals are transmitted normally from cochlea to the auditory nerve. BAHA are suggested for persons with bilateral/unilateral conductive or mixed hearing loss resulting from conditions such as chronic ear infection and congenital middle ear or outer ear abnormality.[14] Some features of conventional hearing aids such as telecoil and DAI can be included in the sound processor of BAHA. Compared to conventional hearing aids, a BAHA is small in size, less visible and produces fewer feedback problems and ear infections. It also provides better sound quality than traditional bone conduction hearing aids.

Middle Ear Implants (MEIs)   A middle ear implant (MEI) is a small transducer that is implanted into the middle ear to act directly on an ossicle. The transducer makes sounds louder by enhancing the chain movement of ossicles. Two types of transducers can be used: magnetic and piezoelectric. Typically, a microphone, implanted or visibly place behind the ear, transmits vibrations to the transducer via an implanted receiver. Unlike the other implant approaches, MEI amplifies sound as it is transmitted via middle ear. Then sound is passed to the cochlea and auditory nerve through the normal pathway.[15] An MEI is only suitable for adults with moderate to severe sensorineural hearing loss who are unable to use conventional hearing aids.[14] Users of MEI must have intact anatomy structure in the middle ear. An MEI allows users to hear their own voice more naturally without sound distortion. Other advantages of using an MEI are less feedback and increased comfort, and an MEI is less visible.[16]

Cochlear Implants (CIs)   Use of cochlear implants (CIs) is appropriate for persons with severe to profound sensorineural hearing loss that cannot benefit from conventional hearing aids. Profound sensorineural hearing loss results from the loss of hair cells in the cochlea so that sound cannot be effectively transmitted to the intact auditory nerve. A CI bypasses the impaired inner ear and stimulates the auditory nerve directly with electrical impulses, which produces and sends hearing sensations to the brain.

Most CIs include two major parts: the external component includes a microphone, a sound processor, and a transmitter; and the internal component of CIs includes a receiver and an array of electrodes that are implanted in the user's ear. The microphone and sound processor are placed in a BTE or a BW hearing aid unit to pick up and process sound signals and then covert them into electrical signals. The electrical signals are sent to the receiver implanted under the skin through the transmitter placed behind the ear. The electrical signals are then transmitted from the receiver to an electrode array placed in the cochlea through implanted wire. The electrodes stimulate the auditory nerve fiber directly to create sound perception. People who receive CIs must have an intact auditory nerve.[12] A CI does not "restore" hearing; and hearing through CI is different from normal hearing. However, it provides persons with profound hearing loss improved hearing ability, increased accuracy of lip-reading, and environmental sound recognition.[12]

Auditory Brainstem Implants (ABIs)   For some people with profound hearing loss or even total hearing loss that cannot benefit from CIs due to auditory nerve absence or damage, ABIs can be considered. ABIs provide hearing sensation by stimulating the neurons of the cochlear nucleus located in the auditory brain stem, bypassing the cochlea and auditory nerve.[10] ABI is similar to the CI approach in that a microelectrode array is implanted to provide electrical signals that stimulate the auditory processing center.[17] The reduced hearing sensation provided by ABI can help people with profound hearing loss in lip-reading and relief from total sound isolation.[10]

Assistive Listening Devices (ALDs)

Assistive listening devices refer to devices that help people hear and communicate in situations when hearing aids are insufficient.[18] ALDs have three basic functions: capture the desired sound, carry sounds to receiver, and couple the receiver with ears or hearing devices.[19] The desired sound is sent to the listener's ears directly with improved signal-to-background noise ratio and reduced effects of poor room acoustics and diffused sound. ALDs can further be categorized into two groups: personal hand-held amplifiers and assistive listening systems.

Personal ALDs   Personal ALDs are relatively inexpensive, hard-wired devices used for one-to-one conversations or with television or telephone. This type of device can be used alone or with hearing aids. Basically, a personal ALD consists of a small portable microphone, an amplifying receiver, and a coupling device, such as a headphone or a neckloop. Different kinds of microphone can be wire-connected to the receiver worn by the person with hearing loss. The amplified output from the receiver then can be transmitted to the user by direct wiring, such as earphone and headphone, or coupled with hearing aids with DAI or induction system, such as neckloop or silhouette. Telephone listening can also be amplified by personal ALDs with a proper connection. This device is designed for personal applications at close range, such as a conversation in a car or restaurant. It is also useful for small group conversations.

Some personal ALDs have a wireless FM and infrared (IR) function. For example, the SoundWizard II personal listening system by Hitec Group offers a telephone or an IR module to the basic system for extended functionality. The add-on IR module allows users to listen to TV programs (requires an IR transmitter plugged into TV), movies, or a play in theater. SmartLink by Phonak is a personal FM system, which has an integrated microphone system and digital signal processor (DSP). SmartLink has different microphone settings and capacity for external microphone connections to let users select the best microphone mode to improve signal quality. The integrated DSP can enhance the loudness of the sound and reduce the effect of noise (noise cancellation). SmartLink can also remotely control the setting of hearing aids, such as program selection and FM control. This personal FM system needs to be used with BTE hearing aids that have FM reception capacity. Other types of personal ALDs are used for specific purposes, such as an IR headset for TV and stereo listening.

Assistive Listening System (ALS)   An ALS is an assistive listening device used in group settings. An ALS provides a function similar to that of a personal ALD. It amplifies and transmits sound directly to the users' ears or hearing aids in a large room, such as a church, a theater, or classroom. ALS can provide amplification for several users at the same time. Basic components of the ALS include microphone(s), transmitter, receiver, and coupling devices for the ears or hearing aids. There are three types of wireless ALS available: FM, IR, and inductive loop systems. Each system has its own strengths and disadvantages.[19,20]

FM System   Free-field wireless frequency modulated (FM) system transmit sound captured from a microphone through radio frequency to a receiver worn by users. FM systems can be portable or permanently installed. These systems are usually connected to public announcement (PA) systems in churches or meeting rooms. Because sunlight has no effect on the transmission of the radio wave, FM systems can be used indoors or outdoors with more than 100 feet of coverage.[19] FM signals can travel through walls and are not affected by obstacles between the speaker and the listener; therefore, it can be used in settings where the speaker needs to move around, such as in a classroom. However, radio frequency can receive interference from other transmitters or other electromechanical devices nearby. A specific radio-frequency band has been assigned for use by persons with hearing impairments.[12] In some cases, FM receivers are built into BTE hearing aids or can be added on to BTE hearing aids, so no additional coupling is needed. Hearing aid users can use an induction system (when telecoil equipped) or DAI to couple with FM receivers. Otherwise, a pair of earphones or a headset can be used to bring the sound from the receiver to the ears for persons with hearing problems.

IR System   Infrared (IR) systems transmit sound through IR light waves to user-worn receivers. The IR signals do not work well in natural light; therefore, IR systems are generally for indoor use. When using an IR system, the IR receivers must point directly toward the transmitter with no obstacles in between.[20] The advantage of an IR system is that IR signals cannot go through a wall; confidentiality of the conversation can be preserved in the room where the IR system is used. IR systems allow an unlimited number of receivers to be used at the same time. Usually, IR systems are used in live theaters, courtrooms, and movie theaters.

Inductive Loop System   Inductive loop systems (also called audio loop systems) transmit sound through an electromagnetic field that is built by a wire loop surrounding the listening area. For hearing aid users equipped with telecoil, no additional receivers are necessary for listening within the looped area. Receivers with earphone or headset are available for people who do not have telecoils. Most likely, induction loop systems are installed permanently, but portable loop systems are also available.

Telecommunication

Telecommunications is the process of people at some distance from each other communicating with each other.[21] In the past, telephones were the most convenient telecommunication device for verbal conversations. Now, wireless technology and the internet have changed the way people communicate. For example, text-messaging, emailing, online chatting, and online conferencing are some popular methods that allow people around the world to perform voice and/or visual communication through mobile phones or computers. Communication information now includes voice, text, graphics, and video images.[21] This innovation enables people with hearing impairments to telecommunicate via various mainstream or specialized technologies.

Talking on Telephone and Mobile Phone   Today, telephones in the United States, both wired and cordless, are mandated to have built-in volume control. Many new model telephones have a headphone jack that can be connected to a headphone, an ALD, or a BTE hearing aid with DAI feature for amplification. With a telephone coupler, ALDs can also be used on any telephone. When a telephone user needs more amplification than that provided with the volume control, or he/she is using an old model telephone, add-on amplifiers or a special telephone can be used for persons who do not wear a hearing aid. Three types of add-on amplifiers are available: portable amplifiers, amplification handsets, or in-line amplifiers.

A portable amplifier is a device that the user can put on the earpiece and secure with a strap for most wired or cordless phones. This device also works well for traveling. Amplification handsets or in-line amplifiers only work on modular phones where the dialing mechanism is separated from the handset, and they cannot be used on cordless phones.[21] The two devices are connected to the phone receiver jack on the telephone. The amplification handset replaces the original handset. The in-line amplifiers is connected to the original handset. Specialty phones are available in corded or cordless models with many accessible features, such as volume control, ringer control, output jacks for headset or ALDs, and a flash ringer indicator. Specialty phones provide better amplification than the add-on units.

Using a telephone acoustically with the hearing aid on is the most common way for people with hearing impairment to use telephones.[21] However, direct, acoustic telephone use through a hearing aid can cause feedback and increased background noise. Using DAI and inductive coupling can reduce this problem.[22] In the United States, hearing aid compatibility (HAC) of all wired and cordless phones is required by law. Telecoil-equipped hearing aid users can use induction systems, such as neckloop or silhouette inductors, with ALDs to listen to HAC telephone binaurally. Using hearing aids with DAI or using a high-quality speaker phone are other ways for hearing aid users to use telephones.

Using mobile phones may also be problematic for hearing aid users. Most mobile phones have built-in volume control, and many mobile phone receivers can emit a magnetic field that can be captured by the telecoil equipped hearing aid. Even though these two features make mobile phones more accessible for people with hearing impairment, mobile phone users with hearing aids experience problems of interference. A digital wireless phone, which is now the most common type of mobile phone, causes radio-frequency interference to the hearing aid no matter which coupling method is used. Hearing aid users hear frequent buzzing sounds when the wireless phone is communicating with its network through an antenna.[23] In addition to the electromagnetic interference, the environment for using a mobile phone, such as in a car or a public place, produces a higher level background noise.[24]

Some solutions are available to eliminate interference problems while using a mobile phone with a hearing aid.[25] The types of wireless network technology adopted by the mobile phone service provider can make a difference in the severity of interference.[26,27] Among the current used technologies, including CDMA (code-division multiple access), TDMA (time-division multiple access), GSM (global system for mobile communication), and iDEN, CDMA produces less interference on mobile phones than other technologies. Another possible solution is choosing a flip-style mobile phone rather than standard bar phones. The antenna of a flip-style mobile phone is further away from the receiver, which could reduce the interference from the magnetic field to the hearing aid. Finally, hearing aid users can use hearing-aid-compatible accessories for mobile phone use. Using an inductive system or DAI connected to the mobile phone, placed at a distance from the hearing aid, can eliminate the electromagnetic interference. Hearing-aid-compatible accessories for mobile phones have built-in microphones to allow hands-free use of a mobile phone (Figure 4.13).

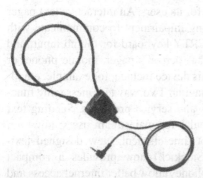

Figure 4.13   Neck loop accessory for Nokia cell phone. Photo courtesy of Nokia.

The Bluetooth wireless technology (two-way radio transmission) are now incorporated into newer mobil phones. ALDs, or even hearing aids to permit greater application and sound quality with a hearing aid. Phonak had added Bluetooth technology on their FM system ALD, SmartLink, for mobile phone use. In Europe, a Bluetooth headset developed by GN ReSound can transmit a phone signal from a Bluetooth-equipped mobile phone directly to a hearing aid through a t-coil.[28] These two Bluetooth devices allow hearing aid users hand-free mobile phone use.

Visual System for Telephone and Mobile Phone Use   Telephone communication for persons who are deaf, hard of hearing, or speech impaired is made possible through using visual text display by a device called the telecommunication device for the deaf (TDD). TDD users can connect their device to phone line directly or through a coupler. A TDD transforms text messages into sound-based code and sends out through the phone line. If the other party on the phone also uses a TDD, he or she can use a TDD to decode the sound code into text. When a TDD user calls a hearing person, telecommunication relay services (TRS) are needed with an operator who reads the text message to the hearing person or vice versa.[29] For an individual who wants to speak with their own voice on the phone but cannot hear the other party, a voice carry-over (VCO) phone allows him or her to talk on the phone and read text display from the other party through a relay service. If the two persons on the phone both have VCO phone with TDD keyboard, no relay service is needed to place the call. Functional options available on TDDs are large print display, printer, TDD call announcement, and portability. With proper software and hardware installation, such as TDD software and modem, computers can also be used as a TDD to communicate with another person.

Problems also exist for persons with hearing impairment or deafness in using a TDD with mobile phones. Now major mobile service providers have made the network service compatible for TDD. Newer model mobile phones have built-in TDD compatibility features' and are connected to TDD with a special cable. Interference problems with using a mobile phone with a TDD have been reported.[21] Kozma-Spytek (2002) further indicated that using a TDD with a mobile phone does not provide better portability and convenience for its users. An interactive text pager provides an easier way for people with hearing impairment to communicate with text messaging. This device has a small QWERTY keyboard for thumb input, and it enables users to send text message to another person's pager, mobile phone, or computer. Additional functions available for this device include, for example, emailing, sending faxes, TDD chat, and instant messaging. Two-way text messaging function is now available on most mobile phones and service providers. Sending text messages through mobile phones is very popular for mainstream users; however, using a numeral keypad for text input is not time-efficient. New designed text-messaging mobile phones (e.g., T-mobile Sidekick) now provides a compact QWERTY keyboard with large screen. These phones allow better internet access and instant messaging. In addition to text messaging, sending email and instant messaging are other popular ways to communicate through text. Online instant messaging requires both users to be online and using the same instant messaging program at the same time. However, text-messaging mobile phones free their users from the restraints of time and place.

Video Communication Although current technology provides various text messaging options for persons with profound hearing impairments, text input takes more time than natural speech. TDD telephone transmission is one-third to one-fourth slower than speech communication.[30] On the other hand, using sign language is more efficient than text communication providing a similar communication rate to speech.[12] In addition, persons who are deaf use sign language prevalently. Using a videophone permits people who are deaf to communicate with sign language. Video relay services provide an interpreter to translate sign language when a deaf individual places a video call to a hearing person through a videophone or computer. To use a videophone successfully, a digital telephone service: ISDN (Integrated Services Digital Network) is required for large video signal transmission.[21] Other forms of videoconferencing can be carried out on the internet using a computer. High Speed Internet services and local area networks (LANs) now provide enough bandwidth for transmitting large video signals. People can easily use individual videoconference program or the videoconference features provided by most instant messaging programs to carry out online sign language communication. A web cam and (or) a headset with microphone are required for online videoconferencing. In the near future, mobile video calls are expected to be a common communication method used by persons who are deaf or hard of hearing.

4.4 SMART TECHNOLOGY FOR PEOPLE WITH MOBILITY AND MOVEMENT IMPAIRMENTS

The Administration on Aging (2004) reported that 41.9% of noninstitutionalized Americans aged 65 and above had some disability in 2000. The most frequent disability (28.6% of older people) among older Americans relates to mobility and movement defined as substantial limitations in walking, climbing stairs, reaching, lifting, or carrying.[31]

Devices for Self-Care

ADL and IADL limitations are highly prevalent among the elderly. In 2004, the U.S. Department of Health and Human Services reported that, in 1999, 27.3% of community-dwelling Medicare beneficiaries over the age of 65 had difficulty in performing one or more ADLs,[31] and 40% reported difficulties with IADLs. According to an earlier census report, the most frequently reported ADL limitation was transferring (getting in/out of bed/chair), followed by showering/bathing and getting around inside their house.[32] Similarly, going outside alone was the most prevalent IADL limitation reported by older adults, followed by doing light housework and meal preparation.

Many low-tech devices are designed for persons with disabilities to carry out self-care activities, such as bath/shower chair, long-handle shower brush, dressing aids, large-handle spoon and fork, and so on. These low-tech self-care devices, described in more detail in Chapter 6, can eliminate some of the physical effort needed to carry out movement activities. Now, more high-tech devices are available with various automated features that allow people with physical limitations to perform daily activities.

Food Preparation   Automated small kitchen appliances for food preparation are now available. Black & Decker introduced their automatic jar opener in 2003 through the cooperation with the RERC on Technology Transfer at the University at Buffalo (Figure 4.14).[33] The automated jar opener was designed with functions and features identified by consumers. The automatic jar opener is operated electrically by pressing and holding a button to activate a motor driven gear system until the jar lid is loosened. The automatic jar opener is compact (similar to a coffee maker), and it is adjustable to a wide range of different jar and lid sizes.

There are other automated small kitchen appliances that provide hands-free or one-handed operation. For example, a cordless electric can opener that is placed on top of a can automatically moves around the can to cut the lid (Figure 4.15). Another type of can opener providing hands-free operation is mounted under the cabinet. Many under-cabinet can openers also serve as bag and bottle openers, knife sharpeners, and clock/timers. Some manufacturers state that their under-cabinet can openers are able to hold up to a 36-ounce can and require only light support for opening cans heavier than 36 ounces. Hands-free automatic can openers are priced at $10 to $40.

Electronic graters and slicers are available. These small kitchen appliances make food preparation easier, with single-hand operation.

House Chores   Technology has also been applied to house chores. One example is a robot vacuum cleaner. The first automatic robot vacuum cleaner emerged in the late 1990s. Using room mapping and sonar technology, the high-priced robot vacuum ($1500–$2000) can detect objects in the room and recognize a room and its objects, automatically cleaning a room without hitting objects. More affordable home robot vacuums have been available since 2002. At least three different brands of robot vacuums are in the market now, and they work in the same way, vacuuming the floor unattended with little effort from their user. Affordable robot vacuums use touch sensors in the front bumper to notify the robot vacuums about obstacles it is approaching. These less expensive robot vacuums have infrared (IR) sensors to detect floor drops such as stairs, so they can avoid falling down stairs. One recently introduced robotic vacuum uses sound transducers to determine whether there is dirt in the cleaning area; if dirt is detected, it will spend extra time on that area.

Robot vacuums are user-friendly and easy to operate. Without expensive sensors, affordable robot vacuums are preprogrammed with systematic or random movement patterns and different cleaning modes to cover almost all the floor area in a room.[34] Robot vacuums can be used with different kinds of flooring (from hardwood to carpets) and hard-to-reach areas like under bed or cabinet because of their compact size (height from 3 to 5.5 inches). Some models use timers and others use room-size or automatic detection to determine the area that needs to be cleaned. Newer models come with an IR or radio-frequency (RF) remote control so the user can operate and control the direction of the vacuum. It takes 15 to 30 minutes for a robot vacuum to clean a medium-sized room. Limited rechargeable battery life (from about 45 minutes to 1.5 hours) is one drawback of robot vacuum. However, the latest robot vacuum automatically returns to its charge base for recharging when batteries are low. It does this through detection of an IR beam emitted from the base. Similarly, an IR virtual wall is used to set the cleaning area for some robot vacuums. New models provide easier unit cleaning systems. In addition to remote control and easy-cleaning features, robot vacuums use different sound modes to indicate operation conditions. Different sound indicators are especially helpful for users with vision impairment.[35]

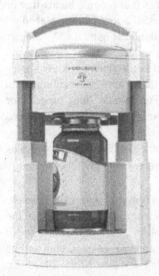

Figure 4.14 Black & Decker automatic jar opener.

Figure 4.15 Gizmo cordless can opener. Photo courtesy of Black & Decker.

Similar to a robotic vacuum cleaner, robotic lawn mowers can be simply operated by pressing buttons after several setup procedures for calibration and mowing time setup. One important preparation procedure for using a robot mower is to define the lawn area by putting perimeter wiring around lawn unless the lawn is fenced. Like the concept of virtual wall for robotic vacuums, robot mowers can detect the magnetic field produced by wiring and then avoid exceeding the wired area. Before operating robot mowers, obstacles on the lawn that are lower than 4 inches must be removed. However, unlike the compact and lightweight robot vacuum, robot mowers are relatively bulky and heavy (weight range from 7 kg to more than 30 kg) so that automatic programming becomes an important feature for robot mowers. The price range of robot mowers is from $500 to more than $2000.

Toileting   Many older adults experience difficulty getting on and up from a toilet.[36] In addition to most common used devices, such as toilet grab bars and raised toilet seats, more high-tech devices are available to assist with transferring and hygiene tasks. A mechanical or powered self-lift seat can provide external assistance with sitting-down or resuming a standing position from the toilet (Figures 4.16). A toilet lift seat assists an individual in standing up by elevating the seat. Some models also combine forward tilting movement. Mechanical toilet lifts use springs adjusted to the user's weight. Users of mechanical toilet lifts need enough strength in their arms and hands to initiate the lifting mechanism or to trigger the safety release mecha-

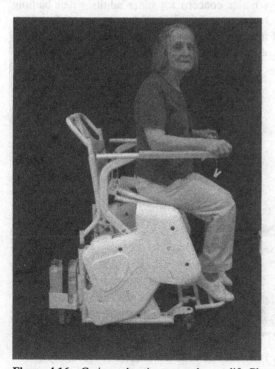

Figure 4.16   Cariana electric commode seat lift. Photo courtesy of Apexlift.

nism.[36] Powered toilet lifts provide automatic movement for sitting down and standing up. Users of both types of toilet lifts need to have enough lower-extremity strength to weight-bear and rise with the seat. Some toilet lift seats can be used as mobile or stationary bedside commodes. For transfer and space-saving purposes, toilet lifts are equipped with swivel or foldable armrests. The height of a toilet lift seat is adjustable to accommodate personal needs and to fit most toilets. Pant clips for preventing pants from falling are optional. Remote controls are available for some powered toilet seats, which can be operated by the individual or a care provider. Maximum weight is from 270 to 375 pounds, depending on the make and model.

Hygiene may also be difficult for persons with movement and mobility impairment. Long-handle toilet aids are a low-tech solution. An electronic bidet can be added to an existing toilet (Figure 4.17). While not in wide use in the United States, bidet use is common in other regions of the world such as Europe and Japan. The basic functions of an electrically powered bidet are seat warming, warm-water cleaning, and warm-air drying afterwards. The control unit is usually located at the right-hand side of the bidet and conjoined to the toilet seat. Remote control is available for newer bidet models. More advanced models allow users to control the position of the water jet, different cleaning modes, and temperature of the heated water and seat. Some toilet lift models offer a bidet function, such as the Aerolet ToiletLift by Economic Mobility, Inc.

Bathing/Showering Safety is a major concern for older adults when bathing or showering. Simple bath bench/chairs and grab bars are common low-tech approaches to increasing safe and independent bathing or showering. Using simple assistive devices to get into or out of a bathtub may not be sufficient for some people

Convenient Remote Control

Washlet S300 shown on Pacifica One Piece Toilet (MS904114)

A

B

Figure 4.17 (A) Washlet S300. (B) The remote control of Washlet. Photo courtesy of ToTo USA.

with disabilities. In this case, a mechanical or electrical bath lift may be warranted. Mechanical bath lifts are hydraulic, using the body weight of an individual to lower the lift and also utilizing the buoyancy of the water to elevate the bath lift. Most electrical bath lifts use rechargeable batteries, although some do use main electricity as the power supply for lifting. Several models of bath lifts are available. Bath lifts are available with or without a backrest, although backrests generally provide better support and comfort. Bath lifts may be installed permanently, while other models are removable, providing other family members access to the bath. However, the suction cups for fixation, along with the heavy weight of bath lifts, make them difficult to remove. Users of most bath lifts need to be able to move their legs in and out of the tub independently. Bath lifts are also available with a transfer function (manual or automatic swivel movement to assist moving legs in/out of tub), for persons who have difficulty moving their legs. Most transfer bath lifts have armrests and a fixed backrest. Both mechanical and automatic bath lifts can be operated by the user to enhance independent bathing.

Use of an alternative type of bathtub is another way to facilitate bathing or showering independently. Walk-in tubs have a door in front for entry (Figure 4.18). One disadvantage of a walk-in tub is that the user must sit in the tub while it fills and drains. Walk-in showers provide another alternative. In Japan, an automatic showering system is convenient for persons with physical limitations. The shower unit includes a foldable chair and two easy controls for water flow and temperature. Two large arching arms of spray not only avoid the need to hold the hand-held shower, but also keep users warm as if they are taking a bath. The arching spray arms fold back for space saving.

Figure 4.18   Walk-in bath by Safety Bath, Inc.

Device for Bed and Chair Transfer

Transferring is not only difficult in the bathroom, but can be problematic with beds and chairs for 10% of elderly population.[32] Common solutions include low-tech devices such as bedside rail/poles, using a hoist, or providing personal assistance.

MOBIL   A team in Germany developed a prototype for a powered walking and lifting aid called MOBIL (Figure 4.19). This device assists older adults with transferring difficulty.[37] MOBIL, which looks like a four-wheel walker, can be used as a powered lifting device to raise/lower the user from/to a sitting position and can be used as a rolling walker when a user is upright. During the battery-powered lifting process, the user controls the lifting or lowering movement with two switches in the handles. To assist with standing up, MOBIL first moves the rear wheels backwards followed by a side-spreading movement. By doing so, MOBIL lowers its handles, widens the frame to provide better stability, and allows users to pull MOBIL as close as possible. The user simply holds on to the handles and stands up with assistance from the powered lifting movement. During walking, MOBIL partially supports the user's weight as a rolling walker. MOBIL has a unique breaking system. Armrest brakes activate when users apply more body weight on the armrest or when a user tends to fall either forward or backward. The armrest-braking system may make the walker mode of MOBIL difficult to operate if a user tends to support more weight on the armrests. While still under development, MOBIL represents a new perspective for mobility aids combining the functions of two different devices.

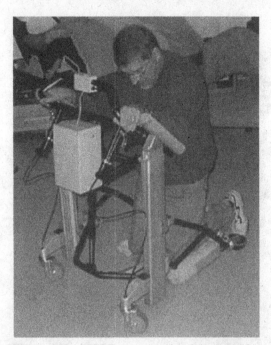

Figure 4.19   MOBIL, a powered walking and lifting aid. Photo courtesy of Forschungsinstitut Technologie-Behindertenhilfe.

Lift Chairs   The comfort provided by a recliner is an important reason many people enjoy this kind of chair. However, most recliner seats are low to the ground and too deep, which makes standing up from or sitting down to a recliner very difficult for older adults and people with physical impairments. Lift chairs provide an integrated and powered lifting function for what looks like a typical recliner. Users press buttons to elevate the backrest end of the lift chair while the front side of the seat remains the same height. The advantage of this lifting movement is that total support is provided to the person during the sit-to-stand process. The price range of a lift chair is from $500 to $1500. A power-operated seat-lifting base that can be attached to an existing recliner is an economic alternative for a similar lifting function. More simple and portable devices such as lift seat and power lift seats cushions could initiate the momentum and assist users in standing up.

Device for Mobility

In addition to the mobile device described above, other new-wheeled mobility devices to assist people with mobility difficulties are available as product or are under development.

Pushrim-Activated Power Assist Wheelchairs   A new feature for manual wheelchairs already available in practical form is called the pushrim-activated power assist wheelchairs (PAPAWs, Figure 4.20). PAPAW is a new category of wheeled devices offering an alternative between traditional manual and power wheelchair[38,39] PAPAWs use battery-powered motors to amplify the power produced by the wheelchair user while propelling or slowing down a wheelchair. Torque applied to the pushrims when propelling a wheelchair activates the in-wheel motors, which provide

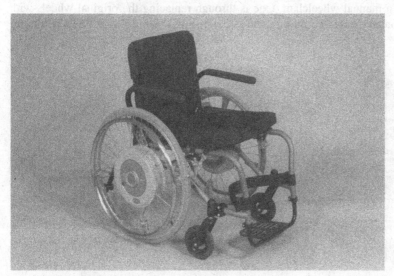

Figure 4.20   Pushrim-activated power assist wheelchairs (e-motion by Alber). Photo courtesy of Dr. Charles Levy.

brief bursts of power to augment propulsion. A micro-controller is used to control both rear wheels for simulating inertia, compensating discrepancies between wheels, and activating automatic braking when detecting reverse torque on pushrims.[39] An optional electronic control can be used to set power assist level and turn the power assist function on or off. Some models allow setting different power assisting levels on each wheel, which is useful for people with imbalance, strength, and coordination problems.[12,39] PAPAWs are relatively lightweight (between 50 and 70 pounds) compared to a power wheelchair, making them more portable than a wheelchair or scooter. Most PAPAWs use quick-release axes and can accommodate a standard wheelchair. PAPAWs assist in many environments such as carpet and inclines that are usually inaccessible by a manual wheelchair. PAPAWs impose exercise challenges to users with less physiological stress than a manual wheelchair.[40] Potential users of PAPAWs are people who have difficulty propelling a manual wheelchair due to reduced cardiopulmonary function, insufficient upper-extremity strength/endurance, possible risk for upper-extremity joint degeneration,[40] and inability to maintain posture during propulsion.[39] Levy and Chow pointed out that significant differences could be found across different models, including mechanisms and algorithms of motor output, programmability, ease of wheel removal, downhill safety, motor noise, and others.[38] They further suggested that the price of PAPAWs (ranging from $5900 without frame to $7500 with frame), difficulty in loading/unloading them in vehicles, and unfamiliarity of both consumers and practitioners are reasons for limited acceptance to date.[38]

Manual Wheelchair Add-on Devices There are other add-on features available for manual wheelchair users and their caregivers to propel or push the wheelchair more easily. An add-on power system can transform a manual wheelchair into a powered wheelchair (Figure 4.21). There are different approaches to adding a power system to a manual wheelchair. One is through replacing the original wheels with in-wheel battery-operated motors with a control unit. Similar to a PAPAW, the in-

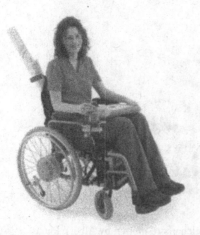

Figure 4.21 Alber e-fix. Photo courtesy of Alber.

wheel motors of an add-on power system are interchangeable with the wheels of a standard wheelchair. The control unit provides functions similar to a control unit of a power wheelchair, such as horn, LCD battery indicator, and programmable modes. When mounted to a handgrip, the control unit can be used by caregiver. Total weight of this type of add-on power system is about 60 pounds, with each component weighing less than 19 pounds for easy assembling/removing and transporting. Another approach to add-on power systems is connecting the manual wheelchair to a tiller steering system, and then the users "drive" their wheelchairs like scooters. Current available add-on steering systems are different across models in the following areas: the weight of the system, mounting method, steering method, the power the system provides, and the stability when operating.[41] The price range is also high, from around $2000 to $6000. Maximum speed produced by the add-on power system varies form 3.5 to 11 mph, but usually its maximum speed is lower than a power wheelchair. The travel distance per battery charge is about 20 miles.

One type of power assist unit is designed for a caregiver. This unit consists of a motor unit, a battery, and a controller (Figure 4.22). The battery-powered motor unit integrates motor, gear, and brake functions together into the wheel hub of a manual wheelchair. The motor unit operates a powered wheel to assist with propelling and braking. The controller includes an on/off switch, a speed-controlling lever, a battery indicator, and a direction control switch, all mounted to the wheelchair handgrip. The unit is especially helpful for adding power when pushing a wheelchair up an incline (up to 18°), as well as for braking when propelling downhill.

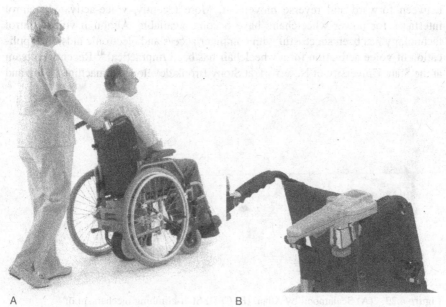

A   B

Figure 4.22   Alber viamobil. Photo courtesy of Alber.

Negotiating stairs is traditionally impossible for wheelchair users. Stair lifts, elevator, or other environmental modifications are used to overcome problems with stairs. A portable, relatively low-weight (total weight under 25 kg), powered add-on device can be considered as another way to ascend or descend stairs for manual wheelchair users. The main component of the stair-climbing device is a motor unit that connects and controls the four-wheel climbing unit. The detachable battery and handles increase the portability of the device. The switches on the handles control the power on/off and movement direction. When using the device to climb or descend stairs, two pairs of wheels operate with an orbiting movement pattern on two different axes (shown in Figure 4.23). There are limitations for height and depth of each stair for successful use of this stair-climbing device. Every stair should be at least four inches deep and no more than 10 inches high. Before attaching the stair-climbing device to a wheelchair, the rear wheels need to be taken off and an attachment bracket must be installed if no brackets are available on the wheelchair.

Control Method for Power Wheelchairs The most common control interface of a power wheelchair is a proportional joystick. The direction and magnitude of displacement of the stick controls the speed and direction of wheelchair movement.[12] Alternatives to the proportional joystick control include a single switch control with indirect scanning, a four-position switch activated by joystick, or a multiswitch array. The variety of alternatives of control interfaces and their positions allow users with limited movement to control wheelchair movement independently. For example, proximity switches can be installed in the headrest to detect slight head movements of the user, which determines the desired direction of travel without the necessity of actual contact with the headrest. This type of proportional head control method must be combined with other switches to activate/stop the wheelchair or to switch between forward and reverse movement. More recently, voice-activated control interfaces for power wheelchairs have become available. Although voice control technology has been successful with computer access and electronic aids, the application of voice activation for a wheelchair has been impractical.[42] Recently, a team at the State University of New York at Stony Brook developed a machine vision and

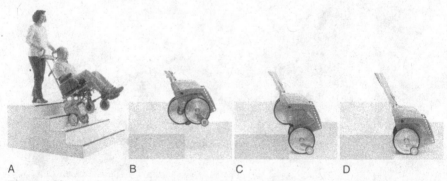

A   B   C   D

Figure 4.23 (A) Scalamobil by Alber. (B, C, D) Stair-climbing mechanism of Scalamobile. Photo courtesy of Alber.

voice controller for power wheelchairs.[43] By integrating current available technology—laptop computer, Microsoft voice recognition technology, and computer-aided speckle interferometry—they developed a system that allowed users to control a power wheelchair using voice commands and head movements, successfully integrating existing voice recognition and video technology into a wheelchair control interface.

Existing control interfaces provide another important capacity, allowing users to control multiple assistive technology devices, such as power mobility, augmentative and alternative communication (AAC), EADLs, and computer access, with a single control unit. This is called integrated control. A processor, connected to an integrated control, can operate several devices under different modes. Users operate the integrated control to select designated mode and control a single device under each mode. For example, a power wheelchair user is able to use a joystick to drive the wheelchair under wheelchair mode, and it can turn on the TV under the environmental control mode. An integrated control can reduce the massive hardware and electronic devices around a person, lower the demand of learning different operating systems, enable persons with very limited motor control and increase independence.[12,44]

New Features of Power Wheelchairs Advances in power wheelchairs offer increased possibilities for persons with physical impairment to perform various activities for self-care, work, and leisure. Power wheelchairs now perform better in negotiating obstacles and uneven terrain, and they offer a smaller turning radius.[40] Wheelchair users now have a wide range of selections for power wheelchairs that meet their individual needs for indoors or outdoors. Drive systems have advanced beyond traditional rear wheel drive and offer mid-wheel drive, front-wheel drive, and all-wheel drive. Modular power bases commonly used on new power wheelchairs provide flexibility in configuring the wheelchair to individual users and user activities. Another advantage of a modular base is that the seating system is a separate unit from the power base. Different functions of the seating system, such as reclining, tilt-in-space, can be interfaced to the power base.[12]

Long periods of sitting by power wheelchair users can lead to pressure sores, back pain, and poor posture, especially for users with decreased sensation. Powered reclining backrests and tilt-in-space features of a seating system independently operated by users can significantly reduce static seating pressure.[45] Reclining results in pressure redistribution by lowering the back of the wheelchair and elevating the leg rests simultaneously or separately. Physiological benefits of changing the seating position with a reclining backrest results in redistribution of pressure on weight-bearing surfaces, altering the load of postural musculature, improved circulation, and facilitation of respiration.[39] On the other hand, the tilt-in-space function changes the relative position of a wheelchair user relative to gravity with a preset seat-to-back angle. In addition to relief of seating pressure in the tilted back position, the tilt-in-space feature can assist in proper seating posture especially for persons with increased muscle tone.[12] However, the reclining system produces shear force on the back and buttocks that could result in skin breakdown.[12] The tilt-in-space system produces less shear force than the reclining system, but it adds seat height and length to the wheelchair. This system also adds more weight to the wheelchair and results in decreased stability and a larger turning radius.

Power seat elevation is another automatic feature available for seating systems. Power seat elevation systems allow seat height to be elevated or lowered within a certain range. An elevated/lowered seat is helpful for users in accomplishing tasks like reaching for an object on higher or lower shelves, talking to people at eye level, transferring to different level surfaces, and easily accessing tables. Power seat elevation also provides greater adaptation and flexibility for wheelchair users in achieving various tasks without further home modification.

Another available feature of automatic seating systems is the passive stand-up function that provides the same flexibility of an elevated seating system in carrying out activities at a standing level. The standing position offers wheelchair users improved circulation and facilitates renal and bowel function, and it prevents consequences of prolonged seating. Passive stand-up systems reduce the need for environmental modification especially in work settings.[12,39] Being able to carry out tasks in a standing position also offers improved social interactions for wheelchair users.

Robotic Wheelchairs Independence 3000 iBOT Transporter (iBOT) represents a breakthrough technology in the field of power mobility (Figure 4.24). The iBOT uses a dynamic balance system that integrates various sensors, electronics, and software to automatically adjust wheel position and seat orientation according to the change of user's center of gravity. The iBOT also includes redundant computer systems to maintain stability and safe operation. The iBOT has two coaster wheels and four primary wheels, with each wheel controlled by an individual set of motors. The two wheels on each side of the wheelchair form a cluster. The cluster of wheels

Figure 4.24   Stair function of the Independence 3000 iBOT. Photo courtesy of Independence Technology.

can operate around the center of a cluster while every single wheel rotates around its own hub. This special operation of the wheels allows iBOT to overcome uneven surfaces, inclines, and even stairs.

The iBOT provides five different operation functions: balance, four-wheel, stair, standard, and remote function. The balance function of iBOT raises the seat height for eye-level communication with others or for reaching high objects. The stairs function allows users to drive the iBOT up or down stairs independently; however, users need to have good upper-body and extremities control to maintain stability using handrails. When driving on grass, sand, uneven terrain, or street curbs, users can switch to four-wheel function to handle these obstacles. Under the remote function, users or caregivers can drive the iBOT to a designated location using its detachable control interface (with cable connected to the iBOT), such as directing it into a van for transportation. In their study of use of the iBOT in the community, Cooper indicated that the balance and four-wheel functions were used more frequently by the users. They suggested that the major advantage of iBOT was in overcoming outdoor challenges. They found that the iBOT was too high for most tables and desks even in standard mode, and it required attention to control under the standard mode.

The continued development of power wheelchairs has provided more functions that allow users to independently carry out activities in self-care, work/education, and leisure. Attali and Pelisse suggested that the future trend for power wheelchair development would come in the form of robotic mobility devices. Robotic wheelchairs, also called "smart wheelchairs," contain either (a) a standard power wheelchair base with an add-on computer and different types of sensors or (b) a mobile robot base with a seat.[46] Smart wheelchairs will assist users in the following areas: obstacle detection and avoidance, assistance for specific activities, providing users efficient and adaptable interface, and automatic transportation.[46,47] Yanco[47] summarized some robotic wheelchairs that were still in development stage in his review.

4.5 DEVICES FOR COGNITIVE IMPAIRMENT

What Are Cognitive Prostheses?

Previous studies demonstrated limited applications and limited use of AT by people with cognitive impairment. Older adults with cognitive impairment use less assistive technology compared to those with other types of disabilities.[48] Elders with cognitive impairment also reported less satisfaction of the AT devices they used. For persons with traumatic brain injury (TBI), studies also showed that few clinicians have the experience in applying portable electronic devices with their patients.[49,50] Use of portable computer devices as memory aids is helpful for general population, as well as for persons with cognitive impairment.

AT that is specifically for cognitive support may also be referred to as "cognitive prostheses" or "cognitive orthoses." More recently, cognitive prostheses were defined as devices that employ computer technology to serve the needs of persons with cognitive impairments in functional activities.[51] Cognitive prostheses need to be designed with highly customizable and user-friendly features when used for rehabilitation purposes. AT for cognition can provide external assistance to persons with cognitive impairment, ranging from a simple device such as a reminder alarm for taking medications to high-tech robotic caregivers. Low-tech devices for cognitive impairment provide limited storage of information and present users with few interaction or cueing methods.[52] For example, a digital watch can produce an audio cue at the specific time when its user needs to perform a task, but it provides no information about the content or procedure of the task. New technologies—whether (a) products marketed for the mainstream population or (b) products designed especially for persons with cognitive impairment—are now integrated with more functions to assist people with cognitive defects in memory, problem solving, communication, and others.

Devices for Memory

Medicine Reminders   Today, older people with chronic conditions often take several medications. The increased complexity of taking multiple medications can result in nonadherence, misuse, and treatment failure.[53] Memory impairment is one important reason for medication nonadherence or misuse among older adults.[54] Various off-the-shelf products that provide storage, reminding, and monitoring of medication use are targeted at this problem. Simple devices, such as a medication reminder watch, can produce multiple (up to 12 alarms per day) audio and/or vibrating alarms to remind its user on a daily basis. Some models allow data entry and storage to give short notes about medications along with alarms. However, the medication note provided by a wristwatch is limited by the display size and memory. A paging system can overcome this limitation. Carrying a pager or mobile phone with paging services is another method to get medication reminders. Similarly, PDA users can get medicine reminders by installing specially designed software. Functions provided by the medication reminder software include (a) alarms with relatively detailed pill information (such as name, dosage, and directions), (b) a medication log that can be uploaded and saved to keep track of medication history, (c) a refill reminder, and (d) emergency information. Caregivers or users themselves need to set up the alarms and input the information into the devices before they function effectively. The shortcoming of these devices is that users may forget to bring pill cases along because the medication is stored separately from the devices.[54]

Information on these device is available on the internet:

1. Medication reminder watch: The Cadex Medication Reminder Watch (http://cadexproducts.com/).
2. Paging service: MedPrompt's Medical Paging System (http://www.medprompt.com).
3. Medication software: On-Time-Rx for Palm OS (http://www.ontimerx.com/).
4. E-pill PillPAL for Pocket PC (http://www.epill.com/pillpal.html).

Electronic pill organizers/dispensers now provide the function of both pill storage and medication reminder. Pill storage capacity ranges from four compartments for one-day use, to 28 compartments for weekly use, to 60 compartments. Alarms can be set to either beeping sounds, voice, light, or vibration. Some pill dispensers control the pills and dose available to the users to avoid mistakes. Most of the electronic pill dispensers are portable in size, but provide no medication notes and directions. Monitored Automatic Medication Dispenser (MD.2) by E-pill is a nonportable device that provides both medication reminder and monitoring services. MD.2 can store 60 medication cups, each holding up to 25 pills. It produces alarms up to six times a day or twice a day for 30 days. Due to its large capacity, MD.2 is about the size of a coffee maker and is AC-powered. In addition to reminders (with alarm, text, and flashing light) and dispensing functions, MD.2 can monitor if medications have been taken. When reload of medication is needed or missed medications are detected, MD.2 will call a caregiver (one needs to subscribe to the service and connect MD.2 to a phone line). Electronic medication organizers/dispensers usually need to be prepared and set up by a caregiver, but provide better medication safety features for persons with more severe cognitive impairment.

Memory Aids for General Purposes Many electronic or computer-based devices used by the general population are now used by persons with cognitive impairments. Research has demonstrated the successful effect of providing those commercial products to persons with mild to severe cognitive impairments. The majority of studies were conducted on persons with TBI, who usually experienced nonprogressive prospective memory deficits.[55] Current available off-the-shelf products include a wide range of devices, such as electronic organizers, voice recorders and organizers, software for computers, electronic communication devices (mobile phones and pagers), and PDA.

Electronic Organizers Electronic organizers are compact-sized and economical devices that provide: alarm system, daily schedule planning, temporary storage (e.g., to-do lists or notes), permanent storage (e.g., contact lists or phone books), and upload/download information in some high-end.[56] The compact size of an electronic organizer, however, is also its disadvantage. The display area of this device sometimes is difficult for people with visual impairment to read, and the mini keyboard on the device is also difficult to operate. Voice recorders and organizers can be used as alternative electronic organizer devices. Some voice organizers described in earlier sections are available for persons who have difficulty using the display or input method of an electronic organizer. The advantage of a voice recorder is its ability to store long voice auditory messages and the ability to store speech in discrete, labeled files for fast retrieval.[56] Using voice organizers for five individuals with TBI, van den Broek and colleague demonstrated improvement of a memory task and performing a house chore.[57]

Computer Applications Computer applications such as Microsoft Outlook or Lotus Notes are examples of organization programs available for computers that can provide functions such as alarm reminders, daily schedule, and storage for contact information. PDAs can usually synchronize with these personal organization applications to share information and provide portability.

Electronic Communication Devices Electronic communication devices such as pagers and mobile phones can be used as memory aids. Both pagers and mobile phones provide built-in alarm and storage functions. Commercial paging companies also can provide reminder services. A paging system called NeuroPage was used in studies about its effectiveness in improving independence in the United Kingdom. The NeuroPage system used microcomputers linked to a paging company to send out reminders of tasks to be carried out at the proper date and time. Wilson reported that 80% of participants ($n = 143$) with memory deficits had significant improvement from baseline.[58] The effects could also sustain after 7 weeks of returning the pagers.

PDAs Current PDAs with time management software hold the potential for use as an alarm and schedule system for persons with memory deficits. Kim reported that 9 out of 12 participants with TBI considered the PDA to be helpful for them in assisting daily activities.[59] All participants in their study suggested the use of palmtop computer for outpatient rehabilitation. PDAs now are available with a wide range of functions and designs. Basic appearance differences among PDAs are found in the keyboard.

Although studies have demonstrated favorable results of using those devices for persons with cognitive impairment, limitations exist in both software and hardware aspects of current technology.[55] Software that is not designed for people unfamiliar with computers or for people with memory problems may cause difficulty in use.[55] Software should be designed with error-free features and customized to meet the needs of specific user groups. Hardware considerations of currently available products are portability, storage space, visual display, input method, and ease of use. PDAs seem to be the device that provides the capacity and flexibility for software installation and for other accessible hardware features such as large display screen and touch screen input. The future development of PDA with powerful capacity of wireless communication features, such as internet access, mobile phone function, and GPS, suggests the potential power of PDAs as memory aids for persons with cognitive impairment.

Specially Designed Software and Hardware Essential Steps by Mastery Rehabilitation Systems[60] is a desktop computer program designed to provide cueing and guidance to complete ADL tasks for persons with cognitive impairments. Essential Steps was found to be successful in task-skill training for individual with cognitive impairments by providing on-screen reminder or computer-generated voice reminders.[61]

Another example of specialized desktop computer software is the Cognitive Orthosis for Assisting Activities in the Home (COACH) developed by Mihailidis.[62] The prototype COACH system used a single video camera connected to a computer and associated software for artificial neural networks and plan recognition to monitor and provide auditory prompts to persons with cognitive impairments for carrying out daily activities. Using single-subject design with 10 elders with moderate to severe dementia, Mihailidis reported significant improvement in completion of hand-washing tasks without caregiver assistance with the presence of COACH system.[63]

The Planning and Execution Assistant and Training System (PEAT) is a palmtop application designed to provide cuing and planning for persons with cognitive impairments. The cueing system provided by PEAT is either auditory or graphical. The PEAT system automatically cues its users, monitors task performance according to users' input, and adjusts the schedule when delays, interruptions, or other calendar changes occur. Another function of PEAT is activity modeling for different types of daily tasks such as standard tasks. Users' performance can also be recorded and uploaded to a desktop computer for further monitoring and training by caregivers or clinicians.

A wearable cognitive prosthesis, ISAAC™, is an example of a specially designed computerized device that stores behavior initiation prompts and procedural information for persons with cognitive impairment. The ISAAC™ automatically delivers individualized synthesized speech audio prompts to its user to initiate routine actions such as taking medication, preparing for work/school, etc. The procedural cueing provided by the device can be simple text, interactive sequential text list, graphics, or auditory. Users select and access their procedural and information content by operating the ISAAC™ touch screen. When the ISAAC™ is connected to ISAAC Author™ software on a desktop computer, its content can be customized to meet individual needs. A case study involving two individuals with TBI who used ISAAC™ showed improved independence in ADLs, better communication with caregivers, and psychosocial adjustment.[64]

Other New Technology for Memory Aids Timex Ironman Data Link is a digital watch with built-in PDA features to provide extended time-keeping and personal organization functions. Basic functions available on this PDA watch are alarms and reminders, to-do list, phonebook, timers, and schedule planner. Similar to a PDA, the Timex Data Link watch can connect to a PC, using USB connection, for data upload/download through special software that comes with the watch. Using

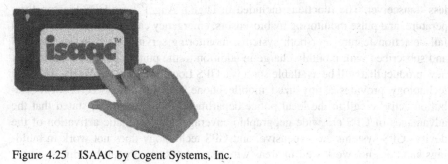

Figure 4.25   ISAAC by Cogent Systems, Inc.

currently available Microsoft Outlook is another option for the users for download-ing personal information to the watch. Through the PC software, all the settings, functions, and options can be set easily without the trouble of pushing small buttons on the watch. Users can allocate memory space to most frequently or importantly used functions such as contact information or schedule planner, but the watch still holds the maximum storage space for each data type. In addition, new applications and modes can be downloaded and added to the watch.

This watch provides three practical features for persons with cognitive impair-ments. First, the Data Link watch provides both alarms and reminders simultane-ously to inform users of the task that needs to be performed at that time. Traditional wristwatches provide only auditory alarm with task reminder. Second, it is a wrist-watch that users can wear all day long and it is less likely to be misplaced or lost. Finally, Timex Data Link watch is inexpensive (the retail price is under $100). Another similar product, called WatchMinder, also provides a vibration alarm along with text reminders for use as a memory aid. Although WatchMinder cannot be linked to a computer for customized functionality, it provides preset text reminders.

Devices for Preventing Wandering

GPS Wristwatch   In the early stage of Alzheimer's disease, people often experi-ence forgetfulness and disorientation. They may get lost when traveling in an unfamiliar area. The spatiotemporal disorientation further results in wandering behavior that poses threats to their safety and increases caregiver burden. More than 60% of people with Alzheimer's disease have exhibited wandering behavior.[65] To keep track of people with Alzheimer's disease at high risk of wandering, use of GPS technology offers promise.[65] Products available in the market include wrist-wear GPS locator watches (GPS Locator Watch by Werify, and Digital Angel for Senior Wanderers). The GPS Locator Watch includes an integrated GPS and wireless transceiver that points out the exact location of the watch wearer and allows care-givers to remotely communicate with the Locator Watch. Other functions provided by this device are built-in pager, automatic clock, removal prevention and alarm, remote safety lock/unlock for watch removal, basic watch functions to display time and date, and emergency call function activated by pressing two buttons simultaneously.

While providing slightly different functions than the GPS Locator Watch, Digital Angel[TM] has two components: a wristwatch and a pager-sized clip-on wire-less transceiver. The functions included in Digital Angel[TM] are GPS locator, tem-perature, and pulse monitoring by biosensors, emergency call, and an add-on sudden fall detection feature. For both systems, monitoring services need to be activated and subscribed with monthly charge in addition to the purchase of GPS devices. A new product that will be available soon is a GPS Locator Phone by Werify. The new technology provides a tiny-sized mobile phone with GPS transceiver with one-button activate call to the local police department. Paterson (2003) stated that the advantages of GPS are wide geographic coverage and automatic activation of the device. GPS systems are expensive, and GPS technology does not work in build-ings and does not work well in areas with many trees or very tall buildings.

A   B

Figure 4.26   Activity compass. (**A**) Version 4. (**B**) Version 5.

Activity Compass   GPS technology was also used to integrate with artificial intelligence in providing prompts to a destination. Researchers at the University of Washington designed a prototype of Activity Compass that recorded the GPS reading into a PDA.[66] The Activity Compass monitors which activity paths stored in the server it believes are in progress based on the time, user location, and activity path. Visual guidance (arrows for direction) then were provided on PDA monitor. The arrows guide the user for the correct route to his/her most likely destination. The technologies used in Activities Compass are hand-held computer, GPS receiver, and wireless technology. The most recent version of Activity Compass uses only a smartphone and GPS receiver.

Other Wireless Systems   Other wireless solutions to prevent wandering are available. HomeFree Systems Ltd. provides a radio-frequency transmission system to monitor elders wandering behavior. A watch worn by elders produces a silent signal. A monitoring unit is installed at the entrance(s), and a caregiver wears a local pager. When the elder wearing a transducer moves near or walks out the door, the monitoring unit detects the signal from the watch. A message is sent to the caregiver's watch to inform the caregiver. In senior facilities with multiple entrances and multiple watch transducer users, a computer-linked monitoring station is used to provide detailed information about the wanderer and his/her position to the caregiver. An emergency response system can be added to the system for further safety monitoring.

4.6   OTHER DEVICES

Wireless and the Internet

Using video-telephone technology is a common strategy for providing telehealth or telerehabilitation services for the elderly. In Japan, studies demonstrated that using a video phone could increase ADL functioning and social communication and at the same time decrease loneliness and a negative attitude.[67,68]

Suggesting that elders have critical social interaction needs, a design team at Carnegie Mellon University developed an innovative robotic design, Hug, to enhance commutation for all people.[69] Hug looked like a sea-star-shaped pillow with two longer arms that functioned as a mobile phone with extensive sensory feedback produced during communication. Hug is best used for distance communication between family members and friends. To activate Hug, the user squeezes the left arm and says the name of the person they want to talk to, and Hug connects to the other Hug. When the connection is established, users just talk as talking on a phone while holding the Hugs. Any movement such as stroke, hug, or pet will activate a pressure sensor and accelerometers then will be translated by the other Hug into heat and vibration. This design is still under development; however, it provides an opportunity for distant communication using a simple, tactile interface.

Personal Emergency Response Systems

Personal emergency response systems (PERS) are electronic communication devices that allow emergency contact for persons who live alone or are at risk of accidents. PERS have three components. The first is a small battery-operated radio transmitter worn or carried by user. The second component is an automatic dialing console connected to a phone line. An emergency response center that monitors calls is the third component. The emergency response center can either be a manufacturer-based operation located in one national center, or a regional provider-based center. When an accident happens or emergency help is needed, the PERS user presses the button on the transmitter to send out a signal that is received by the console. Then the console automatically dials out to the preset emergency phone number, usually an emergency response center. The center responds to the call and check out the condition of the user. Some PERS have the function to dial emergency numbers even when the phone line is in use or off the hook. If the emergency center cannot contact the user and determine that the user is safe, it will inform emergency service providers to go to user's home. PERS can be rented, leased, or purchased. Purchasing price ranges from $200 to $1500. In most case, users need to pay an installation fee and monthly service charge ($10 to $30).

PERS can significantly reduce hospital admissions and inpatient days, but does not appear to affect the number of emergency room visits.[70] Over 90% of the PERS users in one study were very satisfied with the features provided by PERS.[71]

Financial Management and Smart Cards

For older adults and people with disabilities, making financial transaction at automatic teller machines (ATMs) can be problematic. People with vision problems, poor dexterity, or cognitive impairments or who are using wheelchairs or scooters state that ATMs are hard to see and operate. Recently, more and more banks have talking ATMs that provide voice output prompting users at each step of ATM transaction. These machines have an earphone jack to allow privacy during the transaction. Another possible and available solution for banking is using telephone or on-line banking. People with vision impairment find on-line banking accessible because they can use computers equipped with screen magnification/reading applications or refreshable braille output to complete the transaction remotely. Using touch screens can reduce the demand of dexterity; however, persons with visual problems prefer using keypads to a touch screen.[72] Researchers in Japan suggested adding tactile features with raised signs and numerals around the screen that correspond to their positions on the screen along with auditory output to make ATMs more accessible for people with visual impairment.[73]

There are many future possibilities for ATMs and smart card are endless. In Canada, a prototype ATM equipped with iris identification for consumer recognition, speech recognition of user's selection, and speech synthesized output for transaction prompting allows users a full cardless and contactless environment for ATM transactions.[74] The receipt and transaction record could then be sent to the user's PDA from the prototype. The emergence of the touchless ATM shows great accessibility potential for persons with disabilities.

Another trend is the use of smart cards for personal ID, health system, financial transactions, and more. For example, with smart cards used for ATM transactions, the ATM could easily be customized based on user preferences and needs stored on the smart card.[72] A smart card is a credit-card-sized plastic card with an electronic chip that can hold large amounts data, including security information. Smart cards have different functions for various uses. A memory-only smart card can be used for prepay phone service. Another type of smart card has a memory function plus a microprocessor to be used as credit or debit cards. A contactless smart card can be used for public transportation and can be useful for persons with coordination or dexterity problem when accessing public transportation gates. Another example of smart card use is found in the Canadian health sector. Canada began using smart cards, called "Health Cards," in their health system. The use of Health Cards is expected to enable information communication between doctors, pharmacists, and other health-care professionals.[75] Other advantages of smart card use in health-care systems are (a) cost reduction through prevention of unnecessary exams and (b) prevention of adverse drug interactions.

4.7 CONCLUSION

In this chapter, a variety of new and developing assistive technologies for people with different types of impairment are presented. The innovations of microprocessor, artificial intelligence, and communication technology play an essential role in the advancement of AT. AT provides people in needs with greater possibility of achieving independence and promoting social participation. In addition, some AT devices have the potential to eliminate care-giving burdens. AT can be a commercially available device or a specifically designed technology for a certain type of disability. It is important for both the potential AT users and AT practitioners to be aware of the current available technology and resources in order to benefit from it.

REFERENCES

1. Shoval, S., Ulrich, I., and Borenstein, J. (2001). Computerized obstacle avoidance systems for the blind and visually imapired. In: *Intelligent Systems and Technologies in Rehabilitation Engineering*, Teodorescu, H.-H. L., and Jain, L. C., eds. Boca Raton, FL: CRC Press LLC, pp. 413–448.
2. Bentzen, B. L., Barlow, J., and Franck, L. (2002). Determining recommended language for speech messages used by accessible pedestrian signals: Final report. Retrieved August 15, 2004, from www.ite.org/library/APS_Speech.pdf
3. Carroll, J., and Bentzen, B. L. (1999). American Council of the Blind survey of intersection accessibility. *The Braille Forum* **38**, 11–15.
4. Uslan, M. M., Peck, A. F., and Waddell, W. (1988). Audible traffic signals: How useful are they? *Institute of Transportation Engineers Journal* **58**(9), 37–43.
5. VTT Industrial Systems. (n.d.). Navigation and guidance for the blind. Retrieved August 15, 2004, from http://www.vtt.fi/tuo/53/projektit/noppa/noppaeng.htm
6. Lindo, G., and Nordholm, L. (1999). Adaptation strategies, well-being, and activities of daily living among people with low vision. *Journal of Visual Impairment and Blindness* **93**(7), 434–446.
7. Leventhal, J. D. (1996). Assistive devices for people who are blind or have visual impairments. In: *Evaluating, Selecting, and Using Appropriate Assistive Technology*, Galvin, J. C., and Scherer, M. J., eds. Gaithersburg, MD: Aspen Publishers, pp. 125–143.
8. Keller, B. K., Morton, J. L., Thomas, V. S., and Potter, J. F. (1999). The effect of visual and hearing impairments on functional status. *Journal of the American Geriatric Society* **47**(11), 1319–1325.
9. National Institute on Deafness and Other Communication Disorders (February 2001). The basics: Hearing aids. Retrieved September 1, 2004, from http://www.nidcd.nih.gov/health/hearing/thebasics_hearingaid.asp
10. Campbell, D. (2003). Hearing-aid principles and technology. In: *Assistive Technology for the Hearing-impaired, Deaf and Deafblind*, Hersh, M. A., and Johnson, M. A., eds. London: Springer, pp. 71–116.
11. e-Michigan Deaf and Hard of Hearing (n.d.). Hearing aids. Retrieved September 1, 2004, from http://www.michdhh.org/assistive_devices/hearing_aids.html
12. Cook, A. M., and Hussey, S. M. (2002). *Assistive Technologies: Principles and Practice*, 2nd ed. St. Louis: Mosby.
13. American Speech-Language-Hearing Association. (n.d.). Hearing aids. Retrieved September 15, 2004, from http://www.asha.org/public/hearing/treatment/hearing_aids.htm
14. Weber, P. C. (2002). Medical and surgical considerations for implantable hearing prosthetic devices. *American Journal of Audiology* **11**(2), 134–138.
15. The Royal National Institute for Deaf People (RNID). (February 2002). Implantable middle ear hearing devices. Retrieved September, 1, 2004, from http://www.rnid.org.uk/pdfs/factsheet_pdfs/implantable_middle_ear_hearing_devices.pdf
16. Spindel, J. H. (2002). Middle ear implantable hearing devices. *American Journal of Audiology* **11**(2), 104–113.
17. Rauschecker, J. P., and Shannon, R. V. (2002). Sending sound to the brain. *Science* **295**(5557), 1025–1029.
18. Holmes, A. E., Saxon, J. P., and Kaplan, H. S. (2000). Assistive listening devices and systems: amplification technology for consumers with hearing loss. *Journal of Rehabilitation* **66**(3), 56–59.
19. National Information and Training Center for Hearing Assistive Technology. (October 9, 2003). Assistive Listening Devices. Retrieved September 15, 2004, from http://hearingloss.org/hat/assistive_listening_devices.HTM
20. e-Michigan Deaf and Hard of Hearing. (n.d.). Hearing assistive technology. Retrieved September 15, 2004, from http://www.michdhh.org/assistive_devices/hearing_assistive_tech.html
21. Kozma-Spytek, L. (October 31, 2002). Accessing the world of telecommunications. Retrieved August 15, 2004, from http://tap.gallaudet.edu/AccessTelecomLKS/AcTel.htm
22. Compton, C. L. (1991). *Assistive Devices: Doorways to Independence*. Annapolis, MD: Vancomp Associates.
23. Kuk, F. K., and Nielsen, K. H. (1997). Factors affecting interference from digital cellular telphones. *The Hearing Journal* **50**(9), 1–3.

24. Qian, H., Loizou, P. C., and Dorman, M. F. (2003). A phone-assistive device based on Bluetooth technology for cochlear implant users. *IEEE Transactions on Neural System and Rehabilitation Engineering* **11**(3), 282–287.

25. Kozma-Spytek, L. (2001). Digital wireless telephones and hearing aids. Retrieved August 15, 2004, from http://www.audiologyonline.com/articles/arc_disp.asp?id=278&catid=1

26. Rogers, R. J. (1996). Interference in hearing aids caused by digital wireless telephones: An opportunity for improvement. *Hearing Journal* **49**(7), 25–26.

27. Skopec, M. (1998). Hearing aid electromagnetic interference from digital wireless telephones. *IEEE Transactions of Rehabilitation Engineering* **6**(2), 235–239.

28. Aarts, N. C. (2004, August 30, 2004). T-coils: Getting the most out of your hearing aid. Retrieved September 15, 2004, from http://www.healthyhearing.com/healthyhearing/newroot/articles/arc_disp.asp?article_id=250&catid=1054

29. e-Michigan Deaf and Hard of Hearing. (n.d.). TTY or TDD: The text telephone. Retrieved September 13, 2004, from http://www.michdhh.org/assistive_devices/text_telephone.html

30. Galuska, S., and Foulds, R. (1990). A real-time visual telephone for the deaf. *Proceedings of 13th Annual RESNA Conference*, 267–268.

31. U.S. Department of Health and Human Services, Administration on Aging (2004). A profile of older americans: 2003. Retrieved August 15, 2004, from http://www.aoa.gov/prof/Statistics/profile/2003/2003profile.pdf

32. U.S. Census Bureau. (2001, Feburary). Americans with disabilities, 1997. Retrieved July 27, 2004, from http://www.census.gov/prod/2001pubs/p70-73.pdf

33. Applica Consumer Products, Inc. (2003). Introduces Black and Decker Lidsoff automatic jar opener. Retrieved August 15, 2004, from http://www.householdproductsinc.com/pressroom/DisplayRelease.asp?id=35

34. Gade, L. (August 20, 2004). Review: Roomba the affordable vacuuming robot. Retrieved September 1, 2004, from http://www.everydayrobots.com/index.php?option=content&task=viewandid=2

35. Kendrick, D. (2004). Dancing the Roomba: Artificial intelligence that sweeps the floor. Retrieved August 15, 2004, from http://www.afb.org/afbpress/pub.asp?DocID=aw050206

36. Disabled Living Foundation. (2003). Choosing toilet equipment and accessories. Retrieved August 20, 2004, from http://factsheets.disabledliving.org.uk/printpdf.php?factsheetid=51

37. Bühler, C., Heck, H., Nedza, J., and Wallbruch, R. (2001). Evaluation of the MOBIL walking & lifting aid. In: *Assistive Technology Added Value to the Quality of Life,* Marincek, C., Bühler, C., Knops, H., and Andrich, R., eds. Amsterdam: IOS Press, pp. 210–215.

38. Levy, C. E., and Chow, J. W. (2004). Pushrim-activated power-assist wheelchairs: Elegance in motion. *American Journal of Physical Medicine and Rehabilitation* **83**(2), 166–167.

39. Cooper, R. A., and Cooper, R. (2003). Trends and issues in wheeled mobility technologies. Retrieved August 20, 2004, from http://www.ap.buffalo.edu/idea/space%20workshop/Papers/WEB%20%20Trends_Iss_WC%20_Cooper_.pdf

40. Cooper, R. A., Fitzgerald, S. G., Boninger, M. L., Prins, K., Rentschler, A. J., Arva, J., et al. (2001). Evaluation of a pushrim-activated, power-assisted wheelchair. *Archives of Physical Medicine and Rehabilitation* **82**(5), 702–708.

41. Bauer, S. M., and Stone, V. I., eds. (1999). Proceedings for the stakeholders forum on wheeled mobility. Retrieved August 20, 2004, from http://cosmos.buffalo.edu/t2rerc/pubs/forums/mobility/mobility.pdf

42. Simpson, R. C., and Levine, S. P. (2002). Voice control of a powered wheelchair. *IEEE Transactions on Neural System and Rehabilitation Engineering* **10**(2), 122–125.

43. Antonakakis, J., Azeloglu, A., Chiang, F., Ge, Q., and Theophilou, T. (2003). A smart wheelchair with machine vision and voice control. Retrieved September 1, 2004, from http://icadi.phhp.ufl.edu/2003/presentation.php?PresID = 253

44. Ding, D., Cooper, R. A., Kaminski, B. A., Kanaly, J. R., Allegretti, A., Chaves, E., et al. (2003). Integrated control and related technology of assistive devices. *Assistive Technology* **15**(2), 89–97.

45. Hobson, D. A. (1992). Comparative effects of posture on pressure and shear at the body–seat interface. *Journal of Rehabilitation Research and Development* **29**(4), 21–31.

46. Simpson, R. C., Poirot, D., and Baxter, F. (2002). The Hephaestus Smart Wheelchair System. *IEEE Transaction of Neural System and Rehabilitation Engineering* **10**(2), 118–122.

47. Yanco, H. A. (1998). Integrating robotic research: A survey of robotic wheelchair development. Retrieved August 20, 2004, from http://www.cs.uml.edu/~holly/papers/sss98.pdf

48. Mann, W. C., Hurren, D., and Tomita, M. (1993). Comparison of assistive device use and needs of home-based older persons with different impairments. *American Journal of Occupational Therapy* **47**(11), 980–987.

49. Hart, T., O'Neil-Pirozzi, T., and Morita, C. (2003). Clinician expectations for portable electronic devices as cognitive-behavioural orthoses in traumatic brain injury rehabilitation. *Brain Injury* **17**(5), 401–411.

50. O'Neil-Pirozzi, T. M., Kendrick, H., Goldstein, R., and Glenn, M. (2004). Clinician influences on use of portable electronic memory devices in traumatic brain injury rehabilitation. *Brain Injury* **18**(2), 179–189.

51. Cole, E. (1999). Cognitive prosthetics: An overview to a method of treatment. *NeuroRehabilitation* **12**(1), 39–51.

52. LoPresti, Mihailidis, A., and Kirsch, N. (2004). Assistive technology for cognitive rehabilitation: State of the art. *Neuropsychological Rehabilitation* **14**(1), 5–39.

53. Muir, A. J., Sanders, L. L., Wilkinson, W. E., and Schmader, K. (2001). Reducing medication regimen complexity: a controlled trial. *Journal of General Internal Medicine* **16**(2), 77–82.

54. Logue, R. M. (2002). Self-medication and the elderly: How technology can help. *The American Journal of Nursing* **102**(7), 51–55.

55. Inglis, E. A., Szymkowiak, A., Gregor, P., Newell, A. F., Hine, N., Wilson, B. A., et al. (2004). Usable technology? Challenges in designing a memory aid with current electronic devices. *Neuropsychological Rehabilitation* **14**(1), 77–87.

56. Kapur, N., Glisky, E., and Wilson, B. A. (2004). Technological memory aids for people with memory deficits. *Neuropsychological Rehabilitation* **14**(1), 41–60.

57. van den Broek, M. D., Downes, J., Johnson, Z., Dayus, B., and Hilton, N. (2000). Evaluation of an electronic memory aid in the neuropsychological rehabilitation of prospective memory deficits. *Brain Injury* **14**(5), 455–462.

58. Wilson, B. A., Emslie, H. C., Quirk, K., and Evans, J. J. (2001). Reducing everyday memory and planning problems by means of a paging system: A randomized control crossover study. *Journal of Neurology, Neurosurgery, and Psychiatry* **70**(4), 477–482.

59. Kim, H. J., Burke, D. T., Dowds, M. M., Jr., Boone, K. A., and Park, G. J. (2000). Electronic memory aids for outpatient brain injury: Follow-up findings. *Brain Injury* **14**(2), 187–196.

60. Bergman, M. M. (1996). Computer orthoses: Fostering self-sufficiency in people with cognitive challenges. *Disability Today, Fall* 54–55.

61. Bergman, M. M. (1997). People with cognitive challenges can enjoy rapid success in acquiring skills and managing their lives: The exciting breakthrough of Cognitive Orthoses. Paper presented at the California State University, Northridge, Technology and Persons with Disabilities Conference (CSUN), Los Angeles, CA.

62. Mihailidis, A., Fernie, G. R., and Barbenel, J. C. (2001). The use of artificial intelligence in the design of an intelligent cognitive orthosis for people with dementia. *Assistive Technology* **13**(1), 23–39.

63. Mihailidis, A. (2004). The efficacy of an intelligent cognitive orthosis to facilitate handwashing by persons with moderate to severe dementia. *Neuropsychological Rehabilitation* **14**(1), 135–171.

64. Gorman, P. (2003). Effectiveness of the ISAAC cognitive prosthetic system for improving rehabilitation outcomes with neurofunctional impairment. *NeuroRehabilitation* **18**(1), 57–67.

65. Parnes, R. B. (2003). GPS technology and Alzheimer's disease: Novel use for an existing technology. Retrieved August 15, 2004, from http://www.cs.washington.edu/assistcog/NewsArticles/HealthGate/GPS%20Technology%20and%20Alzheimer's%20Disease%20Novel%20Use%20for%20an%20Existing%20Technology%20CHOICE%20For%20HealthGate.htm

66. Patterson, D. J., Etzioni, O., and Kautz, H. (2002). *The activity compass.* Paper presented at the UbiCog '02: First International Workshop on Ubiquitous Computing for Cognitive Aids, Göteborg, Sweden.

67. Ezumi, H., Ochiai, N., Oda, M., Saito, S., Ago, M., Fukuma, N., et al. (2003). Peer support via video-telephony among frail elderly people living at home. *Journal of Telemedicine and Telecare* **9**(1), 30–34.

68. Nakamura, K., Takano, T., and Akao, C. (1999). The effectiveness of videophones in home health-care for the elderly. *Medical Care* **37**, 117–125.

69. Gemperle, F., DiSalvo, C., Forlizzi, J., and Yonkers, W. (2003). The Hug: A new form for communication. Paper presented at the Proceedings of the 2003 Conference on Designing for User Experiences, San Francisco, California.

70. Roush, R. E., Teasdale, T. A., Murphy, J. N., and Kirk, M. S. (1995). Impact of a personal emergency response system on hospital utilization by community-residing elders. *Southern Medical Journal* **88**(9), 917–922.

71. Hyer, K., and Rudick, L. (1994). The effectiveness of personal emergency response systems in meeting the safety monitoring needs of home care clients. *Journal of Nurse Administration* **24**(6), 39–44.

72. Noonan, T. (2000). Barriers to using automatic teller machines: A review of the usability of self-service banking facilities for Australians with disabilities. Retrieved August 15, 2004.

73. Wake, H., Wake, T., and Takahashi, H. (1999). Tactile ATM controls for visually impaired users. *Technology and Disability* **11**(3), 133–141.

74. Johnson, G. I. C. L. (2001). "You talking to me?" Exploring voice in self-service user interfaces. *International Journal of Human–Computer Interaction* **13**(2), 161–186.

75. Aubert, B. A., and Hamel, G. (2001). Adoption of smart cards in the medical sector: The Canadian experience. *Social Science and Medicine* **53**(7), 879–894.

CHAPTER 5

TELEHEALTH

Jessica Johnson and Roxanna Bendixen

5.1 INTRODUCTION

In this chapter we define telehealth, explain the technology used for telehealth applications, and discuss government programs that promote telehealth. We describe a number of telehealth products, and we conclude with an examination of legal issues and current limitations.

Definition

The 2001 Report to Congress on Telemedicine defines telehealth as the "use of electronic information and telecommunications technologies to support long-distance clinical health care, patient and professional health-related education, public health and health administration."[1] Telehealth technology can, therefore, be defined as the devices and software that facilitate the transferring of information to health-care providers and educators to remotely diagnose, consult, monitor, treat, and/or educate patients and consumers. Telehealth is an approach that connects individuals and health-care providers through the use of telecommunications technology. Specialized medical devices, video-conferencing, computer networking, and software management systems allow for the evaluation, diagnosis, and treatment of patients in locations other than hospitals or clinics.

Other terms such as telemedicine, telerehabilitation, and telehomecare reflect a narrower population or professional focus within telehealth. Telemedicine seeks: (1) increased access to services for individuals who live in rural areas or have disabilities that make it difficult for them to easily travel to a doctor's office, hospital, or clinic; (2) cost effectiveness by avoiding unnecessary emergency room and clinic visits; (3) preventative medicine and early intervention of medical complications that might otherwise go unreported; (4) better diagnostic and prognostic capabilities, as patients submit vital health information daily, allowing for tracking of trends; (5) increased patient involvement, as patients are more aware of their vital parameters (blood pressure, blood glucose levels, oxygen saturation, body weight, and temperature) and able to become actively involved in the process of managing their care and treatment interventions.[2] Telehomecare promotes aging in place, providing supports for living at home and enhanced quality of life through prevention of chronic illnesses.

Smart Technology for Aging, Disability, and Independence, Edited by William C. Mann

Telehealth Today

Today, telemedicine and the use of telecommunications technology is widely used by the United States federal sector through the Department of Veteran's Affairs (VA), the Department of Defense (DoD), especially the army, and the Department of Health and Human Services' Office for the Advancement of Telehealth (OAT). These departments view telehealth as integral to the delivery of health services and education within their systems. A recent Technology Administration Report (2004) entitled "Innovation, Demand and Investment in Telehealth"[3] provides information on these programs, which is discussed below.

The VA implemented an expansive telemedicine initiative, and it now operates the nation's largest telehealth program. Because the VA is federally funded and constitutes a "closed system" for patients, providers, and payers, it does not have a need to annually seek alternative funding for its initiative. With a stable funding base, the VA has proven to be a leader in telehealth in such areas as research, clinical efficacy and cost effectiveness, development of standards, and needs assessment. Although the VA has conducted numerous high-quality, cost-effectiveness studies, to date there has not been a coordinated effort to catalog and distriubte these clinical studies for other health-care providers.[3]

Within the DoD, the Telemedicine and Advanced Technologies Research Center (TATRC), a section of the United States Army Medical Research & Material Command (USAMRMC) Headquarters, manages Congressional Special Interest (CSI) extramural research programs encompassing technology research areas. Since 1990, the USAMRMC has managed over 100 CSI programs totaling over $3 billion. The programs are awarded via extramural contracts and cooperative agreements. In 2001, TATRC received a budget of over $104 million to fund research in innovative health-care technologies and telemedicine programs. Such programs included the Disaster Relief and Emergency Medical Services (DREAMS), which tests interactive telemedicine technologies to treat patients in both urban and rural settings, develops chemical sensors for on-site diagnosis of toxic substances and biological decontamination, and provides medical treatment to patients who are unable to receive advanced care quickly. The National Medical Testbed (NMT) focuses on applying defense and aerospace technology to advanced health-care delivery, and it supports projects that focus on improving and assessing the delivery of health care to underserved populations, including the civilian population in general, as well as deployed active duty service members. The Center for Innovative Minimally Invasive Therapy (CIMIT) combines the clinical and technical expertise of a consortium of nonprofit institutions with the primary aim of developing technologies to diagnose and treat patients using minimally invasive approaches. The CIMIT concentrates on five key areas: cardiovascular disease, cancer, stroke, trauma and critical care, and new initiatives.[4]

The Department of Health and Human Services' (HHS) Office for Advancement of Telehealth (OAT) and the U.S. Department of Agriculture's Rural Utility Service (RUS) are the largest federal telehealth programs. Their focus is more civilian-oriented, and they provide grants for telehealth programs. They expect grantees to study the value of telehealth as an effective health-care technique, as well as to disseminate information to increase awareness of telehealth. OAT is a consortium of experts from a variety of fields, including clinicians, telehealth grant administrators, multimedia producers, distance learning consultants, and telehealth policy analysts. In 2002, OAT administered approximately 100 telehealth/telemedicine grants in 43 states, awarding new funds totaling over $39 million. These grants focused on interactive training and education, the development of "best practice" models, and telehealth policy development. Congress did not appropriate funds to OAT for new telehealth grants in fiscal year 2004.[5]

Through RUS, grants continue to be funded to finance rural America's telecommunications infrastructure, which supports distance learning and rural telehealth projects. For fiscal year 2002, $20 million in grants were made available through a national competition to provide broadband transmission service on a "community-oriented connectivity" basis. The "community-oriented connectivity" approach targeted rural, economically challenged communities and offered a way for broadband transmission services to be provided to rural schools, libraries, health-care facilities, law enforcement agencies, and public safety organizations, as well as residents and businesses. This initiative provided small, rural communities a way to benefit from the advanced technologies, fostering economic growth, providing quality education and health-care opportunities, and increasing and enhancing public safety efforts. RUS's focus is on rural citizens, who often have inadequate health-care including lack of health-care providers, few hospitals, and inadequate health education resources.[6]

Many states and local governments also fund telehealth research, project development, and/or feasibility studies. The University of Arizona Telemedicine Network, which is funded through a variety of state and local sources, is currently assessing cost containment with telemedicine, as well as the use of telemedicine for providing health-care services for its state corrections system. The Statewide Health Coordinating Council (SHCC) in Texas brought together entities throughout the state to develop a strategic plan, and subsequently prepared a comprehensive report entitled "The State of Telemedicine and Telehealth in Texas," and has been piloting telehealth projects and the use of telecommunications for distance learning initiatives. The Florida Department of Elder Affairs, the National Institute on Disability and Rehabilitation Research (NIDRR), and the Department of Veteran Affairs support projects within the University of Florida's Center for Research on Telehealth and Healthcare Communication. In 1997, private funding sources created the California Telehealth and Telemedicine Center for the purpose of strengthening telemedicine applications and consumer health education delivery in California, especially for its rural populations. California is one of the first states to allow Medicaid reimbursement for telemedicine services.

Telehealth Technology

The need to lower health-care costs, especially for individuals with chronic diseases and disabilities, has provided much of the impetus for a change in health-care delivery. This change is also being driven by our changing demographics (aging population) and by advances in technologies that support the development of telemedicine systems, internet access, and electronic patient record systems.[7] With increased use of the internet, health-care providers are able to communicate more readily and effectively with their clients.

Telemedicine by definition utilizes medical devices that enable health-care providers to remotely evaluate, diagnose, and treat patients. Specialized application software, data storage devices, database management software, and medical devices capable of electronic data collection storage and transmission are all key components of a telemedicine infrastructure. These components are enhanced through the use of telecommunications technology, network computing, video-conferencing systems, and CODECs. The term CODEC is short for compressor/decompressor, and it describes any technology used for compressing and decompressing data. In telecommunications, this is a device that encodes and decodes various types of data, particularly data that take up a very large amount of disk space, such as sound and video files.

Telehealth uses either a "live" or "store and forward" method for transmitting data or sound information. With live transmission, the health-care provider participates in the evaluation of the patient, who is in another location, while diagnostic information is being viewed, collected, and transmitted to the facility. With the store and forward method of transmission, the health-care provider views the data collected at a later time. Some telehealth programs use both approaches.

Many companies offer software for data and image management. This allows for electronic interfacing with such devices as ultrasound machines, ECGs, and spirometers, and transfer data along with patient demographics directly into a reporting database. Through the database, digital video recording can be compressed, and the production of final reports can be provided through the internet anywhere in the world.

Sensors   Mobile monitoring systems may include sensors that are attached to patients and can monitor a variety of physiological parameters. Sensors placed discreetly on a patient are able to monitor and record an individual's movement patterns, medication compliance, and nutritional and fluid intake. It is also possible, as discussed in more detail in Chapter 2, to place sensors throughout the home to monitor the environment, such as temperature and adjust the heat settings, ensure that the stove is turned off, or that the doors and windows are locked.

Patient End Unit   A patient end unit is the device that collects and sends information on the patient's status. Depending on the purpose of the telehealth system, the components of the patient unit will vary. The unit may require sensors on the patient. Alternatively, it may consist of a computer station or small device for the person to enter information or measurements that are transmitted to a health-care center. The patient end unit may also be a video camera and a computer system for video conferencing with a health-care professional.

Call Center or Health Professional Unit   Data transmitted from a patient unit is typically transferred to a secure server at a health-care facility. The receiving center has a computer station to access and analyze the information. From this station, the information is forwarded to the appropriate specialist through an intranet, fax, email, or to a cell phone.

Wired Connections   Wired technology from the sensor to the patient's processing unit consists of leads or hard wires that go from the device that is taking the measurement to the device that is recording and storing the data. These systems require the patient to be in a particular location with limited movement when taking measurements. They are not optimal for continuous measurement of a physiological parameter. However, in some settings, wireless may not be an option because of interference with other equipment.

The unit may also be hardwired from the patient monitor to the receiving centers' server (Table 5.1). These wires include standard telephone lines, which are commonly referred to as plain old telephone service (POTS).[8] "POTS" are limited to about 56 kbps. "POTS" are also called "public switched telephone networks" (PSTN). When transferring data over a POTS system, the user is not able to receive or send regular telephone calls on that line. A benefit of POTS is that the system is widely available.

ISDN or (integrated services digital network) is a method of sending data over digital or regular telephone lines.[9] The ISDN transfer rate is up to 1.5 Mbps in North America and Japan.[10] "Digital subscriber lines" (xDSL) are similar to ISDN in that they both send data over telephone lines and both require the user to be within 20,000 wire feet of the telephone company's central office.[11] For distances over approximately 18,000 wire feet, phone lines need load coils to transmit "voice grade service."[12] However, these load coils interfere with internet service. ADSL, which is used by AT&T, is able to upload data at speeds up to 128 kbps and download data up to 1.5 Mbps.[13]

Another wired option is a cable modem, which transfers data at speeds from 512 kbps to 5 Mbps.[14,15] This method of transmitting data is not available in all areas, especially rural areas. Wired systems are not mobile, and this has limited flexibility. For example, the person may need to be home to transmit health information at a time when they were invited to have lunch with friends. These wired systems, however, do offer better security than wireless systems.

The system may also be hardwired from the receiving center's server to computers within the facility. This requires the health professionals or data analysts to

TABLE 5.1   Wired Technologies for Connecting Home User to Health-Care Center

Wired technologies	Data transfer rate
POTS	~56 kbps
ISDN	~64 kbps to 1.5 Mbps
XDSL	128 kbps to 1.5 Mbps
Cable modem	512 kbps to 5 Mbps

physically be in the facility and at a computer station to view the data and respond appropriately.

Wireless Connections The number of wireless devices in health care is expected to triple by 2005, with an increase from 18% to 55% of physicians utilizing handheld wireless devices.[16] The advantages of wireless communication are numerous. Physicians and health-care providers are able to obtain information from almost any location. This not only increases access to databases that contain patient health information, such as recent lab results, pharmaceuticals, and insurance information, but also increases the ability to connect to patients in distant locations such as in their homes, at accident sites, or in transport to emergency rooms. Facilities such as nursing homes are typically without the resources to set up every room with a computer and/or video-conferencing capabilities, making wireless telemedicine a more cost-effective approach.

Wireless technologies may be used to transmit data from the sensor to the patient's processing unit. For example, there are several cardiac sensors that measure cardiac function and then transmit the data to a monitor that stores the data and transmits it to a health-care facility. There are a few different ways that sensors can wirelessly connect to a patient processing unit including infrared and Bluetooth. Infrared requires the sensor to be in line-of-sight and within a few feet of the patient processing unit, while Bluetooth does not require line of sight and has a greater range.[15,17] Through a Bluetooth interface a device sensor can connect with a mobile phone, which in turn can transfer data to a health care facility. The device may also send the data to a PDA or laptop equipped with Bluetooth. The Bluetooth ECG Shirt (Figure 5.1) is a prototype that monitors cardiac activity without the individual

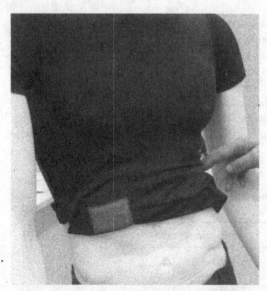

Figure 5.1   The Bluetooth ECG Shirt[19] by the Institute for Information Processing Technology (ITIV), University of Karlsruhe.

having to put on additional electrodes or put forth any effort other than putting on the shirt. The shirt has sensors within the fabric and may be washed in a washing machine.[18]

Another device that uses Bluetooth technology is a blood pressure monitor that continuously monitors blood pressure noninvasively without the use of a cuff.[20] The blood pressure is calculated from other cardiac parameters, including blood flow and pulse wave velocity. The sensors wirelessly transmit data using Bluetooth technology to a computer or PDA. A clinical trial was performed to assess reliability of this method compared to traditional blood pressure measurement using a blood pressure cuff. Invasive methods, while less convenient for the patient, are considered to be the most precise. The correlation between measuring with a blood pressure cuff and the invasive method is 0.80 with a standard deviation of 12 mmHg for systolic and 0.70 with a standard deviation of 10 mmHg for diastolic. The correlation between the continuous monitoring device with Bluetooth technology and the invasive method was 0.90 with a standard deviation of 5.8 mmHg for systolic and 0.81 with a standard deviation of 2.3 mmHg for diastolic.

Wireless Local Area Network (WLAN) and Personal Area Network These modes of data transmission are able to reach up to 100 meters and speeds of 1.6 Mbps to 54 Mbps.[15] A problem with using WLAN in sensors is that the cards are not made to fit into small devices, unlike Bluetooth transceivers.

The wireless link from the patient unit to the health center's server may link to a wired network access point once it has left the home. Some types of wireless transmission include a GSM (Global Systems for Mobile Communication) modem, satellite communication, and wireless WAN (Wide Area Network). GSM is the standard for digital cellular communication.[21] The transfer of data speed is usually 10–30 kbps. GSM takes up bandwidth for the duration of the connection. Eight calls can occur on one radio frequency at a time.[22] General packet radio service (GPRS) is used for data transfer as opposed to voice transfer.[23] GPRS is able to transfer data at speeds from 30 to 70 kbps. Using GPRS, bandwidth is only used when data are being transmitted, not for the duration of the connection. It is a good system for people who send or receive data intermittently. A universal mobile telephone system (UMTS) provides coverage by combining different-sized cells, from in-building to global, which is provided through satellite.[24] Data may be transmitted at speeds from 220 to 320 kbps.[25] The types of information transmitted include voice, streaming audio and video, and data. Enhanced Data GSM environment (EDGE) is based on GSM wireless, but can transfer data at speeds up to 384 kbps.[26] In the United States, EDGE is currently the fastest nationwide wireless data network.[27] In satellite transmission of data, a user may be connected to a transceiver that sends and receives signals from a satellite. The satellite then sends and receives signals from a ground station computer that acts as a hub for the system.

More and more health-care providers are using the internet for communicating with patients (Figure 5.2). The internet provides the means for consultation, education, and information exchange between patients from their homes and health-care providers from their clinics.[28] Through the internet, specially designed web "portals" or gateways to clinical and patient record systems allow for remote access to patient

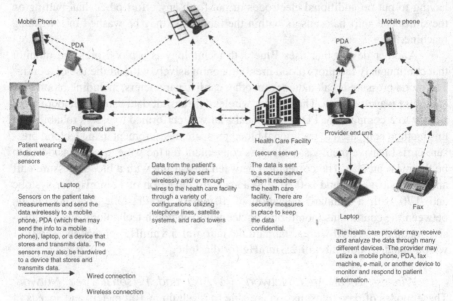

Figure 5.2 Example of Telenealth Network.

records for electronic signature, certification, referrals, or verbal orders.[29] Currently, access to the internet is accomplished mostly through computers, but the use of cell phones for transmission of data is expected to increase in the future.

History of Telehealth

Access to health care has been the primary driving force for the development of telemedicine. In the 1950's, Montreal, Quebec, Canada was the site for the first successful transmission of radiograms, which pioneered teleradiology.[30] The University of Nebraska, College of Medicine reported in 1959 that they had performed the first telemedical consultation with video communications.[31] In 1964, the same group received a $480,000 grant from the National Institute for Mental Health, which allowed the use of two-way, closed-circuit TV using microwave technology for telepsychiatry consultations between the Nebraska Psychiatric Institute in Omaha, Nebraska, USA, and the state mental hospital approximately 112 miles away. The link was mainly used for consultations and education. In 1971, the Nebraska Medical Center expanded the link to the Omaha Veterans Administration Hospital, as well as veteran's facilities in two other towns.

The National Aeronautics and Space Administration (NASA) provided much of the technology and funding for early telemedicine demonstration projects, initially through a pilot project utilizing communications satellites to transmit physiological information from both the spacecraft and the space suits of astronauts during space missions.[32] NASA, in conjunction with Lockheed Corporation, initiated the Space Technology Applied to Rural Papago Advanced Health Care (STARPAHC) project in 1972, which continued until 1975. The STARPAHC project was based in southern Arizona and provided remote care on the Papago Indian Reservation where two Native American paramedics utilized radiographic and ECG peripherals to transmit data by microwave to a public health service facility by two-way microwave telemedicine and audio transmission.[33]

In 1968, Logan International Airport in Boston, Massachusetts and Massachusetts General Hospital (MGH) began the transmission of medical data from first-aid stations at the Logan airport to provide health services and emergency care to airport employees and travelers. Physicians at the MGH were provided with ECGs, blood pressure readings, stethoscope sounds, and blood smear images for consultation and intervention. The first-aid stations were staffed 24 hours/day by nurses, and supplemented with physicians during peak passenger use. As this system developed and matured, it was eventually used by Massachusetts General Hospital and the local Veterans Administration medical center for psychiatric consultation.[34]

In 1964 at the New York World's Fair, AT&T unveiled a new product called the Bell System Picturephone, which combined the audio capabilities of the telephone with the picture capabilities of a tiny television. In the early 1970's, picturephones were provided to Tethany Brethren-Garfield Park Community Hospital in Chicago, Illinois for a pilot project. These initial picturephones lacked clarity and color.[35] Despite demonstrations by high-profile advocates such as Lady Bird Johnson, and videophone scenes in the 1968 classic film "2001: A Space Odyssey," the picturephone never went beyond trial tests in Pittsburgh and Chicago. AT&T attempted to revive the picturephone in 1992, but the cost, as well as the concern about having to "get dressed" to answer the phone, continued to preclude it from being successful. Today, the picturephone is called a videophone, and is experiencing some success, especially with businesses using it for video conferencing. Cell phone companies are developing cellular phones with video screens. A new version of a videophone called ViaTV, is being marketed, which sits atop a television set and displays the picture in color.

In 1971, the National Library of Medicine's Lister Hill National Center for Biomedical Communications funded a field trial in Alaska, choosing 21 sites in an attempt to determine if village health care could be improved through the use of reliable communications technology. The technology chosen for this project was NASA's ATS-1, the first in their series of Applied Technology Satellites. The Alaska Native Medical Center in Anchorage used black and white, one-way television, which received information from satellite ground stations at four rural locations. All sites were supplied with two-way audio. Following the trial, the Institute for Communications Research at Stanford University evaluated the project and found that the satellite system was effective and could be used for most medical problems except for emergency situations. It was also concluded that although the use of video may play a role, there was little measurable difference between the outcomes from the use of video compared to audio consultation.[36]

Interest in telemedicine grew by the 1980s, as costs related to communication technologies decreased.[37] By the early 1980s, the Navy began testing a system to support their personnel while at sea or other remote sites. In 1982, the University Hospital of Cleveland, Ohio and the Intensive Care Unit (ICU) at Forest City

Hospital of Cleveland were using real-time, interactive video for consultations. In the 1980s, telemedical consultations were provided for many major casualties. For example, in 1988, NASA, through the Spacebridge Project, was able to assist with remotely connecting specialists in the United States with Armenian physicians during a massive earthquake that hit the Soviet Republic of Armenia, causing more than 150,000 casualties. With the support of the U.S./U.S.S.R. Joint Working Group on Space Biology, one-way video, voice, and facsimile was used to conduct consultations between a medical center in Yerevan, Armenia and four medical centers in the United States.[38] The North–West Telemedicine Project was created in 1984 in Australia to pilot the Q-Network, a government satellite communications network. The Q-Network, based at the Mount Isa Base Hospital, included 20 two-way and 20 one-way (television receivers only) earth stations. The project provided health services to Aborigines or Torres Strait Islanders in five remote towns south of the Gulf of Carpentaria. Although they were unable to separate the operating costs of the project from other operations of the network, health-care costs were reduced, mostly due to a decrease in travel expenses for routine visits along with fewer emergency situations.[39]

Significant growth in telehealth occurred in the 1990s, with the advancement of underlying technologies. Emerging technologies enabled video, audio, and other imaging information to be transmitted digitally over telephone lines, in lieu of expensive satellites or newly developed cable or fiber-optic lines.

5.2 STATE OF SCIENCE: TODAY'S TELEHEALTH DEVICES

The telehealth approach has been applied to a broad range of clinical specialties. Populations most commonly served include the elderly, individuals living in rural areas, and veterans.[40] In this section, we discuss the devices used today, along with model programs organized by the disease categories for which they were designed.

Cardiac Telehealth

Heart disease is the leading cause of mortality in the United States, and it is the most common reason for hospital admission for people aged 65 years and older (Figure 5.3).[41] The American Heart Association reports that 64.4 million Americans have some form of cardiovascular disease (CVD), including diseases of the heart, stroke, high blood pressure, congestive heart failure, congenital heart failure and other congenital defects, hardening of the arteries, and other diseases of the circulatory system.[42] Americans will pay $368 billion in 2005 for CVD-related medical costs and disability.

Some types of heart disease progress without showing obvious signs or symptoms, making the disease difficult to diagnose, monitor, and treat. Telecardiology is highly effective in not only the diagnosis and treatment of heart disease, but also the essential aspect of disease management.[43] Quality of care can be improved when patients are quickly and accurately diagnosed, ensuring those individuals that require

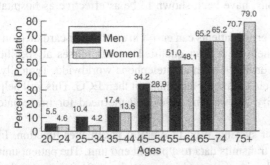

Prevelance of Cardiovascular Diseases in Americans Age 20 and Older by Age and Sex NHANES III:1988–94

Note: These data include CHD, CHF, stroke and hypertension
Source: CDC/NCHS.

Figure 5.3   Prevalence of cardiovascular diseases in Americans age 20 and older by sex and age.

transport to a medical facility receive the necessary services. Telecardiology also allows individuals, who are able to manage their symptoms in their homes, to be provided with the information and means to do so effectively.

Most telecardiology programs are designed for the home environment. Primary cardiology care may include blood pressure management, blood lipid control, and the monitoring of heart functions, all of which can be performed remotely with technology. Electrocardiography (ECG) is widely used for cardiac analysis. A resting 12-lead ECG is used to provide information on rhythm, presence of heart block, previous myocardial infarction, and myocardial hypertrophy and ischemia. The presence of an abnormal ECG supports a clinical diagnosis of coronary artery disease. Tele-echocardiography is the transmission of cardiac ultrasound exams over telecommunication lines, and it is effective and reliable in both resting 12-lead ECG and continuous ambulatory recordings.[44] Telestethoscopy allows the remote physician to auscultate from a distance. Tele-electrocardiography, tele-echocardiography, and telestethoscopy are effective at transmitting diagnostic-quality information.[44–46] Ruling out the possibility of cardiac problems through laboratory tests, referrals to specialists, and other ancillary tests is expensive. Tele-consultation with a cardiologist is simple, reliable, and effective in improving patient treatment and in reducing costs.[47] Teleconsultation prevents unnecessary emergency room visits and reduces hospital admissions.

Cardiac rehabilitation is essential to the management of heart disease. It includes monitoring outpatients' physical activity, as well as providing education and counseling, all of which can be effectively accomplished with a telehealth approach. Individuals who reside in rural or remote areas are often unable to access outpatient facilities for their rehabilitative needs. Over 50% of home nursing visits related to heart failure and hypertension in the United States could be replaced by telehealth visits, with a significant cost savings.[48] Exercise is a vital aspect of cardiac rehabilitation, but is typically provided in rehabilitation facilities where dropout rates are high, due to travel time, scheduling difficulties, and other commitments. Home-based exercise programs using real-time monitoring, which include ECG and interactive voice communications, have been shown to be as effective as hospital outpatient programs.[49,50]

Ambulatory cardiac monitoring patients can enroll in a variety of cardiac monitoring services, which allow them to contact qualified cardiac nurses at specific control centers at any time day or night, from any telephone worldwide. Typically, they will be asked to describe their symptoms and transmit their ECG. This will help the experienced nurse to identify the warning signs and the need for immediate medical emergency care.

There are several different systems used to monitor pacemaker function. In general, the internal pacemaker transmits data to a patient end unit. The patient unit then sends the data either wirelessly or through wires to the receiving center that monitors and analyzes the data. Below is an example of a wireless monitoring system that uses a cell phone like device to transmit data to the receiving center. A system through Medtronic is also described briefly to provide an example of a wired system.

Biotronik Home Monitoring System[51]   The U.S. Food and Drug Administration (FDA) recently approved the Biotronik Home Monitoring System, which transmits data from an implanted pacemaker, through radio-frequency communication to a special wireless cell phone, which then delivers the information to a service center (Figure 5.4). The service center analyzes the data and confidentially forwards it to the patient's doctor. This allows doctors to check patients who have the Biotronik pacemaker between office visits. A benefit of transferring the data to the

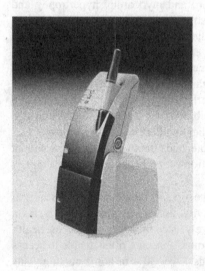

Figure 5.4   Cardio Messenger that receives messages from the implant and sends them to the Biotronik Service Center.

receiving center wirelessly is that it can be done any time and anywhere cell phone service is available. The device is designed to submit information to the service center once each day, but can be programmed to send data whenever the patient is experiencing certain symptoms, such as shortness of breath, dizziness, or an irregular heartbeat. This allows the doctor to more closely monitor the patient and make changes in the treatment plan, should it be required. Because early intervention is essential to the management of heart disease, the ability to report cardiac information from implantable devices linked directly to the internet allows physicians to have more control over many aspects of the early detection and management process.

A nationwide study led by physicians at the Stanford Medical Center in California will determine whether continuous monitoring through the Biotronik system allows the patient's clinician to respond more quickly and more efficiently to their patient's constantly changing cardiac status.

Medtronic Carelink Network   The Medtronic Carelink Network also allows physicians to monitor cardiac patients with internal pacemakers.[52] The patient has a scheduled time that they are to transmit data. At that time, the patient connects the Medtronic CareLink Monitor to a telephone line and presses the monitor's "power" button. The patient then places the monitor's antennae over the implant and the monitor reads and stores the data. Then the monitor dials a phone number and sends the information to a secure server. The clinic uses the internet to view and analyze the data. The health-care provider may use the Medtronic Carelink Programmer to record data for all of their patients with a Medtronic cardiac device. If a patient is experiencing unusual symptoms, the data may be gathered and transmitted at an unscheduled time. Using this system, the patient must be connected to a telephone line to send the data to the receiving center. The person has to connect devices and be in a specific location to transfer data.

There are several different telehealth systems used to collect and analyze electrocardiograms (ECGs) remotely. In general, the systems utilize electrodes that send data to a patient monitoring unit that records ECGs. The data from the monitoring unit is then transferred to the receiving center through either a wired or wireless connection. The receiving center monitors and analyzes the data.

CardioNet's Mobile Cardiac Outpatient Telemetry (MCOT)[53]   The CardioNet technology uses sensors that are invisible under clothing, worn as a pendant or a belt clip, which continuously monitor the patient's ECG during normal daily activities. With continuous monitoring of cardiac activity, the health-care provider gets a better clinical picture of the patient's cardiac status. The sensors constantly communicate with a monitor small enough to fit in a pocket or a purse. The monitor is capable of automatically detecting and transmitting abnormal heart rhythms to the CardioNet monitoring center, where certified cardiac technicians are available all day, every day to analyze the transmissions and respond appropriately. If the patient experiences an episode, they are also able to use the monitor's touch screen to send the data. Physicians receive daily and urgent telemetry reports from the CardioNet monitoring center by fax, mail, or email or remotely accessed through the internet, and they use the data to make diagnoses and treatment decisions. The CardioNet's technology/service is unique in that it detects and transmits events automatically, whether or not patients sense they are occurring. CardioNet, Inc. is a private, venture-backed company headquartered in San Diego.

Cardiolert[54]   The Cardioalert system requires the patient to be very involved and invested in monitoring their cardiac activity. The system is based on proven technology called impedance cardiography. A very small current is passed through the chest and changes are detected by sensors pads: one each on the forehead, neck, chest, and abdomen. These sensor pads are connected to a small impedance monitor device (about the size of a deck of cards) that is plugged into the serial port of a personal computer. After signing on to the Cardiobeat.com website and requesting the "Cardiolert" test, a test collection code is downloaded to the patient's PC for implementation. Two or three tests of 25 heart beats, which last about four minutes, are conducted in two positions: standing and supine position. When completed, the information is transmitted to the website for compilation. The procedure can be conducted anywhere, and there is a version of the product that supports store and forward testing where there is no access to the Internet. Once the data is received by the server, it is processed into reports that can be transmitted immediately or stored. The patient is sent a summary of the report with a brief explanation about the results. If requested by the patient, the results will be sent to their physician immediately. The physician evaluates the information for diagnosis and treatment. "Cardiolert" (Figure 5.5) enables individuals to take greater responsibility for their own cardiovascular health management and provides readily available direct access to their cardiovascular health history at a moments notice, for themselves and for their physician.

Medic4All[55] *(www.medic4all.com)*   The Medic4All is a telehealth system that remotely monitors several physiological parameters, including the pulse wave from the radial artery, monitored through a wireless wristwatch-like sensor. The pulse wave is used to determine heart and respiration rates. The sensor transmits heart and respiration rates through a wireless gateway, installed in a nearby location in the patient's home, to a medical call center computer. At the call center, medical personnel analyze the transmitted signals to identify heart rate irregularities, respiration rate, and other vital signs. Moreover, the center has the medical history of the patients' vital signs for comparison. The gateway can also serve as a speakerphone or a videoconferencing unit providing interactive communication between the patient and the medical staff at the call center.

The accuracy of this new technology was tested on two groups of patients undergoing cardiac catheterization, as well as on healthy patients in their homes. A group of 44 patients had the sensor fastened to their left wrist, and vital signs were recorded continuously throughout the catheterization. Simultaneously, regular ECG and intraarterial blood pressure monitoring was conducted and sampled against the sensor's data. A second group of 100 healthy patients utilized the sensors in their own homes, with ECG and spirometer devices connected as well. The patients were instructed to sit down, push the activation button on the wrist sensor, and remain still during the measurement procedure. These signals were wirelessly transmitted

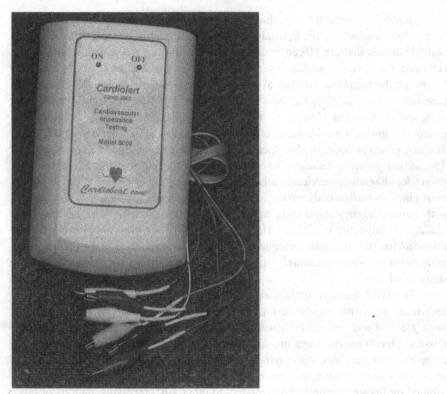

Figure 5.5   The Cardiolert.

via the gateway to a server and stored in a file. ECG and spirometer measurements were collected at the same time and stored in a separate file. The mean heart rate measurements from the wrist-worn sensor's pressure signal, along with the measurements from the ECG and spirometer signals, were then plotted against each other for all 144 patients. The Medic4All system measurements were highly correlated to measurements performed with standard ECG and spirometer devices, suggesting that this could be a promising, noninvasive tool for monitoring vital signs in the home.

Visual Telecommunications Networks, Inc., ViTel Net[56]   ViTel Net provides home and resident care monitoring, as well as clinician-based telemedicine applications. A referring physician or sonographer may transfer echocardiograph clips, full motion videos, and still images to a consulting cardiologist with the Med-Vizer Tele-Echocardiography. The cardiologist is able to examine a patient's heart "hands-free" with remote control cameras and medical device selection tools. Images can be real-time or store and forward, and image analysis is provided to assist with the consultation and consists of measurement using video and still images, plus zooming, magnification, and annotating. Once an interpretation is complete, the consulting cardiologist uses an automated report feature to generate a health assessment report to fax back to the referring facility. This type of system is often used to bring a specialty service to remote or under-served areas.

Aerotel[57] Aerotel's Heartline™ monitors (Figure 5.6), which transmit and receive information, are small, hand-held devices (similar in size to a cellular phone) with electrodes that are placed in designated positions on the patient's body. Once activated, the device modulates the acquired ECG signal and acoustically transmits it through the telephone handset to a medical center. At the center, PC-based ECG receiving station acquires the transmitted ECG in real-time through acoustic coupling and display. The Heartline™ range consists of numerous models divided into groups designed for a wide range of diagnostic and emergency service applications. The first group includes models specifically designed for on-line ECG transmission. The second group is dedicated to off-line ECG recording transmitted via the telephone for diagnostic services. In both groups, the number of electrodes a patient must place on his/her body varies, as do other operational features. When combined with alert/emergency out-dialing equipment, some models offer wireless telephone dialing. Through the use of the Heartline™, continuous heart monitoring can be provided for patients with infrequent arrhythmia, unexplained chest pain, cardiac rehabilitation, post-myocardial infarction follow-up, and drug research or case study monitoring.

The HRS features application software for access and management needs. Individual subscriber files allow for cross-reference breakdowns by type of monitor used, medical and general information parameters, demographics, and ECG transmission. Operational features include instant review of ECG transmission received, comparison to previous transmission of the same subscriber, ECG pattern review, physician's interpretation, and report generation. All information can be printed, distributed by fax, or transmitted via modem to other HRS receiving stations or other destinations for update or consultation. Several systems can also be networked to support a large-scale service operation.

Telecare's ProTime Microcoagulation System[58] American TeleCare's ProTime Microcoagulation System for prothrombin time testing is designed to manage Coumadin therapy at home. This test is done to check the status of patient's oral anti-coagulation therapy. Results are reported in both INR and PT seconds. The

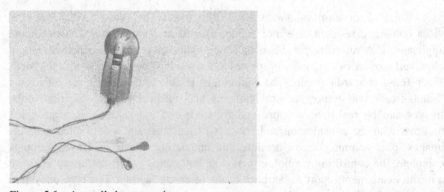

Figure 5.6   Aerotel's heart monitor.

reagents (substances used to run the test) are inside the specially designed cuvette. The patient places a drop and a half of blood in a fresh cuvette to run the test. This device is a peripheral that is wirelessly connected to a patient monitoring station. The patient monitoring station transfers data to the health-care provider through telephone wires.

Ambulatory Blood Pressure Systems[59] Ambulatory blood pressure (ABP) monitoring is becoming a routine procedure in many European countries and is increasing in the United States. Many physicians are using ABP to detect "white coat" hypertension and to adjust drug therapy for their hypertensive patients. Space-labs Medical Ambulatory Blood Pressure Monitoring products (Figure 5.7) are used in pediatric, adolescent, adult, and elderly populations, as well as in diabetic, pregnant, renal, and transplant populations.

Cardionics (www.cardionics.com/productdescriptions.htm) Many companies utilize telecommunications for teaching and education. Learning to recognize heart sounds requires many hours of listening and practice. The physician/instructor must be present to explain the differences in location, pitch, timing, and quality of each sound and murmur. The SimulScope was developed for teaching auscultation at the bedside or in the classroom. It consists of a small, portable, battery-operated infrared transmitter with a low-frequency stethoscope that is taken to the bedside. Each student and the instructor wear a specially designed headphone. The instructor knows exactly what each student is hearing as everyone hears the same patient simultaneously. The SimulScope (Figure 5.8) has a series of discrete filters that allow the accentuation or reduction of eight different frequency bands. This permits the instructor to accentuate a heart murmur or any other sound for purposes of teaching. Sounds can be recorded at the bedside and played back through the SimulScope in the classroom, if desired. The physician can teach multiple students simultaneously with the same patient. Software is provided which allows editing of

Figure 5.7   Spacelab's Ambulatory Blood Pressure System: monitor model 90217 and ABS cuffs.

Figure 5.8   The SimulScope is a bedside auscultation teaching device. It is also used in telemedicine and allows multiple listeners with wireless, infrared headphones.

the recordings to remove unwanted baseline noise. For example, if a patient moves during the final seconds of the recording, then this portion can be edited. If there is excessive baseline noise, the baseline noise can be edited to improve the identification of remaining sounds and murmurs. There is a library of stored sounds, which allows the user to see and hear any common heart sound or murmur. Also, any two sounds recorded from a single patient can be compared. This allows the physician to note any changes that may have occurred.

Cardionics also provides a telecoder for use with their stethoscope systems. It interfaces analog sound and ECG signals to a codec, terminal adapter, or other device that communicates data over a high-speed telephone network, such as T1, ISDN, or DSL. The telecoder can either send or receive serial data. In the send mode, it digitizes the analog signals and converts them to serial data. In the receive mode, it converts the serial data to analog signals. The telecoder can also be used over POTS lines or with IP.

TeleCardio-FBC—Brazil   In Brazil, a telemedicine system called TeleCardio-FBC was developed to allow cardiologists to communicate with other physicians.[60] The purpose of this system is to bring increased access to specialized medical services to people in remote areas. This system is more attractive to sites that are not able to make large financial investments in telemedicine systems. The system uses the internet to provide services. TeleCardio-FBC links cardiologists at the Unidad de Cardiologia e Cirurgia Cardiovascular/Fundacao Bahiana de Cardiologia, a unit of the University hospital, with physicians in remote locations to help them make diagnoses of cardiovascular diseases, set up a treatment plan, and help them follow-up with patients who have been discharged home after hospitalization at the University hospital. Telecardio was originally designed for desktop computers, but now has evolved with third-generation wireless technology to allow mobile utilization.[16] The new mobile system is called TeleCardio Mobile and uses PDAs and cell phones connected to the internet through wireless modems.

Congestive Heart Failure

Many telehealth systems for monitoring patients at home have scales that may be added as peripherals. The scales may be used to monitor fluctuations in body weight, a common practice in managing congestive heart failure. An example of a telehealth system in which the scale is the main component is the Cardiocom Telescale.

Cardiocom[61]   The Cardiocom TELESCALE (Figure 5.9) is used for home monitoring of patients with congestive heart failure (CHF). TELESCALE is an interactive home monitoring device with an electronic scale. TELESCALE'S measurement can provide early detection of as little as 45 ccs of change in fluid volume. TELESCALE attaches to the patient's existing telephone line. Each morning, patients use their Cardiocom TELESCALE to answer a series of questions about their current symptoms and to measure their weight. This is referred to as their "Health Check." The Health Check provides two-way communication between patients and health-care providers and can be customized by a physician for a patient's specific needs. The Health Check data are automatically transmitted over the patient's telephone line directly to the computer server in a physician's office, or to the CARDIO-PLAN nursing staff.

Figure 5.9   The TELESCALE is an interactive home monitoring device integrated with a precision electronic scale.

MindMyHeart is an ongoing Medicare-supported telehealth demonstration project at Georgetown University Medical Center.[62] The project is designed to provide comprehensive care management to patients with congestive heart failure.[63] The program aims to improve the patients' clinical outcomes, quality of life, and satisfaction with care.

Subjects in the program must be 65 years of age or older, have a primary diagnosis of congestive heart failure, have Medicare parts A and B, and have a primary physician who also agrees to participate in the program. The demonstration involves a control group and a treatment group. The control group receives traditional interventions. The treatment group receives a HomMed Sentry Monitor for home use. The monitor alerts the participants at a specified time each day to take measurements of their weight, blood pressure, and pulse oximetry. The monitor also asks a few subjective, "yes" or "no," health-related questions. The data are sent to a Home Med central monitoring station and reviewed by a case manager. The case managers perform routine assessment of the participants regularly, and interventions are implemented when necessary. The case managers utilize a web-based tool to manage day-to-day care of the patients.

Chronic Obstructive Pulmonary Disease (COPD)

Remote monitoring of COPD uses many of the home-care telehealth systems with a spirometer attachment or accessory. Some examples of spirometers that attach to home-care systems follow.

AMD 3920 Digital Spirometer   This is a PC-based spirometer able to test expiratory reserve volume (amount of air forcibly expired at the end of a normal expiration), relaxed vital capacity (maximum amount of air that can be expelled starting at full lung capacity), forced vital capacity (total volume of air that can be exhaled during a forced expiration after a maximum inspiration), forced expiratory volume, peak expiratory flow, and maximal voluntary ventilation.

The Veterans Administration in Boston uses a telephone-linked computer system to monitor patients with COPD in their homes.[64] The patients call the automated system one time per week and answer questions generated by the system. A phone call typically takes 5 to 10 minutes. The computer asks questions about symptoms the patient has been experiencing in the last week and about the severity of the symptoms. The computer generates questions based on the patient's previous answers. The computer also asks questions about the patient's medication regimen and compliance to the treatment plan. In addition, the patients are instructed to call the system when they think they may be experiencing respiratory symptoms. After this type of call, the system sends a fax to the patient's physician to alert the doctor of the patient's status. The computer system provides education to the patient during all telephone calls and attempts to catch exacerbations early to prevent hospitalization.

Dermatology

Because it is a visually-based specialty, dermatology is well-suited for the telehealth arena. Advances in technology permit accurate viewing of skin images electronically, making teledermatology more feasible. Teledermatology has become more widely utilized, but its impact has not been clarified.[65] As the rates of malignant melanoma continue to rise, early diagnosis and excision are essential for effective treatment.[66] Dermoscopy is a method of examination of cutaneous lesions with an incident light magnification system and fluid at the skin magnifying lens interface.[67] Dermoscopy can be acquired through the use of a regular digital camera and special dermoscopy attachment (Figure 5.10).

A University of Pennsylvania study sought to determine if dermatologists could effectively assess a patient's need for a biopsy using teledermatology, compared to face-to-face assessment.[68] A primary care physician recruited 61 subjects with skin growths requiring dermatologist diagnosis. Forty-nine completed the study. The primary care physician took digital photographs of the growths using the maximum zoom with an Olympus D-600L camera, which provided images with a resolution of 1280 × 1024 pixels. An overlay grid was placed next to some of the images to allow measurement of the growth. The images were transmitted from the primary care physician to the dermatologist via email. The subjects also met in-person with a dermatologist within a month of their teledermatology appointment. The teledermatologist reported back to the primary care physician the diagnosis and whether a biopsy was indicated. The primary care physician then put the teledermatologists response in a sealed envelope. The face-to-face dermatologist completed the assessment and filled out a consultation form including the diagnosis and whether a biopsy was indicated. Then he opened the envelope containing the teledermatologist's diagnosis and decision on biopsy. If either the teledermatologist or in-person dermatologist decided the growth needed to be biopsied, the in-person dermatologist performed a biopsy at their assessment session. There was 100% agreement between the teledermatologist and the face-to-face dermatologist in their decision to biopsy. The teledermatologist was usually available to patients within 7 days for assessment, and the wait time to see a dermatologist face-to-face was about a month.

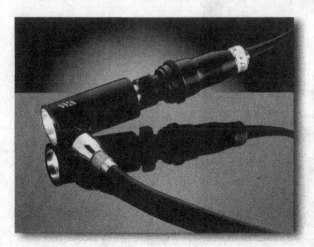

Figure 5.10 Dermascope: The AMD-2030 is a skin surface contact microscope for use in primary care, pediatrics, or dermatology. Manufactured for AMD by Welch Allyn.

As with most telehealth clinical specialties, there are two basic modes of consultations: Store and forward teledermatology utilizes digital images and clinical information that are obtained at a prescribed time and place, then forwarded to the physician for diagnosis; video teleconferencing provides synchronous video and audio communications for a live and interactive consultation between the patient and dermatologist. Each method has advantages and disadvantages.[69] Advantages of store and forward teledermatology include practicality, low cost, and the fact there is no need for a consulting physician to be available at the same time as the patient and referring physician. The disadvantages are that the consulting physician can only work with the images provided and is unable to ask for more clinical information or to reposition or palpate the lesion site to aid in diagnosis. The main advantage of video teleconferencing is that it can emulate a face-to-face consultation and allows for the specialist to ask the referring physician and patient clinical questions. Its disadvantages are the expense and the fact that it requires coordination between the physicians and the patient.

Apollo's Telemedicine System[70]   Apollo's Teledermatology system combines a dermatology examination camera with Apollo's Windows Image Management System and Apollo's Video Conferencing Module (Figure 5.11). Combining this hand-held camera with the capability of sending still and full motion imaging allows a remote site to send a wide variety of dermatologic images from any angle. The camera provides power zoom, freeze frame, integrated light, and auto focus, and it uses light polarization to eliminate reflection from surface skin to diagnosis. A special dermascope camera for viewing melanomas is also available.

Figure 5.11 The AMD-2500 general examination camera combines power zoom, auto focus, freeze frame, and electronic image polarization in one diagnostic device.

Radiology

Because this is mostly a diagnostic service which relies on imaging, with little patient contact, teleradiology, along with telepathology, is one of the most well-established clinical specialties in the telehealth area.[71] The American College of Radiology–National Electronic Manufacturers Association has agreed on a set of standards for teleradiology, which have facilitated the acceptance and implementation of programs. These standards address image quality and how images are submitted, examined, and interpreted. Established industry-wide standards such as these have been important for third-party reimbursement in the field of teleradiology.[72]

Rehabilitation

The 2000 U.S. Census report estimates that approximately one in five Americans has a significant disability that limits functional ability in activities of daily living (eating, dressing, bathing, toileting, grooming) and impacts their ability to work and participate in the community.[73] As the number of persons with disabilities increases due to factors such as aging and increased survival rates for illnesses and injuries, the challenge of providing rehabilitation also increases.[74]

Telerehabilitation is defined as the remote delivery of rehabilitation services through consultation, training and education, monitoring, and long-term care of individuals with disabilities using telecommunications technology. The focus of telerehabilitation is to increase access to rehabilitation services and to allow individuals to remain safe and independent in their home. Typically, rehabilitation focuses on individuals with impaired motor, cognitive, perceptual, and social abilities and assists them with regaining function or providing compensatory strategies to enhance participation in work-related activities, community activities, and personal relationships. Outpatient or home health therapy is usually provided over an extended period of time, with the goal of increasing strength, endurance, and functional abilities necessary to complete such activities of daily living as dressing, grooming, bathing, toileting, and mobility. Telerehabilitation offers clinicians the ability to provide therapy in an environment or setting that is more relevant to the patient: their home.

There are numerous methods for providing telerehabilitation. A recent project for stroke rehabilitation consisted of videoconferencing sites at hospitals and senior community centers where education, exercise programs, and social support were provided. This allowed seniors to view the therapist at the hospital and ask questions about medical management of their disease, rehabilitation methods, risk factors and their management, psychosocial impact of disabilities, available community support, and home and environmental safety. Exercise programs to increase strength and balance were also provided, with the recording of blood pressure and heart rate before and after the exercise.[75]

Virtual reality (VR) has been incorporated in therapy and rehabilitation in a wide range of physical, psychological, and cognitive rehabilitation areas.[76] VR can deliver treatment through precisely controlled, dynamic three-dimensional and interactive methods. By creating a virtual environment (VE) based on a patient's needs and abilities and where success is more achievable, the therapeutic value of reha-bilitation can be improved.[77] Current advances in computer speed and power, graph-ics and imaging, interface devices, movement tracking, and voice recognition have supported the development of VR systems. Typically, patients are provided with high-resolution, head-mounted displays (HMD) with tracking systems. A connec-tion can be made directly to a rehabilitation facility or through an internet-based company that provides the prescribed software. Most applications are games that require the patient to engage in reaching with arms and hands and proper position-ing for increased range of motion, strength, and motor dexterity. Programs can also focus on perceptuomotor activities, visual tracking, selective attention, and other mental or visual challenges. Information from these programs can be sent directly to the rehabilitation facility to track and monitor progress. Cybersickness and per-ceptuomotor after-effects have been reported as potential side effects from the use of VR, particularly with the HMD-delivered applications.[78] Although the potential for increased use of VR telerehabilitation may exist, there remain practical chal-lenges for clinicians, health-care providers, and users before this will become an established practice.[76]

Other applications for telerehabilitation have included distance consultation by clinical rehabilitation specialists for seating and positioning, provision of and monitoring the use of assistive technology,[79] or remote stroke or brain injury reha-bilitation management and teleconsultation by physiatrists and therapists utilizing videoconferencing systems.[80]

Ophthalmology

Diabetic retinopathy (DR) is the leading cause of blindness and visual impairment in adults in developed societies.[81] Approximately 2% of all individuals who have diabetes become blind after 15 years, and severe visual impairment develops in nearly 10% of individuals with diabetes. Early diagnosis of DR before visual loss has occurred is essential.

Advances in technology and improvements in digital cameras have made it possible to accurately capture retinal images and transmit them over the internet for diagnosis and grading of DR. The presence or absence of DR can be correctly assessed by inspection of the images.[82] Agreement has also been found between retinopathy gradation made from the images and the gradation made by direct exam-ination of the eyes. In addition to the ease of diagnosis for the physician, digital pho-tography requires low illumination; therefore, patients may not need to have their eyes dilated for examination. This results in quicker recovery time, ability to drive themselves, and less time from work or home.

Psychiatry

Based on a 1999 report of the American Telemedicine Service Providers, telepsy-chiatry is one of the most frequently utilized applications of telemedicine, with an estimation of over 12,000 consults conducted annually in the United States.[83] In a study conducted to evaluate the health outcomes and costs associated with telepsychiatry, there were no significant differences found between face-to-face psychiatric care and telepsychiatry in the areas of well-being and quality of life.[84] This study also determined that costs associated with telepsychiatric care were less than conventional psychiatric care. Telepsychiatry has been used extensively with the prison population as an effective way to deliver mental health services.[85] Telepsychiatry has also demonstrated benefits in the management of negative emotions for cardiac patients. Patients who reside in remote areas, and who have been prescribed home-based cardiology rehabilitation programs, have reported significant reduction in mental stress and improved self-confidence through receiving remote counseling.[86] Because interpersonal relations, body language, and other physical signs are essential in this area, real-time or synchronous exchanges appear to be the preferred mode of telecommunication.

Several studies have documented the reliability of telepsychiatry compared to face-to-face intervention. Ruskin et al. conducted a study to compare outcomes of depressed adults treated through telepsychiatry and depressed adults treated in-person.[87] Patients improved significantly on the Hamilton depression scale, and they did not differ significantly from each other. There was no significant difference between groups, and both groups improved significantly from baseline in scores on the Beck Depression Inventory, the GAF, the state anxiety scale, the CGI, and the Short Form Health Survey. One study assessed children through face-to-face interviews and also through telepsychiatry.[88] One group received telepsychiatry first and then face-to-face evaluation, and the other group received the interventions in reverse order. There was 96% agreement in diagnosis and treatment regimen between videoconferencing and face-to-face intervention.

Baigent et al. and Ruskin et al. in separate studies also found high inter-rater reliability in diagnosing clients comparing video consulting with face-to-face interviews.[89,90] Twenty-six participants were given face-to-face and telepsychiatric assessments on the same day.[91] Half of the participants received the face-to-face consultation first, and the other half received telepsychiatry first. The researchers used two desktop video conferencing units that were connected by ISDN at 128 kbps. During each session, the participant completed cognitive assessments. The correlation between the Quick Test results was .80, for the National Adult Reading Test the correlation was .97, and for the Information Processing A the correlation was .75. The researchers state that an increased bandwidth would decrease time delay and may increase reliability.

Several studies have reported on the reliability of telepsychiatry with different types of equipment. Quality of equipment may impact reliability. Montani et al. reported that good audio and video transmission is necessary for effective telepsychiatry consultations.[92] Chae et al. and Zarate et al. in separate studies found the use of a low-bandwidth system (128 kbps) produced "motion echoes."[93,94] Motion echoes were considerably reduced with use of higher bandwidth (384 kbps). Live interviews, low-bandwidth video conferencing, and high-bandwidth video conferencing were all found equally reliable for assessment of global severity and positive symptoms of schizophrenia; however, assessing negative symptoms was less reliable using low-bandwidth equipment. Yoshino et al. found that telepsychiatry using a narrow bandwidth resulted in a lower correlation of positive symptoms with total score than a live interview, while use of a broad bandwidth was more similar to the live interview.[95]

Several studies have addressed patient and staff satisfaction with telepsychiatry. Bose et al. found that the majority of their subjects preferred telepsychiatry services to waiting or traveling for a face-to-face interview.[96] Brodey et al. and Ruskin et al. found that patient satisfaction was similar for both a telepsychiatry approach and in-person interviews.[97,98] Kennedy and Yellowless found that patients using a telepsychiatry approach were moderately or greatly helped in treatment management: Ninety eight percent of patients wanted to have the option of using videoconferencing along with local services.[99] Elford et al. studied children with mental illness, their parents and staff.[88] While the staff and parents were satisfied with the telepsychiatry approach, they preferred face-to-face contact. The children were satisfied with the use of video-teleconferencing. Interviewers preferred face-to-face interviews, but this may have been related to their use of low-bandwidth equipment.[100]

Three studies have reported functional outcomes with the use of telepsychiatry. Rohland examined the use of telepsychiatry in a general mental health population using a mixed design with one group receiving telepsychiatry and face-to-face intervention, a second group receiving only telepsychiatry, and a third group receiving only face-to-face interviews.[101] Global Assessment of Functioning (GAF) scores varied very little for the group as a whole, but GAF scores improved more for the telepsychiatry-only group and the face-to-face interview-only group. D'Souza studied the use of telepsychiatry in discharging patients from an inpatient psychiatric hospital.[102] One group used videoconferencing during discharge planning, followed by psycho-educational programming. A comparison group received conventional discharge planning and no psycho-educational programming. Participants in the videoconferencing group had less frequent re-hospitalizations, experienced fewer medication side effects, and had better treatment compliance. Zaylor did a retrospective review of two groups of patients diagnosed with schizoaffective disorder or major depression.[103] One group was seen in an outpatient clinic, the other group was seen using telepsychiatry. There was no significant difference in GAF scores between the two groups.

The American Psychiatric Association (APA) provides equipment guidelines for videoconferencing.[104] The major components of a system include monitors, cameras, coder–decoder or CODEC, a desktop computer, microphones, speakers, and other audiovisual technology such as videophones. Many different camera options are available for videoconferencing. Options include fixed lens cameras, cameras that zoom in and out, cameras that pan around the room, remote site cameras that may be controlled by the psychiatrist at the health facility, and document cameras to transmit written materials. The coder–decoder or CODEC turns the picture picked up by the camera into a digital signal and compresses it. The compression algorithms are responsible for the quality of the signal received. The CODEC also turns the digital signal back to an analog signal that is viewed as a picture on the monitor. Appropriate bandwidth for telepsyhchiatry is between 128 and 384 kbps according to the APA. The lower bandwidth may be used successfully in many clinical applications, but the higher bandwidth may be necessary to capture more detailed information required in some situations. In addition, higher-quality microphones and speakers will facilitate optimal audio communication.

Email Crisis Intervention   The internet continues to play a key role in providing health information, diagnostics, and purchasing of pharmaceuticals. Email is currently being utilized as a modality for crisis intervention in the mental health arena. The use of email provides rapid response, accessibility, and practical, effective interventions. Polauf (1997) reported on the aspects of email-based crisis intervention, and he defined it as "time-limited counseling that is structured into distinct stages, with concrete goals and problem-solving exercises, and the overall mission is to return the individual to pre-crisis, stabilized behavior."[105] He also makes an important distinction that this type of intervention is different than trauma services, which typically require hospitalization or immediate response hotlines.

Surgery

Telesurgery has been utilized effectively for mentoring and educational sessions. Through telecommunications, surgeons receive consultative advice from specialists, videos are utilized during difficult operative procedures, students receive training from specialists, and updated and enhanced surgical procedures are easily provided to hospitals for education.[106]

The first major telesurgery involved surgeons in New York removing the gallbladder of a woman in France in 2001 through the use of robotic arms.[107,108] The procedure involved two medical teams linked through video and high-speed fiber-optic connection. The surgery was successful and without complications.

The Brady Urological Institute at Johns Hopkins Medical Institute is involved in telesurgery for the purpose of mentoring surgeons in other countries.[109] They are also researching the use of robotics in surgery, a necessary component in performing surgery remotely unless the goal of the telesurgery is in mentoring surgeons in another location. The researchers use 4 ISDN lines to establish an audio and video connection with a remote medical facility, to have remote control of the electrocautery machine and surgical instruments, and to control the position of the camera.

Currently, telesurgery is mainly limited to mentoring and education applications because the reliability of the communication connections and time delay interfere with safely operating on a patient remotely.[110] A feasibility study performed in 2002 sought to demonstrate that remote surgery could be performed safely. The patient was a 68-year-old woman who received a laproscopic cholecystectomy. The Zeus system was used in the operation. The surgeon remotely operated two robotic arms that manipulated instruments and a third arm that moved the endoscopic camera. The surgeon and the patient were connected through asynchronous transfer mode technology, which has a low transport delay and low packet loss ratio. A backup connection of exactly the same type was also established for emergency use. The robot motion data was guaranteed a rate of 512 kbps and the video packets were guaranteed 7 Mbps. The operation took 54 minutes. There were no complications and no interruptions in data transfer and communication. The authors identified several limitations in performing remote surgeries. One limitation is that most hospitals are not equipped with asynchronous transfer mode technology. Another limitation is the cost of the system; the authors stated that a robotic machine costs about 1 million dollars. Another issue is malpractice because the patient may be in one state or country and the surgeon in another creating conflicts of jurisdiction. Currently, operating on a patient remotely on a boat or on a space station is not possible due to time delay in using a satellite connection.

Diabetes

Education programs for diabetes care are effective in encouraging self-management, which leads to improvement in diabetes control and fewer diabetes-related complications.[111,112] Unfortunately, patients residing in rural areas, or who are ill and unable to travel, must overcome the barriers in receiving face-to-face education or consultation for their diabetic condition. Telediabetes has the potential to increase access to education and consultation for improved diabetic care. The use of technology to provide diabetic education reduces staff time, reduces expense of travel for patients, and improves patient compliance with fewer missed appointments.[113]

A review of the literature shows that many telediabetes programs utilize real-time transmission of diabetes education material from a diabetic center at a district hospital to local health-care clinics. Programs such as these provide a means for community nurses in primary care clinics to link with nurse specialists in larger hospitals, and they enable interactive education to groups of individuals in lieu of one-on-one encounters. Digital images of diabetic wounds can be successfully stored and forwarded for evaluation.[114,115] Videophones have been used for interactive discussions and to send still images for assessment of wounds.[116] Real-time two-way video is also useful in the reduction of costs for evaluation and management of lower-extremity ulcerations, which are often a complication from unmanaged diabetes.[117] Individuals, from the comfort of their homes, can also submit information daily on their blood glucose levels, injected insulin, meals, and exercise in a device that stores and forwards the data via modem to a diabetes center for review and necessary action.[118] Diabetic patient outcomes and compliance are improved when there is collaboration between the patient and health-care provider, and telemedicine provides a means for increasing this collaboration.[119,120]

MyDiabetes Team is a program at Georgetown University that focuses on improving health outcomes for people with diabetes through the use of telehealth.[121] The participants in the program use electronic blood glucose meters and personal computers to transfer their readings weekly over the Internet to a secure database.[122] The database is protected by a firewall and authentication techniques to prohibit unauthorized access. The participants and their practitioners have access to the information using standard web browser technologies. After the data are transmitted, participants and practitioners are automatically notified if their measurements are outside an acceptable range. Practitioners also provide feedback to the patient regarding their readings and blood glucose status and trends. Through MyDiabetes Team, practitioners are able to catch problems earlier because they have access to the participant's data between visits. The participant and the practitioner are also able to communicate through secure instant messaging regarding glucose readings or other issues related to diabetes care.

A pilot study was conducted to assess the impact of the MyDiabetes Team program on HbA1c. Participants in the study included 18 patients age 18–65 with diabetes. The participants were split into two groups depending on how often they checked their data on-line. They were divided for data analysis purposes into heavy or light users. As one complete group, the reduction of HbA1c by 2.22 percentage points was significant. The heavy users had a reduction in HbA1c by 3.15 percentage points, which was also significant. The light users, however, had a reduction of 1.28 percentage points, which was not significant.

Emergency Medical Services

Ambulances can now use a wireless telemedicine system that transmits vital signs (such as blood pressure and pulse) and video of a patient to the hospital. The hospital is able to see the patient's condition in real-time during ambulance transport. The system uses wireless digital cellular communications and in-hospital intranet technologies.

Life Support for Trauma and Transport (LSTAT) was created for use by the military because of increased medical evacuation times during the Gulf War due to rapidly advancing military troops.[123] LSTAT can also be used in civilian situations to stabilize a patient before transporting them to a medical facility, decrease evacuation time, and expedite in-hospital care. LSTAT is a portable intensive care unit, which contains a ventilator, defibrillator, three-channel infusion pump, oxygen, rapid infusion pump, suction device, blood chemistry analyzer, and physiologic monitor. Each component in the LSTAT is connected to the LSTAT computer system and has its own IP address. The data may be downloaded, locally displayed, or transferred to another location for analysis.

The data stored on the LSTAT hard drive can be remotely downloaded using a password-protected file transfer protocol (FTP) application. This helps to ensure that other FTP applications do not access patient information inappropriately. The LSTAT can be secured to a stretcher for patient transport. It has a rechargeable battery that can be hooked up to a variety of different power sources. With the LSTAT the clinician is able to monitor the patient, monitor the LSTAT mechanical status (platform temperature, oxygen supply levels, and battery charge status), and monitor all device settings. Typically, device settings were not altered during transport because equipment was not easily accessible as it was secured for safety. With the LSTAT having compact devices and a secondary display, the clinician is more able to make changes to address small problems before they become big problems.

Previously all documentation was completed by hand. With the LSTAT device settings and patient status are automatically recorded, which leaves the clinician free to evaluate and treat the patient. The secondary display of the LSTAT can be used for electronic documentation using a keypad or screen-pen touch technology. The electronic documentation reduces duplicate information from different health professionals, which is more efficient.

The LSTAT is priced at about $165,000 and can be leased for about $125 per day. For this price the company gets the LSTAT, an equipment bag (with a second display and user's manual), adaptor cables, complete patient disposable supply prepack, stretcher, reusable shipping container, familiarization training course, and 12-month warranty.

A study of time from diagnosis to treatment using the LSTAT versus traditional equipment found no difference in the time to diagnose or treatment between the LSTAT and the traditional equipment. This was expected because the LSTAT is made up of traditional equipment components in a portable design.

The LSTAT has been used in many civilian transport experiences. A mother and infant were transported in western Alaska to a larger medical facility, a critically ill spectator at a speedway in Fontana, California was transported to a local trauma center, and a crew member at the Long Beach Grand Prix was stabilized and transported. The LSTAT was part of the equipment used by the Championship Auto Racing Team's medical team in Laguna Seca, California and at Glen Helen Raceway in California to stabilize and transport an injured motocross rider.

In Canada, the Integrated Emergency Medicine Network (IEMN) program uses mobile satellite technology to provide emergency response capabilities with real-time communication and patient data transfer. Through the mobile satellite connection patient information may be transmitted, health-care providers may communicate, and the location of the ambulance may be tracked.

Home Care

The number of home health-care referrals, as well as the cost of providing home health-care services, has increased significantly in the past 10 years.[124] This provides an impetus for health-care organizations to seek more efficient and less costly methods for providing these types of services. Using telemedicine technology, video visits and monitoring of vital signs can be accomplished electronically, medication compliance can be verified, and patient education can be enhanced.[125] Through the use of telecommunications, medical technology, and computer devices, telehomecare can remotely monitor individuals within their home environments, including those with chronic diseases such as congestive heart failure or diabetes, provide medical services at home to high-risk patients who are at risk during transport to the hospital or doctors offices, or provide access to health-care providers for persons with disabilities. Telehomecare has shown promise in decreasing home health-care costs, as well as cost savings through the elimination or reduction of providers' travel costs.[126,127] Numerous telemonitoring programs have reported decreased emergency room visits, reduced hospital admissions and hospital bed days of care, and decreased hospital readmission rates.[128–130]

Some important issues related to home monitoring include the patient's ability to use the technology, acceptance of the technology, and the sense of intrusiveness that may occur with home monitoring. One of the most important considerations is compatibility of the technology with the patient and their abilities.[131,132] Patients are more willing to accept technology in their homes if they have prior experience with it, and if the experience was positive, which increases their sense of control over the technology. Acceptance of technology increases when it is promoted as applicable to the patient's health and well-being, when the length of time and frequency of interaction with the technology is limited, and if the technology is less visible or less apparent in the home.[132,133]

The ability to have chronically ill patients check in with a health-care provider every day and answer questions about their current symptoms allows for immediate intervention. Numerous Telehomecare devices have been developed to allow health-care providers the ability to manage follow-up care of the chronically ill. This technology allows patients to sit in the comfort of their own homes while health-care providers conduct routine and comprehensive medical monitoring procedures in their offices. Many of these units utilize telephone lines, and they can be specifically tailored to the patient's individual disease state and comorbidities. Data are automatically recorded and transferred through regular telephone lines to a monitoring service center. The information allows for monitoring of patient adherence to medication regimens, as well as tracking blood pressure readings, weight, and other medical parameters (such as blood glucose levels, oxygen saturation, and pulmonary function tests).

One example of this type of technology is Aerotel's Medical Parameters Monitoring (MPM) devices (Figure 5.12), which allow data to be stored for immediate consultation and treatment, as well as for future reference. The health-care provider can set individual alarm values for each patient. Aerotel's system provides supporting software and operators at a central monitoring service center. Operators ensure that the information is entered into the computerized patient files, and they can immediately notify health-care providers if a specific physiologic parameter has been flagged. Patient data can be presented in graph form, and a report can be generated if needed.

QRS Diagnostic[134]   QRS Diagnostic offers patented PC Card devices that turn personal home computers, laptops, or hand-held computers into medical

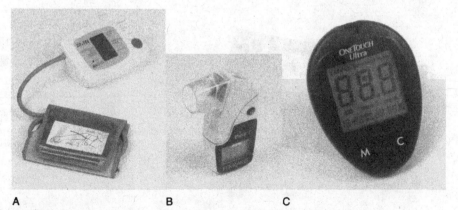

A   B   C

Figure 5.12   Aerotel's blood pressure monitor (a), spirometer (b), and glucometer for home monitoring (c).

devices, including Spirometry, Oximetry, and ECG (Figure 5.13). QRS also provides patient management software for understanding physiological data. This technology turns computers on a web-based network into full-function medical devices simply by sliding a QRS PC Card device into the PC Card drive of an existing network workstation. Access to test results is provided to the patient, and the data are stored real-time in a central database.

Cardiocom's CARESTAR (Figure 5.14) uses a "tree branching" Smart Logic System that automatically adapts health questions based on each answer entered by the patient. Severity scoring identifies the patients most in need of immediate intervention for the case manager. CARESTAR can also monitor such parameters as temperature, peak flow, oxygen saturation, blood pressure, and blood glucose.

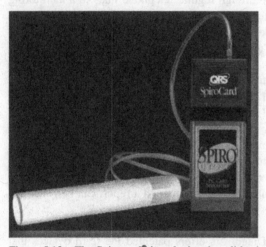

Figure 5.13 The Spirocard® is a device that slides into a PC card drive of a laptop, desktop, or hand-held PC making it a fully functioning spirometer.

Figure 5.14 CARESTAR is a home monitoring device for multiple disease states that require interactive symptom monitoring.

CARESTAR has a scoring system that identifies patients in need of intervention so that treatment can be initiated quickly.

Well@home Telemanagement System from Patient Care Technologies, Inc.[135]   The *Well@home* device has an interactive function similar to a bank ATM. This technology reminds patients to take their medication; instructs patients through text, illustrations, and the spoken word on what, when, and how to take their medication; asks patients if they would like to learn more about their medication; provides administration, purpose, side effect, and storage information to the patient; and documents the date, time, and the amount of medication the patient took. *Well@home* provides patients with health education tailored to their clinical needs, collects information about patient compliance with specific medical orders, and assesses their comprehension of the educational information, as well as their clinical status. The system contains "clinical alerts" that allow the agency to identify specific events that need to be brought to a clinician's attention. *Well@home* incorporates physiological measurement devices to collect patient vital signs such as a digital scale, sphygmomanometer, glucometer, pulse oximeter, electrocardiogram/respiration, and thermometer. Physician orders are automatically sent to *Well@home* to (a) ensure that the device accurately reflects the patient's current treatment program and (b) decrease manual or duplicate data entry. Data collected by *Well@home* is accessible to clinicians through their office or home computers.

American TeleCare® Telehealth System[136]   This system also utilizes telephone lines to connect patient stations with provider stations, but it allows for real-time, two-way personal conversations via an integrated camera, video monitor, microphone, and speakerphone. The video patient monitoring systems can be customized with various medical peripherals including a stethoscope, blood pressure and pulse meter, glucometer, pulse oximeter, digital scale, and digital thermometer. This combination of the live, two-way audio/video system and the medical peripherals allows the health-care provider to assess a patient's health status through real-time pictures. This technology provides either a movable color video camera or high-resolution digital snapshots to give health-care providers the ability to assess such areas as surgical incisions, wound care, skin conditions, and edema. The Telehealth System also manages patient data through the TeleChart®/Patient Record Manager software, which transmits information to the provider and provides permanent data storage.

American TeleCare® also provides a one-way monitoring station developed for patients with such chronic conditions as heart failure, diabetes, COPD, and hypertension. The monitoring station is placed in the patient's home where it gathers objective (numeric) and subjective patient information. It reminds patients to take their vital signs and/or physiological measurements (including blood pressure, pulse, weight, temperature, blood glucose, oxygen saturation levels, and blood coagulation) through available peripherals if recommended. The monitoring station asks the patient a series of simple clinician selected questions relating to their health-care status. After the monitoring session is completed, the system connects via the patient's telephone line to the NX Server to upload data into the patient's record. Patients can also utilize wireless connections to submit data to the NX Server. The NX Server can either store the measurements in its electronic medical record (EMR) TeleChart® database or forward the measurement data to a third-party EMR database via a Health Level Seven® (HL7) interface.

Should a patient require more specific and frequent symptom monitoring, American TeleCare® offers a Disease Management (DM) monitoring station. The DM Monitoring Station guides the patient through their disease-specific program(s) containing a series of questions about their health status and self-management habits, reminds them to take their vital signs and/or other physiological measurements, and then takes them through education modules including reinforcing questions. The DM monitoring station includes a modular algorithm building tool for patients with multiple diseases including congestive heart failure, COPD, diabetes, chronic depression, hypertension, and palliative care. The DM station captures, stores, and transmits patient responses using branching logic, whereby the patient's response to certain questions determines the path of the algorithm. Patients answer health questions using a touch screen and take physiological measurements (such as vital signs), which are captured via wired or wireless medical peripheral connections or through manual entry of measurements. The NX Server Software™ located on the American TeleCare Provider Station automatically prioritizes patient responses based on stratification established by the provider, using a color coding system.

I-Trax Health Management Solutions[137]   *Health-e-Coordinator*™ is a web-based application designed to support disease management, patient care management, education, and referral according to current published clinical guidelines. This system manages the care of patients by connecting all health-care professionals involved with that patient. This application is connected to another web-based platform called the *MyFamilyMD*™. This application was designed to allow a patient to record his or her daily health routine, including medications, allergies, exercise, and achievement of health goals, as well as collaborate, via a secure and confidential messaging system, with their health-care provider. With permission, health-care providers are able to access patients' personal health records kept in the MyFamilyMD™ application. *CarePrime*® is a web-based communication tool for physicians and their staff that permits secure messaging between the physicians, their staff, and patients and facilitates on-line appointment requests and referrals.

I-talk™ is specifically designed to interact with individuals through the telephone using conversational speech recognition. I-talk™ technology is a disease intervention program that monitors patient compliance, collects data between office visits in an effort to reduce data entry costs, provides access to data for analysis, and offers access for patients from any location any time of the day or week.

MyNurseLine™ is a technology-enabled, clinical nurse triage service that is available 24 hours per day, 7 days per week. It allows for assessment of callers' condition, triaging them to the appropriate level of care ranging from emergency care referral to guided self-care at home. By utilizing state-of-the-art information technology, MyNurseLine™ provides consumers with health and wellness information through I-trax's Care Communications Center.

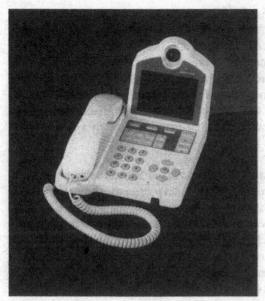

Figure 5.15   The AMD-9940 Video Phone is as familiar and easy to operate as a telephone and has a speaker phone function for hands-free operation.

Videophones are also very useful devices for home monitoring (Figure 5.15). AMD Telemedicine, Inc.[138] offers both video communication and data transmission capabilities in its design. It supports connection to an integrated electronic stethoscope allowing real-time transmission of heart, lung, and bowel sounds. The medical professional can use video to guide anatomical placement for accuracy of audio. The videophone facilitates a face-to-face relationship between caregiver and patient. This capability allows monitoring patient compliance to medications and prescribed regimens, allows the health-care provider to make medication adjustments, provides timely medical intervention to minimize acute events requiring emergency room visits, and even lends emotional support for coping with chronic and acute illness.

TERVA: System for Long-Term Monitoring of Wellness at Home   The Terva system was created to monitor psychological and physiological data as indicators of wellness in the home environment. If clients experience an illness, the TERVA can monitor their progress and the effects of treatment. The Terva system consists of a laptop computer, blood pressure monitor, thermometer, RRI (time between 2 consecutive R waves of ECG) and activity monitor, scale, static charge sensitive bed, diary, and software. The system guides the client through taking the blood pressure measurement with the semiautomatic monitor. The arm cuff reports heart rate as well as blood pressure. The client takes the auxiliary temperature with the thermometer while being guided through the process by the computer software program. The RRI and activity monitor measures beat-to-beat heart rate through an electrode belt worn around the chest and motor activity through a piezoelectric accelerometer. A digital scale that automatically transfers the measurement to the computer measures the client's body weight. The static charge-sensitive bed monitors heart rate and other "ballistocardiographic parameters," respiratory rate and amplitude, and movements while the client is in bed. The bed could also perform sleep stage classification. Data from the bed are automatically stored whenever the client goes to bed during the programmed recording period. Through the structured diary the client tracks emotional and psychosocial wellness and intake of alcohol, tobacco, coffee, and tea. The client must initiate taking all of the measurements—except for the bed measurement, which starts on its own. The software will alert the person when a measurement needs to be performed.[139]

Low ADL Monitoring Program　A Department of Veteran's Affairs Community Care Coordination Service clinical demonstration project uses home monitoring and communication technology to address the needs of veterans who are dependent in some aspect of activities of daily living (ADL).[140] The project utilizes a combination of traditional and advanced technologies to promote independence and help the veterans maintain the skills they need to remain at home. The target population for LAMP includes veterans with decreased functional status who require personal assistance with at least two basic ADLs (eating, bathing, dressing, toileting, transferring, and mobility). Institutional care and other health-care utilization is reduced through the use of LAMP services.

Veterans are monitored through one of three technologies, computers with video teleconferencing capabilities, a combination of phone and computer/internet-based communications, and the SmartPhone. The introduction of innovative technology, such as the SmartPhone, to monitor and assist patients in their homes allows contact with individuals who may be isolated and have difficulty accessing medical services due to their remote location. Through the use of communications technology, the patients are able to become actively involved in managing their care and treatment interventions. The integration of care coordination and high technology for home monitoring provides improved patient compliance, improved service delivery to the home, early intervention of medical complications that may previously have gone unreported, and the avoidance of unnecessary emergency room and clinic visits. LAMP services effectively utilize care coordination and the very latest available technology to enable safe and independent living, enhance quality of life, increase access to services, and reduce health-related costs to functionally impaired veterans.

Consortium for Health Outcomes, Innovation, and Cost-Effectiveness Studies (CHOICES)　Located at the University of Michigan School of Medicine, this team conducted a study to determine the patterns of email usage and the attitudes concerning the use of email between primary care providers and their outpatient clinic patients.[141] A survey was completed by 476 consecutive outpatient clinic patients, 126 general medical and family practice physicians, and 16 clinical and office staff individuals from two large primary care centers. More than half the patients had knowledge of and used email. Although 70% of the patients reported that they would be willing to use email to communicate with their doctors, only 10.5% had ever done so. Overall, the patients were more concerned about whether the message would get to the appropriate person, how long it would take to get a response, and the effect it would have on the doctor–patient relationship. Physicians and clinical staff, on the other hand, were much more optimistic about the potential for email to improve the doctor–patient relationship. All participants reported low levels of concern about the issues of security and privacy of the email. CHOICES concluded that if managed care organizations plan to build email and web-based patient portals, they needed to educate both the patients and providers about the efficiency, effectiveness, and appropriate use.

Automatic Message Routing System Three parts to the email model of telemedicine are used with general practitioners to contact specialists regard patients.[142] The three parts include distributing emails to the appropriate specialist, ensuring that the specialist's response is returned to the appropriate referring physician, and tracking emails to ensure proper follow-up and that the specialist responds within a reasonable amount of time. There are also three main components to an automated message-handling system. They include a storage area for all messages that are sent and received, a database of all of the doctors, specialists, and patients, and an automatic routing program that makes decisions about where to send the message. It is also important that the router program send the message to the appropriate specialist and not to every specialist, so that people receiving emails do not get bogged down in emails that do not pertain to them.

In a study at the University of Queensland in Australia, each new patient referral was termed a "case." A case is processed through three stages. It can be "unallocated" (waiting for a decision about which specialist to send it to), it can be in progress, or it can be closed (referring doctor determines the case has been resolved). Allocating a referral to a specialist is done manually or automatically. After the referral has been allocated to a specific specialist, it is tracked as *unanswered* (the specialist has not yet responded to the initial email), *in progress* (the specialist has sent at least one return email), or *closed*. This study found that it took, on average, one day to allocate a referral to a specialist and 0.7 days to get a response back from a specialist. Some of the problems with manual email allocation systems that the automatic routing system was created to solve included:

- Providing a single point of contact for all users
- Removing the need to keep multiple lists of email addresses at all sites
- Avoiding the need to install and maintain special software at all the sites
- Automatic tracking of cases
- Having a system that could be operated by multiple system operators in different time zones
- Decreasing the decision-making and procedural requirements at user sites
- Allowing the system operators to monitor all traffic

This study took place in 2002, and at that time there were still unsolved problems with the email telemedicine system. These problems included: the referral appearing as answered when the specialists forwards it on to a colleague, a duplicate referral appearing as a unique referral, or a message being sent by the automatic router and the specialist not receiving it.

A summary of technologies is presented in Table 5.2.

TABLE 5.2   Descriptions of Technologies

Company	Product	Use
AMD Telemedicine, Inc. 650 Suffolk Street Lowell, MA 01854 www.amdtelemedicine.com	CareCompanion	Transmit vital monitoring information from the home to caregivers.
	Dermoscope	Skin surface contact microscope used to diagnose conditions and to document and archive lesions.
	General Examination Camera	Multipurpose analog camera used in primary care, emergency medicine/trauma care, dermatology, ophthalmology, wound care.
	Spirometer	Supports diagnostic cardiac and pulmonary applications including expiratory reserve volume (REV), relaxed vital capacity (VC) and forced vital capacity (FVC), forced expiratory volume (FEV), peak expiratory flow (PEF), and maximal voluntary ventilation (MVV).
	Videophone	Capable of both video communication and data transmission, and supports connection to an integrated electronic stethoscope. The videophone facilitates a face-to-face relationship between caregiver and patient.
Aerotel Medical Systems 5 Hazoref Street Holon 58856, Israel www.aerotel.com	Blood pressure monitor	Noninvasive, blood pressure measuring device; automatically transmits the data via built-in communicator over the telephone line to the receiving center.
	Chest Electrode	Post-event recorder for emergency and diagnostic purposes; primarily used for monitoring of arrhythmia; uses single lead recorder with 30 or 60 second event memory.
	Heart Monitor	Single lead loop event recorder/transmitter for continuous heart monitoring, such as postmyocardial infarction follow-up, detection of infrequent arrhythmia, unexplained chest pain (ST-Segment analysis), cardiac rehabilitation, anti-arrhythmic therapy monitoring, drug research/case study monitoring.
American TeleCare, Inc. 7640 Golden Triangle Drive Eden Prairie, MN 55344	ProTime Microcoagulation System	Used for prothrombin time testing, consists of the ProTime instrument, the three-channel reagent cuvette, and the Tenderlett® Plus LV sample collection system. This device is a peripheral that is wirelessly connected to a patient monitoring station.

(Continued)

TABLE 5.2 *Continued*

Company	Product	Use
	Telehealth System	Customized monitoring system with various medical peripherals; utilizes telephone lines to connect patient stations with provider stations, and allows for real-time, two-way personal conversations via an integrated camera, video monitor, microphone and speakerphone; provides health-care providers with either a movable color video camera or high-resolution digital snapshots.
	Disease Management System	Utilizes branching logic whereby the patient's response to certain questions determines the path of an algorithm to guide the patient through their disease-specific program(s); patients uses a touch screen to answer questions regarding physiological measurements that are captured via wired or wireless medical peripheral connections or through manual entry.
	Health-e-Coordinator™	A web-based application to support disease management, patient care management, education and referral; manages the care of patients by connecting all health-care professionals involved with that patient.
	MyFamilyMD™.	Designed to allow a patient to record his or her daily health routine and collaborate, via a secure and confidential messaging system, with their health-care provider.
	CarePrime®	A web-based communication tool for physicians and their staff that permits secure messaging between the physicians, their staff, and patients and facilitates on-line appointment requests and referrals.
	I-talk™	Designed to interact with individuals through the telephone using conversational speech recognition; disease intervention program that monitors patient compliance, collects data between office visits, provides access to data for analysis, and offers access for patients from any location any time of the day or week.
	MyNurseLine™	A technology-enabled, clinical nurse triage service that is available 24 hours per day, 7 days per week.

(Continued)

TABLE 5.2 *Continued*

Company	Product	Use
Apollo Telemedicine, Inc. 7700 Leesburg Pike, Suite 209 Falls Church, VA 22043	Teledermatology System	Combines a Dermatology Examination Camera with an image management system and videoconferencing module. Has the ability to send still and full motion dermatologic images; the use of unique light polarization eliminates reflection from surface skin; a dermoscope camera for viewing melanomas can also be added to the system.
Biotronik GmbH & Co. Woermannkehre 1 D-12359 Berlin, Germany www.biotronik.com	CardioMessenger	An integral component of the BIOTRONIK Home Monitoring® System. This mobile patient device receives messages from an implant (in the form of trend, event, or patient-triggered messages) and forwards them to the BIOTRONIK Service Center via a cellular telephone network.
Cardiobeat, Inc. 8070 Morgan Trail, Suite 210 Scottsdale, AZ 85258 www.cardiobeat.com	Cardiolert	Four sensor pads are connected to a small Impedance Monitor that is plugged into the serial port of a personal computer; it collects, digitizes, and stores cardiovascular impedance test data in the computer for transmission to the server over the web.
Cardiocom Minneapolis,MN www.cardiocom.net	CareStar	Home monitoring device for multiple disease states that require interactive symptom monitoring; uses a "tree branching" Smart Logic System that is specifically tailored to the patient's individual disease state and comorbidities.
	TeleScale	Interactive home monitoring device integrated with an electronic scale; requires patients to answer a series of customized questions about their current symptoms and to measure their weight; provides two-way communication between patients and health-care providers.
Cardionet 1010 Second Ave., Suite 700 San Diego, CA 92101 www.cardionet.com	Mobile Cardiac Outpatient Telemetry	A lightweight three-lead sensor worn as a pendant or belt clip records two channels of ECG; the sensor constantly communicates with the Cardionet Monitor, which is the size of a palm pilot.
Cardionics, Inc. 910 Bay Star Blvd. Webster, TX 77598 www.cardionics.com	SimulScope	Device for teaching auscultation at the bedside or in the classroom so that each person hears the same patient simultaneously.

(Continued)

TABLE 5.2 *Continued*

Company	Product	Use
Medic4all Services International, Ltd. 14 Merrion Square Dublin 2, Ireland	Telehealth System	Monitors physiological parameters, including the pulse wave from the radial artery to determine heart and respiration rates, through a wireless wristwatch-like sensor; the sensor transmits information through a wireless gateway installed in a nearby location in the patient's home to a medical call center computer.
Medtronics 710 Medtronic Parkway Minneapolis, MN 55432-5604	Carelink Monitor	Works with an internal pacemaker, and it plugs into a standard phone line; the patient puts the monitor's antennae over the implant and the monitor reads and stores the data, then dials a phone number and sends the information to a secure server. The clinic uses the internet to view and analyze the data.
	Carelink Programmer	Health provider unit that is used to record information. One programmer is able to support all of a provider's patients with a Medtronic cardiac device.
Patient Care Technologies, Inc. One Northside 75 Atlanta, GA 30318	Well@home	Provides clinical reminders and health information, collects data about patient compliance and clinical status; incorporates physiological measurement devices to collect vital signs such as a digital scale, sphygmomanometer, glucometer, pulse oximeter, electrocardiogram/respiration, and thermometer and contains "clinical alerts."
QRS Diagnostics 14755 27th Avenue, North Plymouth, MN 55447 www.qrsdiagnostic.com	SpiroCard	Device slides into any PC card drive of a laptop, desktop, or hand-held PC to make it a fully functioning spirometer; creates a variety of graphs and reports
Spacelabs Medical www.spacelabs.com	Medical Ambulatory Blood Pressure Monitor	Remote communications capability permits telephone modem transfer from outlying locations; data can be exported to ASCII data files, and reports can be emailed as PDF files.
ViTel Net 8201 Greensboro Drive, Suite 820 McLean, VA 22102	MedVizer Tele-Echocardiography	Provides consultations with diagnostic-quality echocardiograms, full motion videos, and still images; referring physicians or sonographers can transfer data to a consulting cardiologist. Uses hands-free capture of echocardiograph studies to simplify data entry.

5.3 CAREGIVER ISSUES

Elder care has become an important issue as our population increases in age. Many researchers have sought to determine the effects of caring for a relative suffering from chronic diseases, especially those with Alzheimer's disease and related disorders. Caregivers in rural settings may experience many more difficulties acquiring necessary health information, skill training, and ongoing support. Transportation issues have often been reported as barriers to the access of services, but studies have shown that even if transportation is available, the need to travel long distances reduces the benefit.[143,144]

The demands faced by caregivers, especially wives, of individuals with dementia-related disorders are greater than the demands of caregivers of persons with other chronic diseases.[145-147] Caregiver's of individuals with dementia-related disorders, especially Alzheimer's disease (AD), experience substantial psychosocial, emotional, and physical health concerns, which are difficult to address due to limited financial resources, large geographic areas, and limitations in available health-care professionals. Caregivers are faced with a variety of emotional and behavioral difficulties, such as agitation, wandering, depression, and repetitive behaviors and questions, as well as monitoring or assisting with personal hygiene and other self-care activities. Many ongoing projects are demonstrating that the internet is a promising way to meet the educational and support needs of caregivers.

The Resources to Enhance Alzheimer's Caregiver Health for Telephone-Linked Care (REACH for TLC) was a randomized controlled trial designed to test a computer-mediated telecommunications system with a sample of caregivers of individuals with AD.[148] The system included an automated interactive voice response (IVR) intervention that provided caregivers with stress monitoring and counseling information, personal voice-mail linkage to AD experts, a voice-mail telephone support group, and a distraction call for care recipients. This computer-mediated system operated with the use of ordinary telephones and telephone lines in order to facilitate access to individuals who may be underserved, such as those of lower socioeconomic status, members of racial or ethnic minorities, females, and the elderly. Modules were supplied which provided automated conversation to monitor the caregivers' stress levels and provide (a) information on managing recipients' behavioral problems, (b) personal voice mail to send to others involved in the study or to communicate with a clinical nurse, (c) a bulletin board to post and receive messages, and (d) an activity–respite conversation. The activity–respite conversation was utilized as a distraction module to reduce disruptive behaviors and provide the caregiver with respite. This was a computer-generated conversation that lasted approximately 18 minutes and was designed to engage the care recipient in a comforting activity. Wives who demonstrated high anxiety and limited mastery in their caregiving roles benefited the most with the IVR intervention. It was also determined that the disturbing behaviors exhibited by individuals with AD were less bothersome to caregivers, demonstrating the suitability for this type of telecaregiver application.

Alzonline.net is an internet and telephone-based education and support service for caregivers of elders with Alzheimer's and other progressive dementias.[149] Alzonline is a partnership between the State of Florida Department of Elder Affairs and the University of Florida (UF) Center for Telehealth. Alzonline is available in English and Spanish, providing education, support classes, and up-to-date information on caregiving via the internet. Caregiver classes are facilitated by the UF College of Pharmacy, the UF College of Public Health and Health Professions, and the NW Florida Area Agency on Aging. Alzonline addresses a wide range of topics such as performing daily tasks, medication management, and dealing with the challenges and stress of caring for a person with dementia. Expert forums are also available through AlzOnline, which includes a powerpoint and phone presentation featuring speakers from a variety of health-care and service organizations. The topics discussed focus on practical considerations in dementia caregiving, the latest developments in dementia research, and strategies for increasing caregiver quality of life. Reading room topics include information in such areas as bathing, behavior management, caregiver issues and perspectives, depression, disaster preparation, driving, legal issues, grief, guilt, incontinence, medications, memory loss, nutrition/eating, safety, sleeping, stress, and wandering. The site also lists available resources for caregivers who are in need of additional assistance.

Hanson and Nolan described the Assisting Carers using Telematics Interventions to meet Older person's Needs (ACTION) program at ICADI.[150] ACTION helps people who want to care for their relative at home feel more prepared to take on the role of a caregiver. The ACTION program had five goals: (1) Allow caregivers access to multimedia caring programs and internet service to increase their skills and abilities as carers; (2) increase the positive aspects of being a caregiver; (3) increase the caregiver's sense of control over the situation and allow them to make informed decisions about the future; (4) decrease stress of being a caregiver and create opportunity to reflect on satisfying aspects of being a caregiver; (5) decrease hospital utilization and costs. The initial ACTION services included multimedia caring programs, videophones for access to professional caregivers and families in the project, and internet access. The television in the homes of participating families was connected to a personal computer that stored the caregiving programs. A video camera was attached and ISDN2b was used for videoconferencing. A remote control was used to browse services. The multimedia programs contained information on transferring and handling, incontinence care, assistance with food preparation, eating, and drinking. For families with a narrow social network and who are homebound, ACTION may provide a source of support.

Focus groups of families helped design the caregiving programs and videophone interface. They were then tested by families and quality-tested by professional caregivers. The services were then tested with frail elderly and their caregivers in Sweden, England, Northern Ireland, the Republic of Ireland, and Portugal. A call center was established in western Sweden and operated by two nurse assistants. The call center allowed families to access professional advice through the videophone.

Data was presented at ICADI from one municipality in western Sweden, where 21 families used the ACTION services for a minimum of 3 months and an average of 12 months. The average age of the cared for person was 84 years and the average age of the caregiver was 72 years. Most families felt that the ACTION services helped them feel more prepared, increased the predictability of the caregiving experience, and increased their satisfaction with being a caregiver. One group of participants felt that the program increased their effectiveness of being a caregiver and increased their self-confidence and sense of control. A second group felt that the program helped them to see the rewards in being a caregiver and helped them to feel more prepared to find out about services and to arrange services for their family member. They also felt more comfortable in performing tasks to care for their family member. There was a third group who did not find benefit in using the ACTION program. Some of the reasons given for this included being unsure about how much longer they could continue being a caregiver, not having time to view the programs, dealing with specific medical conditions not included in the programs, and having an extensive support system that included professional caregivers.

5.4 LEGAL AND FINANCIAL ISSUES

Legal Issues

State Licensure Individuals who provide health-related services, such as physicians, nurses, and therapists, are typically required to be licensed and/or certified in the state in which they are practicing. Therefore, if a clinician is providing services to a client within the state in which they are licensed, then the practice is authorized. With the introduction of telemedicine, what are the "rules" if the client is in another state? For example, if a clinician is licensed and practicing in Florida, yet is providing telemedicine services to a patient in Georgia, should the state of Georgia have some jurisdiction over the clinician? The answer depends on whether the law considers that for services provided over a distance the client is "transported" electronically to the clinician, or, alternatively, the clinician is transported to the client.[151] Some states have determined that the professional services take place where the client is located; other states have determined that practitioners are subject to (a) the jurisdiction of the location where their clients are receiving those services and (b) the jurisdiction from which they are physically providing the services. Thus, multistate licensure requirements may be an impediment to health care and telemedicine, because often the health-care provider and the patient are in different jurisdictional locations. The burdens of multistate license requirements may include initial application fees, satisfying other states' examination requirements, annual renewal fees, and the expenses necessary to fulfill other states' continuing education requirements.[152]

States are required to establish laws for the protection of individuals within their boundaries, which also implies that states are responsible for establishing standards of practice for health-care workers who provide services to the citizens of that state.[152] States have an established system for providing licensure to health-care providers in their states, but no state has the authority to regulate a practitioner who resides and practices outside of their state. Standards of care may be different in some states than others, and may even be different within some states themselves.

A potential remedy to counter state barriers to the interstate operation of telehealth is to establish national regulations. It has been argued that a national license is warranted for telemedicine, or the delivery of health services through telecommunications, in an attempt to eliminate barriers to access. However, the U.S. Constitution applies a limitation on congressional power over states. "Therefore, unless Congress acts to regulate telemedicine licensure, the states themselves must decide to harmonize their standards and laws."[153] Unfortunately, this doesn't appear to be occurring. In its 2001 Report to Congress, the federal Office for the Advancement of Telehealth reported that many state's boards appear to be moving toward more restrictive regulatory policies in lieu of cooperation regarding multistate licensure.

The Center for Telemedicine Law (CTL) is a nonprofit entity that gathers and analyzes information related to the legal and regulatory aspects of telemedicine. Figure 5.16 identifies licensure laws and practices by states related to telemedicine and practice across state lines. This map demonstrates that a number of states have taken action to require full licensure or special-purpose licensure or have considered alternatives for granting authority to practice.

Section 330I(p) of the Health Care Safety Net Amendments of 2002 (S 1533) (http://thomas.loc.gov/cgi-bin/query/F?c107:2:./temp/~c107sVEVJQ:e36853:),

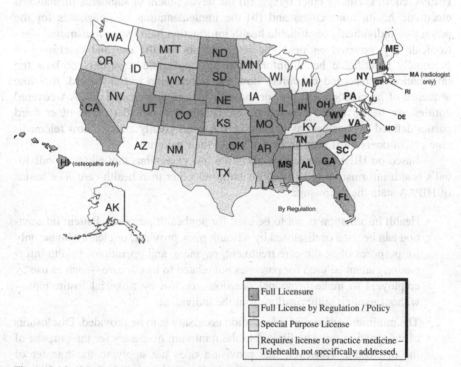

Figure 5.16 Medical licensure laws affecting telehealth. Copyright 2004. Center for Telemedicine Law. CTL © 2004. All rights reserved.

signed into law in October 2002, provides for incentive grants to be awarded to state professional licensing boards to cooperate, develop, and implement state policies that will reduce statutory and regulatory barriers to telemedicine. The specific language follows:

> It is the sense of Congress that, for purposes of this section, States should develop reciprocity agreements so that a provider of services under this section who is a licensed or otherwise authorized health care provider under the law of 1 or more States, and who, through telehealth technology, consults with a licensed or otherwise authorized health care provider in another State, is exempt, with respect to such consultation, from any State law of the other State that prohibits such consultation on the basis that the first health care provider is not a licensed or authorized health care provider under the law of that State. (S 1533, Section 330I, p)

Congress, several states, and even the Federation of State Medical Boards agree in principle to less restrictive rules for interstate telemedicine, although most prescribe different models.

HIPPA: Health Insurance Portability and Privacy Act (HIPPA)

HIPPA requires, among other things, (a) the development of standards for national electronic health transactions and (b) the implementation of safeguards for the privacy of individually identifiable health information held by, or transmitted electronically by, covered entities. The requirements for the use and disclosure of personally identifiable health information are applicable regardless of how the information is recorded or stored, how the information is transmitted, the time sequence of its creation and use, or the way it is communicated. HIPAA-covered entities are health plans, clearinghouses, health-care providers, and other third parties defined as "business associates." HIPAA has greatly affected how telemedicine practitioners must protect the privacy of their patients.

Based on HIPAA regulations, there are few exceptions that allow an individual's health information to be used for purposes other than health care. The basics of HIPAA state the following:

- Health information is not to be used for nonhealth purposes. Patient information can be used or disclosed by a health plan, provider, or clearinghouse only for purposes of health-care treatment, payment, and operations. Health information cannot be used for purposes not related to health care—such as use by employers to make personnel decisions, or use by financial institutions—without explicit authorization from the individual.

- The minimum amount of information necessary is to be provided. Disclosures of information must be limited to the minimum necessary for the purpose of the disclosure. However, this provision does not apply to the transfer of medical records for purposes of treatment, since physicians, specialists, and other providers need access to the full record to provide best quality care.

- Ensure that informed and voluntary consent is obtained. Nonroutine disclosures with patient authorization must meet standards that ensure that the authorization is truly informed and voluntary.

Potentially, one of the most challenging aspects for clinicians employing telehealth is how to comply with HIPAA when state law privacy requirements are in conflict. The law states that HIPAA privacy requirements preclude state law only when state provisions provide less protection. Where state privacy requirements are in conflict with federal law, the rules providing the client the most privacy protection take precedence over the less stringent standards. But, if a physician in one state was consulting with physicians in two or three other states, then which state privacy laws would take precedence? This creates a frustrating mix of state privacy requisites whereby the more extensive a clinicians' telehealth practice is, and the more states involved, the more burdensome it becomes to determine the controlling privacy requirements. In 2002, a 50-state survey of health privacy laws governing the use and disclosure of health information was conducted by the Health Privacy Project, and it demonstrates how wide the discrepancies are in the areas of state privacy protection, complexity, and coverage.[154]

According to the Advanced Technology Institute's preliminary research, which utilized information and input from grantees in the Office for the Advancement of Telehealth, other privacy concerns for telemedicine practitioners may include:

- A need for a heightened level of concern for patient privacy in the telemedicine environment, especially where patient visits are occurring in realtime. A clinician must be careful to only collect personal data for specific, legitimate purposes.
- The potential for more complicated informed consent requirements under HIPAA that could inhibit obtaining the necessary patient consent signatures that are necessary prior to initiating telehealth activities. Patients are entitled to receive sufficient information in a way that they can understand the proposed treatment, the possible alternatives, and any substantial risk or risks that may be special in kind or in magnitude or special to the patient so that they can make a balanced judgment. A clinician must be satisfied that, wherever possible, the patient has understood what is proposed and consents to it.
- The presence of outsiders or nonclinical persons in teleconsultations.
- Nonclinical technicians, camera people, schedulers, and so on, located on either side of a telemedicine consultation or at the site of a service provider, either physically or via the technology they support.
- Clinical personnel who may not be visible or observable by the patient in a teleconsultation.
- Patient information that is transmitted in electronic and physical form on a regular basis across organizations and political (state and national) borders.
- Patient information routinely stored electronically and/or physically at each of the sites involved in the encounter, often unintentionally, may not be protected

by policies or procedures as effectively as information used in on-site encounters. Health-care providers are responsible for confidential electronic information they receive, and they must make sure that it is effectively protected against improper disclosure when it is disposed of, stored, transmitted, or received.[155]

Telehealth practitioners can refer to a document published by the Federal Office of Civil Rights to understand the key aspects of the standards for privacy of individually identifiable health information of HIPAA that apply to all aspects of their practice. The publication, entitled Medical Privacy: National Standards to Protect the Privacy of Personal Health Information, is comprehensive and intended to guide and explain specific aspects of the privacy rule, such as: incidental uses and disclosures; disclosures for treatment, payment, and health-care operations; marketing; research; and disclosures for public health activities.[156]

European Union Privacy Enhancement in Data Management in e-Health (PRIDEH)

PRIDEH is a demonstration project partly funded by the European Commission, focused on privacy enhancing technologies within the health domain.[157] Privacy-enhancing technology (PET) uses mature cryptographic methods. Although there is increased privacy violation risk due to the use of the internet, as well as the increased need for data to support evidence-based medicine and management decisions, acceptance and utilization of privacy enhancement is slow. They are seeking solutions that are based on "Trusted Third Party" provision of privacy services and the incorporation of privacy enhancing modules into application software. PRIDEH reports that privacy-enhancing services delivery through the use of intermediary trusted third parties has been discussed in the literature, but they determined that seldom has the technology made it into actual practice, and the technology often remains in closed domains. They also state that the existing solutions appear to have questionable "trustworthiness." PRIDEH plans to enhance PET, based on sound privacy principles, and find ways for delivery into the health-care system.

Reimbursement

Reimbursement continues to be a key issue for proponents of telehealth. Although the cost of the technology and setup of equipment for telehealth can be initially expensive, one of the overall assumptions of telehealth is that it could positively affect total cost of treatment over the lifetime of the patient. Unfortunately, prevention rather than short-term treatment is not typically the focus of health-care payers. The Capitol Hill Steering Committee on Telehealth and Healthcare Informatics on behalf of the Department of Commerce's Office of Technology states in their report entitled *Innovation, Demand and Investment in Telehealth (2004)* that the market for telehealth goods and services is estimated at $380 million in 2004, less than 1% of the $80 billion spent on domestic healthcare technologies.[158] The Capitol Hill Steering Committee reported that there has been very little telehealth research on clinical and cost outcomes, and therefore, a business case has not been made for reimbursement.

Although Medicare pays for only a portion of health-care services in the United States, its policies influence other third-party payers. Historically, Medicare has paid for such telemedicine applications as teleradiology and telepathology, which do not require face-to-face interaction with patients, although until 1999, these services were not reimbursable if consultations and office visits were not face-to-face. The Balanced Budget Act of 1997 (BBA) required the Health Care Financing Administration (HCFA), effective January 1, 1999, to reimburse Medicare recipients for telemedicine services under special circumstances, which include face-to-face encounters through real-time interactive videoconferencing.[159] Although the telemedicine community viewed this legislation as important, its effectiveness was reduced through the many administrative limitations written into the bill. Examples of telemedicine reimbursement restrictions included patients limited to locations in rural health professional shortage areas, reimbursement for telephone consultation, email, or video that had been previously taped, stored, and forwarded at a later time, and home health services. As well, nurses could not be presenters, defined as those individuals forwarding or presenting the information to a physician for consultation, even though nurses are the primary health-care staff at most rural clinics. The Medicare, Medicaid, and State Children's Health Insurance Program (SCHIP) Benefits Improvement and Protection Act of 2000 (S.B. 2505) attempted to address and resolve some of these limitations. Medicare reimbursement guidelines changed effective October 1, 2001. Some of the changes include: eligibility for teleconsultation services to Medicare patients who reside in all counties outside of a metropolitan service area, as well as federal demonstration projects; elimination of the qualified presenter requirement; store-and-forward consultations are eligible for reimbursement only for federal demonstration projects in Alaska and Hawaii; and the inclusion of office or other outpatient visits, psychotherapy, and pharmacologic management. Home health services (telehomecare) continue to be ineligible for Medicare reimbursement.

Insurance   First Health is a unique national managed care company serving the group health, workers' compensation, and state public program markets. First Health has become one of the first national managed care companies to establish reimbursement for web-based internet consultations between patients and their physicians. At this time, consultations are limited to chronic conditions, such as diabetes, asthma, and congestive heart failure. They limit consultations to 24 per year at a cost of $25.00 per consultation. First Health assumes that the initiative will enhance well-being of their clients and will potentially reduce the rate and length of stay for hospitalizations.

Industry-wide Standards

There has been little coordinated effort within and between the telehealth community for developing and implementing industry-wide standards. As a result, technology, information, and the dispersion of services lacks coherence. Manufacturers, providers, payers, and an array of others must agree upon and demonstrate the determination to work together to meet the opportunities and the needs of the health-care system. The American Telemedicine Association (ATA) and the National Institute for Standards and Technology (NIST) are currently working together to address the development and marketing of acceptable standards. They have developed and initiated a demonstration project with telehealth standards for diabetic retinopathy, which is currently underway.

5.5 CURRENT LIMITATIONS AND THE FUTURE

Limitations

Telehealth is advancing rapidly, incorporating the latest advances in the underlying technologies, and reflecting a viable market for cost-effective health related devices and services. However, there are limiting factors associated with technology. The telehealth system is built around many different factors. Who will be using the equipment? What type of information needs to be captured and transferred? Does the system need to be live or can it be store and forward? When does the information need to be captured? If measurements are taken, do they need to be continuous, hourly, daily, or some other time increment? In answering these questions, the limitations in today's technology can be seen.

One limiting factor in the use of telehealth may be requirements of the user to initiate use of the equipment. If a patient is at their home and needs to apply devices to take physiological measurements and then connect equipment to send the data to their health-care provider, there may be a limitation in compliance and acceptance of the telehealth program. Some equipment is user-friendly and other equipment is very complex. The choice of equipment will be guided by the goals of the program. As technology advances and the use of telehealth increases, more equipment should be available to choose from. As well, the equipment may be easier to operate, potentially initiating measurements and operations independently.

Capturing the quality or quantity of data or information that is of importance may also be limited by today's technology or the availability of the technology. For example, transatlantic surgeries have been performed, but they are certainly not routine. For some types of surgeries, equipment does not exist to perform them remotely, and for others the cost of the equipment is a limiting factor. Earlier in the telesurgery section of this chapter, a robotic arm was estimated at costing around one million dollars. Telesurgery also requires a connection that is very fast with virtually no delay. The use of dedicated lines and a backup connection is needed to prevent the loss of connection, which may have fatal consequences.

If a physiological parameter needs to be measured continuously, wireless devices are generally preferred. Primarily, it is important to have the sensors wirelessly transmit the data to a patient unit that sends the data to a receiving center. Then the patient does not have to be tethered to the unit. Ideally, the patient unit would also send data wirelessly and the patient would be free to move not just around their home but around the outside world as well. Mobile technology is limited in how big of an application it may handle and how fast it transfers data. As the speed and ability for mobile technology increases, telehealth applications will also advance. Security issues with mobile technologies may also limit their use in telehealth applications.

The Future

In concluding this chapter, we discuss a system under design for the soldier of the future by BioControl Systems, Inc. (BCS)[160]. In the Remote Monitor, Control, and Identify Input Suit (REMCIIS) system, future soldiers will have complete communications, control, and data analysis/display capabilities available in a head-mounted display (HMD). Individual soldiers will be networked with other members of their unit as well as central command. In addition to exact location via GPS, command will know the physiological state of the soldier and can monitor state of alertness, determine stress levels, and even deduce information about the nature of injury via the soldier's personal status monitor (PSM).

The future soldier will also be able to interact with command or other networked personnel and equipment, by using hand gestures, arm and leg movements, or eye movements, or any combination of muscle movements in the body. Eye movement pointing technology is ideal for an HMD user with occupied hands, wherein the user can interact with menu-driven software by positioning the cursor with eye movements. The BCS eye controlling system is biosignal-based, thus all required sensor elements can be mounted in the HMD's cushion that contacts the forehead and face. This allows for silent control that might be required under battlefield conditions. One of the keys to the biosignal-based REMCIIS is the dry electrode sensors, which passively monitor vital biosignals and are incorporated into the fabric of the body suit, located in physiologically strategic positions.

BCS has demonstrated the feasibility of a hand gesture recognition system using a sensor array on the forearm, which leaves the hand unencumbered. These applications can be implemented in software without the need for expensive extremity-mounted movement detectors, such as a data glove. The biosignal data can also be used to gain additional information about a user. By monitoring the magnitude and dynamics of muscle tension, performance and fatigue parameters can be established. Thus, a variety of motor skill tasks can be individualized and designed for training and achievement. All of these monitor and control capabilities may be provided by the REMCIIS system worn comfortably and inconspicuously by the soldier. BCS's overall goal is to create a prototype input suit with multiple monitor and control capabilities. The input suit can be used for monitor and control in actual combat or other operational environments, and it is currently being assessed for human representation in virtual environments (VEs).

BCS also has an ongoing research and development effort devoted to (a) advancing the state of the art in electro-oculography (EOG) controller technology and (b) developing several application areas for the eye controller. EOG is a recording technique, which allows the standing potential between the cornea and the posterior pole of the eye to be recorded. For instance, BCS has developed eye-controlled joystick and mouse applications that allow users to control graphical objects with eye movements. The mouse applications give users the ability to do hands-free word processing or use other menu-driven software. This type of system may be ideal for persons with physical disabilities.

REFERENCES

1. *2001 Report to Congress on Telemedicine, Executive Summary*, Office for the Advancement of Telehealth, http://telehealth.hrsa.gov/pubs/report/2001/exec.htm, May 20, 2002.
2. Celler, B. G., Lovell, N. H., and Basilakis, J. (2003). Using information technology to improve the management of chronic disease. *Medical Journal of Australia* **179**, 242–246.
3. U.S. Department of Commerce, Office of Technology Policy, Technology Administration Report, Innovation, Demand and Investment in Telehealth, February 2004, p. 10.
4. Telemedicine and Advanced Technologies Research Center (TATRC, 2004). Retrieved July 15, 2004, from http://www.tatrc.org
5. Office for the Advancement of Telehealth (AT, 2004). Retrieved July 15, 2004, from http://telehealth.hrsa.gov/grants.htm
6. U.S. Department of Agriculture, Rural Utility Service (RUS, 2004). Retrieved July 15, 2004, from http://www.usda.gov/rus/telecom/dlt/dlt.htm
7. Strategies for the Future: The role of technology in reducing health care costs, Saudia National Laboratories (1996), SAND 60-2469, November 1996.
8. Webpedia (June 2003). POTS. Retrieved August 17, 2004 from http://www.webopedia.com/TERM/P/POTS.html
9. Webopedia (July 2003). ISDN. Retrieved August 17, 2004 from http://www.webopedia.com/TERM/I/ISDN.html
10. Cisco (February 2002). Integrated service Digital Network. Retrieved August 30, 2004 from http://www.cisco.com/univercd/cc/td/doc/cisintwk/ito_doc/isdn.htm
11. Webopedia (July 2003). XDSL. Retrieved August 17, 2004 from http://www.webopedia.com/TERM/x/xDSL.html
12. Maryland Public Service Commission (2001). DSL FAQs. Retrieved August 30, 2004 from http://www.psc.state.md.us/psc/Info/brochures/dslfaqs.htm
13. AT&T (2004). AT&T DSL service FAQs. Retrieved August 30, 2004 from http://www.usa.att.com/dsl/faqs.jsp#how_work
14. Cox Communications (n.d.). High speed internet: Compare services. Retrieved August 17, 2004 from http://www.cox.com/HighSpeedInternet/Compare.asp
15. Herzog, A., and Lind, L. (2003). Network solutions for home health care applications. *Technology and Health Care*, **11**, 77–87.
16. Tachakra, S., Wang, X. H., Istephanian, R. S. H., and Song, Y. H. (2003). Mobile e-Health: The unwired evolution of telemedicine. *Telemedicine Journal and e-Health* **9**(3), 247–257.
17. Webopedia (October 2001). IrDA. Retrieved August 17, 2004 from http://www.webopedia.com/TERM/I/IrDA.html
18. Universitat Karlsruhe Institut fur Technik der Informationsverarbeitung (December 2003). ITIV Telemetry Platform: Bluetooth Sensors. Retrieved August 17, 2004 from http://www-itiv.etec.uni-karlsruhe.de/opencms/opencms/en/research/workgroups/MST_Optik/telematik/Sensoren.html
19. Universitat Karlsruhe Institut fur Technik der Informationsverarbeitung (December 2003). Smart Clothes Technologies. Retrieved August 17, 2004 from http://www-itiv.etec.uni-karlsruhe.de/opencms/opencms/en/research/workgroups/MST_Optik/wear_comp/index.html
20. Universitat Karlsruhe Institut fur Technik der Informationsverarbeitung (December 2003). Strainless blood pressure monitor. Retrieved August 17, 2004 from http://www-itiv.etec.uni-karlsruhe.de/opencms/opencms/en/research/workgroups/MST_Optik/vitalsensorik/blutdruck.html
21. Wordiq (n.d.), Encyclopedia: Definition of global system for mobile communications. Retrieved August 23, 2004 from http://www.wordiq.com/definition/GSM

22. Webopedia (July 2004). GSM. Retrieved August 23, 2004 from http://www.pcwebopedia.com/TERM/G/GSM.html

23. Wordiq.com (n.d.). Encyclopedia: definition of general packet radio service. Retrieved August 23, 2004 from http://www.wordiq.com/definition/GPRS

24. UMTSWorld.com (1999–2003). 3G and UMTS frequently asked questions. Retrieved August 24, 2004 from http://www.umtsworld.com/umts/faq.htm#f5

25. AT&T Wireless (2004). UMTS: features and benefits. Retrieved August 24, 2004 from http://www.attwireless.com/umts/features_and_benefits.html

26. Webopedia (July 2001). EDGE. Retrieved August 25th from http://www.pcwebopedia.com/TERM/E/EDGE.html

27. 3G Americas (August 2004). EDGE fact sheet. Retrieved August 25, 2004 from http://www.3gamericas.org/pdfs/edgefactsheet.pdf

28. Bovi, A. M., Council on Ethical and Judicial Affairs of the American Medical Association. (2003). Use of health-related online sites. American Journal of Bioethics 3(3), W-IF3.

29. Waldo, B. H. (2003). Connecting for compliance: Improving satisfaction and care coordination by extending the home care record to the physician. Home Healthcare Nurse 21(10), 674–679.

30. Jutra, A. (1959). Teleroentgen diagnosis by means of videotape recording. American Journal of Roentgenology 82, 1009–1012.

31. Wittson, C. L., Affleck, D. C., and Johnson, V. (1961). Two-way television group therapy. Mental Hospital 12, 2–23.

32. Bashshur, R., and Lovett, J. (1977). Assessment of telemedicine: Results of the initial experience. Aviation Space and Environmental Medicine 48(1), 65–70.

33. Bashshur, R. (1980). Technology Serves the People: The Story of a Cooperative Telemedicine Project by NASA, the Indian Health Service and the Papago People. Superintendent of Documents, US Government Printing Office, Washington, DC.

34. Murphy, R. L., and Bird, K. T. (1974). Telediagnosis: A new community health resource; observations on the feasibility of telediagnosis based on 1000 patient transactions. American Journal of Public Health 64(2), 113–119.

35. Rosen, E. (1997). The history of desktop telemedicine. Telemedicine Today 5, 16.

36. Foote, D. R. (1977). Satellite communication for rural health care in Alaska. Journal of Communication 27(4), 173–182.

37. Perednia, D., and Allen, A. (1995). Telemedicine technology and clinical applications. Journal of the American Medical Association 273(6), 483–488.

38. Doarn, C. R., Nicogossian, A. E., and Merrell, R. C. (1998). Applications of telemedicine in the United States Space Program. Telemedicine Journal 4(1), 19–30.

39. Watson, D. S. (1989). Telemedicine. Medical Journal of Australia 151(2), 62–71.

40. Hersh, W. R., Helfland, M., Wallace, J., Kraemer, D., Patterson, P., Shapiro, S., and Greenlick, M. (2001). Clinical outcomes resulting from telemedicine interventions: A systematic review. BMC Medical Informatics and Decision Making 1(5).

41. Rich, M. W. (1997). Epidemiology, pathophysiology, and etiology of congestive heart failure in older adults. Journal of the American Geriatrics Society 45, 968–974.

42. American Heart Association (2004). Heart and Stroke Statistical Update. Dallas: American Heart Association.

43. Rogers, M. A., Small, D., Buchan, D. A., Butch, C. A., Stewart, C. M., Krenzer, B. E., and Husovisky, H. L. (2001). Home monitoring service improves mean arterial pressure in patients with essential hypertension: A randomized, controlled trial. Annuals of Internal Medicine 134, 1024–1032.

44. Delborg, M., and Anderson, K. (1997). Key factors in the identification of the high-risk patient with unstable coronary artery disease: Clinical findings, resting 12-lead electrocardiogram, and continuous electrocardiographic monitoring. American Journal of Cardiology 80, 35e–39e.

45. Rendina, M. C., Downs, S. M., and Carasco, N. (1998). Effect of telemedicine on health outcomes in 87 infants requiring neonatal intensive care. Telemedicine Journal 4, 345.

46. Hooper, G. S., Yellowlees, P., Marwick, T. H., Currie, P. J., and Bidstrup, B. P. (2001). Telehealth and the diagnosis and management of cardiac disease. Journal of Telemedicine and Telecare 7, 249–256.

47. Shanit, D., Cheng, A., and Greenbaum, R. A. (1996). Telecardiology: Supporting the decision-making process in general practice. *Journal of Telemedicine and Telecare* **2**, 7–13.

48. Allen, A., Doolittle, G. C., and Boysen, C. D. (1999). An analysis of the suitability of home health visits for telemedicine. *Journal of Telemedicine and Telecare* **5**, 90–96.

49. Squires, R. W., Miller, T. D., Harn, T., Micheels, T. A., and Palma, T. A. (1991). Transtelephonic electrocardiographic monitoring of cardiac rehabilitation exercise sessions in coronary artery disease. *American Journal of Cardiology* **67**, 962–964.

50. Shaw, D. K., Sparks, K. E., and Jennings, H. S., III (1998). Transtelephonic exercise monitoring: A review. *Journal of Cardiopulmonary Rehabilitation* **18**, 263–270.

51. Department of Health and Human Services, U.S. Food and Drug Administration (2004). Home monitoring system with the BA03 DDDR pulse generator—P950037/S19. Retrieved August 25, 2004 from http://www.fda.gov/cdrh/mda/docs/p950037s019.html

52. Medtronic (n.d.). Tachyarrhythmia: Frequently asked questions remote device monitoring. Retrieved August 16, 2004 from http://www.medtronic.com/servlet/ContentServer?pagename= Medtronic/Website/FAQ&ConditionName=Tachyarrhythmia&FAQ_Category=Remote+Device+ Monitoring#1067264780838

53. Cardionet (2004). Retrieved July 15, 2004 from http://www.cardionet.com/device.html

54. Cardiobeat, Inc. (2004). Retrieved August 16, 2004 from http://www.cardiobeat.com/sw_serve.htm

55. Kornowski, R., Zlochiver, S., Botzer, L., Tirosh, R., Abboud, S., and Misan, S. (2003). Validation of vital signs recorded via a new telecare system. *Journal of Telemedicine and Telecare* **9**, 328–333.

56. Visual Telecommunications Network, Inc., ViTel Net (2004). Retrieved August 15, 2004 from http://www.vitelnet.com/Telemedicine/tm_echo.htm

57. Aerotel Medical Systems, Ltd. (2004). Retrieved August 15, 2004 from http://aerotel.com/ Products/ProductsFamily.asp?iProductsFamilyID=1

58. American Telecare. (n.d.). Peripherals. Retrieved September 27, 2004 from http://www. americantelecare.com/prod_peripherals.html

59. Spacelabs Medical, Inc. (2004). Retrieved August 5, 2004 from http://www.spacelabs.com/abp/abp_ monitors.asp

60. Villela, K., Montaoni, M., Blaschek, J., Rocha, A., and Rabelo Jr., A. (September 2000). Tele Cardio-FBC: an Application of Telemedicine for Cardiology. Retrieved August 16, 2004 from http://www.mdf.be/mednet2000/program/op89.html

61. Cardiocom (2004). Retrieved August 5, 2004 from http://www.cardiocom.net/prod_inhouse_ telescale1.html

62. Georgetown University Medical Center. (n.d.). MindMyHeart: Medicare Demonstration Project. Retrieved August 2, 2004 from http://www.isis.georgetown.edu/groups/Ehealth/medicare/index.htm

63. Beauchene, P., McAlinden, E., and Levine, B. (2003, December). Home health technologies for congestive heart failure patients [Abstract]. *International Conference on Aging, Disability, and Independence*, Washington, D.C.

64. Young, M., Sparrow, D., Gottlieb, D., Selim, A., and Friedman, R. (2001). A telephone-linked computer system for COPD care. *Chest* **119**(5), 1565–1575.

65. Weinstock, M. A., Nguyen, F. Q., and Risica, P. M. (2002). Patient and referring provider satisfaction with teledermatology. *Journal of the American Academy of Dermatology* **47**(1), 68–72.

66. Braun, R. P., and Saurat, J. H. (2003). Teledermoscopy. *Telemedicine and Teledermatology* **32**, 201–206.

67. Coras, B., Glaessl, A., Kinateder, J., Klövekorn, W., Braun, R., Lepski, U., Landthaler, M., and Stolz, W. (2003). Teledermatoscopy in daily routine—results of the first 100 cases. *Telemedicine and Teledermatology* **32**, 207–212.

68. Shaprio, M., James, W., Kessler, R., Lazorik, F., Katz, K., Tam, J., Nieves, D., and Miller, J. (2004). Comparison of skin biopsy triage decisions in 49 patients with pigmented lesions and skin neoplasms. *Archives of Dermatology* **140**, 525–528.

69. Whited, J. D. (2001). Teledermatology: Current status and future directions. *American Journal of Clinical Dermatology* **2**(2), 59–64.

70. Apollo Telemedicine (2004). Retrieved August 5, 2004 from http://www.apollotelemedicine.com/ solutions/teledermatology

71. Krupinski, E., Nypaver, M., Poropatich, R., Ellis, D., Safwat, R., and Sapci, H. (2002). Clinical applications in telemedicine/telehealth. *Telemedicine Journal and e-Health* **8**(1), 13–34.

72. Goldberg, M. A. (1996). Teleradiology and telemedicine. *Radiology Clininics of North America* **34**(3), 647–665.

73. U.S. Census Bureau. Disability labor force status-Work disability status of civilians 17 to 74 years old, by sex: 2000. http://www.census.gov/hhes/www/disable/disabstat2k.html

74. Schopp, L. H., Hales, J. W., Quetsch, J. L., Hauan, M. J., and Brown, G. D. (2004). Design of a peer-to-peer telerehabilitation model. *Telemedicine Journal and e-Health* **10**(2), 243–251.

75. Lai, J. C. K., Woo, J., Hui, E., and Chan, W. M. (2004). Telerehabilitation—A new model for community-based stroke rehabilitation. *Journal of Telemedicine and Telecare* **10**, 199–205.

76. Rizzo, A. A., Strickland, D., and Bouchard, S. (2004). The challenge of using virtual reality in telerehabilitation. *Telemedicine Journal and e-Health* **10**(2), 184–195.

77. Winters, J. (2002). Telerehabilitation research: Emerging opportunities. *Annual Review of Biomedical Engineering* **4**, 287–320.

78. Kennedy, R. S., Lane, N. E., Lilienthal, M. G., Berbaum, K. S., and Hettinger, L. J. Profile analysis of simulator sickness symptoms: Applications to virtual environment systems. *Presence: Teleoperators Virtual Environment* **1**, 295–301.

79. Burns, R. B., Crislip, D., Daviou, P., Temkin, A., Vesmarovich, S., et al. (1998). Using telerehabilitation to support assistive technology. *Assistive Technology* **10**, 126–133.

80. Burgiss, S. (2001). Physiatry and other services provided by telehealth for the rehabilitation patient. In *Proceedings of the State of the Science Conference on Telerehabilitation and Applications of Virtual Reality.* Washington, D.C.: NRH Press, pp. 14–18.

81. National Diabetes Data Group (1995). *Diabetes in America,* 2nd ed. Bethesda, MD: National Institutes of Health, National Institute of Diabetes and Digestive and Kidney Diseases.

82. Gomez-Ulla, F., Fernandez, M. I., Gonzalez, F., Rey, P., Rodriguez, M., Rodriguez-Cid, M. J., Casanueva, F. F., Tome, M. A., Garcia-Tobio, J., and Gude, F. (2002). Digital retinal images and teleophthalmology for detecting and grading diabetic retinopathy. *Diabetes Care* **25**(8), 1384–1389.

83. Grisby, B., and Brown, N. (1999). *Report on US Telemedicine Activity.* American Telemedicine Service Providers.

84. Kennedy, C., and Yellowless, P. (2000). A community based approach to evaluation of health outcomes and costs for telepsychiatry in a rural population: Preliminary results. *Journal of Telemedicine and Telecare* **6**, 155–157.

85. Zaylor, C., Nelson, E. L., and Cook, D. J. (2001). Clinical outcomes in a prison telepsychiatry clinic. *Journal of Telemedicine and Telecare* **7**(1), 47–49.

86. Trott, P., and Blignault, I. (1998). Cost evaluation of a telepsychiatry service in northern Queensland. *Journal of Telemedicine and Telecare* **4**(1), 66–68.

87. Ruskin, P., Silver-Aylaian, M., Kling, M., Reed, S., Bradham, D., Hebel, J., Barrett, D., Knowles, F., and Hauser, P. (2004). Treatment outcomes in depression: Comparison of remote treatment through telepsychiatry to in-person treatment. *American Journal of Psychiatry* **161**(8), 1471–1476.

88. Elford, R., White, H., Bowering, R., Ghandi, A., Maddiggan, B., St. John, K., House, M., Harnett, J., West, R., and Battcock, A. (2000). A randomized, controlled trial of child psychiatric assessments conducted using videoconferencing. *Journal of Telemedicine and Telecare* **6**, 73–82.

89. Baigent, M., Lloyd, C., Kavanaugh, S., Ben-Tovim, D., Yellowlees, P., Kalucy, R., and Bond, M. (1997). Telepsychiatry: "tele" yes, but what about the "psychiatry"? *Journal of Telemedicine and Telecare* **3**(Suppl 1), 3–5.

90. Ruskin, P., Reed, S., Kumar, R., Kling, M., Siegel, E., Rosen, M., and Hauser, P. (1998). Reliability and acceptability of psychiatric diagnosis via telecommunication and audiovisual technology. *Psychiatric Services* **49**, 1086–1088.

91. Kirkwood, K., Peck, D., and Bennie, L. (2000). The consistency of neuropsychological assessments performed via telecommunication and face-to-face. *Journal of Telemedicine and Telecare* **6**, 147–151.

92. Montani, C., Billaud, N., Couturier, P., Fluchaire, I., Lemaire, R., Maltere, Ch., Lauvernay, N., Piquard, J. F., Frossard, M., and Franco, A. (1996). "Telepsychometry": A remote psychometry consultation in clinical gerontology: Preliminary study. *Telemedicine Journal* **2**, 145–150.

93. Chae, Y. M., Park, H. J., Cho, J. G., Hong, D. K., and Cheon, K. (2000). The reliability and acceptability of telemedicine for patients with schizophrenia in Korea. *Journal of Telemedicne and Telecare* **6**, 83–90.

94. Zarate, C. A., Weinstock, L., Cukor, P., Morabito, C., Laehy, L., Burns, C., and Baer, L. (1997). Applicability of telemedicine for assessing patients with schizophrenia: acceptance and reliability. *Journal of Clinical Psychiatry* **58**, 22–25.

95. Yoshino, A., Shigemura, J., Kobayashi, Y., Nomura, S., Shishikura, K., Den, R., Wakisaka, H., Kamata, S., and Ashida, H. (2001). Telepsychiatry: Assessment of televideo psychiatric interview reliability with present and next generation internet infrastructures. *Acta Psychiatrica Scandinavica* **104**, 223–226.

96. Bose, U., McLaren, P., Riley, A., and Mohammedali, A. (2001). The use of telepsychiatry in the brief counseling of non-psychotic patients from an inner-London general practice. *Journal of Telemedicine and Telecare* **7**(Suppl 1), 8–10.

97. Brodey, B. B., Claypoole, K. H., Motto, J., Arias, R. G., and Gross, R. (2000). Satisfaction of forensic psychiatric patients with remote telepsychiatric evaluation. *Psychiatric Services* **51**, 1305–1307.

98. Ruskin, P. E., Reed, S., Kumar, R., Kling, M. A., Siegel, E., Rosen, M., and Hauser, P. (1998). Reliability and acceptability of psychiatric diagnosis via telecommunication and audiovisual technology. *Psychiatric services* **49**, 1086–1088.

99. Kennedy, C., and Yellowless, P. (2000). A community-based approach to evaluation of health outcomes and costs for telepsychiatry in a rural population: Preliminary results. *Journal of Telemedicine and Telecare* **6**(Suppl 1), 155–157.

100. Montani, C., Billaud, N., Tyrrell, J., Fluchaire, I., Malterre, C., Lauvernay, N., Couturier, P., and Franco, A. (1997). Psychological impact of a remote psychometric consultation with hospitalized elderly people. *Journal of Telemedicine and Telecare* **3**, 140–145.

101. Rohland, B. M. (2001). Telepsychiatry in the heartland: If we build it, will they come? *Community Mental Health Journal* **35**(5), 449–458.

102. D'Souza, R. (2002). Improving treatment adherence and longitudinal outcomes in patients with a serious mental illness by using telemedicine. *Journal of Telemedicine and Telecare* **8**(Suppl 2), 113–115.

103. Zaylor, C. (1999). Clinical outcomes in telepsychiatry. *Journal of Telemedicine and Telecare* **5**(Suppl 1), 59–60.

104. American Psychiatric Association. (2004). APA resource document on telepsychiatry via videoconferencing. Retrieved September 13, 2004 from http://www.psych.org/psych_pract/tp_paper.cfm#equip

105. Polauf, J. (1997). Telehealth: Email as a modality for crisis intervention. Retrieved June 25, 2004 from http://www.telehealth.net/articles/email.html

106. Rosser, J. C., Wood, M., and Payne, J. H. (1997). Telementoring: A practical option in surgical training. *Surgical Endoscopy* **11**, 852.

107. BBC News (2001). Doctors claim first in telesurgery. Retrieved September 15, 2004 from http://news.bbc.co.uk/1/hi/sci/tech/1552211.stm

108. MedicineNet, Inc. (2001). Med Terms Dictionary: Telesurgery. Retrieved September 15, 2004 from http://www.medterms.com/script/main/art.asp?articlekey=18479

109. Brady Urological Institute (n.d.). Urobotics: Telesurgery. Retrieved September 15, 2004 from http://urology.jhu.edu/urobotics/projects/telesurgery.html

110. Marescaux, J., Leroy, J., Rubino, F., Smith, M., Vix, M., Simone, M., and Mutter, D. (2002). Transcontinental robot-assisted remote telesurgery: Feasibility and potential applications. *Annals of Surgery* **235**(4), 487–492.

111. Yin, M. P. (2000). Telemedicine to improve patients' self-efficacy in managing diabetes. *Journal of Telemedicine and Telecare* **6**, 263–267.

112. Wilbright, W. A., Birke, J. A., Patout, C. A., Varnado, M., and Horswell, R. (2004). The use of telemedicine in the management of diabetes-related foot ulceration: A pilot study. *Advances in Skin & Wound Care* **17**(5), 232–238.

113. Whittaker, S. L., Adkins, S., Phillips, R., Jones, J., Horsley, M. A., and Kelley, G. (2004). Success factors in the long-term sustainability of a telediabetes programme. *Journal of Telemedicine and Telecare* **10**, 84–88.

114. Lowery, J. C., Hamill, J. B., Wilkins, E. G., and Clements, E. (2002). Technical overview of a web-based telemedicine system for wound assessment. *Advances in Skin & Wound Care* 15, 165–166, 168–169.

115. Visco, D. C., Shalley, T., Wren, S. J., et al. (2001). Use of telehealth for chronic wound care: A case study. *Journal of Wound Ostomy Continence Nursing* 28, 89–95.

116. Vesmarovich, S., Walker, T., Hauber, R. P., Temkin, A., and Burns, R. (1999). Use of telerehabilitation to manage pressure ulcers in persons with spinal cord injuries. *Advances in Skin & Wound Care* 12, 264–269.

117. Kobza, L., and Scheurich, A. (2000). The impact of telemedicine on outcomes of chronic wounds in the home care setting. *Ostomy Wound Management* 46, 48–53.

118. Liesenfeld, B., Renner, R., Neese, M., and Hepp, K. D. (2000). Telemedical care reduces hypoglycemias and improves glycemic control in children and adolescents with type 1 diabetes. *Diabetes Technology & Therapeutics* 2(4), 561–567.

119. Smith, I., and Weinert, C. (2000). Telecommunication support for rural women with diabetes. *Diabetes Educator* 26, 645–655.

120. Hayes, J. T., Boucher, J. L., Pronk, N. P., Gehling, E., Spencer, M., and Waslaski, J. (2001). The role of the certified diabetes educator in telephone counseling. *Diabetes Educator* 27, 377–386.

121. Levine, B., Hu, T., Alaoui, A., Fang, M., and Choi, J. (2003, December). MyCare Team: home monitoring technologies for individuals living with diabetes [Abstract]. *International Conference on Aging, Disability, and Independence*, Washington, D.C.

122. Georgetown University Medical Center (n.d.). MyCare Team: Project description. Retrieved August 4, 2004 from https://mycareteam.georgetown.edu/default.html

123. Hudson, T. (2003). Maximizing a transport platform through computer technology. *Computers, Informatics, and Nursing* 21(2), 72–79.

124. Johnston, B., Wheeler, L., Deuser, J., and Sousa, K. H. (2000). Outcomes of the Kaiser Permanente Tele-Home Health Research Project, *Archives of Family Medicine* 9, 40–45.

125. Warner, I. (1998). Telemedicine in Home Health Care: The Current Status of Practice. *Home Health Care Management & Practice* 62, 62–63.

126. Mann, W. C., Ottenbacher, K. J., Fraas, L., Tomita, M., and Granger, C. V. (1999). Effectiveness of assistive technology and environmental interventions in maintaining independence and reducing home care costs for the frail elderly. *Archives of Family Medicine* 8, 210–217.

127. Siwicki, B. (1996). Home Care Market Offers Telemedicine Opportunities. *Health Data Management*, available in 1996 WL 9609664.

128. Stensland, J., Speedie, S., Idelker, M., House, J., and Thompson, T. (1999). The relative cost of outpatient telemedicine services. *Telemedicine Journal* 5(3), 245–246.

129. Jerant, A. F., Azari, R., and Nesbitt, T. S. (2001). Reducing the cost of frequent hospital admissions for congestive heart failure: A randomized trial of a home telecare intervention. *Medical Care* 39(11), 1234–1245.

130. Frantz, A., Colgan, J., Palmer, K., and Ledgerwood, B. (2002). Lessons learned from telehealth pioneers. *Home Health Nurse Journal* 20(6), 363–366.

131. Frantz, A. (2001). Evaluating technology for success in home care. *Caring* 20(7), 10–12.

132. Fisk, M. J. (1997). Telecare equipment in the home. Issues of intrusiveness and control. *Journal of Telemedicine and Telecare* 3(1), 30–32.

133. Mann, W. C., Marchant, T., Tomita, M., Fraas, L., and Stanton, K. (2001). Elder acceptance of health monitoring devices in the home. *Care Management Journal* 3(2), 91–98.

134. QRS Diagnostic (2004). Retrieved August 5, 2004 from http://www.qrsdiagnostic.com/NewFiles/Products.html

135. Patient Care Technologies (2004). Retrieved July 17, 2004 from http://www.ptct.com/wah_Telemanage.html

136. American TeleCare (2004). Retrieved July 17, 2004 from http://www.americantelecare.com/prod_main.html

137. I-Trax Health Management Solutions (2004). Retrieved July 15, 2004 from http://www.i-trax.com/OurSolutions/CareCoordination.asp

138. AMD Telemedicine, Inc. (2004). Retrieved August 20, 2004 from http://www.amdtelemedicine.com/products_list.cfm?Specialty_ID=HOC500

139. Korhonen, I., Iivainen, T., Lappalainen, R., Tuomisto, T., Koobi, T., Pentikainen, V., Tuomisto, M., and Turjanmaa, V. (2001). TERVA: System for long-term monitoring of wellness at home. *Telemedicine Journal and E-Health* **7**(1), 61–72.

140. Bendixen, R. (2003, December). Care coordination and technology to promote independence through project L.A.M.P [Abstract]. *International Conference on Aging, Disability, and Independence*, Washington, D.C.

141. Moyer, C. A., Stern, D. T., Dobias, K. S., Cox, D. T., and Katz, S. J. (2002). Bridging the electronic divide: patient and provider perspectives on e-mail communication in primary care. *American Journal of Managed Care* **8**(5), 427–433.

142. Wootton, R. (2003). Design and implementation of an automatic message-routing system for low-cost telemedicine. *Journal of Telemedicine and Telehealth* **9**(Suppl 1), 44–47.

143. Connell, C. M., Kole, S. L, Avey, H., Benedict, C. J., and Gilman, S. (1996). Attitudes about Alzheimer's disease and the dementia service delivery network among family caregivers and service providers in rural Michigan. *American Journal of Alzheimer's Disease* **May/June**, 15–25.

144. Krout, J. A. (1997). Barriers to providing case management to older rural persons. *Journal of Case Management* **6**(4), 142–150.

145. Hooker, K., Manoogian-O'Dell, M., Monahan, D. J., Frazier, L. D., and Shifren, K. (2000). Does type of disease matter? Gender differences among Alzheimer's and Parkinson's disease spouse caregivers. *The Gerontologies* **40**, 568–573.

146. Ory, M. G., Hoffman, R. R., III, Yee, J. L., Tennstedt, S., and Schultz, R. (1999). Prevalence and impact of caregiving: A detailed comparison between dementia and nondementia caregivers. *The Gerontologies* **39**, 177–185.

147. Hooker, K., Monahan, D. J., Bowman, S. R., Frazier, L. D., and Shifren, K. (1998). Personality counts for a lot: Predictors of mental and physical health of spouse caregivers in two disease groups. *Journal of Gerontology: Psychological Sciences* **53B**, 73–85.

148. Mahoney, D. F., Tarlow, B. J., and Jones, R. N. (2003). Effects of an automated telephone support system on caregiver burden and anxiety: Findings from the REACH for TLC intervention study. *The Gerontologies* **43**, 556–567.

149. Glueckauf, R. L., and Loomis, J. S. (2003). Alzheimer's caregiver support online: Lessons learned, initial findings and future directions. *NeuroRehabilitation* **18**, 135–146.

150. Hanson, E., and Nolan, M. (2003, December). Working with older people and their carers to research and develop responsive ICT support services [Abstract]. International Conference on Aging, Disability, and Independence, Washington, D.C.

151. Denton, D. R. (2003). Ethical and legal issues related to telepractice. *Seminars in Speech Language*, 313–322.

152. Wojtylak, M. A., Bartholomew, K. C., Bell, P. A., Farrell, M. J., Ferrell, M. K., Ganci, A., Horne, N. R., Jones, C. M., King, R. C., Lynch, P. J., McMenamin, J. P., Turner, C. D., and White, T. J. (2004). Recent developments in medicine and law. *Tort Trial Insurance Practice & Law Journal* **39**(2), 597–628.

153. 2001 Report to Congress on Telemedicine. Health Resources and Services Administration, Office for the Advancement of Telehealth Available at: http://telehealth.hrsa.gov/pubs/report2001/main.htm

154. Health Privacy Project (2002). The State of Health Privacy, 2nd ed. Web site: www.healthprivacy.org

155. Advanced Technology Institute (2003). Retrieved July 15, 2004 from http://www.aticorp.org

156. U.S. Department of Health and Human Services, Office for Civil Rights (2002). Medical Privacy—National Standards to Protect the Privacy of Personal Health Information @ www.hhs.gov/ocr/hipaa/privacy.html

157. De Meyer, F., Claerhout, B., and De Moor, G. J. (2002). The PRIDEH project: Taking up privacy protection services in e-health. *Study in Health Technology Information* **93**, 171–177.

158. Capitol Hill Steering Committee on Telehealth and Healthcare Informatics, Department of Commerce's Office of Technology (2004). *Innovation, Demand and Investment in Telehealth.*

159. Whitten, P., and Kuwahara, E. (2003). Telemedicine from the payor perspective: Considerations for reimbursement decisions. *Disease Management Health Outcomes* **11**(5), 291–298.

160. BioControl, Systems Inc. (2004). Retrieved August 15, 2004 from http://www.biocontrol.com/personnel.html

PART II

RELATED ASPECTS OF AGING, DISABILITY, AND INDEPENDENCE

CHAPTER 6

BASIC ASSISTIVE TECHNOLOGY

Cristina Posse and William Mann

6.1 INTRODUCTION

Assistive devices are "technological tools that restore or extend human functions. . . ."[1] The term "low-technology devices," or basic assistive technology, includes simple items, with few moving parts, that aid in the performance of everyday activities and are of relatively low cost.[1,2] While we continue to see rapid advances in smart technology, basic assistive technology devices continue to be widely used and have a positive impact in promoting independence. Basic assistive technology devices can lower health-care costs also[3], and shorten hospitalizations,[4] making it easier to function in the physical and social environment.[1,5-7] The effectiveness of this technology is, however, dependent on the interaction of several factors, from the tangible characteristics of the devices, the needs, interests, and activities of the person, and the training and accessibility of information and resources.[5,8-10]

This chapter provides an overview of basic assistive technology devices, organized by the impairment type they primarily address. We also discuss basic devices used by persons who have arthritis or who are experiencing the long-term effects of stroke. A review of all diseases of later years is not possible in this chapter. However, two are selected because of the many older persons impacted by one (arthritis), and the severity of impact and resultant impairments of the other (stroke). More than half of persons 65+ have arthritis, and, while its severity varies from person to person, for many it impacts on performing everyday activities. Stroke has the potential to result in multiple impairments: vision, hearing, mobility, speech, and cognition. Arthritis and stroke represent diseases of aging that often result in impairments—impairments that can be addressed through the use of assistive technology. With thousands of assistive devices available, this chapter presents an overview of some of the most widely used devices. Research on the use and effectiveness of basic assistive technology is also reviewed in this chapter.

6.2 LOW-TECHNOLOGY DEVICES AND IMPAIRMENT

Mobility Impairment

With increasing age and its inherent chronic conditions, the ability to move is often limited. This impacts basic daily activities, such as dressing, bathing, and walking.[1,11]

Smart Technology for Aging, Disability, and Independence, Edited by William C. Mann
Copyright © 2005 John Wiley & Sons, Inc.

The use of basic assistive devices can improve performance in these everyday activities. We discuss mobility devices in this section.

Canes and Walkers   Overall, mobility devices provide support and stability.[5,12] Canes and walkers can, respectively, support up to 25% and 50% of a person's weight. These devices can be lightweight if made from aluminum or carbon fiber. Proper fit relative to posture and positioning is an important consideration with these mobility devices. There should be 20 to 30 degrees of elbow flexion when holding a cane or walker.[12,13] An improper fit can result in a stooped posture.[5,12,13]

Canes and walkers rank high on non-use and dissatisfaction among older adults.[9] Problems with canes often reported by elders, include heavy weight and fear of falling while using the device.[12] Proper fit and appropriate training is important for safety and to meet individual needs. Proper footwear along with avoidance of uneven surfaces and stairs are also important.[13] While canes and walkers can be purchased from catalogs or drug stores without prescription, professional guidance from a physical or occupational therapist will help ensure successful use.[5,12]

Cane designs vary in types of handles; types of bases, and types of tips. Handles can be crooked, ball-topped, straight, T-shaped, or shoveled[12] (Table 6.1). A cane with

TABLE 6.1   Functional Mobility Devices[14]

Devices	Types	Device price
Canes	Handles	$10.95–$89.95
	• Crooked	
	• Ball-topped	
	• Straight	
	• Shovel	
	• Pistol	
	Shaft	
	• Traditional wood	
	• Aluminum	
	• Carbon fiber	
	Bases	
	• Single	
	• Four-point base	
	Tips	
	• Suction	
	• Stabilizer	
	• Metal	
	• Rubber	
Walker	Rigid	$29.95–$519.95
	Side	
	Wheeled	
Wheelchair	Manual chair	$179.95–$3995
	Power chair	

a single-point base can benefit people with balance deficits, osteoarthritis, or vision impairment. Typically, people who have mobility impairment as a result of stroke require more stability and walk more slowly and thus are better candidates for canes with multiple-point bases.[5] These canes are called quad high profile, quad wide, or quad narrow.[12] The wider and higher the base, the more support it provides, yet canes with larger bases are heavier (Figure 6.1). Cane tips are most commonly made from rubber. They require good maintenance and timely replacement.[5,12] Some cane tips are designed for icy or snowy surfaces.[12] Other cane accessories include seats, wrist straps, cane holders, forearm cuffs, and forearm platforms. Some canes also integrate a reacher at the end of the leg, which can help pick up items off the floor.[14]

Walker designs include rigid, folding, or wheeled (two, three, or four wheels).[14] Rigid walkers require lifting to move forward. Wheeled walkers are simply pushed forward. Folding walkers make transport easier. Most two-wheeled walkers have automatic breaks and some have an auto-glide feature that skims the surface. Three- and four-wheeled walkers have hand brakes and even though they are heavier, they require less strength and energy. Today's walkers include features such as seats, trays, baskets, and platform arm supports (Figures 6.2 and 6.3).[13]

Wheelchairs Wheelchairs come in hundreds of varieties, but their basic design is similar: a seat with two side frames joined by a cross brace. Most wheelchair

Figure 6.1   Canes and walkers can be used indoors and outdoors.

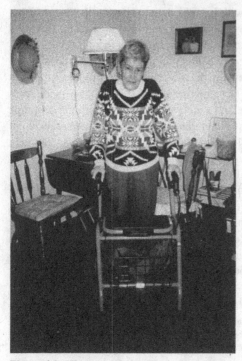

Figure 6.2 Two-wheeled walker with basket and tray.

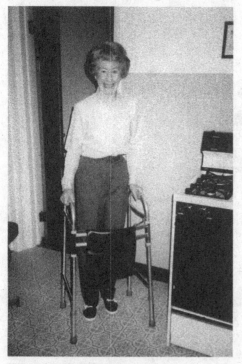

Figure 6.3 Walker with accessory.

frames are built using aluminum, stainless steel, chrome, steel tubing, titanium, or other lightweight composite materials. Frame weight and overall strength is dependent on the type of material used to construct the frame.

The wheelchair's seat, back, arms, and leg- and footrests provide support for the body. Armrests may be short, for ease in pulling up to a desk, or longer to support the entire arm. Some arms are detachable or swing out of the way, making transfers and transporting the chair easier. Foot and legrests support the legs for comfort or medical reasons (relieve of edema). Some footrests are removable or swing under the seat. The height, depth, and angle are usually adjustable.

Wheelchair wheels both drive and steer the chair. Tire materials affect the wheelchair's rolling resistance. Generally, pneumatic tires (inflated like bicycle tires) are better for outside use. Solid tires (rubber or polymer) work better on carpeted floors. Pneumatic tires generally give a more comfortable ride, but require more maintenance than solid tires. A pneumatic tire that is low on air will make it much harder to push the wheelchair. The small wheels in front of the chair are called "casters." Larger casters give a more comfortable ride and clear obstacles more easily. Small casters provide better maneuverability, but are easily caught in cracks and rough terrain.

Hand rims and brakes provide control. Hand rims, used to drive a manual wheelchair, are mounted outside the back wheel. Brakes are required on all wheelchairs. Wheelchair anti-tipping devices can be added to the front or back of a wheelchair to prevent tipping forward or backward. The "Natural-Fit™"[15] (Figure 6.4) hand rim is an innovative design for wheelchair hand rims that provides an ergonomic grip that has reduced fatigue and pain, while increasing satisfaction among customers. The same inventors have created "The Smart Wheel™" (Figure 6.5), a tool that measures wheelchair propulsion biomechanics and has research and clinical applications such as assistance with wheelchair selection, insurance justification, and propulsion training. This wireless technology can measure how forces are applied to the hand rim and other parameters including distance traveled, acceleration, and velocity. Also see Figure 6.5.

A tilt and recline feature is available for wheelchairs. This can provide pressure and postural relief. Recline refers to changing the angle of the seat to the chair's

Figure 6.4   "The Natural Fit"™ Hand rim.

Figure 6.5 "The Smart Wheel"™.

back. A reclining back can help people who need a change of position because of poor head and trunk control, circulation problems, or respiratory problems. Reclining frames come in both manual and powered models. Tilt refers to tilting the back and seat backwards. The angle of the seat and back remains the same, but the angle of the seat and back to the floor changes. Tilting takes the pressure off the buttocks and onto the back. Wheelchair cushion design is important both for comfort and to prevent sores. There are now many new wheelchair cushion designs available.[16]

Common complaints of older adults regarding their wheelchairs include width (too narrow or too wide), seat comfort, weight, and difficulty with special features such as armrests, back support, and problems with tires. As with all assistive devices, the use of wheelchairs depends on various personal and environmental factors. Considering that elders own their wheelchairs for a long period of time, their design should be as individualized as possible.[5,17,18] Wheelchair accessories can enhance use and include lapboards, arm trays, gloves for pushing, seatbelts, and transfer boards (Figures 6.6 and 6.7). Other attachable devices are bags or side pouches, safety flags to be more visible when riding, umbrellas, and cup holders.[19]

Other Issues with Seating   Many elders have difficulty coming to a standing position, once seated. A portable lift seat (includes a cushion with a gentle spring) is a useful device for standing from a seated position (Figure 6.8). It requires no switches or installation, can be easily transported, and weighs approximately 8 pounds.[20]

Mobility and Self-Care Activities of Daily Living (ADLs)

Reachers   Reachers are helpful, low-cost devices for older adults designed to pick up small or large objects (e.g., cans, pans, dishes, books, CDs), and can be used in a variety of activities such as dressing, cooking, and gardening (Figure 6.9).[2,18] These devices can be used to reach for items stored on high shelves, preventing the more risky approach of climbing on a chair, stool, or ladder.[11] Reachers extend the range of motion of a person with disabilities (e.g., low back problems, arthritis,

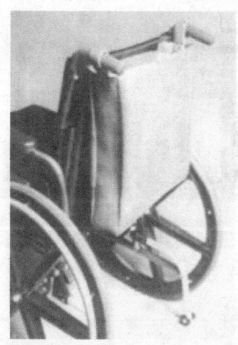

Figure 6.6   Wheelchair with tote bag and anti-tipping device.

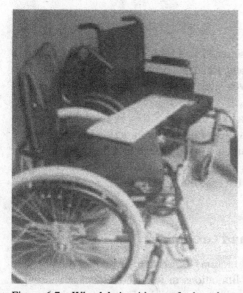

Figure 6.7   Wheelchair with transfer board.

Figure 6.8   Portable lift seat.

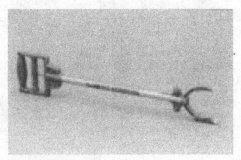

Figure 6.9   A basic reacher.

hypertension, stroke).[2,18] Older adults use reachers to pick up remote controls and to take cups and dishes in and out of cabinets. Reachers can be purchased from department stores, ordered from catalogs or web sites, or prescribed in a medical rehabilitation setting.[11]

A study of reacher use by older adults found that they preferred lightweight reachers with adjustable length, a lock system for grip, lever action trigger, forearm and wrist support, life-time guarantee, and one-hand use. One of the most important criteria for reachers used by elders is that they are lightweight. Self-closing or locking mechanisms are also important because they eliminate the need to grasp the handle for a prolonged period of time.[11]

Assistive Devices for Dressing and Grooming[5,21]

Many older adults have limited range of motion (ROM) in their joints, and they may also have limitation in strength. These limitations in joint movement and strength can make dressing and grooming difficult or impossible. Fortunately, there are a number of basic assistive devices for use with dressing tasks. Dressing sticks are used to pull up pants and for donning shirts. Other devices include sock aids for putting on socks, zipper pulls, buttonhooks, and long-handled shoe horns. Table 6.2 provides a list of ADL devices, types, and prices. Devices for grooming include extensions to brushes, combs, razors, or makeup. Stands for hair dryers, files, nail clippers, and toothpaste are also available.

Toileting and Bathing   Bathing, toileting, dressing, and mobility tasks are the most common activities for which older adults use assistive devices.[22-25] More household accidents occur in the bathroom than in any other room in the house. Using assistive devices can help a person maintain independence while bathing safely and independently. There are a number of different devices that allow for seated bathing in a tub. Bath stools provide a seat while bathing or showering. They are economical and lightweight and are suitable for people of slight to medium build. The seat is approximately 15 inches and rests on rustproof legs. With no backrest, the stool allows easy access to the person's back for easy washing. Compact in size,

TABLE 6.2   A Sample of Assistive Devices for Self-Care[27-29]

Activities	Device	Types	Price
Dressing	Sock and stocking aids	Wood, plastic, built-up	$13.75–$40.95
	Button hook	handle	$5.95–$9.95
	Shoehorns	Plastic, stainless steel	$4.95–$11.95
	Dressing stick		$4.95–$45.95
Eating and food preparation	Built-up utensils	Various grips and angles	$7.49–$16.49
	Jar and bottle openers	Hand-held, wall-mounted,	$10.49–$30.49
	Rocking knife	under-cabinet	$10.35–$23.95
	Nonslip cutting board		$32.15–$71.25
Bathing	Long-handled brushes		$4.95–$31.95
	Nonslip mats		$13.45–$44.95
	Hand-held shower		$19.95–$25.95
	Seating	Stools, chairs, benches	$29.75–$239.95
Toileting	Seats	Raised commodes	$24.15–$285.00
	Toilet safety frame		$44.95–$49.95
	Transfer benches		$94.95–$274.95
Grooming	Long-handle brushes		$16.95–$44.95
	Long-reach toenail scissors		$14.95
Leisure	Gardening tools with ergonomically designed handles		$15.95
	Card holders		$5.95
	Automatic card shuffler		$11.95
	Book holder		$6.45–$45.95
Writing	Adjustable pen		$5.49–$49.45

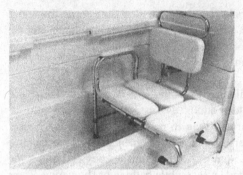

Figure 6.10   A bath seat designed for seated transfer into the tub.

the bath stool provides a good solution for narrow tubs, and it can be stored easily when not in use. However, its small base contributes to somewhat poor stability.

Bath chairs (Figure 6.10) provide a contoured seat and backrest, and they are helpful for people with poor back strength. The chair is stronger than a bath stool, and is able to support people weighing up to 400 pounds. Stability is enhanced with rubber-capped legs and a wide base, but the wide base may limit its use in narrow tubs. Bath chairs are available with a soft padded seat, providing more bathing comfort, and providing protection for people with sensitive skin.[22] Other models of bath chairs allow for adjustments in seat height.[26]

Other bathing devices include mats and treads, grab bars, tub boards, and lifts. For seated bathing, hand-held showers, long hand-held brushes, and sponges aid in reaching the legs, feet, and back.

For toileting, commodes are available in several designs for use at bedside or over the toilet.[21] Male or female urinals are another option, but require good hand coordination to hold the funnel and empty urine in the bag.[5] Frames can also be placed along the sides of a toilet to facilitate standing and bending. Long-handled toilet paper holders are available for assistance in cleaning the perineal area.[5]

Devices for Eating

A wide variety of assistive devices are available to make eating easier. Built-up utensils with nonslip rubber or foam grips make grasping easier. These devices also come in different forms, such as angled, curved, or bendable. Rocker knifes assist people with stroke in cutting food with one hand.[5]

Leisure and Other Devices for Mobility Impairment[21,27]

Table 6.2 lists several assistive devices used for gardening, card playing, reading, and writing. These include built-up handle devices, as well as holders for pens and cards (Figure 6.11). Devices for other activities, such as unlocking doors, include key holders and levered door handles.

Figure 6.11   Card holders.

Cognitive Impairment

The definition of dementia has four components: a decrease in short-term memory, a deficit in one other area of cognitive function, no clouding of consciousness, and severe enough to impair function. The leading cause of dementia in the elderly is Alzheimer's disease,[30] but there are other forms of dementia. Other forms include multi-infarct dementia, secondary dementias such as occur with multiple sclerosis, and forms that are reversible such as pernicious anemia. It is estimated that close to 7% of the 65+ population has some form of dementia, and this increases to over 17% for persons 85+.

Most persons with Alzheimer's disease live at home throughout most of the course of this disease. The early stages reflect mild cognitive symptoms, progressing to the final stage where the person is both severely physically and cognitively impaired and is unable to get out of bed without assistance. Alzheimer's disease even at the early stages can impact on memory, decision-making, judgment, and comprehension of ideas or instructions (Figure 6.12).

People with Alzheimer's disease tend to reduce their use of assistive devices as the disease progresses.[31] Caregivers often make home modifications to control wandering or behaviors such as turning faucets on, or constantly opening the refrigerator. Persons with moderate to severe cognitive impairment who live in the community are in most cases living with someone, in part due to the level of personal assistance they need.[31] Some caregivers prefer to take responsibility for some tasks, such as medication intake, regardless of available assistive devices. This is due to the safety factor related with taking all medications daily and on time, which can be difficult for a person with a cognitive impairment.[32]

Vision Impairment

Most older persons with vision impairment are not totally blind, but have partial or low vision. Advances in ophthalmic surgery and more effective medical control of

Figure 6.12   Picture phone for cognitive impairment.

eye diseases have contributed to the greater proportion of older persons who have low vision, rather than those who are blind. The sharp increase in the 65+ age group has also contributed to a steady increase in the number of persons with useful partial sight. Although persons with a visual impairment may retain usable vision, loss of sight requires spending more time and effort in accomplishing tasks. Techniques and devices are available that maximize remaining visual ability.

Approximately 4.4% of the population of the United States experiences activity limitation due to visual impairment.[33] Among elderly persons, the incidence is higher. Visual impairment in older persons has been documented and described by numerous authorities.[34-36] Older persons are a heterogeneous population, which makes it difficult to determine the exact number of persons who are blind or who have a severe visual impairment; however, one study estimated that 82 out of 1000 older persons have a serious visual impairment.[37] One out of five elderly persons has difficulty with reading because of a visual impairment, and one out of 20 persons older than 65 years of age cannot see words or letters on a page.[38]

Visual impairment may result in a restricted field of vision or in a diminished ability to see sharpness of detail, read standard size print, determine color or depth perception, see contrasts, adjust to changes in light or glare, or locate objects.[39] Visual loss can affect a person's activities of daily living (ADLs), leisure pursuits, education, vocation, and social interaction. The severity of visual loss and the resulting limitations vary with such factors as age of onset, support systems available, and coping strategies.[40]

Compensatory strategies for low vision include illumination techniques and use of contrast, magnification, memorization of location, and auditory and tactile feedback. Compensatory strategies may include the use of optical, nonoptical, low-technology, and high-technology devices to improve functional visual performance. Optical devices, such as high-powered lenses and telescopic spectacles, are items prescribed by an ophthalmologist or optometrist and may require specialized training and periodic reevaluation. Nonoptical devices include items that are readily available and require no special training, such as felt-tip markers and large-print books. Low-technology devices, such as a standard cassette recorder, require little training and may include simple adaptations such as large-print or raised-line indicators on the controls. High-technology devices refer to more sophisticated electronic technology, such as computers and reading machines; these are described in Chapter 4.

Assistive devices are playing an increasingly important role in improving the functional performance of visually impaired persons. In the special issue of the *Journal of Visual Impairment and Blindness* on technical issues for the 1990s, Dixon and Mandelbaum[41] described how technological advances in the use of printed material have improved communication for persons with severe visual impairments. In *Technology and Disability*, Orr and Piqueras[42] raised several issues related to the use of assistive technology by older persons with visual impairments and suggested that some devices may be intimidating. "Low-tech" devices, such as magnifiers, writing guides, and mobility canes, have been available for many years.

Hearing Impairment

Hearing impairment is one of the five most common chronic conditions of aging. It is estimated that one out of three persons over age 64 has some hearing impairment; this increases to almost one out of two persons over age 84.[43] There are many assistive devices available for persons with hearing impairment (Table 6.3), but often loss of hearing is so gradual that many elders accept the loss as simply a normal process of aging, and do not seek assistance. Hearing loss impacts negatively on communication, and decreased communication can in turn result in isolation and depression.[44] Hearing loss can also impact on safety and health in other ways as well, such as failing to hear a fire alarm or not being able to clearly understand a pharmacist's directions for taking medications.

Hearing loss can be the result of exposure to excessively loud noise over time, to hypertension, to neurological diseases such as stroke, or to the side effects of medications. The three major types of hearing loss are conductive, sensorineural, and central. Many older people experience "mixed hearing loss," a combination of conductive and sensorineural impairments.

Conductive hearing loss occurs when sound waves cannot reach the inner ear; the impact of conductive hearing loss is similar to wearing ear plugs. Hearing aids are often quite effective for persons with conductive hearing loss. Sensorineural hearing loss relates to damage to the cochlea and surrounding hair cells—the cells that send electrical signals to the brain. Many people refer to sensorineural hearing loss as nerve deafness; one common type among older persons is presbycusis. Presbycusis first causes loss of hearing in high-pitched sounds; over time, lower and lower pitch sound loss occurs. Tinnitus is also a sensorineural disorder, causing ringing or buzzing in the ears and impacting more than 90% of persons 65+. Central

TABLE 6.3 Environmental Alerting Devices for Hearing Impairment[20]

Device	Function	Picture
Vibrating alarms	Allows person with hearing impairment to wake from vibration rather than by auditory alarm	
Door knock alert	Allows person with hearing impairment to see a blinking light rather than hearing an auditory "knock" sound	
Smoke detectors	Allows person with hearing impairment to see fire alarm rather than hearing auditory fire emergency sound	

hearing loss relates to damage of nerves leading to the brain or damage to the brain itself. Stroke, traumatic brain injury, or vascular disorders can result in central hearing loss.

A *Consumer Assessments Study*[45] report on 35 older persons with hearing impairment found that they used an average of 11.5 assistive devices per person. They used devices that addressed hearing impairment, but more of the devices addressed physical impairments other than hearing, underlining the complexity of multiple impairments faced by older persons. This study found a high rate of dissatisfaction with the devices they were using, almost one out of three devices. Must of the dissatisfaction was targeted at hearing aids. Cognitive impairment also has an impact on assistive device use: Older hearing-impaired persons with severe cognitive impairments use about half as many assistive devices as those older hearing-impaired persons who are not severely cognitively impaired. Results of this study underline the need for: (1) providing consumers with more information on assistive devices, including product comparisons and up-to-date information on new products, and (2) audiological follow-up care.

Arthritis

Arthritis is a serious disabling condition affecting large numbers of persons. It is estimated that 37 million people in the United States have some form of arthritis, with the prevalence greatest among elderly persons.[46] Data from the Longitudinal Study on Aging indicated that 55% of elderly persons have arthritis.[47] Arthritis also has a major impact on our economy: The cost of rheumatic disease (one of several forms of arthritis) was estimated at $35 billion for 1991, or 1% of the gross national product.[48]

The impact of arthritis on activities of elderly persons has been documented in several studies. Using the Longitudinal Study on Aging, Yelin and Katz[49] determined that for those elderly persons who had arthritis and no other chronic conditions, 66% experienced limitations in physical activities, with 25% reporting limitations in activities of daily living (ADLs) or instrumental activities of daily living (IADLs). For those elderly persons who had arthritis and at least one other chronic condition, 82% had limitations in physical activity, and 41% were limited in ADLs. When these same persons were examined 2 years later, the percentage of persons with ADL/IADL limitations increased significantly for both groups.

Korsorok et al.[50] studied the number of restricted activity days of elderly persons. Using data from the 1984 Supplement on Aging of the National Health Interview Survey, they determined an annual average of 31 restricted activity days for elderly persons: 6 days were associated with falls; 4 days with heart disease; 4 days with arthritis and rheumatism; 2 days each with high blood pressure, cerebrovascular disease, and visual impairment; and 1 day each with atherosclerosis, diabetes, major malignancies, and osteoporosis. Arthritis was ranked in this study as the second most important cause of restricted activity days among elderly persons.

Verbrugge et al.[51] concluded that elderly persons with arthritis had more difficulty in physical functions, personal care, and household care than did elderly persons without the disease. Disability was greatest in the areas of walking, reaching, stooping, and other physical functions, especially those that require endurance and strength. The symptoms of arthritis (joint pain, stiffness, reduced range of motion) contribute to a reduction in activity. Eventually, reduced activity can result in loss of physical function. The impact of activity and exercise for persons with arthritis is a frequent topic in the literature. After review of 97 articles, Buchner et al.[52] concluded that exercise and activity can impact positively on functional status and can reduce pain. Assistive technology can help many people with arthritis in maintaining a higher level of activity than would otherwise be possible.

Disability is closely linked to functional status. Verbrugge et al.[53] suggested that a long duration of arthritis, recent medical care for arthritis, and obesity were risk factors for disability. Abyad and Boyer[46] confirmed the association of disability and obesity in elderly persons with arthritis. Additionally, disability rates for persons with arthritis appear to be increasing.[47]

An article from the Consumer Assessments Study reported on assistive device use by home-based older persons with arthritis (Figures 6.13 and 6.14).[54] Sixty-six persons were assigned to a moderate or a severe arthritis group according to the impact of arthritis on their activities. Study participants in the severe arthritis group

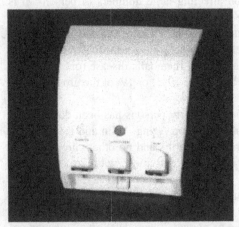

Figure 6.13   Soap and shampoo dispenser facilitate grasp.

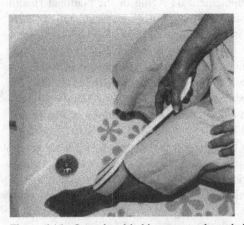

Figure 6.14   Long hand-held sponge and treads in tub.

had more chronic diseases, a higher level of pain, and a lower level of independence in self-care activities than did study participants in the moderate arthritis group. Similarities between the groups included relatively poor health, high rate of medication use, depression, use of a high number of assistive devices (about 10 per person), and an expressed need for additional devices, such as reachers, magnifiers, grab bars, jar openers, and hearing aids. Generally, there was a high rate of satisfaction with the assistive devices used. Most study participants missed being able to participate in at least one activity; most of these activities were active and many related to leisure time. Findings also revealed that study participants had inadequate information on assistive devices, which suggests the importance of information dissemination initiatives for older persons with disabilities.

Stroke

Stroke is defined as *rapidly developing clinical signs of focal (or at times global) disturbance of cerebral function lasting more than 24 hours or leading to death with no apparent cause other than that of vascular origin.*[55] A more recent definition adds the term "RIND" (resolvable, intracerebral, neurological defici), which can last several days; "stroke" would now be defined as lasting more than just a few days. The most outstanding feature of stroke is weakness or paralysis of the extremities on one side of the body. Other common symptoms include dysphasia or aphasia (51%), memory impairment or disorientation (47%), and loss of or altered sensation (36%).[56] More than half of individuals who experience stroke live longer than 1 year, and these stroke survivors typically die from causes other than stroke.[57] Most stroke survivors are not institutionalized, but live in their own homes or with relatives. Coping with the long-term effects of stroke while living at home often requires the use of assistive devices and home modifications. There has been significant study of the rehabilitation of individuals who have survived a stroke,[58] suggesting that older stroke survivors have much difficulty in coping with the long-term effects.

Two papers from the RERC-Aging *Consumer Assessments Study* focused on assistive technology and the needs of older persons with stroke living at home.[1,2] The first study report found that these individuals owned 16 assistive devices, on average, and used about 80% of them. In examining the home environment, the bathroom presents the largest number of problems for older stroke survivors, followed by the kitchen—rooms where many basic ADLs and IADLs are carried out. In the follow-up study one year later, 20% of the sample had either moved into a nursing home or died. The remaining study participants experienced significant declines in physical and health status and demonstrated coping strategies such as acquiring additional assistive devices. The use and cost of devices for patients in a stroke unit were compared with use and cost of devices for stroke patients in a general ward in a study of 249 patients in Sweden. Only 2.1% of the overall health costs were attributed to assistive devices. The prescription of simple devices and training in the first three months after stroke had an impact on lower costs for the patients assigned to the stroke units.[25]

6.3 FUNDING FOR ASSISTIVE TECHNOLOGY IN THE UNITED STATES

Some assistive technology is funded through government programs (federal, state, and local), private health insurance, and private nonprofit organizations. While there are many funding sources for assistive technology, most spending to purchase assistive devices is out of pocket. In 2001, the Medical Expenditure Panel Survey indicated that 61% of spending on "other medical supplies and services" was out of pocket. This survey was aimed at gathering information from the civilian, noninstitutionalized U.S. population. "Other medical supplies and service" is a category that includes many items that would be considered assistive devices, such as visual aids, hearing aids, prosthetics, wheelchairs, and bathroom aids. In 2002, the National Health Expenditure Study estimated that 45% of the spending for "Durable Medical Equipment" was out of pocket. Durable medical equipment is defined as including "the retail sales of items such as contact lenses, eyeglasses and other ophthalmic products, surgical and orthopedic products, equipment rental, and hearing aids." These items would all be considered assistive devices. These high percentages of out-of-pocket expenditures suggest that assistive technology is not adequately covered by third-party payers in the United States.

Government Funding of AT   The major government programs that provide funding for assistive technology are Medicare, Medicaid, and Veteran's benefits. For Medicare and Medicaid, assistive technology typically falls under the category of durable medical equipment, prosthetics, orthotics, and supplies. Durable medical equipment is defined as equipment that can withstand repeated use, is primarily and customarily used to serve a medical purpose, generally is not useful to a person in the absence of an injury or illness, and is appropriate for use in the home. Both of these programs are health-care programs and therefore are not necessarily aimed at improving function, but at improving health status. Medicare and Medicaid require that assistive devices be "medically necessary" to qualify for funding. This means that the device must improve the individual's medical condition. Many people require assistive devices to increase their functional ability, not necessarily improve their medical condition.

Medicare   Assistive devices are typically paid for under Medicare part B, which is a supplemental health-care plan that covers outpatient expenses. The types of assistive technology that Medicare covers includes mobility aids (such as walkers, canes, and wheelchairs), orthotics, and prosthetics. Hearing and vision aids are typically not covered under Medicare. These three qualifiers must be met to fund an assistive device under Medicare. (1) The equipment is used in the patients' home. (2) The equipment is necessary and reasonable for the treatment of the patient's illness or injury or to improve functioning. (3) The equipment meets the definition of durable medical equipment. In 2000, Medicare spent over 2 billion dollars on assistive technology.

Medicaid—Standard Medicaid is a health-care program funded jointly by the federal and state governments. This joint funding results in variation of coverage for assistive technology from state to state. Almost all states cover vision aids, some cover hearing devices, almost all cover prosthetics and orthotics, most cover some types of mobility aids like walkers or wheelchairs, and just over half cover augmentative communication devices. In 1999, Medicaid fee-for-service plans spent over $990 million on durable medical equipment and supplies.

Medicaid Home and Community Based Waiver This is an optional waiver that most states offer. The HCBW is designed to provide community-based services to people who need some help to stay in the community and out of an institution. Often, assistive devices are covered under this waiver, but it also varies from state to state. Almost all states cover a personal emergency response system, most cover home modifications, and less than half of the states' waivers cover mobility aids, eyeglasses, or hearing aids.

Veteran's benefits The Medical Benefits Package for Veteran's covers orthotics, prosthetics, eyeglasses, hearing aids, wheelchairs, and some AT for activities of daily living and communication. There are other programs that cover home and vehicle modifications, but are dependent on the Veteran's level of disability.

Other Programs Other government programs that cover AT to some extent include Vocational Rehabilitation, the Older American's Act, social security, and the Assistive Technology Act of 1998.

Private Not-for-Profit Funding for Assistive Technology There are many private not-for-profit organizations that offer assistance in purchasing, or "borrowing" for assistive devices. Some are run by national organizations and some are state specific. However, the programs vary greatly from state to state and even city to city. An excellent way to find programs in a particular location is to call the local Area Agency on Aging or Independent Living Center and inquire about the programs available.

There are many sources of funding for assistive technology, but they are fragmented and often difficult to navigate. Fragmentation of coverage results in part from the fact that government health programs are aimed at improving the person's medical condition rather than funding assistive technology that would improve functional ability. Medicaid's Home and Community-Based Waiver begins to address functional ability by funding some assistive devices needed to help a person remain living independently in the community.

There is a hierarchy of funding sources when seeking reimbursement for assistive devices. The sources sequentially from first tapped to last for a nonveteran is as follows: private health insurance, Medicare B, Medicaid, Medicaid Home and Community-Based Waiver, other government or not-for-profit programs, and private pay. Not all programs have open enrollment and often they have caps on either money dispersed for assistive technology or people enrolled in the program. This often results in waiting lists to receive benefits from programs. Most programs also have qualifications the individual must meet to enroll in the program such as income level, age, or level of disability.

6.4   RESOURCES FOR ASSISTIVE TECHNOLOGY

Hearing

Lion's Club Hearing   The Lion's Club is a service organization involved in humanitarian causes. They provide hearing screenings and communication aids for people who are hearing impaired.

Web site: http://www.lionsclubs.org/EN/content/programs_hear.shtml

300 W 22nd Street

Oak Brook, IL 60523-8842

Hear Now   This foundation promotes hearing health awareness, supports and conducts hearing related research, provides education on hearing health, and gives away batteries and hearing aids.

Web site: www.sotheworldmayhear.org/forms/hearnow.php

Phone: 800-769-2799

Fax: 952-828-6946

Vision

Lighthouse International   Lighthouse International is a worldwide resource on vision and vision impairment. The Low-Vision Super Store equips professionals with the tools they need to care for low-vision patients. The Lighthouse Store has equipment for people with vision impairment, including lighting, mirrors, magnifiers, and talking products.

Web site: http://www.lighthouse.org/about_main.htm

Email: info@lighthouse.org

Phone: 800-829-0500

111 East 59th Street

New York, NY 10022-1202

Vision Connection   Founded by Lighthouse International, this site offers assistive technology buying tips, Braille products, speech products, magnification products, and more.

Web site: http://www.visionconnection.org/VisionConnection/default.htm

Lion's Club Vision   Lion's Club is a service organization involved in humanitarian causes. They are involved in many activities to prevent or reverse blindness and compensate for visual impairment. Their programs offer free quality eye care, eye-glasses, Braille-writers, large-print texts, white canes, guide dogs, and glaucoma screenings.

> Web site: http://www.lionsclubs.org/EN/content/vision_index.shtml
>
> 300 W 22nd Street
>
> Oak Brook, IL 60523-8842

National Federation for the Blind   NFB provides education and advocacy for people who are blind and the community at large, as well as assistive technology for consumers. They provide an on-line catalog of devices and descriptions of technologies available to help people with a visual impairment.

> Web site: www.nfb.org
>
> Phone: 410-659-9314
>
> Fax: 410-685-5653
>
> National Federation of the Blind
>
> 1800 Johnson Street
>
> Baltimore, MD 21230
>
> Email: materials@nfb.org

New Eyes for the Needy, Inc.   This organization's purpose is to distribute eye-glasses to low-income people with visual impairments.

> Phone: 973-376-4903
>
> Fax: 973-376-3807
>
> 549 Millburn Avenue
>
> P.O. Box 332
>
> Short Hills, NJ 07078

General

Abledata   Abledata is a federally funded project to provide information on assistive technology to consumers and health-care providers. Abledata has a database of over 30,000 assistive technology products. The database provides a description of the product, price, and information about the company that creates the product.

> Web site: www.abledata.com
>
> E-mail: abledata@orcmacro.com
>
> Phone: 1-800-227-0216
>
> Fax: 301-608-8958
>
> TTY: 301-608-8912
>
> 8630 Fenton Street, Suite 930
>
> Silver Spring, MD 20910

Easter Seals Easter Seals is an organization that provides services and equipment to children and adults with disabilities. Assistive technology is usually obtained through their job training programs and paid for through a Vocational Rehabilitation program.

Web site: www.easterseals.com/site/PageServer

Phone: 312-726-6200

Toll-free: 800-221-6827

TTY: 312-726-4258

Fax: 312-726-1494

230 West Monroe Street, Suite 1800

Chicago, IL 60606

Eldercare Locator This service by the U.S. Administration on Aging puts older people and their families in touch with state and local area Agencies on Aging, who would be able to provide information about the types of assistive technology programs in a specific area.

Web page: http://www.eldercare.gov/Eldercare/Public/Home.asp

Phone: 800-677-1116

TDD/TTY: Access relay service and ask them to connect to 800-677-1116.

Medicare Typically, Medicare refers to some assistive devices as durable medical equipment. This is a technical site that offers good information about what types of equipment are covered and under what circumstances, but it can be difficult to navigate because it is set up to be used by providers.

Web site: http://www.cms.hhs.gov/suppliers/dmepos/

General web site: www.medicare.gov

Phone: 800-633-4227

Medicaid This site lists the contact information for Medicaid in each state. It provides address, phone number, email, and web site.

Web site: http://www.cms.hhs.gov/medicaid/allStateContacts.asp

Centers for Medicare and Medicaid Services

Toll Free Phone: 877-267-2323

Toll Free TTY: 866-226-1819

The Muscular Dystrophy Association The MD Association has a wide range of programs to benefit people with muscular dystrophy. Some states have associations that have assistive technology programs. The contact information below is for the national association, which can provide contact information for a specific state.

Web site: www.mdausa.org

Phone: (800) 572-1717

3300 E. Sunrise Drive

Tucson, AZ 85718

The National Council on Independent Living This organization advocates for rights and services for people with a disability. They have a directory of all Independent Living Centers across the country that can help in obtaining assistive technology.

Web site: http://www.ncil.org/

Voice: (703) 525-3406

TTY: (703) 525-4153

Fax: (703) 525-3409

Toll-free: (877) 525-3400 (V/TTY)

Email: ncil@ncil.org

1916 Wilson Blvd, Suite 209

Arlington, VA 22201

National Multiple Sclerosis Society The MS Society has a wide range of programs to benefit those living with multiple sclerosis. Some states have chapters that have assistive technology programs. The contact information for the national society is below, which can be use to obtain the contact information for a specific state.

Web site: www.nmss.org

Phone: 800-344-4867

National United Cerebral Palsy UCP is an organization that provides many services to people with cerebral palsy. They have extensive information on their web site about assistive technology. Their foundation does offer assistance in obtaining AT. The national organization has a directory of the state associations.

Web site: www.ucp.org

Phone: 800-872-5827/202-776-0406

TTY: 202-973-7197

Fax: 202-776-0414

1660 L Street NW

Suite 700

Washington, DC 20036

State Technology Assistance Projects The Rehabilitation Engineering and Assistive Technology Society of North America (RESNA) has a web page that lists all of the states technology assistance programs and provides links for each specific state. They also list the mailing address, phone number, TTY, fax number, and web site.

> Web page: http://www.resna.org/taproject/at/statecontacts.html
>
> RESNA's tech assistance email address: resnaTA@resna.org
>
> RESNA phone: 703-524-6686
>
> RESNA fax: 703-524-6630
>
> TTY: 703-524-6639

State Assistive Technology Alternative Financing Programs RESNA also has a web page that lists all of the alternative financing programs for AT in the state's that have such a program.

> Web page: http://www.resna.org/AFTAP/state/index.html
>
> RESNA's alternative financing email address: resnaTA@resna.org
>
> See above for other contact information for RESNA.

Veteran's Administration Veteran's benefits include coverage for many different types of assistive technology.

> Web site: http://www.appc1.va.gov/Elig/
>
> VA Benefits phone: 800-827-1000
>
> TDD: 800-829-4833

REFERENCES

1. Mann, W. C., and Lane, J. P. (1991). *Assistive Technology for Persons with Disabilities: The Role of Occupational Therapy*, 1st ed. Rockville, MD: The American Occupational Therapy Association.
2. Cook, A. M., and Hussey, S. M. (2002). *Assistive Technologies: Principles and Practice*, 2nd ed. St. Louis, MO: Mosby.
3. Mann, W. C., Ottenbacher, K. J., Fraas, L., Tomita, M., and Granger, C. (1999). Effectiveness of assistive technolgy and environmental interventions in maintaining independence and reducing home care costs for the frail elderly: A randomized clinical trial. *Archives of Family Medicine* **8**, 210–217.
4. Mahoney, J. E., Sager, M. A., and Jalaluddin, M. (1999). Use of an ambulation assistive device predicts functional decline associated with hospitalization. *Journal of Gerontology: Medical Sciences* **54A**(2), M83–M88.
5. Axtell, L. A., and Yasuda, Y. L. (1993). Assistive devices and home modifications in geriatric rehabilitation. *Geriatric Rehabilitation* **9**(4), 803–821.
6. Rogers, J. C., and Holm, M. B. (1992). Assistive technology device use in patients with rheumatic disease: A literature review. *The American Journal of Occupational Therapy* **46**(2), 120–126.
7. Tesch-Romer, C. (1997). Psychological effects of hearing aid use in older adults. *Journal of Gerontology: Psychological Sciences* **52B**(3), P127–P138.
8. Mann, W., Hurren, D., Tomita, M., Packard, S., and Creswell, C. (1994). The need for information on assistive devices by older persons. *Assistive Technology* **6**(2), 134–139.
9. Mann, W. C., Goodall, S., Justiss, M. D., and Tomita, M. (2002). Dissatisfaction and non-use of assistive devices among frail elders. *Assistive Technology* **14**(2), 130–139.
10. Wessels, R., Dijcks, B., Soede, M., Gelderblom, G. J., and Witte, L. D. (2003). Non-use of provided assistive technology devices, a literature overview. *Technology and Disability* **15**, 231–238.

11. Chen, L.-K. P., Mann, W. C., Tomita, M., and Burford, T. (1998). An evaluation of reachers for use by older persons with disabilities. *Assistive Technology* **10**(2), 113–125.

12. Mann, W. C., Granger, C., Hurren, D., Tomita, M., and Charvat, B. (1995). An analysis of problems with canes encountered by elderly persons. *Physical and Occupational Therapy in Geriatrics* **13**(1/2), 25–49.

13. Mann, W. C., Hurren, D., Tomita, M., and Charvat, B. (1995). An analysis of problems with walkers encountered by elderly persons. *Physical and Occupational Therapy in Geriatrics* **13**(1/2), 1–23.

14. Canes and Walkers. In: *Helpful Products for Older Persons (booklet series)*. University at Buffalo, NY: Center for Assistive Technology, Rehabilitation Engineering Research Center on Aging.

15. Web site: The smart wheel: technology for rehabilitation science and practice. From www.3rivers.com

16. From www.ridedesigns.com

17. Mann, W. C., Hurren, D., Charvat, B., and Tomita, M. (1996). Problems with wheelchairs experienced by frail elders. *Technology and Disability* **5**(1), 101–111.

18. Mann, W. C. (2002). Assistive devices and home modifications. In: *Encyclopedia of Aging*, E. D. J., et al., eds. New York: Macmillan.

19. Wheelchairs and scooters. In: *Helpful Products for Older Persons (booklet series)*. University at Buffalo, NY: Center for Assistive Technology, Rehabilitation Engineering Research Center on Aging.

20. Weir, J. *Assistive Technology for Lodging Accesibility: A Resource Guide for Hotels and Motels*. University at Buffalo, NY: Center for Assistive Technology, Rehabilitation Engineering Research Center on Aging.

21. Foti, D. (2001). Activities of daily living. In: *Occupational Therapy: Practice Skills for Physical Dysfunction*, 5th ed. Pedretti, L. M., and Early, M. B., eds. St. Louis: Mosby, pp. 124–171.

22. Mann, W. C., Hurren, D., Tomita, M., and Charvat, B. (1996). Use of assistive devices for bathing by elderly who are not institutionalized. *The Occupational Therapy Journal of Research* **16**(4), 261–286.

23. Gitlin, L. N., Levine, R., and Geiger, C. (1993). Adaptive device use by older adults with mixed disabilities. *Archives of Physical Medicine and Rehabilitation* **74**(2), 149–152.

24. Agree, E. M., and Freedman, V. A. (2000). Incorporating assistive devices into community-based long-term care: An analysis of the potential for substitution and supplementation. *Journal of Aging and Health* **12**(3), 426–450.

25. Gosman-Hedstrom, G., Claesson, L., Blomstrand, C., Fagerberg, B., and Lundgren-Lindquist, B. (2002). Use and cost of assistive technology the first year after stroke: A randomized controlled trial. *International Journal of Technology Assessment in Health Care* **18**(3), 520–527.

26. Products to assist with bathing: Bath seats. In: *Safety in the Bathroom*. University at Buffalo, NY: Center for Assistive Technology, Rehabilitation Engineering Research Center on Aging.

27. Enrichments: Special purpose products for enhanced living. (2004). Sammons Preston Rolyan.

28. *Independent living aids*. from www.independentliving.com

29. *Maxi Aids*. from www.maxiaids.com

30. Mortimer, J. A. (1983). Alzheimer's disease and senile dementia: Prevalence and incidence. In: *Alzheimer's Disease: The Standard Reference*, Reisberg, B., ed. New York: The Free Press, pp. 141–148.

31. Mann, W. C., Hurren, D., Charvat, B., and Tomita, M. (1996). Changes over one year in assistive device use and home modifications by home-based older persons with Alzheimer's disease. *Topics in Geriatric Rehabilitation* **12**(2), 9–16.

32. Nochajski, S. M., Tomita, M., and Mann, W. C. (1996). The use and satisfaction with assistive devices by elderly persons with cognitive impairments: A pilot intervention study. *Topics in Geriatric Rehabilitation* **12**(2), 40–53.

33. Pope, A. M., and Tarlov, A. R. (1991). *Disability in America: Toward a National Agenda for Prevention*. Washington, D.C.: National Academy Press.

34. Cristarella, M. (1977). Visual function for the elderly. *American Journal of Occupational Therapy* **31**, 432–440.

35. Kirchner, C., and Scott, R. (1988). *Data on Blindness and Visual Impairment in the U.S.* New York: American Foundation for the Blind.

36. U. S. Senate Special Committeeon Aging, A. A. o. R. P., The Federal Council on the Aging, and the U.S. Administration on Aging (1991). *Aging America: Trends and Projections.* Washington, D.C.: American Association of Retired Persons.

37. National Center for Health Statistics (1990). In: *Current Estimates from the National Health Interview Survey. Vital and Health Statistics,* Series 10, No. 176. Washington, D.C.: U.S. Government Printing Office.

38. U.S. Bureau of the Census (1986). *Disability, Functional Limitation, and Health Insurance Coverage: 1984/1985. Current Population Reports,* Washington, D.C.: U.S. Government Printing Office, p. 70.

39. Marmor, M. (1992). Normal age-related eye vision changes and their effects on vision. In: *The Aging Eye and Low Vision.* New York: The Lighthouse.

40. Bailey, I. L., and Hall, A. (1990). *Visual Impairment: An Overview.* New York: American Foundation for the Blind.

41. Dixon, J. M., and Mandelbaum, J. B. (1990). Reading through technology: Evolving methods and opportunities for print-handicapped individuals. *Journal of Visual Impairment and Blindness* **84,** 493–496.

42. Orr, A. L., and Piqueras, L. S. (1991). Aging, visual impairment and technology. *Technology and Disability* **1**(1), 47–54.

43. Hotchkiss, D. (1989). The hearing impaired elderly population: Estimation, projection, and assessment. In: *Aging and Rehabilitation,* Monograph Series A #1. New York: Springer.

44. Glass, L. E. (1986). Rehabilitation for deaf and hearing impaired elderly. In: *Aging and Rehabilitation,* Brody, S. J., and Ruff, G. E., eds. New York: Springer, pp. 218–236.

45. Tomita, M., Mann, W. C., and Welch, T. R. (2001). Use of assistive devices to address hearing impairment by older persons with disabilities. *International Journal of Rehabilitation Research* **24**(4), 279–290.

46. Abyad, A., and Boyer, J. T. (1992). Arthritis and aging. *Current Opinion in Rheumatology* **4**(2), 153–159.

47. Yelin, E. (1992). Arthritis: The cumulative impact of a common chronic condition. *Arthritis and Rheumatism* **35**(5), 489–497.

48. Arthritis Foundation (1991). *Media Fact Guide.* Atlanta, GA: Arthritis Foundation.

49. Yelin, E., and Katz, P. P. (1990). Transitions in health status among community dwelling elderly people with arthritis: A national, longitudinal study. *Arthritis and Rheumatism* **33**(8), 1205–1215.

50. Korsorok, M. R., Omenn, G. S., Diehr, P., Koepsell, T. D., and Patrick, D. L. (1992). Restricted activity days among older adults. *American Journal of Public Health* **82**(9), 1263–1267.

51. Verbrugge, L. M., Lepkowski, J. M., and Konkol, L. L. (1991). Levels of disability among U.S. adults with arthritis. *Journal of Gerontology* **46**(2), S71–S83.

52. Buchner, D. M., Beresford, S. A., Larson, E. B., LaCroix, A. Z., and Wagner, E. H. (1992). Effects of physical activity on health status in older adults, II: Intervention studies. *Annual Review of Public Health* **13**, 469–488.

53. Verbrugge, L. M., Gates, D. M., and Ike, R. W. (1991). Risk factors for disability among U.S. adults with arthritis. *Journal of Clinical Epidemiology* **1**(44), 167–182.

54. Mann, W. C., Hurren, D., and Tomita, M. (1995). Assistive devices used by home-based elderly persons with arthritis. *American Journal of Occupational Therapy* **49**(8), 810–820.

55. Aho, K., Harmsen, P., and Hatano, S. (1980). Cerebrovascular Disease in the Community: Results of a WHO Collaborative Study. *Bull WHO.* **58**, 113–130.

56. Mayo, N. E. (1993). Epidemiology and recovery. In: Teasell, R. W., ed., *Long-Term Consequences of Stroke: Physical Medicine and Rehabilitation: State of the Art Reviews.* Philadelphia: Hanley & Belfus, pp. 1–25.

57. Abu-Zeid, H. A. H., Choi, M. W., Hsu, P. H., and Maini, K. K. (1978). Prognostic factors in the survival of 1484 stroke cases observed for 30 to 48 months. I. Diagnostic types and descriptive variables. *Archives of Neurology* **35**, 121–125.

58. Ottenbacher, K. J., and Jannell, S. (1993). The results of clinical trials in stroke rehabilitation research. *Archives of Neurology* **50**, 37–44.

CHAPTER 7

ELDER DRIVERS AND TECHNOLOGY

Dennis P. McCarthy

7.1 INTRODUCTION

Mobility and Quality of Life in Old Age

To enjoy a high quality of life in later years, older adults must be able to access needed goods and services and participate in desired social and leisure activities. A fundamental prerequisite for a satisfactory life, therefore, is mobility, or the ability to get wherever one needs to go.[1] Research has shown that mobility and ability to leave home are among the essential components of quality of life of older persons.[2] Americans, young and old alike, rely on the automobile for most of their travel needs.

We can expect to see continued and increased reliance on the automobile as the primary means of transportation for the elderly, because "It is the private automobile that provides them with independence, enables them to get to essential services, and satisfies their need for social contact—it is pivotal to their quality of life."[3] For the disabled, the automobile is the primary source of transportation. It is used by almost 85% of the elderly as drivers and 60% as passengers.[4] The private automobile accounted for about 90% of all travel needs, regardless of age group in a recent study.[5] This reliance on the automobile holds true for European nations and Australasia, although to a somewhat lesser extent. In Europe, the automobile is used for about 60% of all trips.[6] In many developed countries, the private automobile is essential for an older person's mobility.[7]

The definition of mobility differs among countries. However, universally mobility is defined as providing an individual with freedom and independence and the ability to pursue economic opportunities and social interactions. Mobility reduces the need to rely on others for access to needed goods and services, and it offers comfort in the knowledge that transportation is available.[8]

America's infrastructure is centered around the automobile. Large cities and rural areas alike provide limited or no access to needed goods, services, and social contacts without an automobile. Most older persons have a desire to "age in place" within their homes and communities. An increasing number of these communities,

Smart Technology for Aging, Disability, and Independence, Edited by William C. Mann
Copyright © 2005 John Wiley & Sons, Inc.

are in rural or suburban areas, where there are few, if any, alternatives to driving.[9] Most elders will continue to reside in the community.[10] This demographic shift necessitates dramatic changes in social policy and services to meet the needs of this aging population as they face "retirement from driving." Additionally, more and more older adults, especially women, have grown up with the automobile. They will have high expectations for alternatives to the personal car when they are no longer able to drive safely.[9]

The MOBILATE Project is an international study, funded by the European Commission, of how men and women in later adulthood manage their daily commutes, and the subjects also list the conditions they feel promote or hinder their ability to get around in urban and rural areas of five European countries.[1] Patterns of mobility and activity were examined in autumn, 2000 in 3950 men and women in middle and late adulthood (55 years of age or older) from six urban and rural regions in Germany, Finland, Italy, Hungary, and the Netherlands. Standardized questionnaires and a mobility diary were used to assess various forms of mobility (e.g., walking, using private or public modes of transportation) and the essential features of the community (e.g., access to shops, services, and stations). Demographic aspects, personality measures (e.g., control beliefs, subjective well-being, positive/negative mood), and sensory ability or disability (e.g., visual acuity, physical mobility) were assessed as well. This study found an association between mobility and quality of life. Those with reduced mobility reported a lower level of life satisfaction and a desire to be more active and participate in leisure activities. This decrease in mobility was felt to be the result of physical impairment and/or lack of access to acceptable transportation alternatives rather than the individual's free choice.[1]

Increasing Number of Older Drivers

America's elders represent the fastest growing segment of the population. This trend also holds true for other developed nations (see Figure 7.1). We will see a greater proportion of this population continuing to be licensed drivers, increasing from 12.6% of total drivers in 2000 to 20% in 2030 in the United States.[11] Predicted increases in the population of 65+ licensed drivers include the Netherlands, with a 255% increase; Australia, with 173%; and the United States, with 148%.[11] Current trends suggest that this group will also drive more miles than previous cohorts, because those over 65 were the only age group that significantly increased their mileage from 1995 to 2001 (21% verses 8% for those aged 25–64).[12,13]

Approximately 80% of elders hold a drivers license, compared to 93% of those below age 65.[5] With advancing age, travel patterns change. Elders use their cars for travel on about 75% of days, while younger age groups travel on about 91% of days. Also, elders are more likely to be a passenger (26% of the time), versus younger age groups (18%) when making these trips.[5] These numbers show that many elders are transitioning from driver to passenger. The most common mode of travel, other than driving an automobile, is riding as a passenger. Many elders are outliving their ability to drive safely.[12,14] For drivers aged 70–74, males are dependent on alternatives to driving for approximately 7 years and females for approximately 10.[14]

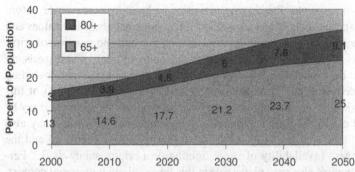

Figure 7.1   Percent of developed world population over age 65 and age 80.

The increasing proportion of America's population represented by elders has societal ramifications, and ". . . assumes the characteristics of a major public health policy crisis" (p.1).[15] Increased numbers of dependent elderly will require increased intervention by both health-care workers and families. In fact, most of the support for frail elders is provided by the family and if curtailed, would significantly impact the ability of the frail elderly to avoid institutionalization.[15,16] The pool of family caregivers is shrinking and the societal burden is growing. In 1990, there were 11 potential caregivers for each person needing care; in 2050, that ratio will be 4 to 1. Twenty-seven percent of the American adult population have provided care for a chronically disabled or aged family member within the past year.[17] A MetLife study calculated that American businesses lose between $11 and $29 billion each year due to employees' need to care for loved ones aged 50 and older.[16]

With recent economic changes that have devalued individuals' retirement funds, together with the decline in number of workers who will pay into the social security fund in America, transportation costs for the elderly are expected to increase as a percentage of total household expenditures. In 2001, American families spent more than 19% of their income on transportation, the second largest expense category (after housing) and more than three times the amount spent on health care.[18] Lower-income families are disproportionately affected: The poorest 20% spent more than 40% of their take-home pay on transportation (95% of these funds were spent on private vehicles).[18]

Conceptual Framework for Driving

Health changes associated with aging may affect the ability to perform the tasks necessary to operate an automobile safely. What are the tasks of driving, then? Michon's[19] conceptual framework of driving, viewed as a hierarchical activity, is useful for examining the requirements of driving and how deficits commonly experienced by elders can affect driving. The three levels of this model include the strategic, tactical, and operational levels.

At the *strategic level*, the highest level, cognition plays the dominant role and one's personal values affect driving decisions. This level includes "pre-driving "and "while-driving" components. Pre-driving activities include decisions made before getting into the car. These decisions are influenced by personal goals and values and include decisions related to when or how much to drive and the purpose of trips. The strategic level of driving activities reflects a balancing of goals. These goals are influenced by just how much the driver perceives driving to be important, including matters of self-identification.[20] Environment is an important consideration at this level. A person who has no walking access to a grocery store, for example, may be forced to drive a car to get food and supplies. Environmental influences may also include socially influenced laws (age-based testing or restricted licensing) and the physical environment (availability of street lighting or a bright, sunny day).[20] Personality and self-control also may play a role at this level[20] along with social context.

While-driving activities associated with the strategic level include changes in choice of route, time urgency (such as when driving to a doctor's appointment), which lane to drive in, and how much of a safety margin is required. These decisions may be influenced by the older adult's perception of their ability to safely control the vehicle, and they may prompt him or her to leave earlier for an appointment or to drive more slowly.

Tactical level tasks, the second level, are also highly cognitive. These driving tasks include performing specific maneuvers in response to the driving environment, such as changing lanes on the freeway and deciding when to pass or slow down. The tactical level of this model is associated with the performance of specific traffic maneuvers that are dependent on the particular driving situation and environment. These maneuvers include when to change lanes, speed up, slow down, or pass another car.

The third level, the *operational level*, deals with perceiving the driving environment and controlling the vehicle's speed, direction, and position.

An examination of these hierarchical components emphasizes the importance of cognition for the driving task because it spans all three levels. Comparison of these tasks illustrates the different types of cognition required. At higher levels, for example, higher thinking and metacognition are important factors. At middle and lower levels, processing of sensory information, physical abilities, and decision-making processes are important.

7.2   ELDERS AND DRIVING

Health-Related Changes and the Effects on Driving Ability

Macdonald described the *general* and *driving-specific* abilities needed for driving.[20] General abilities include sensory perception and processing as well as physical and psychomotor skills. A driver must have adequate visual acuity and sufficient flexibility of the neck and trunk to scan and search the environment. The driver must be able to recognize partially obscured objects, such as a pedestrian emerging from behind a parked vehicle, and have the ability to see and interpret trajectories of moving objects. General functional skills, including sufficient strength, mobility, and endurance to enter and exit the vehicle as well as operate the vehicle's controls and adequate motor response speed and coordination, are also needed.

Driving-specific skills associated with sensory perception and processing include maintaining efficient visual vigilance of the driving environment, including the use of mirrors and "shoulder checks," or turning the head to look behind when backing or changing lanes. One should be able to "read" traffic situations, noting potentially hazardous situations or conditions with sufficient time to react accordingly, and be able to appropriately allocate cognitive resources to the many events that occur when driving. Driving-specific functional abilities include the capability to accurately control the vehicle.[20]

Physical, sensory, and cognitive declines occur during the normative aging process, affecting the performance of everyday tasks, including driving.[21,22] Many of these declines in driving abilities are likely related to the elevated crash rates of older drivers.[23] In addition to normative changes in vision, hearing, cognition, and motor abilities, the elderly are more likely to have multiple medical conditions and take multiple medications, whose interactions may further affect safe driving performance. Over 90% of those over 65 take some form of medication.[24] Elders represent about 12% of the U.S. population, but take over 30% of drugs prescribed in the United States.[25]

Fractures, heart disease, and diabetes are associated with driving cessation, decline in mileage driven, and avoidance of long trips.[26] Increased crash risk was found for drivers with glaucoma[27] and cardiovascular disease.[28] Older, insulin-dependent diabetics had a sixfold increase in crash risk, and those who had diabetes and heart disease were eight times more likely to be involved in motor vehicle crashes.[28] Recent studies have reported an association between back pain and motor vehicle crashes[29] and an elevated risk for crashes among those with medical conditions.[30]

There are conflicting reports regarding the impact of medications on driving. Several studies have shown little correlation between crash rates, antihistamines, frequently used drug ingredients, and the use of multiple medications, all common among older drivers.[29,31,32] Benzodiazepines were found to have little effect on crash risk in one study of older drivers,[32] while another study reported that benzodiazepine users demonstrated impaired performance on a variety of controlled driving tasks.[33] None of these studies included drivers over the age of 60, however. Increased risk for crashes has been associated with the use of antidepressants, opioid analgesics, and nonsteroidal anti-inflammatory medication use.[29,32] One investigator hypothesized that increased risk may have been the result of psychiatric illnesses versus the use of antidepressants or benzodiazepines.[33] Another investigator speculated that the association between increased crash risk and the use of nonsteroidal medications may be linked to other factors such as pain and the presence of arthritic conditions.[29]

With aging we find differences among individuals on performance with cognitive tests, reaction time, sensorimotor functioning, and memory tests, making generalizations about elder drivers difficult.[34-37] Not only do these results have implications for test–retest reliability of older driver performance, but the resulting increase in error measurement decreases probability of achieving statistical significance in studies.

Vision may account for 85–95% of the sensory cues necessary for driving.[38] Visual function declines with age, with some functional declines beginning in one's twenties. The onset and severity of deterioration varies widely with age.[38] A minimum static visual acuity, although varying among licensing agencies, is required for licensure in all countries. Sufficient near static acuity is required for seeing gauges and displays, and adequate distant acuity is necessary to comprehend road signs and visualize other elements of the driving environment. Deficiencies in near and distant visual acuity can often be corrected with prescription lenses. Dynamic visual acuity, thought to be more relevant than static acuity to the driving task, is used to determine the rate of approach of objects and vehicles, such as determining when it is safe to make a left turn against oncoming traffic. Measurement of dynamic acuity is not well established and is seldom used for determining driving capabilities. Contrast sensitivity, which enables one to detect differences in color shadings, is especially problematic for elder drivers. Deficiencies in contrast sensitivity may cause difficulties detecting a white car approaching during a snowstorm or detecting the white line marking the edge of a faded roadway. There is no agreement on the best way to measure contrast sensitivity, but some agencies are assessing this function in drivers. Older drivers also have more difficulty seeing at night and many choose not to drive after dark. Other age-related changes in vision include reduced ability to differentiate colors, reduced peripheral vision (which may affect the ability to detect pedestrians or other cars coming from the sides), reduced glare recovery (such as when exiting a tunnel into bright daylight), and decreased scanning ability and useful field of view (making more difficult the task of obtaining complete information from the driving environment).[38]

The elderly also more frequently experience pathological changes in vision that may affect driving ability. These diseases include cataracts, glaucoma, macular degeneration, and diabetic retinopathy.[39] Cataracts are the leading cause of vision impairment in older adults. About half of the U.S. population aged 75 and over have clinically significant cataracts.[40] These seniors tend to drive less, drive more slowly, venture less far out of their neighborhoods, and are more likely to have received recommendations to stop or limit their driving.[41] In a study examining the effectiveness of cataract surgery and driving safety, those who had the surgery had a significant decrease in crash rates, compared to those that did not have cataract surgery.[42] Some visual deficits may progress slowly, and the person may not recognize these changes and adjust their driving accordingly. Stalvey found that those who recognize their visual deficits are more apt to impose self restrictions and modify their driving behaviors.[43]

Hearing acuity decreases progressively beginning as early as age 40.[38] Although hearing may not have a direct impact on driving performance, detection of emergency vehicles, horns, and auditory information provided by the automobile may be hampered.

The major cognitive functioning components required for driving are attention, memory, information processing, and decision-making.[38,44] Most of these functions are subject to deterioration with aging. Focused attention is important for driving in order to attend to a relevant task, such as changing lanes, while not being distracted by other stimuli, such as a passenger's conversation. Divided attention refers to the ability to attend to two or more tasks simultaneously. An example of a divided attention task might be answering the cell phone while entering the freeway from the on-ramp. Attentional control refers to the ability to switch the focus of attention from one driving task to another.

Memory plays an important role in safe driving performance. Difficulties with short-term memory may impede one's ability to remember the destination or the current speed limit. Long-term memory problems may impede the ability to learn new information, such as street names or route choice, and may make it difficult to retrieve previously learned information, such as landmarks previously used to find destinations.[38] Driving consists largely of procedural memory skills. Since procedural memory may be little affected by the aging processes, this may be one reason that many elders are able to drive safely well into advanced age. Problems may be encountered when changes in well-established routines are required,[38] such as road closures on a normally traveled route.

Age-related cognitive changes produce a general slowing in the ability to process information, which relates to a slowing of response and braking times, especially in response to unfamiliar events.[38] Simple response time, in which there is only one response to a stimuli, is relatively unaffected by age. However, when there are multiple choices to be made in response to a stimuli, such as the decision to veer left, brake, or accelerate in response to a vehicle pulling out from the right, reaction times significantly increase with age.[45] Although age-related changes in decision-making have been identified, Meyer suggested that the decision-making process required for driving appears little affected by age and noted that elders become more safety conscious with age.[38]

Many of the component skills required for safe driving are evident in the performance of basic activities of daily living (ADLs). Good trunk stability, strength, endurance, and coordination are important in performing driving tasks such as holding and manipulating the steering wheel, using the pedals, and other vehicle controls.[46] Muscular strength decreases approximately 12–15% between the ages of 30 and 70 and is accompanied by a loss of speed of muscle contraction and coordination.[38] One study reported an inverse relationship between driving cessation and participation in functional activities such as walking, performing household chores, climbing stairs, and exercising.[21] Maneuvering a motor vehicle becomes more difficult for older drivers with loss of muscle strength and decreased bone density and joint flexibility.[44] Difficulties with access to the automobile may prevent some elderly from driving. Common problems include difficulty entering and exiting, seating, storage for mobility devices, and seat belt use.[47] Drivers with limited flexibility and range of motion in the legs, arms, and neck may be at an increased risk for crashes.[28] With less strength they may have more need for power steering and brakes. Limited head and trunk rotation may cause difficulties looking behind or to the side of the vehicle and may be associated with crashes that occur when backing up or changing lanes.[38] One study reported a high correlation between falls and motor vehicle crashes by older women,[26] while another study found that difficulty in raising the arms above the shoulder increased the likelihood of crashes among older women.[22]

The most important abilities for safe driving (aside from vision) are difficult to determine, because people with even major physical impairments do not usually have a higher crash risk.[20] For each *driving-specific* ability, there are multiple underlying *general* abilities. However, causal links between general abilities and specific driving behaviors are often not clear.[20]

Elder Involvement in Crashes

Older people prefer to drive in their private vehicle as late in life as possible, and generally they do so safely.[48] However, some elders drive longer than they should, due to the lack of acceptable alternatives to the car and the associated consequences of cessation. The most commonly used indicator of unsafe driving is crashes, although use of this measure is problematic.

When crash rates per mile driven are examined, elders are involved in crashes second only to the youngest age groups.[49] However, the elderly, as a group, are among the safest drivers. One reason for increased rates, based on mileage, is the difference in types of roadways driven by elders. While younger groups tend to utilize highways and interstates (which are among the safest roadways, crash-wise) during commutes and trips, the older driver has a tendency to avoid highways, choosing to drive on secondary roads where the odds of experiencing a crash are increased. Consequently, the types of crashes experienced by older drivers are generally different from those of younger age groups. Crash locations for older drivers are highest at intersections. Crashes are more likely when making left turns.[50] Older drivers are also disproportionately involved in crashes at stop signs, where the driver has stopped and then pulls out in front of another vehicle.[12]

The elderly are also more likely to be injured or die in these crashes due to issues of frailty.[51] As people age, their ability to drive safely and to survive a crash begins to decline. Older persons are less able to withstand and recover from the trauma of crashes, and they face a much higher likelihood that a crash will prove fatal.[11,52] When involved in a crash, those over age 80 are more than four times as likely to die than those under 60.[52] Although fatality rates due to automobile crashes have declined in the United States, the over 75-year-old age group is the only age-related segment of our population not to have seen a decline in fatality rates over the last 20 years.[53]

A commonly held belief is that older drivers are a crash risk to other road users. However, the types of crashes experienced by this group differ from that of younger age groups. Older drivers are more likely to be involved in collisions where they are struck in the side of the car, and this probability increases with age.[54] So, although the elderly are more likely to be killed or injured in a crash, they are more likely to be their own victims rather than kill or injure others.[55] Current automobile safety equipment does not seem to offer adequate protection. Air bags appear to offer less protection for elders involved in frontal crashes and may increase the risk of injuries.[56] Even if the death rate were reduced by creating better safety equipment or by removing older drivers from the roadways, the number of older road user deaths would not make a substantial difference because ". . . the absolute level of road deaths represented by older drivers is already close to minimal: More than 99% of older drivers find other ways to die."[55] In Australia, for example, less than 1% of the deaths for elders occur behind the wheel.[55]

Although crash history may have high face validity in determining safe driving ability, the relatively rare occurrence of crashes makes use of crash history unreliable.[20] Additionally, there are significant variations in exposure rates among elder individuals (rural driving versus city driving, for example). Many older drivers compensate for operational level disabilities by adopting strategies that reduce exposure rates.[57] Many errors made while driving do not result in a crash, due in large part to the defensive driving of others.

Driving Reduction and Cessation

As discussed, most older adults ". . . rely upon their ability to drive to maintain their quality of life, mobility and independence and the loss of independence and mobility has been associated with decreased well-being."[58] Age-related declines in visual and sensory abilities, cognition, and/or motor skills often lead to reductions in driving or driving cessation. Many older drivers have made no plans for alternatives to driving. Many of those who have thought about alternatives expect to rely on friends and family for transportation. Elders who live alone, have no close family, and have less money are at a disadvantage when they stop driving.[39]

Where few alternatives exist to personal vehicles, the loss of a driver's license can affect one's quality of life and self-esteem[59] and sense of identity. Isolation resulting from restricted mobility may act to accelerate additional declines in health and psychosocial function.[60] Those isolated by decreased mobility may face social disengagement, a risk factor for cognitive impairment among the elderly.[61] Several studies have linked driving cessation with increased depressive symptoms. Marottoli et al. found that driving cessation was independently associated with increased depression when accounting for cognitive impairment, vision and hearing difficulties, chronic medical conditions, and limitations in ADL performance.[62] Even restricting one's driving or having a spouse available to provide rides for former drivers poses an increased risk for depressive symptoms.[63] Without the social support of family, friends, and neighbors, driving cessation can lead to difficulty obtaining groceries, medications, and health-care services. Isolation may result from inability to attend social functions, church activities, and community events. Without access to social supports, ". . . these people are at significant risk of losing their mobility and independence."[12] Social isolation resulting from driving cessation may adversely affect health and well-being.[62] In one cross-sectional study that examined the differences among 697 elders who were still driving, stopped driving, and never drove, those who still drove fared better on measures of health, cognition, and psychosocial status.[64]

Driving reduction and cessation may also affect the family and caregivers of elder drivers. Among caregivers of former drivers surveyed, over 70% reported that not driving was one of the most, if not the most, difficult aspect of dealing with the condition or illness that led to cessation.[65] Although caregivers are often in agreement with the decision to stop driving, their lives are often changed by this decision. Caregivers have reported changes in work, daily tasks, participation in leisure activities, and even role reversal.[65]

Burkhardt reported that driving cessation resulted in reductions in the number of trips made, in activity levels, and in health and reports of life satisfaction.[66] These former drivers will typically transition to passenger, but their travel patterns differ substantially from current drivers. Many former drivers report that they find it difficult to ask family and/or friends for rides. Generally, former drivers travel shorter distances and make fewer trips; sometimes no trips will be made in certain conditions. Without driving, a great deal of planning may be required to travel.

Travel options after driving cessation are limited for most elders. Burkhardt lists these options as establishing new modes of travel (walking versus driving), changing one's usual travel patterns, reducing activity participation, relying on transportation alternatives, relocation to an area that provides alternatives, or moving in with family members.[66] Eberhard suggested that, for some, especially for those without social or financial support, driving cessation could initiate a downward spiral toward institutionalization.[12]

Some former drivers are able to meet their basic transportation needs under certain conditions. Those found to be most successful at meeting their transportation needs after driving cessation had one or more of the following conditions: (1) they had spouses or others who could drive them; (2) they lived with, or had, children in the area who could provide them with needed goods; (3) they had the financial resources to purchase required transportation; (4) they were able to use available public transportation; (5) they lived in areas that had effective and usable transportation alternatives; and (6) they were involved with religious or social organizations.[8]

Alternatives to Driving

Even if forced to give up driving, whether by frailty or finances, alternatives to the car are often inadequate for this population. Elders in the United States utilize public transportation for fewer than 3% of their trips.[66] Many frail elders cannot use public transportation due to their functional limitations, which may have caused them to stop driving.[12] The incidence of difficulty in using public transportation increases with the number of reported ADL limitations (see Table 7.1).[67]

TABLE 7.1 Number of ADL Limitations and Difficulty with Public Transport

Number of ADL limitations	Percent of people aged 69 and over who reported difficulty using public transport in the previous 12 months
None	3.3
One	19.8
Two	30.1
Three or more	52.1

Source: Ficke, R. Transportation Research Board Annual Meeting Presentation, January 12, 2003.

In another study, of those over 65 who reported a need for specialized assistance or equipment for transportation, more than 30% reported difficulty in obtaining those services.[4] For those older adults who ceased driving, alternative forms of transportation became of paramount importance. Most elders who forfeited their license continued to travel in personal vehicles, but as passengers, and usually with family or friends. In fact, excluding personal vehicle use and walking, all other means of transportation accounted for approximately 2% of daily travel.[5] The use of alternatives to the car by the frail elderly are not encouraging, because only 12% who reported having medical conditions that affected their travel said they use special transit services.[5] People have less difficulty using a car than public transportation or walking.[11,12] Those who cannot drive but live with someone who can drive generally will ride with that person for most of their transportation needs.[12]

Walking is the second-most utilized method of transportation behind the private car. However, older adults have special needs as pedestrians. Pedestrians over age 65 have the highest motor vehicle–pedestrian mortality rate of any age group.[68] Many of the same age-related changes that affect safe driving ability (e.g., changes in vision or cognition) impact older pedestrian safety. With physical changes, older pedestrians tend to spend more time inside the crosswalk, thereby increasing their risk.[69]

Low usage of public transit systems requires special attention. If elders must stop driving, they need public transportation options they can and will use.[12] The MOBILATE Project found that Europe is much less dependent on the automobile than the United States and that, in fact, for elders over 75 years old, walking *is* the primary mode of transportation.[1] Additionally, there is a higher usage rate of pubic transport in Europe, ranging from 8% to 18% of trips.[1]

Elders' reported difficulties utilizing public transport are similar in both Europe and the United States. Some of the commonly listed difficulties include: walking distance to the bus stop or train station and lack of amenities for waiting; getting on and off the bus or train; maintaining balance in the moving vehicle; and perceived sense of insecurity.[70] Other include scheduling availability (services may stop running at a certain time, or not run on weekends); cost to use services; difficulties interpreting the schedule and determining proper routes to take; poor quality of some services; and excessive travel times.[71] A focus group of elders convened to determine specific mobility preferences found that the group valued reliable, on-time, door-to-door service that was flexible enough to change destinations. They expressed a desire for comfortable waiting areas and vehicles that were responsive to one's travel needs.[71] Essentially, these preferences describe autonomy, control and choice,[71] the very same things for which we value the automobile.

Burkhardt provides suggestions to meet the transportation needs of elders making the transition from driver to passenger.[71] First, there is a need to recognize the diverse nature and variability among this group. There is no single solution, and a family of coordinated services, with multiple modes of transport, is needed to address the "submarkets" of special needs travelers. Specifically, Burkhardt recommends that society increase efforts to improve older driver safety, improve public transit services, and integrate private (e.g., taxis) and paratransit services. Volunteer programs, including some that provide "hand-to-hand" services, have been successful.[72] Efforts should be made to improve pedestrian facilities to encourage walking (which would also have added health benefits).

Maintaining Mobility: The Need to Keep Driving

Myth: reducing the numbers of older drivers will be for the good of society, even though it might cause older people some inconveniences.

In all likelihood, older people as consumers will represent one of the main economic mainsprings for society in the immediate future. To consume, you have to be able to move around, e-commerce notwithstanding . . . indeed, mobility itself is a major form of expenditure.

Fact: In the decades to come, society will be unable to afford immobile older people.[55]

Restriction of older people's mobility will be detrimental to society, which will become increasingly dependent upon expenditures by older citizens. Restrictions of older people's mobility will directly impact elders, who will have reduced access to services and social facilities.[73] Therefore, many in the field of older driver safety have promoted the concept of enabling elders to drive safely for a longer period of time. The concept of maintaining mobility in old age is supported by the World Health Organization as a component of active aging and used by developed nations in efforts to manage welfare costs as the population ages.[7]

Keeping elders as independent as possible generally means keeping them driving as long as practical. The goal of Europe's AGILE (*A*Ged people, *I*ntegration, mobility, safety, and quality of *L*ife *E*nhancement through driving) project, for example, is to help older individuals to continue driving safely for as long as possible through the development of training, information, counseling, driving assessment, and support tools.[58] One of the goals of the National Highway Traffic Safety Administration (NHTSA) is to enable the elderly to drive safely as late in life as possible.[74] QUAVADIS is a pan-European initiative to improve the *Q*uality and *U*se *A*spects of *V*ehicle *A*daptations for *D*isabled. One of QUAVADIS' goals is to keep European citizens with a functional impairment (including elderly drivers) safely on the road.[75] This goal is accomplished primarily by adaptation of the vehicle (e.g., left foot accelerator) to meet the needs of the disabled driver.

Methods to accomplish the goal of keeping elders driving safely and longer include improving vehicle occupant safety protection, identifying and removing elders with unacceptably high risk for crashes, improving the roadway infrastructure to allow safer driving, and reducing the need to drive through improved land planning and development of pedestrian-friendly communities.[55] Development of acceptable alternatives to the car is also needed.

Since ". . . society tends to look to technology for solutions,"[76] the use of technological applications can assist with the goal of enabling elders to drive safely for a longer period of time. Since what works for older drivers will benefit all drivers,[77] technology has the potential to increase on-road safety for everyone. Methods to keep older people driving safely include programs to facilitate safe driving, safer roads, and safer vehicles.[12,73]

7.3 OLDER DRIVER INTERVENTIONS AND TECHNOLOGY

Identification and Assessment of At-Risk Drivers

Three approaches have been used to identify at-risk drivers: (1) testing mental competency; (2) examining medical conditions and medications that may affect safe driving; and (3) performance-based measures, that is, assessment of behind-the-wheel abilities. Dobbs suggests that ". . . neither tests of mental competence nor diagnoses are sufficient stand-alone approaches to identify individuals who are unsafe drivers . . ." although those approaches may provide valuable information regarding driving competence (p. 364).[78]

One method to reduce the number of crashes and, consequently, the number of older driver fatalities and injuries is through screening and/or assessment to identify those drivers at an unacceptable risk of crashing. Many questions surround the implementation of such a policy, however. Dellinger highlighted some of these questions during her presentation at ICADI:

- Who will be screened/assessed? Some answers to this question include: drivers when they reach a predetermined age; drivers, in general, who have specific medical conditions or documented impairment; or those for whom there is evidence of poor driving performance, based on a history of crashes.

- Once it is determined that a person will be tested, where is the appropriate place? Possible solutions include: the Department of Motor Vehicles or licensing agency; the physician's office; a driver education school; or a specialty clinic or rehabilitation center.

- Who should perform the screening test/assessment? Some of the professions currently performing tests of safe driving abilities include driving examiners, driving school instructors, driving educators, physicians, occupational therapists and other health-care professionals, and psychologists. There are also methods for a driver to assess their own driving ability.

- What type of screening or assessment should be performed? Most of the tests administered today may be classified as clinically-based tests, which are usually testing function and cognition; on-road or behind-the-wheel tests (also known as "performance-based" tests); and self-administered tests of driving ability.[79]

With regard to age-based testing of older drivers, Langford believes that this method is ineffective for identifying those who may be unsafe to drive and argues that age-based mandatory assessment of older drivers has no demonstrable safety benefits.[73] Age-based testing may, in fact, promote premature driving cessation, forcing the former driver to restrict travel and use travel modes that may be riskier than driving. Macdonald agrees, noting that screening older drivers for those who may be unsafe is unlikely to be cost effective.[57] However, surveys indicate that the general public believe that programs that assess drivers based on age are effective for identifying unsafe drivers.[12] Several U.S. states and other countries have initiated age-based mandatory testing of older drivers. Evidence of the safety benefit of licensing restrictions resulting from this practice has not been shown.[55] Other studies have shown limited value for aged-based testing to identify unsafe drivers.[12]

During the International Older Driver Consensus Conference, held in Arlington, Virginia in December of 2003 and sponsored by the University of Florida's National Older Driver Research and Training Center, a division occurred among panelists with regard to the practice of *screening* versus *assessment* of older drivers (http://driving.phhp.ufl.edu/). Screening was defined as methods employed to quickly identify unsafe drivers, whereas assessment was defined as measurement of drivers' specific skills needed for driving-related tasks. The distinction is important, because screening generally is initiated by the driver reaching a particular age, while assessment of relevant driving skills is generally initiated by the driver or a family member noticing a decline in safe driving ability, by the legal system, or after an adverse event, such as the onset of a medical condition that might impair driving. The process of assessment allows identification of deficiencies in specific driving-related skills that may be amenable to rehabilitative efforts.[80] Middleton et al. stated "It is important that in-depth investigations are conducted to identify the factors influencing driving performance and the critical parameters in assessing ability to drive in older people, in order to address important issues regarding both road safety and mobility."[58]

The American Medical Association (AMA), recognizing the important role that physicians play in their patients' mobility decisions, published the *Physician's Guide to Assessing and Counseling Older Drivers* in 2003.[81] The purpose of the Guide is to increase physician awareness of older driver safety as a public health issue and to "... help physicians maximize their older patients' safe mobility through effective clinical practice."[82] The AMA currently holds educational workshops to instruct physicians in the tool's use and encourages physicians to use the Guidelines as a tool to assist them in helping their patients.[82]

The American Association of Motor Vehicle Administrators (AAMVA) is a nonprofit organization that seeks to develop model programs and serves as an educational clearinghouse for motor vehicle administrators, police traffic services, and highway safely. The AAMVA believes that it is essential that programs be developed to ensure that drivers possess the functional ability to drive safely, and it also believes that impairments due to physical or mental conditions be identified.[83] The AAMVA believes that programs related to drivers' licensing process may have success with reducing crash rates of older drivers. These licensing programs may: establish standards on driver fitness and driver assessment tools; conduct screening and assessment; conduct medical reviews as related to driving safety; examine the possibility of restricted licensing to allow individuals to keep driving safely (e.g., no nighttime driving); and establish renewal requirements (frequency of renewals or documentation necessary for license renewal).[83]

CARA is a unit of the Belgian Road Safety Institute, a nonprofit organization that assesses the driving fitness or those diagnosed with functional impairments. CARA evaluates those identified with functional, cognitive, visual, and/or other disorders to determine if these problems influence driving behavior or driving fitness.[84] Based on the results of testing, clients are categorized as (1) fit to drive without restrictions, (2) fit to drive with restrictions, (3) fit to drive with adaptations, (4) training needed before a final decision is made, and (5) unfit to drive. For those who may be able to continue driving with restrictions or adaptations, CARA provides the required equipment, education, and training needed to do so.[84]

The most common approach healthcare professionals use for testing driving competence consists of a combination of clinically administered tests followed by the "gold standard" for determining fitness to drive: an "on-road" or "behind-the-wheel" test. Clinically administered tests, however, show moderate association, at best, with behind-the-wheel performance. For older drivers as a group, the association between screening and crash reduction is ". . . at best, minimal, (and) in most cases non-existent."[55] Even though the best available evidence relates to on-road testing, Langford believes that except in extreme circumstances, we are technically unable to assess the capacity of an individual to drive safely.[73]

Macdonald points out the variety of dynamic factors that affect required driving abilities. Basic tasks involved with driving a car include observing the driving environment and controlling the car.[20] These tasks occur in the larger scheme of traffic situations, such as negotiating a complex intersection or changing lanes in heavy traffic. The physical environment also affects performance, because roadway conditions vary with time of day (which affects amount of light and amount of traffic) and weather, for example. Finally, the social/legal environment plays an important role. The stereotypic image of the older driver may evoke intolerance by other drivers (such as when driving too slowly). The licensing system in some cases may single out the older driver, as with age-based screening by motor vehicle departments.

Driving Errors Performance-based tests of driving competence generally use a pass/fail rating or a scoring of driving errors. Macdonald notes that there is often poor interrater reliability in the global pass/fail rating. Although most driving errors are not immediately dangerous, many are predictive of unsafe driving.[57] Dobbs et al. discovered a difference in the type of errors that were made when comparing older drivers with cognitive decline with normal elder and younger drivers. Some driving errors ". . . might be the type of error that is characteristic of experienced drivers and not indicative of declining competence" (p. 369).[78] Many of these driving errors that would lose points in a conventional motor vehicle department test may not be indicative of unsafe driving.[57] Examples include "rolling stops," or failure to come to a complete stop at a stop sign, even though no other vehicles are in sight. Driving errors that were found to discriminate between competent and noncompetent drivers included the categories of: "hazardous errors," in which the driving evaluator had to take control of the vehicle or where other drivers took measures to adjust to the error; "scanning errors," in which the driver failed to check for other traffic in adjacent lanes; "positioning errors," in which the vehicle was incorrectly positioned with regards to other vehicles and the driving environment (e.g., lane markings); and "overcautiousness," or driving too slowly.[78]

On-Road Tests Performance-based, on-road testing is thought to be the "gold standard" or criterion for assessing driving abilities.[85] Difficulties exist, however with even this method of testing. Most road tests are unstandardized and, therefore, likely unreliable.[57] Often, test routes may vary for individuals, even when administered by the same evaluator. If, for example, the driver states that they never drive on an interstate highway, many evaluators will not require the driver to prove competence in this environment. Macdonald believes that on-road testing does not target all of the levels of driving performance (strategic, tactical, and operational levels, discussed above). When considering driving errors during a behind-the-wheel test, if we are to identify older drivers who may be unsafe, it is important to place the most weight on hazardous errors, identified above, and not penalize older drivers for "... ordinary bad driving habits."[57]

Methods to Facilitate Safe Driving   Options currently available to older drivers to improve driving safety or regain driving skills are classified into five categories: (1) self-regulatory behavior, (2) educational programs, (3) formal driver rehabilitation programs, (4) simulated driver training, and (5) the use of technology.

Self-Restriction   Although the elderly as a group are more likely to be involved in crashes per mile, there are fewer crashes on a per-person basis.[86] This is due in large part to the self-regulatory behaviors commonly exhibited by elderly drivers[87] and is the result of a decreased sense of confidence experienced in driving in certain conditions.[88] Older drivers tend to adapt their driving to times and situations in which they feel most comfortable.[89] Drivers over age 65, particularly those who have a previous history of crashes, are more likely to engage in self-regulatory driving behaviors.[90] Types of behavioral adaptation can be grouped broadly into behaviors that (1) allow the driver more time (e.g., reducing one' speed), (2) avoid complex or uncertain driving conditions (e.g., rush hour, freeways), and (3) avoid particular conditions (e.g., nighttime driving, driving in the snow, etc.).[76] Other examples of adaptation include driving only on familiar routes, abstaining from unsignaled left turns against traffic, or reducing distractions such as cellular phones or radios.[88,91]

To employ a strategy aimed at increasing driving safety, the driver must recognize his or her deficits. In one study of older adults with mild senile dementia, even those who had failed a driving road test reported they were average to above average drivers.[92] Those unaware of deficits are unlikely to take compensatory actions, which increases the risk of a crash.

Marottoli et al. examined the issues of awareness and self-confidence in relation to self-imposed restrictions.[62] The majority of older drivers (68%) rated themselves as better than their peers. Of those drivers who were rated as having moderate to major difficulties with driving based on a road test, more than one-quarter rated themselves as better drivers than others their age.

In a study that examined the effectiveness of an educational program designed to increase participants' awareness of their visual deficits related to driving, increased knowledge and awareness led to a reported change in driving habits, with subjects engaging in increased self-regulatory behaviors, such as consolidating and thereby reducing trips and reducing miles driven.[93] The participants who reported decreased driving exposure reported no additional dependency on others for transportation despite this reduction in exposure. "This implies that it may be possible to compensate for impairment by reducing exposure, while still maintaining an adequate level of mobility."[93]

It would appear that, given the awareness of a decrease in self-confidence in one's ability to drive under certain conditions, elders appropriately compensate for diminished capabilities. It has been suggested that, without self-restriction of driving behaviors, the elderly would be involved in even more crashes and endure even more disproportionate numbers of injuries and fatalities.[94]

Educational Programs   During the first half of the twentieth century, educating drivers was the primary source of attention. Generally, manufacturers were not concerned with designing vehicles for safety or installing safety equipment until motor vehicle safety legislation passed in the late 1960s. The focus then became vehicle design change with safety in mind and included the development and mandated installation of safety equipment, such as safety belts and, later, air bags. A conceptual shift has occurred, and educational efforts aimed at increasing driving safety are now being directed back toward the driver and can be noted by recent government efforts to increase safety belt use and reduce drunk driving. The Insurance Institute for Highway Safety (IIHS) reports that the current focus of efforts to improve driver safety ". . . has expanded from trying to prevent crashes by educating people to change their behavior."[51]

The question then becomes, "Does education change driving behavior?" Many existing programs provide education to drivers of all ages. The primary goal of most of these programs is to produce "safer" drivers (defined in terms of reduced crash rates). Many make the assumption that those completing a formal educational program on driving safety should have a lower crash rate.[95] Many of these educational programs are not evaluated for effectiveness in reducing poor driving behaviors or increasing driver safety. The IIHS (2001) reports that high-school driver education programs, as well as other educational programs, remain popular due to their "apparent" usefulness as opposed to their proven value. However, no scientific evidence exists that shows that high-school driver education reduces crash rates for younger drivers.[51] They may, in fact, serve to increase perceived confidence in ability and thereby have an adverse effect from the one intended. In a study conducted by the IIHS (2001), it was found that males who received training in driving skills actually had a higher crash rate than those who did not take the training. The investigators speculated that those trained in skills became overconfident and took unnecessary risks. In another study examining driver educational programs, the participants were found to have had little motivation to employ skills learned and became overconfident.[95] The IIHS (2001) states that the most effective (and demonstrable) means of changing driving behavior is through the use of traffic safety laws, evidenced with compliance with safety-belt laws and speed limits (most drivers do not exceed 8 mph over the posted limit).

In a meta-analysis (30 studies, from several countries) of the effectiveness of driver education for reducing crashes, the authors concluded that there was little evidence to support driver education programs.[95] Although this conclusion was based on younger driver performance, there may be similarities between the young and old with respect to driver education.

Despite the lack of evidence supporting the safety benefits of driver education training, these programs remain popular as a means of improving driver safety.[96] In fact, 82% of Americans believe that the number of serious injuries in motor vehicle crashes could be reduced by more public education, and 86% feel that driver education courses are very important in training novices.[97] Several organizations offer driver education classroom courses for the older driver. AARP offers a Mature Driving Program, the National Safety Council offers a Defensive Driving Course (which trains 1.5 million drivers annually),[98] and the American Automobile Association (AAA) has a program entitled "Safe Driving for Mature Operators."

The AARP reported that there were over 717,000 graduates in more that 40,000 courses offered in 2003. Eighty-five percent of graduates were over age 65.[99] Course content includes topics such as age-related changes, aggressive driving, particular conditions or circumstances that have been identified as troublesome for elders, as well as information about the car, the roadway, and retirement from driving.[99] However, as discussed earlier, there is some question about the transfer of education to actual driving. These educational courses take place in a classroom and therefore lack hands-on training. Hunt stated that older adults may have difficulty learning a new skill without practicing that skill and will tend to revert to previous driving habits.[100] In a meta-analysis of educational courses offered to experienced drivers, there was no evidence of reduced crash risk or injuries, although there was a reduction in the issuance of citations for the participants.[101] A California experiment assigned participants to an AARP driver education program or a control group. The study was conducted for 5 years, and each group was followed for 3 years post education. Only two time periods showed significant differences in crash rates; in both cases, the education group had higher crash rates. As in the previous study, there were lower rates of traffic tickets issued to the education vs. control group.[99]

Critics of these types of programs believe that the large number of enrollees are motivated by automobile insurance rate discounts, which are mandated in 36 states, rather than improvements in driving skills. Although these types of programs have been shown to increase *knowledge* of driving, there is a lack of evidence of the transfer of this knowledge to actual driving. Educational courses such as those offered by AARP and AAA are ". . . designed to increase self-awareness of driving abilities and to educate and motivate drivers to adopt compensatory driving strategies."[100] However, these programs have not been shown to improve traffic safety.[102]

Individualized education may be more effective for increasing safety. Stalvey reported on a study in which groups of individuals with visual impairments were assigned to a control group or to a group that received education regarding their conditions. Those that received this training were found to be more aware of their impairments, reported greater difficulty with driving situations, reduced their exposure, and employed alternative strategies more frequently.[43] Education at the operational level could be used to compensate for certain deficiencies (e.g., use of mirrors to compensate for decreased neck rotation). Education at the tactical level should focus on improving performance of routine driving tasks, such as lane-changing or lane-keeping during turns at intersections. Education focused at the strategic level may be the most effective for older driver safety, because it targets exposure to risk.[43] Education at this level would include topics such as where to live, alternative transportation options, driving conditions to avoid, route choice, and the types of vehicles to purchase.[43]

Driver Rehabilitation Programs Driver rehabilitation (rehab) programs employ licensed health-care workers, typically occupational therapists, to work with clients whose functional deficits may prevent safe operation of a motor vehicle. "A driver rehab program assesses persons with disabilities in driving and trains and educates them in the use of adaptive driving equipment and compensatory techniques."[103] Key to driver rehabilitation programs is the inclusion of hands-on training that accompanies education. The purpose of these programs is to determine the person's ability to drive safely as well as to identify those components that may benefit from rehabilitation and/or remediation.[100] Driver rehabilitation may enable elders to remain behind the wheel safely for a longer period of time, which may in turn help them to maintain mobility within their communities.[88]

The typical driving rehabilitation program consists of gathering pertinent medical and personal history and performing a pre-driving assessment of functional abilities and limitations. The pre-driving assessment generally includes an interview and evaluations of cognition and the sensory and motor systems. The pre-driving assessment ". . . yields information regarding safety to perform a road test, what adaptive equipment, compensatory techniques, and further rehabilitation are necessary prior to the driving assessment."[100] Cognitive-perceptual evaluation may provide useful information to help determine the client's capacity for retraining.[103] Some facilities may utilize a driving simulator to further assess clients in the pre-driving assessment phase.

Based on clinical experience, most therapists agree that the behind-the-wheel assessment is essential to determine a client's true driving ability and identify remediable components. It is not uncommon for some elders to do well in clinical tests and poorly on the road, or vice versa. The on-road test is usually conducted in one of, or a combination of, three ways: (1) a course closed to other traffic and pedestrians (which provides the least realistic environment); (2) on a predetermined course, graded for difficulty; or (3) in the client's usual driving environment. There have been few studies to determine what on-road test is best in predicting actual driving ability or safety. The on-road assessment is intended to examine the client's ability to ". . . act appropriately to the environment, drive at an appropriate speed, respond quickly and appropriately to unexpected stimuli, change lanes safely, scan the environment, and other important driving-related skills" (p. 146).[104] The on-road test has been described as the "criterion standard" and ". . . the most widely accepted method for determining driving competency . . ." (p. 153).[85]

Despite the predominance of occupational therapists in this field, there is variability among programs all over the world. French and Hanson conducted a survey of driving rehabilitation programs in the southeastern United States.[103] These programs were most often associated with a rehabilitation hospital (61%). Other programs were affiliated with a hospital (32%), outpatient rehabilitation center (29%), vocational rehabilitation (10%), and private practice (9%). Most of the employees were occupational therapists (69%).[103] Specific methods of evaluation also vary among programs, and the literature regarding assessments that are currently used by occupational therapists is sparse,[103] as is the literature on specific driving programs.[105] Europe also lacks standardized procedures for assessing the driving competence of the elderly.[58]

There is also variability in practice: Some therapists perform the behind-the-wheel road tests from the passenger seat, while some may sit in the back seat, utilizing a driving instructor or driving educator as a co-evaluator. Some clients are tested on fixed courses, while others may be tested in their more familiar, usual driving environment.[101,103] While the importance of vision to driving has been emphasized by many,[106–108] only 90% of surveyed programs assessed vision.[103] Although 100% of respondents recommended an on-road test for those who passed the pre-driving evaluation, 13% did not include one.[103] Only 19% of respondents offered the complete package of clinical assessment, on-road test, and behind-the-wheel training.[103] Standardization of road courses is difficult, making comparative studies problematic, as ". . . matching attributes of the road course leaves questions because it is unlikely that any two road courses can be constructed to be equally difficult."[109]

A treatment plan, based on the results of the evaluation, may include: interventions to increase flexibility or muscle strength; employing compensatory driving strategies; or using adaptive equipment.[88] Problems discovered during the evaluation may lead to referrals to other health-care specialists, such as (a) optometrists or ophthalmologists for certain visual deficits or (b) family physicians for medication correction. A more difficult problem is faced when cognitive deficits are encountered, because these ". . . deficits cannot be remediated with compensatory techniques or equipment."[101] However, recent studies have shown promise for remediation of a component of cognition, visual processing, which has been identified as important to the task of driving. In a randomized controlled trial, 2832 persons aged 65–94 were administered one of four cognitive training interventions. Significant gains were noted for the group that received speed of processing training, with 87% showing reliable improvement.[110] In a study of 97 older adults, the investigators found that speed of processing training resulted in a significant increase for some speed of processing measures and improved performance of instrumental activities of daily living.[111] It was found that ". . . useful field of view, a measure of processing speed and spatial attention, can be improved with training."[112] A recent study sought to determine if speed of processing training could be transferred to driving. Participants went through a speed of processing training program, a driving simulator, and a 14-mile open-road driving evaluation. The authors found that speed of processing training improved a specific measure of useful field of view which transferred to driving and resulted in fewer "dangerous maneuvers."[112] In another randomized control trial of clients referred for a driving evaluation following stroke, participants with right-sided lesions that received useful field of view retraining demonstrated a twofold increase in the pass rate of an on-road evaluation.[113,114] Collectively, these findings suggest that a program of early detection and remediation for both visual and cognitive impairments may be effective. Such a program may help to sustain mobility in older adults.[114]

Other methods employed by driver rehabilitation programs to enable elders to maintain safe driving ability include the use of compensatory strategies to accommodate difficulties, such as the use of different muscles to perform a task and changing driving techniques (such as the manner in which one holds the steering wheel). The client may be educated and instructed in the use of adaptive driving equipment such as hand controls (recommended for some with lower-extremity dysfunction), pedal extenders to allow better access to foot pedals, left-foot accelerators (for those with right lower-extremity difficulty), and spinner knobs to assist with steering. Spot mirrors may be employed to compensate for visual or range-of-motion deficits.

Watson suggested several strategies for improving driving skills. These include increasing following distances (thereby allowing greater braking distances), lane changing strategies, updating one's knowledge of driving laws, and the use of "commentary driving," where the driver verbalizes thoughts while driving to increase attention to the driving task.[115]

For the more severely disabled, vans may be outfitted with a wheelchair lift, motorized captain's seats for easier transfers, joystick or a horizontal steering wheel for upper-extremity difficulties, and toggle switches or touch pads to operate secondary controls such as the heater or headlights.

Driving Simulators   Computer-based simulation has been used for training in many areas including the military, space flight, medicine, the FBI, and the graphic arts and construction industry, for example. Driving simulators range from a PC-based game/program to the $50 million National Advanced Driving Simulator (NADS) at the University of Iowa. The use of laboratory-based simulated driving as a pre-driving evaluation has much better face validity than clinically administered psychometric tests used to assess the cognitive skills needed for driving.[116] One study found the simulator effective for screening for difficulties in speed of visual processing as it related to driving.[117]

Simulators also have the advantage of creating driving situations that could not practically or ethically be reproduced in the actual environment, thereby allowing a safe and economical way of testing driving skills.[118] Driving simulators have been utilized to examine driving patterns and abilities of older drivers.[118,119] While the driving simulator has many advantages, it provides only a fairly realistic simulation of driving and has not been shown to be a predictor of actual behind the wheel driving ability.[94] The simulator, though, has proven to be a useful tool for training skills required of driving.

Simulators were found to be useful in testing a device that assisted elders in determining a safe gap in oncoming traffic in order to make a left turn. This maneuver could not easily, or ethically, be reproduced, or practiced, in the real world.[94] For novice drivers, or those resuming after a period of cessation, the simulator can provide an opportunity to gain awareness and insight into recognition of threatening conditions. Simulation can also provide a means of practicing avoidance tactics.[120] For older drivers, the simulator may provide insight into limitations and driving difficulties.

The driving simulator has the ability to provide measures of multiple outcomes such as vehicle steering, acceleration and braking, lane tracking, and interactions with other cars, pedestrians, and the roadway environment.[120] Typically, the user "maneuvers" the vehicle through progressively more difficult situations, allowing the driver to become familiar with the simulator's steering, braking, and accelerator functions. After the training run, the subject is exposed to the training or assessment scenarios.[120] Simulator training is thought to be effective due to the simulator's capacity to make challenging scenarios that elicit driving errors. Errors, when recognized, produce an element of surprise that leads to introspection into the cause of the error.[121] Employing scenarios that are problematic for older drivers during simulation could be a useful method for facilitating improved performance.[122] In addition, errors encountered while operating the simulator prevent overconfidence and thereby reduce risk-taking behaviors.[121]

In one study, subjects were assigned to one of two groups, error training (where the course is designed to elicit operator error) versus errorless training (where the course is designed *not* to elicit operator error) in a study to look at the effects of each. After training, participants completed a post-test that consisted of simulated driving that required employment of strategies they were exposed to during the training (for example, when a traffic lane was blocked by an obstacle, the correct strategy would be to allow oncoming traffic to pass before driving around the obstacle). The error-trained group scored fewer errors and also reported a lower level of self-confidence of driving ability.[121]

Many traffic safety researchers believe that simulators are unable to accurately represent reality. Advancements in technology may improve the quality of the driving experience and the usefulness of the driving simulator as a training tool and possibly as a valid predictor of on-road performance. Actions taken by simulator subjects have no real safety consequences. Some simulators employ videotaped scenarios to which the operator must react. The subjects' action has no effect whatsoever on the observed scene, however. For example, if a scenario calls for the driver to swerve to the right to avoid a crash, the video continues whether or not the operator made the evasive maneuver. This lack of interaction may cause confusion in an elderly client.[100]

Technology   Just as safety education evolved from the car to the client, technology has also evolved, not only in complexity and function but also in purpose. Most of the technologies introduced in vehicles through the 1980s were focused on ". . . enhancing the capabilities of the vehicle, (whereas) new technologies are aimed at enhancing the capabilities of the driver."[123] The technological advances recently achieved have implications for extending the safe driving life of older adults.[124] Some of these new technologies are ". . . capable of acting as a navigator, a safeguard, and even a second driver."[123] *Telematics*, or technology within vehicles, includes devices such as visual enhancement systems, navigation aids, or route guidance, as well as collision warning and avoidance systems. Most of the literature that has focused on telematics has dealt with the use of Automated Traveler Information Systems (ATIS), which generally include navigational and collision notification systems, and the visual enhancement system known as a heads-up display (HUD). Few studies have looked at the interface of elders and the new technologies being built into our cars. Systems that do not require driver decisions, however, may prove to be more effective safety devices for elders. Caird noted that ". . . interaction with in-vehicle technology that requires fast responses or diverts attention away from the roadway to an interface is incompatible with the declines associated with aging" (p. 249).[76] Technologies to improve older driver safety may be categorized as in-vehicle technology, infrastructure technologies, and technologies that enable communication between the vehicle and infrastructure.

In-Vehicle Technologies

Basic Collision Warning Systems Basic collision warning systems are designed to provide information to the driver with regard to situations in front of the vehicle. These systems check the forward driving environment and include a type of advanced cruise control that monitors the location and speed of nearby vehicles and adjusts the speed to maintain a safe operating distance. Rear-end collision avoidance systems monitor vehicles and objects in front of the vehicle and advise the driver of imminent crashes. Some of these systems provide automatic braking. These systems also can look out for pedestrians and objects within the driver's intended path.[125]

Problems with these systems include questions about false alarms. Should the system provide too many false alarms, the driver may have a tendency to ignore incoming information, rendering the system useless. The most effective methods for conveying this information (e.g., auditory, visual) have yet to be determined and are likely to vary among users.

Advanced Collision-Warning Technologies These systems provide warnings to the driver for a range of driving situations and conditions that occur around the vehicle. This requires that the information from a number of sensors (front, back, side) be integrated in order to provide accurate and consistent collision warning information.[125] Advanced collision warning systems include the capability to monitor lane changes and merging, conditions while driving through intersections, objects and pedestrians while backing, and the status of the vehicle's safety related functions (such as tire pressure, or the integrity of the braking system).[125] Lane changing/merging collision avoidance sensors are activated when the turn signal is engaged and notifies the driver if another vehicle is within the driver's intended path.

Since these systems rely on information obtained from sensors from around the vehicle, development of an integrated system that correctly reads the situation and provides the appropriate response to the situation (turn, brake, etc.) is a key challenge.[125] As in the case of the basic collision warning systems, the appropriate modality for alerting the driver must be determined. One potential problem of these systems is that they may cause "driver complacency", where the driver, believing the system will respond appropriately, fails to take the necessary actions.[76]

Navigation Technologies, Route Guidance Systems Route guidance systems are navigational devices designed to assist in wayfinding, a task identified as problematic for some older drivers, particularly those with cognitive deficits. They provide location information and route guidance, which can be modified to meet the user's preferences (e.g., taking secondary roads versus highways).[125]

After the driver inputs the destination, the route guidance system provides verbalized instructions, announcing upcoming turns and other information. These systems may also be set to display graphic instructions, and they can help avoid getting lost or suggest alternative routes.[76]

Although these systems have been shown to reduce wrong turns and shorten travel time,[123] older drivers have difficulty with this technology. When drivers were asked to utilize this technology while driving, those over age 65 demonstrated an increased number of driving errors even though they traveled at a reduced rate of speed.[126] In a similar study, elders required more time to process information while using navigational systems compared to younger drivers.[127] The author recommended that systems were needed to oversee the cognitive load placed on the driver so that messages would be canceled if roadway conditions warranted such actions.[127] The usefulness of these systems to older drivers is questionable, because some tend to restrict their travels to areas in which they are most familiar. However, systems designed with the older user in mind might encourage travel outside the usual area, as the fear of becoming lost diminishes. These systems may provide the confidence to increase travel areas.

Research is needed to determine the most appropriate interface between these systems and the older driver. Questions include how the flow of information, such as the timing and repetition of messages, or how much information, is delivered.[125]

Automatic Collision Notification or Automatic Vehicle Location Sensors built into the car have the capability of determining when air bags have deployed (indicating a crash). The system automatically transmits vehicle location and position to a dispatch center, which attempts to contact the vehicle occupants. If unsuccessful, or if conditions warrant, the nearest 911 center is contacted and emergency medical services (EMS) are notified to send assistance to the vehicle's location.[76,125] These systems are also useful for tracking stolen vehicles, assisting in contacting emergency roadway services, remote unlocking of doors, and vehicle diagnostics.[76] Immediate notification of EMS may help decrease the number of fatalities. The time delivery of EMS services has been one of the primary reasons that fatal traffic accidents have decreased over the past 40 years.[128]

Vision Enhancement Systems Technologies have evolved that assist drivers with vision during low light conditions or when driving in inclement weather. Information provided by these systems are projected either on a dashboard display or on heads-up display (HUD) projected onto the windshield. These vision enhancement systems (VES) include ultraviolet (UVES) and infrared (IVES) systems. UVES are intended to provide visual assist in detecting roadway features, such as lane striping, not only at night but in adverse conditions (e.g., fog, snow).[76,129] IVES is intended to provide nighttime visual assist by detecting thermal differences between a person or animal and the background and roadway.[76] The system is useful for identifying a pedestrian walking on the side of the roadway when the lights of an oncoming car obscure vision, for example.[130]

These systems hold potential for assisting older drivers with diminished visual capabilities. However, there are problems with the current systems. Caird notes that older drivers may have difficulties switching attention from the driving environment and displays located on the dashboard. Projection on the windshield may be more beneficial, but the display does not take into account pedestrians or animals in the periphery.[76] The area visualized by the system and projected onto the windshield is limited to that in front of the vehicle. Expanding the area to accommodate for elders' decreased useful field of view may be more beneficial, but is currently cost prohibitive.[76] Elders must learn to interpret the thermal representations on the display because they are not intuitively associated with people and animals. When these systems are misaligned, the projected images may not be indicative of the actual location of the pedestrian or animal.[76] Tufano points out that elder drivers might, in fact, be distracted by the HUD, and the display may interfere with concentrating on the entire driving environment.[130]

Other In-Vehicle Technologies Lane changing aids use radar and other technologies to check for other vehicles when making intentional lane changes or provide warnings during unintentional lane changes. Parking aids employ distance sensors and/or camera displays to provide views of the rear of the vehicle and assist with backing maneuvers. These systems could be beneficial for elders whose reduced range of motion prevents turning the head to look for obstacles, other cars, and pedestrians. Devices that also may benefit the elderly include systems that monitor attention and wakefulness: Warnings are provided if the system detects that the driver is falling asleep.

Driver Convenience Devices Driver convenience devices refer to technologies such as integrated cellular telephone and fax systems, email and other web-based capabilities, vehicle diagnostics and monitoring of safety features, and automatic payment of pay tolls. These devices generally provide comfort or entertainment or allow communication.[38] Although these systems may offer convenience, they hold potential for distraction, especially when competing with other technology-based incoming information. Drivers may attend to the messages received from theses convenience devices rather than from safety systems, such as the collision warning system.[76]

Infrastructure and Technology

The roadway infrastructure may have a significant effect on safe driving performance. The design of roadways may help compensate for age-associated difficulties with driving tasks.[69,131] Driving conditions and situations described as problematic for older drivers include night driving, intersections, and freeways.[132] Installation of fixed lighting is not always economically practical to improve visibility during the hours of darkness. Recommendations to alleviate some of these difficulties include making the roadway edges more apparent by painting or using raised delineation, such as median barriers or islands to channel traffic.[69] Retroreflective devices are also helpful for delineating traffic lanes.

The largest percent of fatalities for older drivers occurs during crashes at intersections. Recommendations to compensate for diminished capabilities include limiting the angle of intersections to between 75 and 90 degrees, increasing the sight distance by shifting the left-hand turn lane to the left (creating an offset), using traffic lights to protect those making a left turn across traffic (green arrow), and increasing the width of the lane receiving the turning traffic.[132]

Although many older drivers avoid highway driving, those over 75 years of age are overrepresented in crashes that occur during lane changing and merging required at freeway interchanges.[133] Some recommendations include providing an adequate length of roadway to provide ample time to merge and provide a parallel lane that allows for the driver to make a decision when to merge into traffic, versus a tapered lane that forces a merge.[132]

Although it seems intuitive that these types of design changes to the roadway would increase older driver safety, there is some doubt as to the effectiveness of these changes. One study found that improvements in medical care and safety belt usage was more highly correlated with reductions in fatalities than roadway design changes.[134] The safety benefits of roadway design change reported in many studies may be inflated, because they have not controlled for confounding factors.[135] Noland analyzed data from Illinois' Highway Safety Information System to determine if changes in roadway infrastructure was associated with a reduction in crashes and/or fatalities and found the evidence inclusive.[136]

Technologies may be employed within the driving environment to assist with decision-making. For example, changeable message signs are now frequently seen on roadways, providing up-to-the-minute information on roadway conditions such as construction or congestion that may affect driving. "Smart intersections" are being tested that warn drivers with the right of way that another vehicle may not be yielding, or may provide assistance to the driver to decide when it is safe to make a left turn across traffic.[137] Roadways that communicate with in-vehicle technologies are being developed and tested. For example, real-time traffic conditions may be communicated to the vehicle's navigation system, providing the driver with alternative routes should a roadway become congested or closed. Other information that could be provided to the vehicle from the roadway includes updates on work zones, road surface condition, and environmental conditions that might affect safe driving.[125]

Automobile Design

In the highly competitive automotive industry, automobile design is greatly influenced by marketing. Since younger drivers represent the largest market share, there has been little effort to implement design features to benefit the older driver. Those aged 65 and over account for only 19% of new car buyers.[138] Automobile design impacts the ability of elders not only to drive safely but also to use the vehicle and its features. Design features that could improve usability include easier-to-use and more comfortable safety belts, higher seats, more headroom, improved sun visors, and methods to improve visibility of the driving environment, such as allowing for higher seat adjustment.[139] However, incorporating these design features into automobiles would likely alter the appearance of today's most popular styles.

Entering and exiting motor vehicles has been identified as a serious problem for some elderly users. In their study on frail elders and aging, Steinfeld and colleagues found that about 40% of participants had difficulty with getting their legs in and out of the vehicle.[47] Automobile manufacturers and after-market suppliers are now offering seating options including electronic control of seats that swivel 90 degrees or elevating/lowering seats for models with high floors, such as sport utility vehicles.

Major car manufacturers, including Ford, General Motors, Chrysler, Toyota, Volkswagen, and Volvo, have mobility programs that typically provide financial assistance for selected after-market adaptive vehicle equipment. This trend to design for people with disabilities is more popular in Japan. Most car manufacturers in Japan have developed vehicles equipped with various accessibility features. Toyota, for example, has developed the "Welcab" and "Friendcab" systems designed to assist passengers and drivers and has developed 109 types of adaptive vehicle equipment that can be installed in these cars.

To compensate for changes in physical ability, Watchel suggested the following design considerations. Automobiles should be designed to allow ease of ingress and egress and to have comfortable seating and easy access to all controls, and the safety belt should be comfortable and easy to use.[138] To improve visibility, cabs should be designed to avoid "blind spots" and to reduce headlight glare. Vehicle controls should be placed logically, avoiding clutter to minimize cognitive confusion.[138]

Since elders generally require more time to respond to driving situations, improved seating for increased visibility would facilitate early detection of possible roadway problems. However, "the design of sun visors, windshield glazing, rear view mirrors and headlight systems contribute . . ." to the early detection of these problems[139] Many elders reported that they use seat cushions to increase visibility.[139]

A focus group study[139] found that many older drivers reported difficulty with fastening and adjusting safety belts, which may interfere with their correct use. Fifty percent of the sample had difficulties with vehicle entry and egress. Participants noted difficulty with entering and exiting vehicles with high floors, such as light trucks, vans, and sport utility vehicles. Although elders are commonly not buyers of these vehicles, participants noted that many of their children and grandchildren owned them and senior citizen transportation services commonly use vans and minivans.[139]

Older Drivers and Technology

Older drivers use few in-vehicle technologies. It would appear that there is great potential for these systems to improve safe driving (Table 7.2), however, ". . . given the available empirical evidence, the impact of in-vehicle ITS on older driver safety

TABLE 7.2   Technology that May Benefit Older Drivers

Problem	Potential solution	Issues
Fear or breaking down	Cell phone	Overload if used while driving
Inability to turn head	Back up warning device	Cost
Inability to use right foot	Left foot accelerator	Cost, training
Getting lost	Route guidance system	Cost, overload, lack of understanding
Lane drifting	Lane tracker	Cost
Car following	Intelligent cruise control	Cost, attention lapse
Night vision problems	Vision enhancement systems	Cost, confusion with typical driving
Difficulty with entry/egress[12]	Swivel seats	Conformity with occupant protection systems

and mobility is uncertain" (p. 236).[76] It is important to consider the elder driver when designing these systems given that they are the most likely to benefit or suffer from their use. Many elders lack confidence in their ability to use these systems, citing fear of technology, difficulty in operating a system while driving, comprehending displayed information, or not having received training to correctly operate the systems.[76]

The success and practicality of these systems depends in large measure on designing them to help drivers with special needs without distracting or confusing them. Continued work on specialized vehicle systems to extend the driving capabilities of persons with disabilities is needed.[12] Technology that has potential for increasing older drivers' safety may cause difficulties for those with reduced cognitive capacity since it can complicate the driving task by increasing the demand for the driver's attention or distract and overwhelm the driver.[123] These difficulties have been identified as a contributing factor for increased crash rates for older drivers.[140] Transport Canada reported that driver distraction and inattention were contributing factors in 20–50% of all crashes.[141] Significant changes in driver behaviors, such as reduced visual scanning, were observed even in younger drivers while using telematics.[141] In order to ensure that these new technologies are beneficial, these systems must be designed with older drivers in mind.

The ability to divide attention among a varied number of tasks and driving conditions is more difficult for the elderly. These difficulties are more pronounced when tasks require the same output modality (e.g., a motor response) than when the tasks require different output modalities (e.g., motor response and visual scanning).[38] These difficulties are more evident during increasingly complex cognitive situations, such as left turns at unprotected intersections.[125] Many older drivers have difficulty processing information, especially during divided attention tasks. Therefore, it is important to establish the potential benefits of these new technologies.[142]

Memory difficulties may also affect the ability to fully realize the benefits of new technologies by affecting the ability to learn how to use the new systems and to acquire the new skills necessary to change familiar ways and habits of driving and recalling how to use the systems properly.[38]

Older drivers require a longer period of time to view in-vehicle displays, drive more slowly, have increased reaction times, and have difficulty maintaining lane position, especially when making turns.[125] Mullick et al. recommend that interaction with telematics that require high cognitive demand should be allowed only by the passenger or by the driver when the vehicle is not in motion.[139]

The vehicles of the future will likely be even more technically complex. Although designing these systems with older drivers in mind presents a greater challenger for developers of this equipment,[125] "what works for older drivers will work for the rest of the driving public" but conversely, ITS applications that fail to serve older drivers will leave a large and increasing segment of the driving public at risk.[77]

7.4 SUMMARY

Having the ability to get to where one needs to go, or would like to go, is essential for a maintaining quality of life as we age. More and more people will be faced with a reduction in mobility due to the normative and non-normative changes associated with aging. For most elders in developed nations, mobility is synonymous with the automobile.

The design of cities and towns, especially in America, plus the lack of adequate alternatives to the automobile, make it imperative to enable elders to continue driving safely for as long as possible. Driving cessation has the potential to severely impact the life of the former driver and caregivers. Prolonging safe driving likely contributes to a more satisfactory quality of life, and it allows access to the goods, services, and medical necessities needed to maintain health. However, with age, cognitive, sensory/perceptual, and physical changes may make the driving task more difficult and less safe. Statistics suggest that older drivers, on a per-mile basis, are more likely to be involved in a crash and have an increased risk for injury and fatality when involved in a crash.

There must be a balance, then, between addressing older driver safety and maintaining driving in our later years. There are many questions regarding the best way to identify older drivers who may be at increased risk for unsafe driving behaviors. Age-based testing has been shown to be inefficient and ineffective, and variations in formal assessments and administration make comparisons among programs difficult. Even when these methods identify a driver as needing intervention to prolong safe driving, the effectiveness of remediation strategies is largely unknown.

Several methods are currently employed to facilitate safe driving. Older drivers often restrict themselves to driving situations/conditions in which they feel most comfortable. Some choose not to drive after dark or in heavy traffic, while others may limit themselves to traveling in local areas only. Educational programs are very popular and are perceived to be beneficial. However, the benefits of these educational programs in reducing crashes or improving driving performance have not been demonstrated.

Formal driver rehabilitation programs are typically staffed by licensed health-care providers (usually occupational therapists) who not only have training in the task of driving but also have been trained in the health-related issues and medical conditions experienced by the elderly. These programs have many benefits over other methods of prolonging safe driving, but variation in practice and lack of effectiveness studies casts a shadow over this intervention. Driving simulators have been shown to be effective for the training of particular driving skills and have advantages over on-road training, such as having the ability to visually review a situation to determine what the correct response should have been.

Technology has great potential for assisting elders to prolong their safe-driving lives. However, few elders currently utilize in-vehicle technologies. These systems are not designed with the older driver in mind; consequently, system design and user interface often compete with the driving environment for the driver's attention. Universal design principles need to be employed to facilitate the use of these technologies. Perhaps, during a potential crash situation, systems that take control of a vehicle's functions (e.g., applying the brakes) versus notifying the driver that an evasive action should be taken would be more effective for the older driver.

The roadway infrastructure may play a role in safe driving performance. Guidelines to accommodate older drivers should benefit all drivers. Some studies, however, have cast doubt on the effectiveness of highway design to reduce crashes and fatalities. Technology built into the roadway infrastructure may benefit driver safety. Some of these systems have the capability of communicating with the automobile and provide real-time information regarding roadway conditions and alternate routing.

Many elders have difficulty with entering or exiting the car or using the vehicle's features. As elders represent a relatively small portion of the new car market, there is little incentive for vehicle manufacturers to design cars with higher roofs and seats, lower floors, and other changes that may benefit elder drivers and passengers, because this would affect the appearance of the more popularly styled vehicles.

Future research on elder mobility needs should concentrate on the question of effectiveness of the means we employ to prolong independence. "There is currently a greater need for implementation of what we already know, than for basic research. But to promote implementation, we need evidence of what works, particularly in cost benefit terms."[57]

REFERENCES

1. Mollenkopf, H. (2003). Enhancing mobility in late life. Paper presented at the International Conference on Aging, Disability and Independence, Arlington, VA.
2. Farquhar, M. (1995). Elderly people's definitions of quality of life. *Society for Science and Medicine* **41**(10), 1439–1446.
3. DOT (2003). *Safe Mobility for a Maturing Society: Challenges and Opportunities*. Washington, D.C.: U.S. Department of Transportation.
4. Sweeny, M., and Durant, S. (2003). Transportation patterns of disabled americans. Paper presented at the Driving Decision, Boston, MA.

5. Collia, D. V., Sharp, J., and Giesbrecht, L. (2003). The 2001 National Household Travel Survey: A look into the travel patterns of older Americans. *Journal of Safety Research* **34**(4), 461–470.
6. Mitchell, C. G. B. (2003). Keeping people walking safely. Paper presented at the International Conference on Aging, Disability and Independence, Arlington, VA.
7. Siren, A., and Hakamies-Blomqvist, L. (2004). Private car as the grand equaliser? Demographic factors and mobility in Finnish men and women aged 65+. *Transportation Research Part F: Traffic Psychology and Behaviour* **7**(2), 107–118.
8. Burkhardt, J. E. (2003). The impacts of driving cessation. Paper presented at the International Conference on Aging, Disability and Independence, Arlington, VA.
9. TRB (2002). *Improving Publlic Transit Options for Older Prople*. Washington, D.C.: Transportation Research Board.
10. AARP (2003). *Beyond 50 2003: A Report to the Nation on Independent Living and Disabililty*. Washington, D.C.: AARP.
11. OECD (2001). *Ageing and Transport: Mobility Needs and Safety Issues* (S No. 92-64-19666-8). Paris: OECD: Organisation for Economic Co-operation and Development.
12. Eberhard, J. (2003, December). Enhancing mobility for older people. Paper presented at the International Conference on Aging, Disability and Independence, Arlington, VA.
13. Austin, R. A., and Faigin, B. M. (2003). Effect of vehicle and crash factors on older occupant injury. Paper presented at the International Conference on Aging, Disability and Independence, Arlington, VA.
14. Foley, D. J., Heimovitz, H. K., Guralnik, J. M., and Brock, D. B. (2002). Driving life expectancy of persons aged 70 years and older in the United States. *American Journal of Public Health* **92**(8), 1284–1289.
15. Cox, C. B. (1993). *The Frail Elderly: Problems, Needs, and Community Responses*. Westport, CT: Auburn House.
16. NAC (1997). The MetLife study of employer costs for working caregivers. Retrieved February 28, 2004, from http://www.caregiving.org/metlife.pdf
17. RWJF (1996). Chronic care in America: A 21st century challenge. Retrieved February 27, 2004, from http://www.rwjf.org/publications/publicationsPdfs/Chronic_Care_in_America.pdf
18. STPP (2003). Why a lack of transportation choices strains the family budget and hinders home ownership. Retrieved November 10, 2003, from http://www.transact.org/library/decoder/american_dream.pdf
19. Michon, J. A. (1985). A critical view of driver behavior models: What we know, what should we do? In: *Human Behavior and Traffic Safety*, Evans, E. L., and Schwing, R., eds. New York: Plenum, pp. 485–520.
20. Macdonald, W. (2003). Functional abilities needed to drive safely. Paper presented at the International Conference on Aging, Disability and Independence, Arlington, VA.
21. Marottoli, R. A., Ostfeld, A. M., Merrill, S. S., Perlman, G. D., Foley, D. J., and Cooney Jr, L. M. (1993). Driving cessation and changes in mileage driven among elderly individuals. *Journal of Gerontology: Social Sciences* **48**(5), S255–S260.
22. Hu, P. S., Trumble, D. A., Foley, D. J., Eberhard, J. W., and Wallace, R. B. (1998). Crash risks of older drivers: A panel data analysis. *Accident Analysis and Prevention* **30**(5), 569–581.
23. Eby, D. W., Trombley, D. A., Molnar, L. J., and Shope, J. T. (1998). *The Assessment of Older Drivers' Capabilities: A Review of the Literature* (No. UMTRI-98-24). Ann Arbor, MI: The University of Michigan Transportation Research Institute.
24. McGwin, G., Jr., Sims, R. V., Pulley, L. V., and Roseman, J. M. (2000). Relations among chronic medical conditions, medications, and automobile crashes in the elderly: a population-based case-control study. *American Journal of Epidemiology* **152**(5), 424–431.
25. Williams, B. R. (2000). Avoiding medication mishaps: A pharmacist's perspective. *Geriatric Times* **1**(1) Retrieved February 28, 2004. From www.geriatrictimes.com/g000634.html
26. Forrest, K. Y., Bunker, C. H., Songer, T. J., Coben, J. H., and Cauley, J. A. (1997). Driving patterns and medical conditions in older women. *Journal of the American Geriatric Society* **45**(10), 1214–1218.
27. Owsley, C., Ball, K., McGwin, G., Jr., Sloane, M. E., Roenker, D. L., White, M. F., et al. (1998). Visual processing impairment and risk of motor vehicle crash among older adults. *JAMA* **279**(14), 1083–1088.

28. Koepsell, T. D., Wolf, M. E., McCloskey, L., Buchner, D. M., Louie, D., Wagner, E. H., et al. (1994). Medical conditions and motor vehicle collision injuries in older adults. *Journal of the American Geriatric Society* **42**(7), 695–700.

29. Foley, D. J., Wallace, R. B., and Eberhard, J. (1995). Risk factors for motor vehicle crashes among older drivers in a rural community. *Journal of the American Geriatric Society* **43**(7), 776–781.

30. Vernon, D., Diller, E., Cook, L., Reading, J., Suruda, A., and Dean, J. (2002). Evaluating the crash and citation rates of Utah drivers licensed with medical conditions, 1992–1996. *Accident Analysis and Prevention* **34**(2), 237–246.

31. Stewart, R. B., Moore, M. T., Marks, R. G., May, F. E., and Hale, W. E. (1993). *Driving Cessation and Accidents in the Elderly: An Analysis of Symptoms, Diseases, Cognitive Dysfunction and Medications.* Washington, D.C.: AAA Foundation for Traffic Safety.

32. Leveille, S. G., Buchner, D. M., Koepsell, T. D., McCloskey, L. W., Wolf, M. E., and Wagner, E. H. (1994). Psychoactive medications and injurious motor vehicle collisions involving older drivers. *Epidemiology* **5**(6), 591–598.

33. Ray, W. A., Gurwitz, J., Decker, M. D., and Kennedy, D. L. (1992). Medications and the safety of the older driver: Is there a basis for safety? *Human Factors* **34**(1), 33–47.

34. Christensen, H., Mackinnon, A., Jorm, A. F., Henderson, A. S., Scott, L. R., and Korten, A. E. (1994). Age differences and interindividual variation in cognition in community-dwelling elderly. *Psychology of Aging* **9**(3), 381–390.

35. Li, S., Aggen, S. H., Nesselroade, J. R., and Baltes, P. B. (2001). Short-term fluctuations in elderly people's sensorimotor functioning predict text and spatial memory performance: The MacArthur Successful Aging Studies. *Gerontology* **47**(2), 100–116.

36. Fozard, J. L., Vercryssen, M., Reynolds, S. L., Hancock, P. A., and Quilter, R. E. (1994). Age differences and changes in reaction time: the Baltimore Longitudinal Study of Aging. *Journal of Gerontology* **49**(4), P179–P189.

37. Hertzog, C., Dixon, R. A., and Hultsch, D. F. (1992). Intraindividual change in text recall of the elderly. *Brain and Language* **42**(3), 248–269.

38. Meyer, J. (2004). Personal vehicle transportation. In: *Technology for Adaptive Aging*, Pew, R. W., and Van Hemel, S. B., eds. Washington, D.C.: The National Academies Press.

39. Raymond, P., Knoblauch, R., and Nitzburg, M. (2001). *Older Road User Research Plan* (S No. DOT HS 322). Washington, D.C.: National Highway Traffic Safety Administration.

40. Owsley, C., McGwin, G., Jr., Sloane, M., Wells, J., Stalvey, B. T., and Gauthreaux, S. (2002). Impact of cataract surgery on motor vehicle crash involvement by older adults. *JAMA* **288**(7), 841–849.

41. Owsley, C., Stalvey, B., Wells, J., and Sloane, M. E. (1999). Older drivers and cataract: Driving habits and crash risk. *Journal of Gerontology A Biological Science and Medical Science* **54**(4), M203–M211.

42. Owsley, C. (2003). Enhancing older driver safety and performance: cataract surgery and driver safety. Paper presented at the International Conference on Aging, Disability and Independence, Arlington, VA.

43. Stalvey, B. (2003). Educational programs to improve older driver safety. Paper presented at the International Conference on Aging, Disability and Independence, Arlington, VA.

44. Staplin, L., Lococo, K. H., McKnight, A. J., McKnight, A. S., and Odenheimer, G. L. (1998). *Intersection Negotiation Problems of Older Drivers* (No. DTNH22-93-C-05237). Washington, D.C.: National Highway Traffic Safety Administration.

45. NHTSA (1999). *Safe Mobility for Older People* (S No. DOT HS 808 853). Washington, D.C.: National Highway Traffic Safety Administration.

46. Retchin, S. M., and Anapolle, J. (1993). An overview of the older driver. *Clinics in Geriatric Medicine* **9**(2), 279–296.

47. Steinfeld, E., Tomita, M., Mann, W. C., and DeGlopper, W. (1999). Use of passenger vehicles by older people with disabilities. *The Occupational Therapy Journal of Research* **19**(3), 155–185.

48. Riter, A., Straight, A., and Evans, E. L. (2002). *Understanding Senior Transportation: Report and Analysis of a Survey of Consumers age 50+.* Washington, D.C.: AARP.

49. NHTSA (2002). *Traffic Safety Facts 2001: A Compilation of Motor Vehicle Crash Data from the Fatality Analysis Reporting System and the General Estimates System* (No. DOT HS 809 484). Washington, D.C.: National Highway Traffic Safety Administration.

50. Cerrelli, E. (1989). *Older Drivers: The Age Factor in Traffic Safety* (No. DOT HS 807 402). Washington, D.C.: National Highway Traffic Administration.
51. IIHS (2001). Education alone won't make drivers safer. *Status Report* **36**.
52. Li, G., Braver, E. R., and Chen, L.-H. (2001). *Exploring the High Driver Death Rates per Vehicle-Mile of Travel in Older Drivers: Fragility Versus Excessive Crash Involvement.* Arlington, VA: Insurance Institute for Highway Safety.
53. Burkhardt, J. E., and Eberhard, J. (2003). *Technical Background for a Symposium on Transportation Mobility for the Elderly* (No. NCHRP Project 20–24(24)B): National Cooperative Highway Research Program.
54. Braver, E. R., and Trempel, R. E. (2004). Are older drivers actually at higher risk of involvement in collisions resulting in deaths or non-fatal injuries among their passengers and other road users? *Injury Prevention* **10**(1), 27–32.
55. Langford, J. (2003). Keeping older drivers on the road. Paper presented at the International Conference on Aging, Disability and Independence, Arlington, VA.
56. McGwin, G. (2003). Within vehicle interventions and trauma care to reduce older driver injury and death. Paper presented at the International Conference on Aging, Disability and Independence, Arlington, VA.
57. Macdonald, W. (2003). Driver assessment to maintain mobility. Paper presented at the International Conference on Aging, Disability and Independence, Arlington, VA.
58. Middleton, H., Westwood, D., Robson, J., Arno, P., Eeckhout, G., and Baten, G. (2003). Elderly drivers assessment procedures, criteria and tools currently in use. Paper presented at the International Conference on Aging, Disability and Independence, Arlington, VA.
59. Stutts, J. C. (1998). Do older drivers with visual and cognitive impairments drive less? *Journal of the American Geriatrics Society* **46**(7), 854–861.
60. Eberhard, J. W. (2001). Safe mobility for older Americans: Developing a national agenda. In: *Maximizing Human Potential.* American Society on Aging, p. 1.
61. Bassuk, S. S., Glass, T. A., and Berkman, L. F. (1999). Social disengagement and incident cognitive decline in community-dwelling elderly persons. *Annals of Internal Medicine* **131**(3), 165–173.
62. Marottoli, R. A., Mendes de Leon, C. F., Glass, T. A., Williams, C. S., Cooney Jr., L. M., Berkman, L. F., et al. (1997). Driving cessation and increased depressive symptoms: Prospective evidence from the New Haven EPESE. *Journal of the American Geriatric Society* **45**(2), 202–206.
63. Fonda, S. J., Wallace, R. B., and Herzog, A. R. (2001). Changes in driving patterns and worsening depressive symptoms among older adults. *Journal of Gerontology: Social Sciences* **56B**(6), S343–S351.
64. McCarthy, D. P., Mann, W. C., Wu, S., and Tomita, M. (2003). Health, functional and psychological status and driving. Paper presented at the International Conference on Aging, Disability and Independence, Arlington, VA.
65. Dobbs, B. M. (2003). The role of support groups in helping people adjust to driving cessation. Paper presented at the International Conference on Aging, Disability and Independence, Arlington, VA.
66. Eberhard, J. W. (1998). Driving is transportation for most older adults. *Geriatrics* **53**(Suppl 1), S53–S55.
67. Ficke, R. (2003). Aging and disability: implications for transportation research. Paper presented at the Transportation Research Board Annual Meeting.
68. Koepsell, T., McCloskey, L., Wolf, M., Moudon, A. V., Buchner, D., Kraus, J., et al. (2002). Crosswalk markings and the risk of pedestrian–motor vehicle collisions in older pedestrians. *JAMA* **288**(17), 2136–2143.
69. Staplin, L., Lococo, K. H., Byington, S., and Harkey, D. (2001). *Highway Design Handbook for Older Drivers and Pedestrians* (S No. FHWA-RD-01-103). Lanham, MD: Federal Highway Administration.
70. Dejeammes, M. (2003). Alternative transport services to the private car for elderly people, in France and Europe. Paper presented at the International Conference on Aging, Disability and Independence, Arlington, VA.
71. Burkhardt, J. E. (2003). Improving public transportation options for older persons. Paper presented at the International Conference on Aging, Disability, and Independence, Arlington, VA.

72. Hardin, J. (2003). *Senior Transportation: Toolkit and Best Practices*. Washington, D.C.: Community Transportation Association of America.

73. Langford, J. (2003). Driver licensing and assessment (panel discussion): Some consequences of the different older driver licensing procedures in Australia. Paper presented at the International Conference on Aging, Disability and Independence, Arlington, VA.

74. Harris, J. (2003). Maintaining safe mobility for life. Paper presented at the International Conference on Aging, Disability and Independence, Arlington, VA.

75. Hekstra, A. (2003). Introduction to driver licensing and car-adaptation for elderly and disabled in Europe. Paper presented at the International Conference on Aging, Disability and Independence, Arlington, VA.

76. Caird, J. (1999). In-vehicle intelligent transportation systems: Safety and mobility of older drivers. Paper presented at the Transportation in an Aging Society: A Decade of Experience, Bethesda, MD.

77. Hancock, P. A., Llaneras, R. E., and Vercryssen, M. (2004). *Older Drivers and Smart Cars: Is Technology the Answer?* Baltimore, MD: Johns Hopkins University Press.

78. Dobbs, A. R., Heller, R. B., and Schopflocher, D. (1998). A comparative approach to identify unsafe older drivers. *Accident Analysis and Prevention* **30**(3), 363–370.

79. Dellinger, A. M. (2003). Population trends, risk and assessment. Paper presented at the International Older Driver Consensus Conference, Arlington, VA.

80. Ball, K. (2003). Evaluation of a brief assessment Battery in a Department of Motor Vehicle setting. Paper presented at the International Conference on Aging, Disability and Independence, Arlington, VA.

81. Wang, C. C., Kosinski, C. J., Schwartzberg, J. G., and Shanklin, A. V. (2003). *Physician's Guide to Assessing and Counseling Older Drivers*. Washington, D.C.: National Highway Traffic Safety Administration.

82. Schwartzberg, J. G. (2003). Helping older adults drive safely: The physician's role. Paper presented at the International Conference on Aging, Disability and Independence, Arlington, VA.

83. Cohen, L. (2003). Driver licensing & assessment: What is happening in the U.S.? Paper presented at the International Conference on Aging, Disability and Independence, Arlington, VA.

84. Arno, P. (2003). The elderly driver: What's happening in Belgium and in Europe? Paper presented at the International Conference on Aging, Disability and Independence, Arlington, VA.

85. Odenheimer, G. L., Beaudet, M., Jette, A. M., Albert, M. S., Grande, L., and Minaker, K. L. (1994). Performance-based driving evaluation of the elderly driver: safety, reliability, and validity. *Journal of Gerontology* **49**(4), M153–M159.

86. NHTSA (2001). *Traffic Safety Facts 2000: Older Population* (No. DOT HS 809 328). Washington, D.C.: National Highway Traffic Safety Administration.

87. West, C. G., Gildengorin, G., Haegerstrom-Portnoy, G., Lott, L. A., Schneck, M. E., and Brabyn, J. A. (2003). Vision and driving self-restriction in older adults. *Journal of the American Geriatric Society* **51**(10), 1348–1355.

88. Scott, J. B. (2003). Keeping older adults on the road: The role of occupational therapists and other aging specialists. *Generations* **27**(3), 39–43.

89. Gallo, J. J., Rebok, G. W., and Lesikar, S. E. (1999). The driving habits of adults aged 60 years and older. *Journal of the American Geriatrics Society* **47**(3), 335–341.

90. Ball, K., Owsley, C., Stalvey, B., Roenker, D. L., Sloane, M. E., and Graves, M. (1998). Driving avoidance and functional impairment in older drivers. *Accident Analysis and Prevention* **30**(3), 313–322.

91. Brayne, C., Dufouil, C., Ahmed, A., Dening, T. R., Chi, L., McGee, M., et al. (2000). Very old drivers: Findings from a population cohort of people aged 84 and over. *International Journal of Epidemiology* **29**, 704–707.

92. Hunt, L., Morris, J. C., Edwards, D., and Wilson, B. S. (1993). Driving performance in persons with mild senile dementia of the Alzheimer type. *Journal of the American Geriatrics Society* **41**(7), 747–752.

93. Owsley, C., Stalvey, B. T., and Phillips, J. M. (2003). The efficacy of an educational intervention in promoting self-regulation among high-risk older drivers. *Accident Analysis and Prevention* **35**(3), 393–400.

94. Alexander, J., Barham, P., and Black, I. (2002). Factors influencing the probability of an incident at a junction: Results from an interactive driving simulator. *Accident Analysis and Prevention* **34**(6), 779–792.

95. Mayhew, D. R., and Simpson, H. M. (2002). The safety value of driver education and training. *Injury Prevention* **8**(Suppl 2), ii3–7, discussion ii7–8.

96. Williams, A. F., and Ferguson, S. A. (2004). Driver education renaissance? *Injury Prevention* **10**(1), 4–7.

97. NHTSA (1996). *The Public Favors a Strong Government Role in Highway Safety* (No. 132). Washington, D.C.: National Highway Traffic Safety Administration.

98. Kennedy, J. (2004). National Safety Council: Driver improvement programs. Paper presented at the Transportation Research Board 83rd Annual Meeting, Washington, D.C.

99. Greenberg, B. (2004). AARP Driver Safety Progran: Cultural phenomenon vs. verifiable results. Paper presented at the Transportation Research Board 83rd Annual Meeting, Washington, D.C.

100. Hunt, L. A. (1993). Evaluation and retraining programs for older drivers. *Clinics in Geriatric Medicine* **9**(2), 439–448.

101. Ker, K., Roberts, I., Collier, T., Renton, F., and Bunn, F. (2003). Post-licence driver education for the prevention of road traffic crashes. *Cochrane Database System Review* (3), CD003734.

102. Eby, D. W., Molnar, L. J., Shope, J. T., Vivoda, J. M., and Fordyce, T. A. (2003). Improving older driver knowledge and self-awareness through self-assessment: The driving decisions workbook. *Journal of Safety Research* **34**(4), 371–381.

103. French, D., and Hanson, C. S. (1999). Survey of driver rehabilitation programs. *American Journal of Occupational Therapy* **53**(4), 394–397.

104. Korner-Bitensky, N., Sofer, S., Kaizer, F., Gelinas, I., and Talbot, L. (1994). Assessing ability to drive following an acute neurological event: Are we on the right road? *Canadian Journal of Occupational Therapy* **61**(3), 141–148.

105. Klavora, P., Young, M., and Heslegrave, R. J. (2000). A review of a major driver rehabilitation centre: A ten-year client profile. *Canadian Journal of Occupational Therapy* **67**(2), 128–134.

106. Park, W. (1999). Vision rehabilitation for age-related macular degeneration. *International Ophthalmology Clinics* **39**(4), 143–162.

107. Wood, J. M., and Mallon, K. (2001). Comparison of driving performance of young and old drivers (with and without visual impairment) measured during in-traffic conditions. *Optometry and Vision Science* **78**(5), 343–349.

108. Owsley, C., and Ball, K. (1993). Assessing visual function in the older driver. *Clinics in Geriatric Medicine* **9**(2), 389–401.

109. Dobbs, A. R. (2003). Developing and maintaining standardization of in-car evaluations across assessment centers. Paper presented at the International Conference on Aging, Disability, and Independence, Arlington, VA.

110. Ball, K., Berch, D. B., Helmers, K. F., Jobe, J. B., Leveck, M. D., Marsiske, M., et al. (2002). Effects of cognitive training interventions with older adults: A randomized controlled trial. *Journal of the American Medical Association* **288**(18), 2271–2281.

111. Edwards, J. D., Wadley, V. G., Myers, R. S., Roenker, D. L., Cissell, G. M., and Ball, K. K. (2002). Transfer of a speed of processing intervention to near and far cognitive functions. *Gerontology* **48**(5), 329–340.

112. Roenker, D. L., Cissell, G. M., Ball, K. K., Wadley, V. G., and Edwards, J. D. (2003). Speed-of-processing and driving simulator training result in improved driving performance. *Human Factors* **45**(2), 218–233.

113. Mazer, B. L., Sofer, S., Korner-Bitensky, N., Gelinas, I., Hanley, J., and Wood-Dauphinee, S. (2003). Effectiveness of a visual attention retraining program on the driving performance of clients with stroke. *Archives of Physical Medicine and Rehabilitation* **84**(4), 541–550.

114. Ball, K. (2003). Cognitive interventions to imporve older driver safety. Paper presented at the International Conference on Aging, Disability and Independence, Arlington, VA.

115. Watson, M. (2003). Driver rehabilitation: When remediation is appropriate. Paper presented at the International Conference on Aging, Disability and Indepencence, Arlington, VA.

116. Desmond, P. A., and Matthews, G. (1997). Implications of task-induced fatigue effects for in-vehicle countermeasures to driver fatigue. *Accident Analysis and Prevention* **29**(4), 515–523.

117. Lee, H. C., Lee, A. H., and Cameron, D. (2003). Validation of a driving simulator by measuring the visual attention skill of older adult drivers. *American Journal of Occupational Therapy* **57**(3), 324–328.

118. Rizzo, M., McGehee, D. V., Dawson, J. D., and Anderson, S. N. (2001). Simulated car crashes at intersections in drivers with Alzheimer disease. *Alzheimer Disease and Associated Disorders* **15**(1), 10–20.

119. Janke, M. K., and Eberhard, J. W. (1998). Assessing medically impaired older drivers in a licensing agency setting. *Accident Analysis and Prevention* **30**(3), 347–361.

120. Allen, R. W., Stein, C. A., and Aponso, B. L. (1990). A lowcost, part task driving simulator based on microprocessor technology. Paper presented at the 69th Annual Meeting of the Transportation Research Board, Washington, D.C.

121. Ivancic, K., and Hesketh, B. (2000). Learning from errors in a driving simulation: Effects on driving skill and self-confidence. *Ergonomics* **43**(12), 1966–1984.

122. Rinalducci, E. J., Mouloua, M., and Smither, J. (2003). *Cognitive and Perceptual Factors in Aging and Driving Performance* (No. VPL-03-01). Orlando, FL: University of Central Florida.

123. Little, C. (2002). The Intelligent Vehicle Initiative: Advancing "human-centered" smart vehicles. Retrieved 12/7/02, from http://www.tfhrc.gov/pubrds/pr97-10/p18.htm

124. Ball, K. K., Wadley, V. G., and Edwards, J. D. (2002). Advances in technology used to assess and retrain older drivers. *Gerontechnology* **1**(4), 251–261.

125. Campbell, J. L., Everson, J. H., Garness, S. A., Pittenger, J. L., Kennedy, J., and Llaneras, E. (1998). *Identification of Human Factors Research Needs: Final Report* (No. FHWA-RD-98-178). McLean, Virginia 22101-2296: Federal Highway Administration.

126. Dingus, T. A., McGehee, D. V., Manakkal, N., Jahns, S. K., Carney, C., and Hankey, J. M. (1997). Human factors field evaluation of automotive headway maintenance/collision warning devices. *Human Factors* **39**(2), 216–229.

127. Verwey, W. B. (2000). On-line driver workload estimation. Effects of road situation and age on secondary task measures. *Ergonomics* **43**(2), 187–209.

128. Massie, D. L., Campbell, K. L., and Williams, A. F. (1995). Traffic accident involvement rates by driver age and gender. *Accident Analysis and Prevention* **27**(1), 73–87.

129. Perel, M. (2003). Making vehicles easier and safer for older drivers. Paper presented at the International Conference on Aging, Disability and Independence, Arlington, VA.

130. Tufano, D. R. (1997). Automotive HUDs: The overlooked safety issues. *Human Factors* **39**(2), 303–311.

131. Staplin, L., Lococo, K. H., Byington, S., and Harkey, D. (2001). *Guidelines and Recommendations to Accommodate Older Drivers and Pedestrians* (No. FHWA-RD-01-051). Lanham, MD: Federal Highway Administration.

132. Staplin, L. (1999). Highway enhancements to improve safety and mobility of older road users: Practical applications. Paper presented at the Transportation in an Aging Society: A Decade of Experience, Bethesda, MD.

133. Staplin, L., and Lyles, R. W. (1991). *Age Differences in Motion Perception and Specific Traffic Maneuver Problems*. Washington, D.C.: Transportation Research Board.

134. Noland, R. B. (2003). Traffic fatalities and injuries: The effect of changes in infrastructure and other trends. *Accident Analysis and Prevention* **35**(4), 599–611.

135. Elvik, R. (2002). The importance of confounding in observational before-and-after studies of road safety measures. *Accident Analysis and Prevention* **34**(5), 631–635.

136. Noland, R. B., and Oh, L. (2004). The effect of infrastructure and demographic change on traffic-related fatalities and crashes: A case study of Illinois county-level data. *Accident Analysis and Prevention* **36**(4), 525–532.

137. Penney, T. (1999). *Intersection Collision Warning System* (No. FHWA-RD-99-103). McLean, VA: United States Department of Transportation.

138. Wachtel, J. (2004). Learning from Santa Monica: The role of roads and vehicles for the safety of older drivers. Paper presented at the ASA-NCOA Conference, San Francisco.

139. Mullick, A., Steinfeld, E., and Steinfeld, A. (2003). Designing more effective automobiles for frail older people. Paper presented at the International Conference on Aging, Disability and Independence, Arlington, VA.

140. Institute, N. E. (2003). Vision problems in the U.S.—Prevalence of adult vision impairment and age-related eye diseases in America. Retrieved 03/08/04, from http://www.nei.nih.gov/eyedata/

141. Harbluk, J. L., and Noy, I. Y. (2002). The impact of cognitive distraction on driver visual behaviour and vehicle control. Retrieved 03/08, 2004, from http://www.tc.gc.ca/roadsafety/tp/tp13889/pdf/tp13889es.pdf

142. Caird, J. (2003). In vehicle intelligent transportation systems. Paper presented at the Transportation Research Board Annual Meeting, Washington, D.C.

CHAPTER 8

TRANSPORTATION AND COMMUNITY MOBILITY

Michael Justiss

8.1 INTRODUCTION

The National Household Travel Survey sponsored by the Bureau of Transportation Statistics and the Federal Highway Administration determined that 20% of older Americans do not drive.[1] Major deterrents include: declining health, self-regulation, lack of access to a vehicle, and personal preference. In the United States, independent mobility is often identified with the ability to drive. Many people will outlive the ability to drive safely. Older men live on average 7 years beyond their ability to drive, and older women live on average 10 years beyond their ability to drive. These older adults require alternative modes of transportation for a substantial period.[2] Unfortunately, alternative transportation is all too often inadequate or unavailable.

Elderly Mobility

There are many reasons why older adults cease driving. One reason relates to increased likelihood of disability. With aging comes the increased chance of disability due to age-related decline and associated diseases. Over half (54.5%) of the older adult population in 1997 reported at least one type of impairment. Seventy-four percent of the very old (>85) reported at least one type of impairment or disability.[3] Dellinger et al. conducted a cross-sectional study of community dwelling elders in California ($n = 1950$) and asked study participants why they stopped driving.[4] The main reasons for driving cessation were identified and placed into six categories: medical problems (41%), age-related changes (19.4%), licensing or licensing renewal problems (12.2%), "other" (12.1%), someone else can drive (10.8%), and vehicle maintenance costs (4.3%). Study participants listed vision, slow reaction time/driving, cardiovascular disease, arthritis, Parkinson's disease, and accidents as specific reasons they stopped driving. Approximately 65% of these older adults who stopped driving within the past 5 years were female with a mean age of 85.5 years. Two percent stopped driving in their sixties, 18% in their seventies, 63% in their eighties, and 17% in their nineties.

Marottoli analyzed a number of factors associated with driving cessation among a cohort of older adults (*n* = 309).[5] Medical conditions associated with driving cessation were: Parkinson's disease, stroke, arthritis, hip fracture, cataract, glaucoma, poor vision, and depression. Other factors included *availability of alternative transportation*, being married, inability to perform one or more basic activities of daily living (e.g., bathing, dressing, toileting), decreased physical and social activities, and no longer working. A study of 108 older adults in the United Kingdom reported health reasons (28.6%) and loss of confidence or other psychological reason (17.9%) as reasons for giving up their driving.[6]

Lack of personal transportation and transportation alternatives to the automobile can lead to decreased social interaction. Marottoli et al.'s[7] longitudinal study of older drivers (*n* = 1316) showed an association between driving cessation and decreased social activity outside the home. A number of studies have demonstrated a relationship between decreased out-of-home activities and sense of personal well-being among older adults with arthritis.[8-10] Increased risk for disability and decline in cognitive status have also been associated with disengagement from social activity outside the home.[11,12] A multidimensional analysis using a life satisfaction index measure showed a relationship between activity level and psychosocial outcomes.[13] Social and productive activities provided survival advantages for a group of older adults in Connecticut.[14] Social activities were identified as going to church, cinemas, restaurants, or sporting events; taking a day or overnight trip; playing cards, bingo, or other games; and participation in social groups. Productive activities were identified as gardening, preparing meals, shopping, community work, and paid employment. After controlling for health-related factors related to survival and controlling for physical activity (fitness), social and productive activities showed more survival advantages among the least physically active.

Lack of transportation options can contribute to further isolation. An estimated 50% of all older non-drivers stay at home because they have no transportation alternatives.[1] Many rural communities lack public transportation services and the infrastructure to support walking or bicycling. In addition to geographic differences to accessing transportation alternatives, there are socioeconomic, racial, and ethic differences with the use of these services. More than 25% of African-American households, 19% of Latino households, and 9% of Asian-American households do not own a vehicle. These older adults are more likely than white non-drivers to access public transportation. Only 10% of whites occasionally utilize public transportation compared to African-Americans (21%), Latinos (21%), and Asian-Americans (16%).[15]

Transportation options for older adults may include passengers in a personal vehicle, public transportation, paratransit, private transit, special transit, low-speed vehicles, or personal mobility devices and walking. Arranging a ride with family members, friends, or neighbors as a passenger in a personal vehicle is often perceived by many older adults as an imposition on the driver.[1] A Michigan survey of older driver and former driver use of transportation alternatives (*n* = 1053) reported that a very small percentage of study participants from either group relied on public transportation. Former drivers relied on private vehicles as passengers for their primary community mobility needs (67%), with the majority of these rides provided by an adult child (49%). The other forms of transportation alternatives reported by former drivers were walking (18%), taxis (7%), and special transit services (6%). Sixty percent reported that they had never used public transportation on a regular basis. Primary reasons reported for dissatisfaction with public transportation were unreliability and lack of punctuality. Satisfaction increased with the use of volunteer driver and special transit services, which offered much greater reliability and punctuality.[16]

Public Transportation

Travel behaviors change with age. After age 60, adults make fewer trips as drivers and trips become shorter. As functional abilities decline with age, avoidance of stressful and nighttime driving becomes more common. There is a difference between the United States and European countries regarding travel behaviors (Figures 8.1–8.4). In the United States, older adults rely more on the personal vehicle for transportation than do Europeans of similar age. The percentage of trips by walking remains relatively low and constant across the lifespan for Americans. An estimated 40% of all trips in Europe are taken without a car compared to 10% of trips in the United States.[17]

While the majority of older Americans use a personal vehicle as their primary mode of transportation, approximately 65% walk at least a half-mile once a month and 4% ride a bicycle on a weekly basis.[1]

Use of Public Transportation in Other Countries The United States relies heavily on the personal automobile for daily travel compared to walking and using

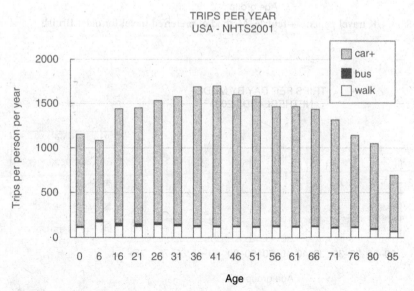

Figure 8.1 U.S. travel patterns. Method of preferred travel (car, bus, or walking) for U.S. citizens across the lifespan.

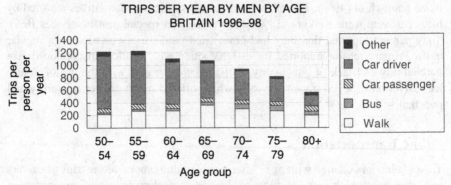

Figure 8.2   UK travel patterns—men. Method of preferred travel for older British men.

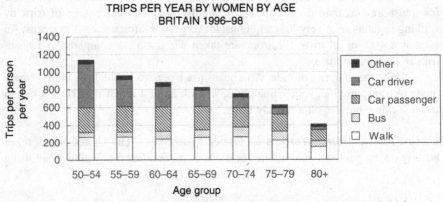

Figure 8.3   UK travel patterns—female. Method of preferred travel for older British women.

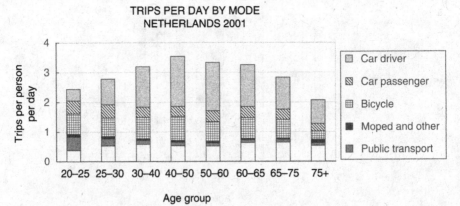

Figure 8.4   Netherlands travel pattern. Method of preferred daily travel for adults in the Netherlands.

public transportation. Accessing public transportation changes little across the lifespan in the United States. In contrast, older adults in the United Kingdom and the Netherlands rely more on walking and use of public transit than do older Americans for their transportation needs. Older adults in the Netherlands use bicycles well into their seventies on a daily basis.[17]

8.2 PUBLIC TRANSIT AND DISABILITY

Technology Use with Public Transportation

Technology has been applied to public transportation in the development of Intelligent Transportation Systems (ITS) that enhance elder mobility by providing better information before and during a journey.[19] Many of the age-related declines in function that contribute to driving cessation can impede mobility independence when using public transportation systems. The application of technology within an ITS can support deficits in vision, hearing, cognition, and sensorimotor function.

Vision of the Future

"Mrs. Smith" can no longer drive and wishes to travel to the local mall. After receiving free travel training through her local transportation service, she is able to access travel information through the internet service in her home. She selects her desired location and a report is generated indicating departure sites and times scheduled for a round trip. She can print the schedule, but would rather download the information to her hand-held device that supports global positioning software. She leaves at an appropriate time to reach the bus stop several blocks from her home.

Her community is designed with benches spaced along main walking routes to provide places to rest. She takes a wrong turn onto an adjacent street and the hand-held device attached to a cord around her neck gives an auditory alarm and vibrates, indicating a deviation from her programmed route. She refers to the device and follows the map to get back on track. Once she arrives at her bus stop, she is able to relax under a pavilion, which shades her from the hot sun. She is able to see the bus schedule on LED signs with large fonts and hear auditory updates of estimated times of arrival for the buses. After waiting several minutes, her hand-held device alarms and vibrates, indicating her bus has arrived.

Mrs. Smith uses a wheeled mobility device similar to a walker that has handbrakes and a basket to hold items while maneuvering around her environment. The bus arrives at her stop, which does not have a curb. Normally, this would increase the height to reach the first step. The transportation service has implemented new bus designs that feature low-riding buses with an extendable step that comes from under the bus to lower the initial step height (Figure 8.5). To further assist entry to the bus, grab bars or rails extend outwardly from either side of the doorway to provide a sturdy handhold (Figures 8.6 & 8.7). With one hand on her walker and the other on the handrail, she doesn't have much room or time to access her purse to count out "exact change." Mrs. Smith's hand-held device interfaces directly with

Figure 8.5 Extendible bus step.[18]

her smart card used for bus fares, which then connects wirelessly with the bus fare system. The power supply in the hand-held device enables the radio-frequency technology in the smart card to access her account information and automatically deducts the "senior discounted rate" for her programmed itinerary.

During her ride she notices that the call buttons to indicate a desired stop are brightly contrasted and at an accessible height. Unfortunately from her seated position, she is unable to read the travel information displayed toward the front of the bus and there is too much background noise to hear the announcements. She plugs her earphone attachment into her hand-held device, which functions as an assistive-listening device connected wirelessly to the announcement system.

As she approaches her destination, the hand-held device sends a signal to the bus driver that a stop is desired. Through her earphone, she receives a warning about the pending deceleration and indication of her desired bus stop for the local mall. The mall has a raised platform for loading and unloading passengers (Figure 8.8). She is able to easily exit the bus without having to navigate the steps.

Figure 8.6   Extendible handrail 2.

Mrs. Smith receives an alarm on her smart device to confirm her lunch appointment with several friends. She looks at her watch and realizes that she only has an hour to complete her shopping. Luckily she programmed her shopping list into her device, which gives her a list of the items with corresponding store locations within the mall. The smart, wireless environment of the mall interfaces directly with her device and assists with navigation. While walking past the pharmacy, she receives an alarm notifying her of a sale on items identified as "routine purchases." She completes her shopping with plenty of time to sit and socialize with her friends. She is having a great time and checks the bus schedule on her device and programs a later departure time.

This is an example of how technology can enhance the mobility independence of older adults. There are many types of technology and service applications that can support aging. Some of the smart technologies described have already been implemented in the U.S. and abroad.

Support for Endurance and Dexterity   Older adults are more sensitive to extreme temperature changes compared to younger adults. Easily read and understandable schedules at bus stops can better inform older adults of the expected

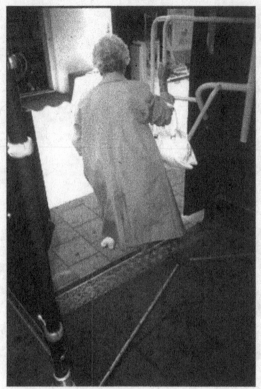

Figure 8.7 Extendible handrail 1.

waiting time. Trip planning can also be supported by smart technology. Hand-held devices such as personal digital assistants (PDAs) and smart phones could provide transit schedules to older adults to decrease the possible waiting time exposed to the elements. Smart card technology can be used to pay for transit fares automatically. Hands-free systems such as these have been introduced in Boston, Massachusetts (MBTA). The smart card can be programmed to automatically pay a fare when in proximity to a sensor or scanned directly into the interface device. The MBTA system, like others across the United States, have upgraded to low-floor buses equipped with wheelchair ramps and automatic audio and visual stop announcement capability.

Support for Vision/Blind and Hearing In public transportation terminals, service displays should be large enough for decreased vision, and auditory announcements of adequate volume to compensate for decreased hearing. Recurring display of the next stop on buses and trains could decrease anxiety for older adults traveling in an unfamiliar environment. For those with impaired vision, talking signs that report routing information can provide increased independence. Smart technology for people with visual and hearing impairment is also possible. Smart card technology will enable users to interface with transit communication systems to provide

Figure 8.8   Elevated loading station.

important information. The effectiveness of advanced fare media for use in the public transportation sector has been tested with smart card and radio-frequency (RF) technology. The newer-generation heavy rail and several light rail systems have implemented magnetic strip cards in Reading, PA (BARTA), Atlanta, GA (MARTA), Washington, D.C. (WMATA), Miami, FL, and Boston, MA (MBTA), to name a few.[20] These cards work similarly to debit cards but have the capacity for fraudulent use and easy duplication. The advancement to smart cards affords greater security against fraud and increased capacity for applications. The smart card contains a small microprocessor that acts like a tiny computer. It contains memory functions and is able to read and write electronic data. Radio-frequency (RF) technology can be applied to these smart cards to create a "hands-free" approach to fare payment systems. This creates an ideal platform for integration with other technology systems to streamline the travel experience.

The performance, cost, and user acceptance of two types of fare technology was studied in Los Angeles.[20] The smart cards used in this experiment have the capability to collect fare and ridership information by vehicle location and time of day.

GPS technology can also be integrated into this system to automatically adjust for distance-based fares. This study compared the use of contact-based and contactless smart cards. The contactless card uses RF technology and has to come within several inches of an interface device, while the contact-based smart card has to be inserted into the interface device. The study assessed the usability of 283 smart cards and 253 RF cards. The smart cards used accounted for 24,564 transactions with a 99.9% success rate and no cases involving multiple transactions. The RF cards accounted for 23,416 transactions, had a 99.99% success rate, and had 10 incidences of multiple transactions. Both of these recording methods produced more successful transaction rates compared to the standard magnetic strip cards (85–93%).[20] For use among older adults, smart card technology has several advantages to enhance mobility. The RF technology has the advantage of keeping the hands free for increased safety and decreased cognitive demand while boarding. The expanded capabilities afforded by the computer chip within the smart card will assist with advanced scheduling and real-time navigation support to further decrease anxiety when traveling in both familiar and unfamiliar environments.

Devices that utilize global positioning systems (GPS) can interface with the transportation system to provide routing information and notify the user of the proper travel information. The hand-held device could vibrate or give an alarm or recorded message indicating the correct stop for requested destination. The hand-held device could also serve as an assistive listening device that ties into the transit announcement system.

Support for Cognition Trip planning can greatly reduce the anxiety associated with community mobility for older adults. Many public transportation systems have enhanced their efforts to inform the public of available services. Many have developed user-friendly web sites for those with computer access. The Federal Transit Administration recognizes the top web sites for dissemination of transportation information. Detailed information about existing services and routing information can be reviewed before ever leaving home. Trip information can be downloaded into hand-held devices to guide the user through their trip from beginning to end. The Boston transit system already has detailed trip information that can be downloaded to a PDA. For those with GPS capability, a PDA in this environment can serve as a personal guide. Most vehicle GPS programs can select a route for a given destination based on ease or directness. The same applies in this transit environment. For the train system, if you were looking for the most direct route, the PDA would display a list organized by departure time from the originating station. The best or easiest route would show a travel itinerary with train departure times and locations. The estimated time of arrival would also be displayed. The PDA can be programmed to vibrate or chime when the train has arrived or destination reached. A similar system works with bus route information.

One reason older adults do not use public transportation systems is perceived lack of reliability. ITS technologies are being applied to increase the reliability, efficiency and safety of public transportation.[19] Examples of these applications include the Advanced Traffic Management Systems (ATMS), Automatic Vehicle Location (AVL), and Automatic Vehicle Identification (AVI). Control systems such as these can provide better communication between individual transport units and control centers to better serve the public in a timely and efficient manner. Alternatives to traditional transportation systems are being studied to supplement the impending transportation crisis expected from the increased number of older adults who will not be able to drive. An innovative method utilizing the internet is the Seattle Smart Traveler (SST). This program was designed to test automated dynamic rideshare matching.[21] The system is differentiated from typical carpooling in that the ridesharing is designed to accommodate the individual as opposed to routine or regularly occurring trips, and trips can be selected close to desired times. The traditional systems assume that the rider has a fixed schedule and fixed locations of origin or destination. The dynamic system considers each trip on an individual basis and must provide the information rapidly. Results indicate a similar rate of usage compared to established carpooling programs. Therefore, the increased demands for specific services required of older adults may be addressed to some degree through an automated matching system.

Mobility Support Services and Key Legislation

The Americans with Disabilities Act of 1990 (ADA) requires all public transit systems that provide fixed route bus and rail service to also provide paratransit (usually vans and small buses) service for people with disabilities who cannot use the fixed route bus and train service.[22]

The United Kingdom established the Disability Discrimination Act (DDA) in 1995. Part V of the DDA addresses issues concerning access to transportation for the disabled. The European Union (EU) has established a Disability Specific Directive to address discrimination for disabled employees. EU countries are expected to comply with the directive guidelines by 2006. The EU is emphasizing the need for comprehensive nondiscrimination legislation (Europeans with Disabilities Act) to ensure that all individuals have access to public transportation, education, and goods and services.

In the United States, the 1991 Intermodal Surface Transportation Efficiency Act (ISTEA) enhanced local transportation decision-making and provided a significant stimulus for surface transportation programs. The 1998 Transportation Equity Act for the 21st Century (TEA-21) is the reauthorization of ISTEA and has promoted many successful transportation programs across the country. TEA-21 allows transit systems to use up to 10% of their annual apportionment of formula funds (at the 80% federal to 20% local matching ratio) to pay for some of their ADA paratransit operating costs.[23] Since its inception, use of public transportation has risen over 20%, which is the highest rate in over 40 years. Ridership rose from 8 billion trips in 1996 to approximately 9.5 billion in 2001. The reauthorization of TEA-21 has been identified as a critical step to sustain the growth of transit users.[24]

The Older Americans Act (OAA) was adopted in 1965 to address societal concerns for the poor and disadvantaged. The OAA provides a statement of the commitment in the United States for ensuring the well-being of older persons. The OAA established the Administration on Aging (AoA) within the Department of Health and Human Services. The duties of the AoA are to serve as an effective and visible advocate for older individuals; collect and disseminate information related to problems of the aged and aging; administer grants; conduct evaluation of programs; provide technical assistance and consultation to states; and stimulate more effective use of existing resources. Title III of the OAA supports State Units on Aging and Area Agencies on Aging (AAA) by providing grants for state and community programs on aging. Title III-B services are directed solely toward improving the lives of older people, which includes issues with transportation.

Administered by the Federal Transit Administration, Section 5310 Elderly and Persons with Disabilities Program funds ensure the right of elderly citizens and people with disabilities to public transportation facilities and services. Since its inception in 1975, it has enabled thousands of Americans to achieve greater mobility and independence. The program also ensures that efforts are made in the planning and design of these facilities and services to guarantee their accessibility and effectiveness for elderly citizens and people with disabilities, and it guarantees that all federal programs offering assistance to public transportation include provisions to implement these policies.

Supplemental Transportation Programs (STPs)

In 2001, a report by the AAA Foundation for Traffic Safety and The Beverly Foundation reviewed Supplemental Transportation Programs for seniors (STPs), which are set up in the United States by grassroots, community, or regional level entities to provide seniors with alternative forms of transportation. This group developed the Senior Transportation Action Response (STAR) Awards for Excellence for groups whose efforts promote senior-friendly transportation. An updated report in 2004 provides extensive information about programs to enhance mobility independence in our aging society.[25]

The STAR recipients provide novel approaches to change or create programs to increase mobility independence for older adults. Strategies implemented by these organizations include both expansion and/or modification of existing services and design of new systems. There is a wide range of participant involvement within these programs. Some are governmental agencies, while others are philanthropic or volunteer networks. Budgets for these groups range from no funding to multi-million dollar projects.

Easter Seals is spearheading Transportation Solutions for Caregivers (TSC), an initiative funded through the Administration on Aging's National Family Caregiver Support Program. The most recent addition to the project is the release of the Senior Transportation Options Template for Communities that was developed in collaboration with the Beverly Foundation. The tool is a customizable electronic template ("drop in the facts") to identify all of the transportation options that are available to seniors in a typical community. It provides a framework for professionals, caseworkers, city and county planners, and other interested groups to take an inventory and assess transportation options, gaps, and needs in their own communities. Customizable supportive materials are included for providing additional information.[26]

Active Living by Design is a national program of the Robert Wood Johnson Foundation created to promote the development of safe environments that support increased physical activity such as walking and bicycling for either transportation or pleasure. Other examples of projects to increase awareness and promote senior friendly environments and transportation are discussed next.

Easter Seals' "Project ACTION"

The Easter Seals project entitled "Accessible Community Transportation in Our Nation (ACTION)" was established in 1988 as a research and demonstration project to improve access to public transportation for people with disabilities. This coincided well with the passage of the ADA two years later, which enhanced goals to help transportation operators implement the law's transportation provisions. This project is jointly funded through the U.S. Department of Transportation and the Federal Transit Administration. Both groups have the goals to promote cooperation between the transportation industry and the disability community to increase mobility for people with disabilities under ADA.

The Beverly Foundation with the Community Transportation Association of America released a profile of these innovative programs that address problems with senior mobility services. Three programs are identified for innovations of excellence, while three are identified for innovations of distinction as part of the United We Ride initiative, and they are described next.

Innovations of Excellence

Council on Aging & Human Services (COAST), Colfax, WA The problem identified in this area was limited transportation services for smaller communities. COAST developed a Community Vans program, using ADA compliant vehicles staffed by trained volunteer drivers. Rider and volunteer driver schedules are coordinated to provide transportation in the community. Funding of the program is offset through donations to the agency and contracting for Medicaid funded service to qualified residents.

Community Association for Rural Transportation, Inc. (CART), Harrisonburg, VA CART identified underutilization of their vehicles during the evenings and over weekends. They developed an approach to make the ADA accessible vehicles available for senior use during these unused periods for travel for daily, overnight, and out-of-town events. Trained drivers volunteer their time and are covered under the CART's insurance policy.

Seniors' Resource Center (SRC), Denver, CO The SRC had difficulties meeting the increasing demands for senior transportation services outside their normal working hours. The SRC brokered transportation services through other providers for essential rides (basic, non-emergency) utilizing existing funding sources such as Medicaid. Rates and type of transportation are negotiated based on the physical and/or cognitive needs of the rider. By brokering agreements for transportation services, the SRC has been able to increase its coverage area and working hours while still acting as the primary contact for service. Other programs of distinction have been identified for similar innovations to address the increased demand on aging society on current transportation systems: Special Transit, Boulder, CO; St. John's Council on Aging, St. Augustine, FL; Community Partnership Program (SMART), Detroit MI.

Walkable Communities　Walkable Communities, Inc. was founded in 1996 with the goal to help communities of all sizes become more walkable and pedestrian friendly. Executive director Dan Burden provides services to federal, state, and local agencies to create communities that are more livable and sustainable.[27] The premise of the organization is as follows[27]:

> Walkability is the cornerstone and key to an urban area's efficient ground transportation. Every trip begins and ends with walking. Walking remains the cheapest form of transport for all people, and the construction of a walkable community provides the most affordable transportation system any community can plan, design, construct and maintain. Walkable communities put urban environments back on a scale for sustainability of resources (both natural and economic) and lead to more social interaction, physical fitness and diminished crime and other social problems. Walkable communities are more livable communities and lead to whole, happy, healthy lives for the people who live in them.

UCP Michigan's "Everyone Travels"　"Everyone Travels" is a public transportation advocacy program developed through the United Cerebral Palsy (UCP) of Michigan. Its purpose is to increase awareness of issues concerning people with disabilities and access to public transportation.[28]

"Communities for a Lifetime" Florida Department of Elder Affairs　"Communities for a Lifetime" is a statewide initiative that advises Florida communities how to make improvements to benefit all ages. Existing state services are used to make improvements in housing, health care, transportation, accessibility, business partnerships, community education, use of natural resources, and volunteer opportunities. Community leaders and partners enter into an agreement to follow program guidelines. A "blueprint" is provided to conduct a comprehensive community assessment of geography, economy, population trends, housing, transportation, health, social, and cultural services and opportunities.[29]

Independent Transportation Network®　The Independent Transportation Network® (ITN®) was developed through cooperative funding by the Federal Transit Administration (FTA), AARP, and the Transportation Research Board (TRB) to address transportation needs of older adults in Portland, Maine. This program is a model to provide consumer-oriented and community-based senior transportation by offering full time-shared, scheduled, and on-demand service through paid and volunteer drivers with cooperative support from local businesses.[30,31]

8.3 PEDESTRIAN INFRASTRUCTURE: ROADWAY AND ACCESS IMPROVEMENTS

Changes in the environment can provide safer and easier access to mobility options. Getting to a bus stop is one problem in which roadway design can provide a major obstacle. The United States has changed over the past century, transitioning to a pre-dominantly suburban society. Walking to a corner market to purchase everyday household goods is a rare occurrence. Walking to stores may be possible based on proximity, but safe access is often impeded by lack of sidewalks and other designs to allow foot or bicycle traffic. A New Urbanism design movement promotes the balanced mixture of urban and residential areas. Housing developments are being designed to include town centers with grocery, pharmacy, medical offices, and other basic need facilities to cater to a local geographic sector.[32] An example of this concept is the Villages in central Florida (www.thevillages.com). The Villages is an active-living, 55+ community designed with all amenities in a localized area focus-ing on safety, convenience and recreation activities. The environment has been designed to support golf cart traffic as an alternative to standard vehicle transporta-tion. Designated cart paths are able to share the roadway safely and still access nec-essary locations. Many of the homes are designed with a separate garage bay to house golf carts.

An integral part of this type of community design is accessibility by alterna-tive forms of transportation as well as walking. Most excursions involve some degree of walking or assisted walking with the use of low-tech mobility devices such as walkers, canes, wheelchairs, and so on. Examples of pedestrian infrastructure required to support independent mobility include ramped curbs, adequately sized sidewalks with hospitable surfaces, protected roadway crossings, rest areas with benches spaced efficiently along routes, and structures with adequate shelter from the elements while waiting for a bus. Recommendations to address decreased vision at intersections are color-contrasted and textured curb cuts. A textured, ramped plat-form provides sensory feedback for approaching an intersection and a safe staging area while waiting to cross. Contrasting colors enhance visibility for the crosswalk by making the scribed pathway more visible.[33]

Technological advancements in roadway infrastructure provide safety meas-ures to decrease vehicle–vehicle related injury as well as vehicle–pedestrian injury. Signalized crossings provide a potential barrier to elder mobility. Not understand-ing the request buttons and inadequate crossing times are common difficulties experienced by pedestrians at signalized intersections.[34] Up to 82% of the pedestri-ans crossing a signalized intersection do not push the indicator button.[35,36] Crossing times allotted for pedestrians range between 6 and 10 seconds. The total time usually given for crossing a typical two-lane roadway is 10 times that of the vehicle; and when a traffic control system is used, the time is often adjusted in favor of the vehicle.[37]

An automated approach to increase pedestrian safety at intersections has been studied with the use of microwave sensors.[34] As part of the DRIVE II project VRU-TOO (Vulnerable Road User Traffic Observation and Optimization), trials were con-ducted at several European locations with emphasis on pedestrian behavior and safety. The goals of the technology were to replace the traditional pushbutton indicators, provide earlier activation upon approach, provide extended times for late approaches, and provide adjustment in crossing times based on quantity of activations. Results indicate a general improvement in the number of vehicle–person conflicts. The authors indicate a complex interaction between pedestrian safety and comfort that cannot be readily solved by pedestrian detectors alone. An impact can be made with combinations of different approaches. Traffic calming devices, such as advanced signal warning (flashing lights indicating pending change), rumble strips to provide feedback of required speed reduction, and speed bumps in high pedestrian volume areas, can enhance pedestrian safety. Smart intersections that provide visual and auditory notification for safe crossing can also improve safety.

A combination of infrared and microwave technology was used to evaluate automated pedestrian detection at several signalized intersections. Infrared detectors were used to detect pedestrians within a crosswalk, and microwave detectors monitored stationery presence on the sidewalk. The system automatically triggered a crossing signal when the microwave detectors were triggered, and the length of the crossing time was adjusted when the ultrasound detectors sensed a presence in the crosswalk. Application of this technology increased appropriate crossing (with WALK signal) by 24% and decreased the inappropriate crossings (with steady DON'T WALK signal) by 81%.

Guidelines for infrastructure design and changes have been applied to the older adult population.[38] Older pedestrians have a slower walking speed and shorter stride length than do younger adult pedestrians. A recommended 0.85 m/sec walking speed should be given to accommodate the functional differences in walking ability. Another reason given for increased walking times for older adults is the starting position before crossing the street. A study of pedestrian behaviors showed that older adults stand farther from the curb prior to crossing than do younger age groups, which accounts for an increased total crossing time among older adults.[39] For larger intersections that may require two-stage crossing, refuge islands are recommended. Placards that explain the pedestrian control signal with warnings for turning traffic should be displayed at the intersection and on any refuge islands. Many communities provide visual countdown timers to let pedestrians know the amount of time remaining for safe crossing.

Traffic-calming devices are an example of designs to promote safe foot-travel for seniors. Speed bumps are one method to slow traffic in areas of increased pedestrian activity. Speed platforms effectively slow traffic and bring the level of the roadway up to meet the level of the sidewalk to provide an even path for walking or wheeled mobility across streets (Figure 8.9).[17] A random sample of 750 households (of 2587) was assessed prior to and following implementation of a traffic-calming scheme in a community.[40] Improvements in perceived health and health-related behaviors were associated with the creation of a traffic-calming scheme.

Level entry from a platform is common when boarding a train. Environmental modification of bus stops can create "loading stations" where the sidewalk is built

Figure 8.9   Traffic calming—speed platform

up to meet the level of the bus for easier entry, similar to a train platform. Some buses provide retractable steps to decrease the distance required to board or exit. Low-floor and kneeling buses provide easier boarding for all people. Many bus designs also incorporate handles that extend outside the door to provide a more stabile support system for ingress or egress.

8.4   USE OF LOW- AND HIGH-TECH MOBILITY DEVICES TO INCREASE COMMUNITY MOBILITY

Low-Tech Mobility Devices

Low-tech devices to enhance elder mobility are common. Canes, walkers, manual wheelchairs, and even bicycles are used by older adults for safer mobility in the home and community environments. One reason that older adults may not access public transportation is lack of strength and endurance to reach bus stops. The walking environment is not always designed to support the decreased functional ability of older adults and others with disabilities. Modifications to these low-tech devices can enhance mobility even more than their original designs allowed. Newer cane designs call for lighter and stronger materials, such as titanium, to decrease fatigue by the user. Grips are becoming more ergonomically designed to decrease pressure and pain associated with prolonged use. Various types of canes such as quad canes and tripod canes add a wider base of support. Some designs allow for prolonged travel. The seat-cane is becoming increasingly popular. This lightweight cane unfolds into a tripod or quad supported seat to provide a resting place any time or location.

Walkers also come in a variety of styles and provide a greater amount of mobility support than the cane. Walkers are also being constructed from lighter and stronger materials to increase safety and decrease fatigue associated with their use. Most walkers are capable of being folded for easier transport to and from vehicles, whether public or private. Many designs have wheels to ease travel and decrease the need for lifting. Wheels provide easier mobility but can render a walker less stabile. Many classic wheeled-walker designs are not built for rough or uneven terrain. Newer styles come with larger, inflatable tires that can travel with ease over most terrains. To increase safety, many of these all-terrain walkers have hand brakes similar to those of a bicycle to provide greater control and stability. Like the seat-cane, many newer walkers can second as a mobile resting spot. The brakes can be locked and the walker used as a chair. Many accessories are also available. Walker baskets support hands-free travel for increased safety while traveling to or from the bus stop.

For more active adults, bicycles provide another means of motor-free travel. An estimated 1.1 million older adults ride a bicycle at least once a week.[1] Many public transportation services provide bike racks attached to the front of buses. This can decrease anxiety associated with longer distances between bus stops and desired destinations by providing this extra level of mobility support. For people with decreased function or fear of injury, the use of a tricycle for increased stability is often preferred. Tricycles are better suited for communities that support direct access to local destinations as most public buses do not support tricycle transport. Baskets for both bicycles and tricycles can also provide easy item transport between locations. The hand-powered tricycle provides another mobility option for those adults with decreased lower-extremity function.

High-Tech Mobility Devices

Power wheelchairs and scooters are becoming increasingly popular among adults with decreased functional mobility. Advancements in power supply technology have greatly increased the range and speed capability of these personal mobility devices. The level of controller sensitivity can be adjusted to accommodate all levels of upper-extremity function. The most common controller for the power chair is the mounted joystick. For decreased function, adaptations can support head and mouth controllers in order to navigate the environment. Many of the wheel designs in either the power chair or scooter designs support mobility across different terrain.

The Segway® Human Transporter (HT) uses technology that provides two-wheeled transport while standing. The same technology has been applied to an all-terrain power chair. The Independence™ iBOT™ 3000 (refer to Figure 3.11) can navigate across sand and climb steps. The rider can also elevate the chair onto two wheels to meet the eye level of friends or family while moving.

With the increase in freedom that the newer technologies provide, the geographic boundaries of travel are extended. Older adults with declining cognitive function may be less able to find their way around in their newly expanded environment. Other applications of high-tech devices to enhance older adult mobility can be seen with the use of smart technology. Hand-held devices such as personal digital assistants and smart phones could be linked to global positioning software to decrease anxiety associated with navigating the environment. These devices can also be linked to monitoring systems to notify caregiver or family members in case of emergency, or to provide the user with information, instructions, and support while moving about the community.

8.5 SUMMARY

Technology can be applied to many different areas of transportation and community mobility. The Beverly Foundation identified five components for senior friendly transportation: availability, accessibility, acceptability, affordability, and adaptability (5 A's). Advancements in technology will continue to increase mobility independence for seniors. Smart cards will keep travelers informed and help compensate for declining function by reducing time to board and will decrease the potential for falls by unburdening the hands. Real-time information about travel routes, transit arrival, and departure schedules are available through hand-held devices. This can reduce the time waiting at a station, exposure to the elements, and level of stress in an unfamiliar environment.

Modification of public transit vehicles to ease boarding or exiting for seniors will decrease the probability for injury. Kneeling and low buses are safer for all passengers, and extended door handles provide increased support. Contrasted colors of bus interiors and call bells will increase safety for visually impaired seniors and designated seating areas for wheelchairs (with wheel locks) will reduce injury during travel. Highly visible travel signage and auditory announcements help compensate for declining sensory function.

Infrastructure changes to make communities more travel-friendly give seniors more transportation alternatives. Safer areas for walking are provided by smooth, wide surfaces with accessible curb cuts. Traffic calming devices are used to decrease vehicle-related injury or fatality in areas with increased pedestrian activity. Highly visible crosswalk signage, auditory cross notification, and smart intersections that detect pedestrians will help make environments friendly for all levels of mobility.

Existing transportation systems are inadequate to meet the demands of our aging society. Supplemental Transportation Programs are an effective means to increase senior mobility by "filling in the gaps" left by existing programs. A combination of technology and policy can increase transportation options for seniors and provide safe alternatives in order to age successfully.

REFERENCES

1. Collia, D. V., Sharp, J., and Giesbrecht, L. (2003). The 2001 National Household Travel Survey: A look into the travel patterns of older Americans. *J Safety Research* **34**(4), 461–470.
2. Foley, D. J., et al. (2002). Driving life expectancy of persons aged 70 years and older in the United States. *American Journal of Public Health* **92**(8), 1284–1289.
3. Ficke, R. (2003). Aging and disability: Implications for transportation research. In: *Transportation Research Board Annual Meeting*.
4. Dellinger, A. M., et al. (2001). Driving cessation: What older former drivers tell us. *Journal of the American Geriatric Society* **49**(4), 431–435.
5. Marottoli, R. A., et al. (1993). Driving cessation and changes in mileage driven among elderly individuals. *Journal of Gerontology: Social Sciences* **48**(5), S255–S260.
6. Brayne, C., et al. (2000). Very old drivers: Findings from a population cohort of people aged 84 and over. *International Journal of Epidemiology* **29**, 704–707.
7. Marottoli, R. A., et al. (2000). Consequences of driving cessation: Decreased out-of-home activity levels. *The Journal of Gerontology Series B* **55**, 334–340.
8. Zimmer, Z., Hickey, T., and Searle, M. S. (1995). Activity participation and well-being among older people with arthritis. *Gerontologist* **35**(4), 463–471.
9. Mor, V., et al. (1989). Risk of functional decline among well elders. *Journal of Clinical Epidemiology* **42**(9), 895–904.
10. Slattery, M. L., Jacobs, D. R., Jr., and Nichaman, M. Z. (1989). Leisure time physical activity and coronary heart disease death. *The US Railroad Study. Circulation* **79**(2), 304–311.
11. Hubert, H. B., Bloch, D. A., and Fries, J. F. (1993). Risk factors for physical disability in an aging cohort: The NHANES I Epidemiologic Followup Study. *Journal of Rheumatology* **20**(3), 480–488.
12. Bassuk, S. S., Glass, T. A., and Berkman, L. F. (1999). Social disengagement and incident cognitive decline in community-dwelling elderly persons. *Annals of Internal Medicine* **131**(3), 165–173.
13. Hoyt, D. R., et al. (1980). Life satisfaction and activity theory: A multidimensional approach. *Journal of Gerontology* **35**(6), 935–941.
14. Glass, T. A., et al. (1999). Population based study of social and productive activities as predictors of survival among elderly Americans. *BMJ* **319**(7208), 478–483.
15. Bailey, L. (2004). *Aging Americans: Stranded Without Options*. Surface Transportation Policy Project. pp. 1–18.
16. Kostyniuk, L. P., and Shope, J. T. (2003). Driving and alternatives: Older drivers in Michigan. *Journal of Safety Research* **34**(4), 407–414.
17. Mitchell, C. G. B. (2003). Keeping people walking safely for local mobility and independence. In: *International Conference on Aging, Disability and Independence*. Washington, D.C.
18. Eberhard, J. (2003). Enhancing mobility for older people. In: *International Conference on Aging, Disability and Independence*. Arlington, VA.
19. Suen, S. L., and Mitchell, C. G. B. (2003). *Applications of Intelligent Transportation Systems to Enhance Vehicle Safety for Elderly and Less Able Travelers*. Transportation Development Centre, 98-S2-O-03.
20. Moore, J. E., and Giuliano, G. (1998). Functional evaluation of the Los Angeles smart card field operational test. *Transportation Research Part C* **6**, 247–270.
21. Dailey, D. J., Loseff, D., and Meyers, D. (1999). Seattle smart traveler: Dynamic ridematching on the World Wide Web. *Transportation Research Part C* **7**, 17–32.
22. Title 49—Transportation, Code of Federal Regulations, Title 49, Volume 1, *Part 38_Americans with Disabilities Act (ADA) Accessibility Specifications for Transportation Vehicles*, Revised as of October 1, 2003, From the U.S. Government Printing Office via GPO Access [CITE: 49CFR38.39], p. 558.
23. U.S. Department of Transportation (1998). http://www.fhwa.dot.gov/tea21/factsheets/ada.htm
24. APTA (2002). *An Investment in America: TEA 21 Reauthorization Proposal*. Washington, D.C.: American Public Transportation Association.
25. Larsen, L. (2004). Methods of multidisciplinary in-depth analyses of road traffic accidents. *Journal of Hazardous Materials* **111**(1–3), 115–122.

26. Seals, E., and Foundation, B. (••). *Transportation Solutions for Caregivers: Senior Transportation Options*.

27. Burden, D. (2001). *Building Communities with Transportation*. Transportation Research Board, Washington, D.C.: p. 14.

28. Miller, J., Wisselink, K., and Thayer, K. (2003). *The Regional Ride*. Beulah, MI: Michigan Land Use Institute and United Cerebral Palsy of Michigan.

29. *Communities for a Lifetime*. (2000). State of Florida Department of Elder Affairs.

30. Burkhardt, J. E. (2003). *Improving public transportation options for older persons*. In: *International Conference on Aging, Disability, and Independence*. Arlington, VA.

31. *ITN: A New Model for Senior Transportation*. (2004).

32. Patterson, P. K., and Chapman, N. J. (2004). Urban form and older residents' service use, walking, driving, quality of life, and neighborhood satisfaction. *American Journal of Health Promotion* **19**(1), 45–52.

33. Staplin, L., et al. (2001). *Guidelines and Recommendations to Accommodate Older Drivers and Pedestrians*. Lanham, MD: Federal Highway Administration, p. 86.

34. Carsten, O. M. J., Sherborne, D. J., and Rothengatter, J. A. (1998). Intelligent traffic signals for pedestrians: Evaluation of trials in three countries. *Transportation Research Part C* **6**, 213–229.

35. Davies, H. E. H. (1992). The Puffin Pedestrian Crossing: Experience with the First Experimental Sites. Crowthorne, UK: Transport Research Laboratory.

36. Levelt, P. M. B. (1992). *Improvement of Pedestrian Safety and Comfort at Traffic Lights: Results from French, British, and Dutch Field Tests*. Leidschendam, Netherlands: SWOV Institute for Road Safety Research.

37. Hunt, J. G. (1993). Pedestrian crossings: Changing the balance of priorities. In: *PTRC European Transport, Highways and Planning 21st Summer Annual Meeting*, Manchester, UK.

38. Staplin, L., et al. (2001). *Highway Design Handbook for Older Drivers and Pedestrians*. Lanham, MD: Federal Highway Administration, p. 380.

39. Harrell, S. (1990). Perception of risk and curb standing at street corners by older pedestrians. *Perceptual and Motor Skills* **70**(3:2), 1363–1366.

40. Morrison, D. S., Thomson, H., and Petticrew, M. (2004). Evaluation of the health effects of a neighbourhood traffic calming scheme. *Journal of Epidemiology and Community Health* **58**(10), 837–840.

CHAPTER 9

HOME MODIFICATIONS AND UNIVERSAL DESIGN

Patricia Belchior

9.1 INTRODUCTION

This chapter complements the earlier chapters on smart technology. It discusses the place where much of that technology is used—the home. The basic structure and design of the home can facilitate or inhibit independence. In this chapter, we will discuss two different approaches to making the home environment conducive to maximizing independence: (1) building the home following principles of *universal design* and (2) adapting existing housing through *home modifications*.

As the population ages, we will need housing that compensates for the declining abilities of its residents. Older adults are reluctant to move in their later years, with 85% preferring to "age in place."[1] Their homes have "emotional meaning," providing a sense of self, family, independence, control, and autonomy.[2] Older individuals experience and assess domestic spaces in terms of routines, such as eating a meal or doing housework; entertaining visitors; and sentiment attached to furniture and objects that keep their memories alive.[2,3]

As they age, many people face impairments while living in homes that lack accommodations to provide support and accessibility. Most single-family homes where older residents live were designed for younger persons, sometimes called "Peter Pan" homes. They typically have inaccessible entrances, difficult-to-climb stairs, unsafe conditions in bathrooms, and narrow hallways and kitchens that do not accommodate the needs of its residents.[4] Subsequently, many older people have difficulty moving around the house.

The built environment plays an important role in facilitating or inhibiting human performance and is critically important for older persons with disabilities. Today, technology is also an important component for aging in place.[5] This chapter focuses on two interventions that help people age in place: (1) home modifications and (2) universal design.

Smart Technology for Aging, Disability, and Independence, Edited by William C. Mann
Copyright © 2005 John Wiley & Sons, Inc.

9.2 HOME MODIFICATIONS

Defining Home Modifications

Home modifications create a safer and more accessible home environment, and increase competence in task performance by adapting a home in such a way as to promote independence in activities of daily living.[6] Even minor, low-cost changes can have a positive impact on a person's safety and ability to perform routine everyday tasks.[7] Varying with the type of adaptations, home modifications may involve architects, builders, and occupational therapists. To address specific needs, the resident and caregivers should be involved in decisions to modify a home.

Several classification schemes have been suggested for home modifications. Pynoos et al. categorized home modifications by type of structural change and type of behavioral change desired.[8] Gitlin categorized home modifications by cost: from no-cost to moderately priced changes, to costly structural changes.[9] Steinfeld and Shea suggested all home modifications address one of the following areas: risk reduction, fire safety, security, accessibility/usability, and home repair and maintenance.[10] Mann et al. suggested that home modifications could be categorized by type of impairment they addressed: hearing, vision, cognition, or movement (upper and lower extremities).[11] Each of these categorization schemes is unique, and any single home modification would fall within one or more categories of each scheme.

Messecar et al. identified 44 strategies to promote independence, many of which are home modifications. They grouped the 44 strategies into seven categories[12]: (1) *organizing the home*, which relates to achieving a harmony in the environment through reduction of demands on the elder and increasing the efficiency of the caregiver—for example, rearranging the elder's kitchen to facilitate meal preparation; (2) *supplementing the elder's function*, by making home modifications and using assistive devices—for example, acquiring a hearing aid; (3) *structuring the elder's day*, that is, structuring the elder's schedule during the day, so activities are not too demanding or too boring—for example, establishing routines and creating activities; (4) *protecting the elder*, which is related to accident prevention and detection of functional decline—for instance, eliminating objects in the environment that are dangerous for the elder; (5) *working around limitations or deficits in the home environment*, that is, decreasing adverse stimuli or ameliorating shortcomings; (6) *enhancing the home environment*, giving meaning to the elder through activities that help them to enjoy life; and (7) *transitioning to a new home setting*.

Common, simple home modifications include[13]: (1) nightlights in hallways and/or bathroom; (2) non-skid strips in bathtub or shower; (3) higher-wattage light bulbs; (4) lever handle faucets and doorknobs; (5) non-slip strips on stairs; (6) secured carpets and throw rugs (using double-sided tape). More expensive home modifications include: (1) installation of light switches at the top and bottom of stairwells; (2) adding a bathroom and/or bedroom to the first floor of a two-story home to make the first floor livable; (3) addition of handrails to both sides of stairs; (4) installation of handrails and/or grab bars in the bathroom; (5) widening of doorways; and (6) addition of a ramp or stair lift.

Need for Home Modifications

The number of older American homeowners is increasing.[13] The majority of Americans over age 45 live in single-family residences. Single-level homes are more common than homes with two or more levels, yet it is not uncommon for multistory homes to have no bathroom or bedroom on the lower level.

While many homes of older adults need modifications, as well as basic maintenance and repairs, often they are not made. Common reasons for not undertaking home modifications include the following[13]: (1) Elders are not able to complete the modification by themselves; (2) elders are not able to afford to hire someone to complete the home modifications; (3) elders are not able to identify reliable contractors or handymen; and (4) many elders are simply not aware of the need to make home modifications.

Home modifications offer many benefits.[14] Basic daily tasks such as bathing, dressing, and cooking can be completed more easily if the home has been appropriately modified. Home modifications also provide caregivers with a more supportive environment, making their caregiving tasks easier to complete. The risk of accidents such as falls can be reduced with even very simple, no-cost modifications. Overall, home modifications are a factor in reducing health-related costs and in preventing or delaying institutionalization.[14]

Caregiver Issues

With home modifications, caregiver burden can be reduced as the care recipient is able to complete more tasks independently or with less personal assistance, thus reducing hours of paid caregiver assistance. Allen and Resnik reported at the International Conference on Aging, Disability and Independence (ICADI) that the more accommodations present in the home, the fewer hours of paid assistance were required.[15] They pointed to the following as important home modifications for promoting independence: railings, bathroom modifications, ramps or street level entrances, and accessible parking or drop-off site.

Overton et al. reported at ICADI on a model program called Caregiver Adaptation to Reduce Environmental Stress (CARES).[16] CARES was developed to reduce physical burden and strain for caregivers through "environmental coping strategies" (ECS), including home modifications and assistive technology. These investigators found that the greatest physical burden for caregivers is experienced during lifting, transferring, and bathing. The most common home modifications used with these activities are grab bars. Several barriers impede caregivers in using ECS more often. Many caregivers are unaware of the benefits of ECS and do not know how to locate ECS products or professionals. Many service providers also lack awareness of the benefits of ECS.

Home Modifications to Reduce Health-Related Costs

In a study of the effectiveness of an approach that provided elders with both assistive technology (AT) and environmental interventions (EI) in maintaining independence and reducing home care costs among frail older adults, it was found that although functional decline occurred over time, even with the use of interventions, functional decline was slowed when using these interventions, and institutional and in-home personnel costs were reduced.[17]

Home Environmental Problems: Rooms, Spaces, and Hazards

Before undertaking home modifications, it is first necessary to determine the functional status of the elder and to assess the potential of the home to facilitate or inhibit independence. Through this assessment process, home environmental problems can be identified, and strategies for modifying the home can be planned. Below we discuss common home environmental problems.[18]

Kitchen Kitchens present more problems for older persons with disabilities than any other room or space in a home. Problems encountered in the kitchen relate to: high and/or small counters and insufficient counter space. Older individuals often do not use the cabinets, or use only the lower shelf and/or the front section of the shelf. Many use a chair or a step tool to gain access, which can be dangerous. For wheelchair users, often there is not enough counter space, and the kitchen is too small to turn in the wheelchair.[18] Modifying the counter space is one of the most common modifications in the kitchen. General guidelines for counter modification includes 28- to 32-inch height for seated users; 36-inch height for general standing users; 42- to 45-inch height for counters raised over appliances, and minimum dimensions for knee spaces of 30 inches wide by 27 inches high[19] (Figures 9.1 and 9.2). Four key issues summarize the problems faced by elders in the kitchen: climbing, reaching, difficulty bending, and forgetfulness. Furthermore, the inability to prepare meals may compromise an older adult's sense of independence and well-being.[20]

Bathroom The second most problematic area in the house is the bathroom. Common problems include the need for grab bars and transfer benches. Often the toilet seat is too low or too small, mirrors are placed too high, there is insufficient storage space, towel bars are too high, and there is difficulty in accessing the sink.[18] A study of bathroom modifications for frail residents found that difficulties with tub transfers (90%) and toilet transfers (62%) were higher than bed transfers (21%).[21] In terms of activities of daily living (ADL) performance, participants reported more problems with bathing (79%) than with feeding or grooming (10%). Grab bars are a very common modification to bathrooms. General guidelines include the following: Install at appropriate height and position, be sure they have a non-slip surface, and ensure they are mounted securely.[22] Faulty installation of grab bars and other devices can create unsafe conditions.[18]

Some illustrations of common bathroom modifications are presented in Figures 9.3–9.6.

Figure 9.1   This adjustable sink system can be raised or lowered to meet the user's needs. Photograph courtesy of ADAS.

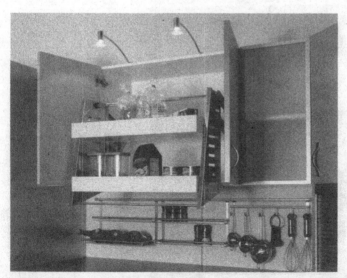

Figure 9.2   Pull-down adjustable shelves make it easier to reach items in upper cabinets. Pull Down Shelf Mechanism Cat. No 504.58.200, Häfele America Co.

Figure 9.3   A shower space without a bathtub accommodates the needs of wheelchair users, eliminating the need for transfers in and out bathtubs.

Figure 9.4   Eliminating the cabinet below the sink provides ease of access for wheelchair users. This Gator-Tech smart house sink also has automatic water and soap dispensers.

Figure 9.5   Grab bars installed in proper spaces are important to help standing from the toilet, transfer from wheelchair and can help to prevent falls. Courtesy of Otto Bock.

Figure 9.6   This system of grab bars was installed to provide safety in the shower. Courtesy of Otto Bock.

Bedroom The bedroom often presents problems for older adults. In two-story homes, it is common to find bedrooms located on the second floor of the house. Size of the bedroom may be a problem for those who use wheelchairs, and getting in and out of the bed can be very challenging for those with mobility impairments.[18] Many elders have difficulty dressing, and simply adding a chair for seated dressing can make the task much easier.

Other Rooms and Spaces Fewer problems are typically encountered in the dining living and family rooms, compared to problems in bathrooms and kitchens.[18] Common problems include clutter, unsafe carpets, and chairs and couches that are difficult to sit down or get up. The laundry area can cause problems if stairs are involved or if the washer and dryer are difficult to operate. Access to the mailbox may also be a problem.

Other general problems frequently encountered in a house occur with[18] (1) operating the thermostat, (2) lack of adequate light, (3) an insufficient number of outlets resulting in an excessive number of appliances plugged into a single outlet, (4) exposed extension cords resulting in falls, (5) appliance controls that cannot be read by persons with visual impairments, and (6) difficulty in lifting pots off the stove.

Stairs Stairs should be designed to be safe even in low light. For wooden stairs, use of a light color wood on the leading edges with a dark wood in the risers and stringers of the stair provides better contrast. "Triple switch design" (having turns in the stairs with intermediate landings) permits resting between risers. If carpet is used, it should be installed carefully to avoid the potential for tripping. Also handrails on both sides of the stairs can improve safety.[23]

Fire and Shock Exposed electrical cords and overloaded electric outlets represent fire and shock hazards and should be eliminated.[24] Whenever possible, furniture should be arranged so lamps and appliances can be plugged in without the use of extension cords. Smoke detectors are essential in all homes, and the risk of injury or death from not having them is even greater in the homes of the elderly, who cannot exit as quickly and are unlikely to use unconventional exits such as windows. Burns can also occur from hot tap water. To control the temperature of the water, an adaptor can be installed under the sink and an anti-scald safety valve can be installed on shower heads and faucets.

Outdoor Spaces Parking areas and entrances to a home must also be considered.[19] Ideally, the distance from parking to the front entrance should be short. Parking spaces should be at least 8 feet wide next to a 5-foot access isle. The slope of the access isle should be less than 1:50, have a smooth and continuous surface, and be directly connected to an accessible route. Curb cuts should have a slope no greater than 1:12, with flared side slopes no greater than 1:10, and the transition from curb cut to road should not exceed ¼ inch. If a flared side is not provided in the curb cuts, plants should be used in these spaces to prevent tripping.

Figure 9.7 This ramp provides access to the home by a person in a wheelchair. Center for Inclusive Design and Environmental Access. Used with permission.

Entries can be modified to enhance accessibility by re-grading the ground when there is enough space, or by adding a ramp or lift (Figure 9.7)[19]. There are several different types of ramps, but in general they should have the least possible slope, a width of at least 36 inches, a non-slip surface, and handrails and level landings at the bottom, top, and every 30 feet of run. If the elevation needed is great, and/or the space where a ramp might go is limited, a lift might be a better solution. Lifts should include (a) a threshold to keep the wheelchair from moving, (b) call buttons in the lift and at each landing, with manually operated switches to stop the lift, (c) protection from the weather, (d) landing gates, and (e) an alternate power source in case their is a power loss.

Barriers to Implementing Home Modifications

There are many barriers to implementing home modifications for older adults with disabilities. Often, older persons find home modifications too expensive and are not able to identify ways to pay for them. Many also lack knowledge about home modifications and the benefits of undertaking them. Older adults who rent may have landlords who are reluctant to make the modifications to meet their needs. In government-subsidized housing, the response to retrofitting older adult homes has been slow, and development and implementation of accessibility codes are inadequate.[14]

A recent study of factors associated with environmental problems among older people living in the community found that demographic factors and functional status are risk factors for problems with the home environment.[25] Five characteristics related to increased numbers of home environmental problems included: young–old, female, minority, have a higher level of disability, and suffer a higher level of pain. Although the exact association of these factors is not known, some factors were explored. People in the young–old range might experience more environmental problems because they may have been experiencing impairments for a shorter period of time and had not yet made necessary home modifications. Women had, on average, four more environmental problems than men. This could be due to limited resources, which could also be true for the minority elders in the study. Individuals who experience pain and have higher levels of disability may experience more environmental problems as a result of their reduced capacity to navigate in the home.

In a study of stroke survivors' perceptions of their environment, participants reported not having problems in managing their self-care activities, but had problems in managing some household activities.[26] The most common difficulties encountered outside the home were uneven ground, poor lighting, and stair access. Inside the home, wheelchair access was a problem for most participants. Many lived on one floor and in some cases in one room because they could not get to the second floor.

Home Modifications

Often several different home modifications are necessary but, due to time or income limitations, cannot be carried out simultaneously. In these situations it is necessary to set priorities. A model for viewing the environmental problems was developed by Mann et al. for use by occupational therapists in prioritizing environmental interventions.[18] The following scheme was developed:

Design + Maintenance + Social Support = Safety + Independence + Comfort

In this model, environmental problems relate to design, maintenance, or social support. Many environmental problems can be addressed by changing the design, which often has a major positive impact on users but is relatively inexpensive. Examples include: changing light fixtures, outlets, thermostats, locks, and shelving in closets. Maintenance is another important area, with problems ranging from basic issues such as pavement surface and condition of carpets to more major issues with roofs, windows, and doors. The third area in this model is social support. Members of a social support network can help the older adult to identify problems and find solutions. This includes spouse, adult children, health-care aids, or therapists. Following this model, if there is good input (design, maintenance, and social support), the output will be a safe and comfortable home where the older occupant can maintain independence.

Pynoos suggests three approaches to enhance aging in place[14]: (1) home modifications, (2) retrofitting existing apartment, and (3) building new accessible housing. He offers suggestions for each of these in Table 9.1.

TABLE 9.1 Three Approaches to Enhance Aging in Place

1. Make Home Modification More Available

A Campaign to Raise Public Awareness About the Benefits of Home Modifications
- Extend HUD's successful public relations campaign on lead paint and homes safety to "Healthy Homes" that support aging in place.
- Support a campaign to inform tenants about their rights under the "Reasonable Accommodations" section of the Fair Housing Amendments Act of 1988.

Enhanced Planning and Coordination Efforts
- Require that HUD's Consolidated Plan, Housing Elements, and master plans by area agencies on aging address the need for home modifications and retrofitting of multi-unit housing.
- Create Aging-in-Place Councils/Coalitions or add aging in place to the agendas of existing coordinating groups to raise awareness about home modifications and develop strategies to create more supportive environments.

Increased Funding for Home Modifications
- Reform Medicare and Medicaid to pay for home environmental assessments by occupational therapists or other health-care professional and allow broader coverage for home modifications.
- Include home modifications in home- and community-based waiver programs, including those intended to implement the Olmstead decision.
- Change IRS and state income tax rules to more easily allow home modifications as deductible expense and/or provide tax credit.
- Encourage states and localities to use revolving loan programs, grants, and housing trust funds for home modification and retrofitting of multi-unit housing.

Demonstration Projects that:
- Test the most effective ways of delivering services to modify single-family homes and apartments.
- Serve as best models that encourage organizations to replicate successful approaches.

Research that analyzes the need for and effectiveness of home modification
- Large datasets that should systematically and regularly collect information about home modifications include: U.S. Census and the Annual Housing Survey as well as longitudinal studies such as the National Long-Term Care Survey Self-Care and Aging, and AHEAD

2. Retrofit Existing Multi-unit Housing to Meet the Needs of Its Aging Residents

- Facilitate the retrofitting of multi-unit housing by
- Provide incentives to owners and sponsors of apartment buildings to modify their buildings to meet needs of persons with disabilities.

3. Promote the Building of Suitable Housing in the First Place

Suitable housing needs to be built in the first place by implementing the principles of
- Visitability
- Universal design

The content of this table has been reproduced and originally appeared in *Meeting the needs of older persons to age in place: Findings and recommendations for action.* Andrues Gerontology Center, University of Southern California.

This section has focused on home modifications. Another strategy to help individuals to age in place is to follow the principles of universal home design.[1] In this approach, the focus is not simply on home design for the elderly, but on a design that accommodates the needs of people of all ages.

9.3   UNIVERSAL DESIGN

What Is Universal Design?

In the early 1980s, architect Ron Mace introduced the concept of universal design: *"Universal Design is the design of products and environments to be usable by all people, to the greatest extent possible, without the need for adaptation or specialized design"* (Definition ¶1).[27] What makes universal design unique? Typically, products are designed for use by "average users." If a person differs significantly from the average, the product will likely have a poor fit for this person. Following the principles of universal design, product developers strive to have their products meet the needs of multiple users. For example, removing thresholds provides ease of mobility for a person in a wheelchair as well as for a parent with a stroller.

In exploring the concept of design, a number of adjectives have been paired with design: accessible, adaptable, transgenerational, and/or universal.[28] Accessible design addresses the needs of special populations, such as special bathrooms in restaurants for people in wheelchairs. "Special bathrooms" and other "special" spaces in the built environment may make people with disabilities feel segregated from others. Adaptable design provides more flexibility in that spaces can be easily changed to meet the needs of individual users. For example, cabinets that are removable under sinks reflect adaptable design. Transgenerational design considers the natural changes that occur as we age, but generally does not consider congenital or injury-related disabilities nor address the full range of possible disabilities. Universal design is the most inclusive and least stigmatizing approaches to designing our environment. Good universal design is invisible—you don't get the feeling that the space is "special." In some cases, universal design may be adaptable and sometimes transgenerational, and it is always accessible. Universal design is an approach that does not emphasize people's differences. For example, "disabled" toilet may be stigmatizing but an "accessible" toilet does not provide the symbol of separateness.[29] Whereas accessible design often focus on the needs of wheelchair users or individuals with visual impairment, universal design considers other differences such as strength, intellect, perception and values. At airports for example, universal design would include signs that can be understood by people of all languages.[30]

History of Universal Design

A number of changes in America led up to the introduction of the concept of universal design: changes in demographics, the economy and legislative initiatives. Over the past century, the United States has passed a number of federal laws requiring spaces in the built environment be more accessible for persons with disabilities.

These acts included the Soldiers Rehabilitation Act passed after World War I and the Vocational Rehabilitation Act of 1920, which recognized the importance of vocational rehabilitation services for U.S. citizens with disabilities.[31,32]

In the 1950s, the importance of incorporating accessibility into public buildings and facilities was recognized in the United States. The disabilities rights movement, which began in the 1960s and gained strength in the 1970s, postulated that the concept of disability is imposed by society, and the main contributors to disabilities were attitudes and inadequacies of the built environment.[29] Accessibility standards were developed by the President's Committee on Employment of the Physically Handicapped, the National Easter Seal Society, and the American National Standards Institute (ANSI), and they were published in 1961 by ANSI (A117.1—Making Buildings Accessible to and Usable by the Physically Handicapped).

In 1965 the National Commission on Architectural Barriers to Rehabilitation of the Handicapped was created, and in 1968 the Architectural Barriers Act was passed, mandating that all buildings and facilities designed, constructed, altered, or leased with federal funds must be fully accessible to individuals with disabilities. To complement this act, the Access Board was created under Section 502 of the Rehab Act of 1973. The original mission was to ensure federal agency compliance with the Architectural Barriers Act and to propose solutions to environmental barriers. Section 504 of the Rehabilitation Act of 1973 provided the first statutory definition of discrimination toward individuals with disabilities. It also introduced the concept of program accessibility and changed the emphasis of disability away from a social service perspective to one that included political and civil rights.[31,32]

In 1988, Congress passed the Fair Housing Amendments Act, an expansion of the Civil Rights Act of 1968. It was the first time in American history that builders were required to incorporate universal design into multifamily dwellings. This meant that individuals with disabilities could expect to find accessible housing in the open market.[31,32]

The Americans with Disabilities Act of 1990 (ADA) was the broadest and the most far-reaching civil rights legislation relating to people with disabilities. It extends full civil rights protection to all people with disabilities. While the ADA covers a wide range of disabilities including mobility, hearing, and speech impairment, it was not developed with people with cognitive impairment in mind. Titles II and III of the ADA encompass accessibility guidelines for buildings, facilities, and transit vehicles and provide technical assistance and training on these guidelines. More information about ADA guidelines can be found at http://www.usdoj.gov/crt/ada/adahom1.htm.

Dramatic changes in demographics also contributed to the development of universal design. Older people and people with disabilities, who were considered a small minority 100 years ago, now comprise a significant segment of our population. People are living longer and more people are living with disabilities.

Ron Mace, who introduced the concept of universal design, was a disabilities rights advocate as well as an academically based architect. He was very much involved in creating environments and products that could be used by all people regardless of their age, ability, or status in life. In 1989, Ron Mace created the Center for Universal Design, at the School of Design at North Carolina State University.[31,33]

Principles of Universal Design

The principles of Universal design were developed at North Carolina State University, based on research conducted from 1994 to 1997.[31,33] This research involved evaluations of consumer products, architectural spaces, and building elements. The principles are posted at http://www.design.ncsu.edu:8120/cud/univ_design/princ_overview.htm and are reprinted below:

1. **Equitable use**—*The design is useful and marketable to people with diverse abilities.*

   Guidelines:

   (1) Provide the same means of use for all users; be identical whenever possible and equivalent when not.

   (2) Avoid segregating or stigmatizing any users.

   (3) Provision for privacy, security, and safety should be equally available to all users.

   (4) Make the design appealing to all users.

2. **Flexibility in use**—*The design accommodates a wide range of individual preferences and abilities.*

   Guidelines:

   (1) Provide choice in methods of use.

   (2) Accommodate right- or left-handed access and use.

   (3) Facilitate the user's accuracy and precision.

   (4) Provide adaptability to the user's pace.

3. **Simple and intuitive**—*Use of the design is easy to understand, regardless of the user's experience, knowledge, language skills, or current concentration level.*

   Guidelines:

   (1) Eliminate unnecessary complexity.

   (2) Be consistent with users expectations and intuition.

   (3) Accommodate a wide range of literacy and language skills.

   (4) Arrange information consistent with its importance.

   (5) Provide effective prompting and feedback during and after task completion.

4. **Perceptible information**—*The design communicates necessary information effectively to the user, regardless of ambient conditions or the user's sensory abilities.*

   Guidelines:

   (1) Use different modes (pictorial, verbal, tactile) for redundant presentation of essential information.

   (2) Provide adequate contrast between essential information and its surroundings.

(3) Maximize "legibility" of essential information.

(4) Differentiate elements in ways that can be described (i.e., make it easy to give instructions or directions)

(5) Provide compatibility with a variety of techniques or devices used by people with sensory limitations.

5. **Tolerance for error**—*The design minimizes hazards and the adverse consequences of accidental or unintended actions.*

   Guidelines:

   (1) Arrange elements to minimize hazards and errors: most used elements, most accessible; hazardous elements eliminated, isolated, or shielded.

   (2) Provide warning of hazards and errors.

   (3) Provide fail-safe features.

   (4) Discourage unconscious action in tasks that require vigilance.

6. **Low physical effort**—*The design can be used efficiently and comfortably and with a minimum of fatigue.*

   Guidelines:

   (1) Allow users to maintain a neutral body position.

   (2) Use reasonable operating forces.

   (3) Minimize repetitive actions.

   (4) Minimize sustained physical effort

7. **Size and space for approach and use**—*Appropriate size and space is provided for approach, reach, manipulation, and use regardless of user's body size, posture, or mobility.*

   Guidelines:

   (1) Provide clear line of sight to important elements for any seated or standing user.

   (2) Make reach to all components comfortable for any seated or standing user.

   (3) Provide adequate space for the use of assistive devices or personal assistance.

Guidelines for Designers

The Center for Universal Design also developed guidelines for incorporating universal design in housing (Table 9.2), which first appeared in an article entitled "Universal Design in Housing,"[34] authored by Mace in 1998.

Home Modification and Universal Design in Other Countries

Differences among cultures, reflected in their values and customs, play a major role in shaping peoples' preferences and types of home modifications they will consider. In this section, we discuss issues about home modifications in different countries.

TABLE 9.2 Guidelines for Incorporating Universal Design in Housing

Entrances

—*No steps at entrances*
- Making all home entrances stepless is best.
- More than one stepless entrance is preferred.
- At least one stepless entrance is essential; if only one, not through a garage.

—*Site design methods for integrated stepless entrances*
- Level bridges to uphill point.
- Garage elevated to floor level so vehicles do the climbing.
- Earth berm and bridge and sloping walk details.
- Site grading and earth work (with founding waterproofing) and sloping walks at 1-in-20 maximum slope.
- Ramps avoided; if used, ramps must be integrated into the design.

—*Maximum rise of ½ in. at thresholds.*

—*View of visitors for all people, including children and seated users*
- Sidelights,
- Wide-angle viewers,
- TV monitors, and/or
- Windows in doors or nearby.

—*A place to put packages while opening doors: built-in shelf, bench, or table with knee space below located on the outside next to the door.*

—*Weather protection shelter while unlocking and opening doors.*
- Porch,
- Stoop with roof,
- Long roof overhang,
- Awning, and/or
- Carpot.

—*A way for visitors to communicate with residents*
- Lighted doorbell,
- Intercom with portable telephone link, and/or
- Hardwired intercom.

—*Space at entry doors: minimum 5-ft × 5-ft level clear space on both inside and outside of entry door for maneuvering while opening or closing door (can be smaller if automatic power door is provided).*

—*Light for operating at entry doors*
- Focused light on lockset,
- General illumination for seeing visitors at night, and/or
- Motion detector controls that turn on lights when someone approaches the door, help eliminate the problem of dark approaches to home, and add to sense of security.

—*Address house number: large, high contrast and located in a prominent place to be easy for friends and emergency personal to locate.*

Interior Circulation

—*At least one bedroom and accessible bathroom should be located on an accessible ground floor entry level (on the same level as the kitchen, living room, etc.).*

—*Minimum of 32-in. clear door-opening width (34- to 36-in.-wide doors) for all doorways.*

—*Minimum of 18-in. clear floor space beside door on pull side at latch jamb: provides spaces to move out of the way of the door swing when pulling it open.*

(Continued)

TABLE 9.2 *Continued*

—*Accessible route (42-in. minimum width): provides maneuvering room in hallways and archways.*
—*Turning space of 5-ft diameter in all rooms.*

Vertical Circulation

—*All stairs to have appropriate width and space at the bottom for later installation of a platform lift, if needed.*
—*At least one set of stacked closets, pantries, or storage spaces with knock-out floor for later use as an elevator shaft; or*
—*A residential elevator with minimum 3-ft × 4-ft clear floor installed at the time of initial construction.*
—*Stair handrails to extend horizontally beyond the top and bottom risers.*

Light and Color

—*Contrast between floor surfaces and trim: color or contrast difference that facilitates recognition of the junction of floor surfaces and walls. Avoid glossy surfaces.*
—*Color contrast difference between treads and risers on stairs.*
—*Ambient and focused lighting: lots of light, lighting that is thoughtful and variable, emphasizing lightning at entrances, stairs, and task lighting.*
—*Contrast between countertops and front edges or cabinet faces.*

Hardware

—*Easy to use, requiring little or no strength and flexibility.*
  • Lever door handles,
  • Push plates,
  • Loop handle pulls on drawers and cabinet doors—no knobs,
  • Touch latches,
  • Magnetic latches in lieu of mechanical, and
  • Keyless locks.

Switches and Controls

—*Light switches at 36–44 in. above floor maximum and thermostats at 48-in. maximum height.*
—*Easy-touch rocker or hands-free switches (see Home Automation, below).*
—*Additional electrical outlets at bed locations and desk for equipment: fourplex boxes one each side for computer and electronic equipment as well as personal use equipment.*
—*Electrical outlets at 18-in. minimum height allow easy reach from a sitting position as well as for those who have trouble bending over.*
—*Electrical panel with top no more than 54 in. above floor located with a minimum 30-in. × 40-in. clear floor space in front.*

Home Automation

—*Motion detector light switches in garages, utility spaces, entrances, and basements.*
—*Remote controls for selected lights.*
—*Remote controls for heating and cooling.*
—*Doorbell intercoms that connect to portable telephones.*
—*Audible and visual alarms for doorbell, baby monitor, smoke detector, etc.*

(Continued)

TABLE 9.2 *Continued*

Plumbing Fixture Controls

—*Single-lever water controls at all plumbing fixtures and faucets.*
—*Pressure balanced anti-scald valves at tubs and showers.*
—*Hand-held shower heads at all tubs and showers in addition to fixed heads, if provided. Single-lever diverter valves, if needed.*
—*Adjustable-height hand-held shower head on 60-in. flexible hose: allows ease of use by people of all heights.*
—*Mixer valve with pressure balancing and hot water limiter: prevents scalds by people who cannot move out of the way if the water temperature or pressure changes suddenly.*

Bathrooms

At least one bathroom must have one of the following accessible bathing fixtures:
—*Minimum 5 ft long × 3 ft (4 ft preferred) deep curbless shower (see wet area shower details below).*
—*Tub with integral seat, waterproof floor, and a floor drain.*
  • Other bathrooms in the same house may have a tub with an integral seat or a 3-ft × 3-ft transfer shower with an L-shape folding seat and $\frac{1}{2}$-in. maximum lip (curb) in lieu of the fixtures described above. When more than one bathroom has the same type of bathing fixtures (a tub, shower, or wet area shower), at least one shower should be arranged for left-handed use and one for right-handed use.
—*Adequate maneuvering space: 60-in.-diameter turning space in the room and 30-in. × 48-in. clear floor spaces at each fixture. Spaces may overlap.*
—*Clear space of 3 ft in from one side of toilet: allows for easy maneuvering to and around toilet.*
—*Toilet centered 18 in. from any sidewall, cabinet, or tub.*
—*Broad blocking between studs in walls around toilet, tub, and shower: allows for future placement and relocation of grab bars while assuring adequate load-bearing capacity (eliminates the need to open up wall to add blocking later).*
—*Minimum lavatory counter height of 32 in.*
—*Clear knee space 29 in. high under lavatory: allows someone to use the lavatory from a seated position. May provide open knee space or removable vanity or fold-back or self-storing doors. Pipe protection panels must be provided to prevent contact with hot or sharp surfaces.*
—*Countertop lavatories are preferred with the bowl mounted as close to the front edge of the counter as possible.*
—*Wall hung lavatories are acceptable with appropriate pipe protection.*
—*Pedestal lavatories are not acceptable.*
—*Long mirrors should be placed with bottom no more than 36 in. above the finished floor and top at least 72 in. high. Full-length mirrors are good choices.*
—*Offset controls in tub/shower with adjacent clear floor space: allows for easy access from outside the tub with no inconvenience when inside.*
—*Integral transfer seat in tub and in 3-ft × 3-ft shower stall allows people to sit in tub/shower without needing additional equipment.*
—*Grab bars: if installed, should not be stainless steel or chrome. Use colors to match decor.*

(Continued)

TABLE 9.2 *Continued*

Kitchens

—*Space between face of cabinets and cabinets and walls should be 48-in. minimum.*
—*Clear knee space under sink 29-in. high minimum: allows someone to use the sink from a seated position. May provide open knee space or removable base cabinets or fold-back, bifold, or self-storing doors. Pipe protection panels must be provided to prevent contact with hot or sharp surfaces.*
—*Adjustable-height (28–42 in.) work surfaces: electrically powered continuously adjustable counter segments, some with cook tops, others with sink and disposal units; or*
—*Mechanically adjustable counter segments, some with cook tops, others with sinks and disposal units, adjustable from 28 in. to 42 in. allows in-kitchen work for people of all heights, those with back trouble, people who are seated, and children.*
—*Contrasting color border treatment on countertops: color or contrast difference that facilitates recognition of the edges of counters and the different heights to prevent accidental spills.*
—*Stretches of continuous countertops for easy sliding of heavy items, particularly between refrigerator, sink, and stovetop for easy one-level food flow.*
—*Full-extension pullout drawers, shelves, and racks in base cabinets for easy reach to all storage spaces.*
—*Adjustable-height shelves in wall cabinets.*
—*Pantry storage with easy access pullout and/or adjustable-height shelves for easy reach to all items stored (e.g., Stor-ease pantry storage system).*
—*Front-mounted controls on appliances to facilitate reach.*
—*Cook top with knee space bellow: allows someone to use the appliance from a seated position. May provide open knee space or removable base cabinets or fold-back or self-storing doors. Pipe protection panels must be provided to prevent contact with hot or abrasive surfaces.*
—*Cook top or range with staggered burners and front- or side-mounted controls to eliminate dangerous reaching over hot burners.*
—*Glare-free task lighting to illuminate work areas without too much reflectivity.*
—*Side-by-side refrigerator: allows easy reach to all items, particularly if pull-out shelving is provided; or*
—*Use under counter or drawer-type refrigerators and install them on raised platforms for optimum access to storage space at 18 in. to 48 in. above finished floor.*
—*Built-in oven with knee space beside. Locate so one pullout oven rack is at same height as adjacent countertop with pullout shelf.*
—*Drop-in range with knee space beside. Locate top surface at 34 in. above finished floor.*
—*Dishwasher raised on a platform or drawer unit so top rack is level with adjacent counter top. This also puts bottom racks within easy reach, requiring less bending.*

Laundry Areas

—*Front-loading washers and dryers with front controls. Washers and dryers raised on platforms to reduce need to bend, stoop, or lean over.*
—*Laundry sink and counter top surface no more than 34 in. above finished floor with knee space below.*
—*Clear space 36 in. wide across full width in front of washer and dryer and extending at least 18 in. beyond right and left sides (extended space can be part of knee space under countertops, sink, etc.).*

(Continued)

TABLE 9.2 *Continued*

Storage

—*Fifty percent of storage to be no more than 54 in. high.*
—*Adjustable-height closet rods and shelves: allows for flexibility of storage options.*
—*Provide lower storage options for children, short, and seated people.*
—*Motorized cabinets that raise and lower.*
—*Power operated clothing carousels.*

Windows

—*Windows for viewing to have 36-in. maximum sill height.*
—*Casements, awning, hoppers, and jalousies are good choices but are not essential.*
—*Crank-operated windows.*
—*Power operators whenever possible.*

Sliding Doors

—*Bypassing closet doors: each panel should create an opening at least 32 in. clear.*
—*Interior pocket doors: when fully open, door should extend 2-in. minimum beyond doorjamb and be equipped with an open-loop handle for easy gripping.*
—*Exterior sliding doors: drop frame and threshold into sub floor to reduce upstanding threshold track or ramp finished flooring to match top of track on both sides.*

Decks

—*Build deck at same level as house floor.*
—*Keep deck clear of house and use slatted decking for positive drainage (e.g., a wood trench drain).*

Garage and Carports

—*Power-operated overhead doors.*
—*Door height and headroom clearances 8-ft minimum for tall vehicles or provide alternative onsite outdoor parking space.*
—*Extra length and width inside for circulation around parked cars.*
—*No ramp in garages.*
—*Sloping garage floor (with wall vents at bottom of slope to release fumes) in lieu of stepped entrance with ramp from garage to house interior.*

This article has been reproduced and originally appeared in *Assistive Technology*, 1998, 10, 21–28. For purchase, subscription and membership information, contact RE SNA, Suite 1540, 1700 North Moore Street, Arlington, VA 22209-1903.

Japan[35] Home modifications in Japan vary from Western countries as a result of significant differences in demographics, politics, culture, living arrangement, and environment. Japan is one of the most rapidly aging nations in the world, and it has a short period of time to adapt for this massive change in demographics. Due to the high population density in Japan, houses are smaller and typically have multiple floors. This is an unsuitable design for frail elders, especially if they are in wheelchairs. Although many houses in Japan have been adapted following customs of Western societies, a great number still use the more traditional Japanese design. Traditional Japanese toilets present another problem for elders. Squatting toilets were prevalent in Japan, and while this has largely changed, some elders still face the problem of using a toilet that is very difficult to use if they have mobility impairment. Also, the Japanese wash their bodies on the floor outside the tubs and then soak in the tub. They also prefer bathtubs filled with water to about 21 inches. This requires more balance when getting in and out of the tub.

In Japan, home modification programs for older adults followed programs for home modifications for younger people with disabilities. Many programs for elders were developed between the 1980s and 1990s with money from Japan's prosperous economy. Municipalities received incentives to support home modifications when the central government introduced a categorical grant for home modifications in 1990.

A compulsory national program called the National Long-Term Care Insurance System (LTCIS) was introduced in Japan in 2000. The goal of LTCIS is to respond to increasing long-term care needs, and it offers support for home modifications. With the introduction of the LTCIS, home modifications have become available nationwide. This program is more restrictive in the types of home modifications covered. The national program restricted benefits to frail older adults, excluded preventive modifications for relatively vigorous elderly, and did not pay for costly features such as lifts.

Australia   The state policies in Australia focus more on public housing or age-specific housing than on private housing.[36] The Disability Discrimination Act (1992) and "AS 1428 Design for Access and Mobility" applies to public buildings and public spaces only. The Australian standard covering access in private housing, AS 4299 Adaptable housing (Standards Australia, 1995), focuses on adaptable design rather than universal design.

Europe   For 30 years, Europe has promoted housing designs that address the needs of people with disabilities, especially wheelchair users. In the last 15 years, Lifetime Adaptable Housing standards were introduced to ensure that new and renovated housing can accommodate the needs of persons of all types of disabilities.[37]

The Importance of Lighting

Age-related vision changes and conditions can seriously impact one's ability to perform basic daily activities, and they increase the risk of accidents such as falls. Modifications of a home's lighting system can reduce accidents and enhance independence.[38] Furthermore, quality of light equates to quality of life. Lighting needs to be of sufficient intensity to promote task completion, should have minimal glare, should be uniform, and should render good color recognition. Many elders are concerned with the cost of electricity, so maximizing the use of daylight within the home may be a solution for at least part of the day.

The Lighting Research Center (LRC) at Rensselaer Polytechnic Institute developed a set of lighting principles and practical guidelines (Table 9.3) to address visual problems associated with age-related visual changes.[39] These principles were developed to provide a more comfortable home where older adults could maintain their independence.

TABLE 9.3 Lighting Principles and Practical Guidelines

More Light

Homes are often under lit in critical areas, such as kitchens. As much as 10 times more light will be required to see fine details (e.g., reading small type) or low-contrast objects (e.g., black thread or black cloth). Directional light sources should be used to maximize visibility and minimize energy use and heat.

Less Glare

Homes often have a single bright light in the center of the room ceiling. Although more light is required for the older eye to see, substituting high wattage light bulbs will not help visibility if the person has a direct sight of the light fixture or if shadows are cast onto the visual task. The location of the light fixture with respect to the person and the visual task is critical.

Balanced Light Levels

Homes often have dark walls or a single point of light that can cause shadows. Due to optical, and perhaps neural changes to the eye, older adults cannot completely adapt to dim lighting conditions, so diffuse lighting should be used in living spaces. Luminance levels in transitional spaces, such as hallways and entrance foyers, should be similar to those of the adjacent spaces.

More Contrast

Because contrast sensitivity is reduced with age, the visibility of important objects, such as edges, curbs, ramps, or doorways, can be greatly improved by increasing their contrast with paint or similar techniques.

The content of this table has been reproduced and originally appeared in *Lighting for older adults: Home modifications that help older adults maintain their independence*. Paper presented at ICADI, December 2003. Washington, D.C.

Evaluating the Home: Home Assessment Instruments

Home assessment is the process of identifying the problems associated with performing activities in the home.[40] The goal of the assessment is to make recommendations for modifying the home and provide a good person–environment fit. Consumers (e.g., homeowners, renters), providers of aging and rehabilitation services (such as occupational therapists and case managers), and building industry personnel (such as contractors and remodelers) generally conduct the assessments. Each has a different approach and use a diversity of instruments for the home assessment. These instruments are generally not interchangeable.

Home assessments conducted by the end user may result in underestimating problems, because residents may be unfamiliar with potential solutions.[40] They may change their behavior rather than changing the environment. For example, they may confine themselves to the first floor to avoid climbing stairs. Building professionals usually focus on evaluating the built environment and are usually guided by accessibility codes and regulations, but do not evaluate functional abilities of the residents. Providers of aging and rehabilitation services may focus more on assessing the person's functional abilities.

Combining these three perspectives could result in a comprehensive assessment approach encompassing all aspects of the problem, and result in better solutions. Pynoos et al.[40] developed a home assessment instrument with the goal of providing information about: (a) consumer priorities, (b) ability to participate in home-specific tasks and activities of daily living and, (c) the space, layout, and design of the residence. The Comprehensive Assessment Survey Process for Aging Residents (CASPAR™) was designed for occupational therapists in conducting functional and environmental assessments.

The Rehabilitation Engineering Research Center on Aging developed a home environment instrument to study the types of problems encountered by older persons with disabilities.[18] One instrument used in the 10-year, longitudinal Consumer Assessments Study is included below.

Rehabilitation Engineering Research Center Environment Survey

1. Type of neighborhood (to be completed by interviewer):

   Describe the predominant land use of the surrounding neighborhood (immediate street and rear yard)

   _____ residential—single-family homes/flats

   _____ residential—apartment buildings

   _____ commercial—neighborhood-oriented

   _____ commercial—regionally oriented

   _____ industrial

   _____ institutional

   _____ other (describe) _____

2. Perceived Safety

   How safe from crime do you consider your neighborhood?

   _____ very safe

   _____ fairly safe

   _____ dangerous

   _____ very dangerous

   Has the safety of your neighborhood changed in the last few years? How has it changed?

   _____ yes, more crime

   _____ yes, less crime

   _____ no

   Have you been a victim of crime in the neighborhood or in your home?

   _____ no

   _____ yes

   If yes, please describe _____

3. Type of living arrangement (to be completed by interviewer):

Standard Community Housing

_____ isolated mobile home

_____ mobile home in mobile home park

_____ single-family detached home

_____ townhouse or row house

_____ 2-unit building

_____ walk-up apartment building (3+ units in building)

_____ elevator apartment building

_____ small boarding home

_____ other (describe): _____

Age Segregated Housing

_____ retirement community (describe type): _____
_____

_____ "elderly" apartments

_____ congregate housing for the elderly (service supported)

_____ foster care home

_____ group home

_____ adult home

_____ other (describe): _____

4. Home Range

Please list all the places you usually visit during a typical week and how frequently you would visit each place.

Distance	Frequency	Places
_____	_____	Church
_____	_____	Grocery store
_____	_____	Other store/shopping (clothing, etc.)
_____	_____	Drug store
_____	_____	Hair/beauty salon
_____	_____	Volunteer work
_____	_____	Visit relatives
_____	_____	Visit friends
_____	_____	Bank
_____	_____	Restaurant
_____	_____	Senior program
_____	_____	Hospital
_____	_____	Doctor's office
_____	_____	Dentist
_____	_____	Other _____
_____	_____	Other _____
_____	_____	Other _____

Are there any other places you would like to go? Why don't you go there now?

Check if Yes	Place	Why You Don't Go
_____	Church	_____
_____	Grocery store	_____
_____	Other store/shopping	_____
_____	Drug store	_____
_____	Hair/beauty salon	_____
_____	Volunteer work	_____
_____	Visit relatives	_____
_____	Visit friends	_____
_____	Bank	_____
_____	Restaurant	_____
_____	Senior program	_____
_____	Hospital	_____
_____	Doctor's office	_____
_____	Dentist	_____
_____	Other _____	_____
_____	Other _____	_____
_____	Other _____	_____

On this street map, help me mark the places you usually go during a typical week with these stickers. After data collection, calculate total distance from home of every destination.

Interviewer: Identify the furthest destination. Compute distance to it on a map.

Distance to furthest destination: _____

5. **Accessibility and Usability:**

A. **Respondent Ratings**

How would you describe the usability and safety of your building and home?

_____ excellent

_____ very good

_____ good

_____ fair

_____ poor

Have you had any accidents in the last 5 years?

Please describe the problems you have:

Total _____ Getting from the street (or parking lot) to the building:

_____ Pavement surface uneven or cracked

_____ Slope

_____ Distance

_____ Wandering behavior

_____ No ramp for wheelchair

_____ Steps (can't handle)

_____ Other _____

NOTES:

Total _____ Using the entry to the house (or building):

_____ Difficulty with locks/keys

_____ Stairs present problems

_____ Lack of needed handrails

_____ Elevator difficulty/impossible to use

_____ Door too heavy

_____ Surface of entry presents problem

_____ Other _____

NOTES:

Total _____ In apartment buildings only, getting to or using common rooms and spaces in the building (e.g., mailroom, laundry, etc.)

_____ Stairs to laundry/basement present problem _____

_____ Difficulty accessing mailbox

_____ Difficulty with trash disposal

_____ Other _____

NOTES:

Total _____ Getting to or using yards or outdoor spaces on the property.

_____ Clutter prevents access/use

_____ Ground surface presents problem

_____ Stairs prevent access

_____ Lacks needed handrails

_____ Other _____

NOTES:

Total _____ Getting to or using your dining room, living room, or family room:

_____ Cluttered

_____ Thresholds are difficult

_____ Carpeting presents problems

_____ Difficulty getting up from chairs

_____ Layout causes confusion
_____ Too small
_____ Halls too narrow
_____ Other _____

NOTES:

Total _____ Getting to or using bedrooms:
_____ Closet shelves too high
_____ No closets in room
_____ Difficulty getting to because of stairs
_____ Rugs prevent danger
_____ Lacks needed telephone
_____ Too small
_____ Cluttered
_____ Difficulty getting into/out of bed
_____ Other _____

NOTES:

Total _____ Getting to or using the kitchen:
_____ Cabinets too high
_____ Appliances difficult to access
_____ Counter too high
_____ Not enough counter
_____ Plumbing problems
_____ Lower cabinets/can't bend to use
_____ Overall too small
_____ Other _____

NOTES:

Total _____ Getting to or using the bathroom(s):
_____ Getting in/out of tub
_____ Lacks needed grab bars
_____ Lacks needed transfer bench
_____ Lacks needed hand-held shower
_____ Bathroom too small for wheelchair
_____ Difficulty with faucets
_____ Bathroom upstairs and stairs are problem

_____ Towel bars too high

_____ Problems with toilet: lacks needed grab bars

_____ ' seat too low

_____ too small

_____ doesn't operate well

_____ Limited storage

_____ Limited counters

_____ Mirror too high

_____ Sink too high

_____ Other _____

Total _____ Getting to or using closets, cabinets, or other storage areas:

_____ Not enough space for storage

_____ Cluttered, inefficient

_____ Shelves too high

_____ Other _____

NOTES:

Total _____ (If relevant) Using stairs:

_____ Can't use independently

_____ Worn out/ill-maintained

_____ Too steep

_____ Cluttered

_____ Need handrails

_____ Need better lighting

_____ Too narrow

_____ Other _____

NOTES:

Total _____ Using appliances:

_____ Cognitive impeded use of controls

_____ Vision impeded use of controls

_____ Motor impairment limits use of appliances (other than wheelchair)

_____ Wheelchair use limits access to appliances

_____ Other _____

NOTES:

Total _____ Using doors:

_____ Not wheelchair/walker accessible

_____ Locks and latches difficult to operate

_____ Difficult to use door knob/pulls

_____ Other _____

NOTES:

Total _____ Using outlets, switches, and other electrical controls:

_____ Difficulty with outlets

_____ Switches too high

_____ Difficulty in seeing/then operating electric devices

_____ Need more outlets

_____ Lamp switch difficult

_____ Other _____

NOTES:

Total _____ Is there enough light during the <u>DAY</u> to see everything safely?

_____ Kitchen

_____ Dining room

_____ Living room

_____ Bedroom

_____ Home office

_____ Hallways/corridors

_____ Bathroom

_____ Entrances

_____ Other _____

NOTES:

Total _____ Is there enough light during the <u>EVENING</u> to see everything safely?

_____ Kitchen

_____ Dining room

_____ Living room

_____ Bedroom

_____ Home office

_____ Hallways/corridors

_____ Bathroom

_____ Entrances

_____ Other _____

NOTES:

Total _____ Is it warm enough in winter and cool enough in summer (check if problem)?

_____ Too cold in winter

_____ Poor insulation

_____ Difficulty with thermostat

_____ Too hot in winter

_____ Too hot in summer

_____ Other _____

NOTES:

Total _____ Are there any other problems that you know about?

_____ Peephole not accessible

_____ Scatter rugs

_____ Extension cords

_____ Windows difficult to open/close

_____ Difficulty crossing street

_____ Leaks in roof/ceilings

_____ Getting in/out of car

_____ Inadequate storage areas

_____ Other _____

NOTES:

_____ **GRAND TOTAL**

B. Interviewer Rating

Describe accessibility and usability of the building and dwelling unit (based on person's condition):

_____ Excellent (completely accessible)

_____ Very Good (all rooms accessible but not fixtures and equipment)

_____ Good (kitchen, bath, loving-dining and bedroom accessible)

_____ Fair (kitchen, bath, living-dining only accessible)

_____ Poor

Describe the safety and security of the building and dwelling unit (based on the person's condition):

_____ No obvious hazards

_____ Minor hazards _____

_____ Major hazards _____

Describe the sanitary condition including presence of garbage, pests, and odors.

_____

6. Home Modifications Related to Disabilities/Impairments

Since you became disabled, have any modifications been made to your home to make it easier use? (Read list, check all that apply):

Total _____ EXTERIOR

_____ exterior ramp at an entrance

_____ porch lift

_____ security system

_____ railings for stairs

_____ improved lighting

_____ other (describe): _____

Total _____ INTERIOR

_____ widened door(s)

_____ bathroom improvements (describe) _____

_____ kitchen improvements (describe) _____

_____ bedroom improvements (describe) _____

_____ level handled door openers

_____ added lighting

_____ other (describe) _____

7. Caregiver Issues

To Caregiver: Do you have any problems using the building or dwelling? Please describe: _____

Interviewer: Describe any modifications which are related to maintenance: _____

Tanner developed an instrument to evaluate home safety for homebound older adults.[41] The instrument addresses falls, violence, and disasters. The Home Safety Assessment Tool has six subscales: risk for falls (external factors); risk for falls (internal factors); history of falls; risk of injury (use of personal precautions); risk and preparation for fire and disasters; and risk for crime. External risk factors for falls include inadequate lighting in the bathroom and dangerous pathways between the bedroom and bathroom. Examples of questions in this category are: "Is the pathway leading from the bedside to the bathroom free of clutter or obstacles?" "Are the stairways in good condition, with no broken, sagging, or slopping steps or loose carpeting/metal edges? Are handrails extending from the top of the bottom of the steps secure and easily grasped?" (p. 252). Internal risk factors for falls include health problems such as decreased vision, equilibrium, sensory perception, and reaction time, as well as decreased strength and mobility. An example of a question in this section of the assessment is, "Do you hold on to grab bars when getting in or out of the tub or shower or when changing position while bathing?" (p. 252). This instrument also assesses history of falls, as well as the use of personal precautions for risk of injury such as the presence of a telephone in a home. The last sections of the assessment address risk and preparation for fire and disaster and risk for crime.

Gitlin et al. recently developed a protocol to assess dimensions of the physical environment of homes of persons with dementia. The home environment assessment protocol (HEAP) measures four dimensions that are considered important for the well being of persons with dementia. The HEAP involves rating 192 items in up to eight areas of the home (entrance, living room/den, dining room, kitchen, bedroom, bathroom, hallway, and stairs) that are used by the person with dementia. This protocol was developed for research and clinical practice[42]: (1) safety or the lack of common home hazards, (2) support of daily functions or performance of everyday tasks through physical adaptation, (3) support of orientation through the use of visual cues, and (4) support of comfort through the presence of meaningful items to touch or observe. The HEAP defines hazards as the presence of three types of conditions: (a) tripping and falling hazards (e.g., glare, torn carpets), (b) electrical problems (e.g., cords draped over oven or water), and (c) access to dangerous items (e.g., medications, sharp objects). Functionality items are based on four types of adaptations: (a) fixed or permanent structural renovations such as changes to wiring, (b) home modification and adaptive equipments such as grab bars, (c) assistive devices such as mobility aids, and (d) nonpermanent adaptations such as removing furniture. For orientation, two elements are observed: (a) the level of clutter in the home (excessive number of objects that can decrease the ability to navigate in the home) and (b) the use of visual cues to help identify common objects such as use of labels and contrasting colors. For comfort, objects that are of interest to participants, objects with symbolic meanings, and items that have ties to the past should be used.

Model Projects Using Home Modifications and Universal Design

Visit-ability Truesdale and Steinfeld described at ICADI a project called Visit-ability.[43] The goal of this project is to improve community accessibility through integration of basic accessibility features in all newly built homes and housing. While making adaptations in one's home is essential to improve functional independence, the adaptation of a home is not likely to contribute to improved social interaction among neighbors. Visit-ability advances universal design at a community level. Three structural features are considered essential for a person with a mobility impairment to live in a home. A Visit-able building must meet the following:

1. One zero-step entrance on an accessible path of travel
2. Doorways that are 32 inches clear throughout the floor plan
3. Basic access to at least a half bath on the main floor" (p. 1)

Visit-ability does not advocate for full access. Its goal is to change the way all new houses are built. The founder of the project, Eleanor Smith, states that if you want to "radically change the way all new houses are built . . . you cannot have a long list of demands" (p. 3). Visit-ability is particularly concerned in providing physical access for single-family detached houses and townhouses. The advantage of Visit-ability in contemporary single-family housing design is that it incorporates a much less comprehensive standard than either accessibility or universal design. It is much easier to apply Visit-ability than universal design on the neighborhood level.

Truesdale and Steinfeld suggest that there are several myths that prevent Visit-ability from being widely adopted:

Myth 1. *Full access in housing is already mandated by existing law.* This is not true because although there are several laws that mandate accessibility, most single-family homes are not covered by regulations.

Myth 2. *The percentage mentality—an accessible house should be constructed for those who need it.* However, we need to consider that people with functional impairments also need to visit other people's homes. Furthermore, those houses that use the Visit-ability floor plans are easier to adapt if it is necessary in the future.

Myth 3. *The equal importance fallacy—all the features in a typical access code are equally important.* This is not true because for a short-term visitor, the two most important needs are getting in and out of the house.

Myth 4. *Aesthetic concerns—accessibility features are unattractive.* Visit-ability features are generally integrated in the project and are not noticeable.

Myth 5. *Expense-accessibility is expensive.* If Visit-ability is incorporated into the housing design, planning its plan is affordable.

Myth 6. *Sitting constraints—a zero-step entrance is not feasible except on a flat lot.* Grading can overcome the need for steps even on sloped lots.

Myth 7. *Design constraint—concrete slabs are necessary for accessible entrances.* Building on a concrete slab is not the only way to make a zero-step entrance feasible.

Application of the principles of Visit-ability has resulted in the construction of many visitable houses. Between 1992 and 2003, 2455 Visit-able homes were built, with the majority of them constructed under mandate tied to financial assistance from one or more levels of government.[44] However, voluntary efforts by dissemination of information and the increased marketability of single-family homes have also resulted in a large number of visitable homes. The Visit-ability project has educated builders and developers on the importance of being able to visit one's friends and neighbors, and taught them the principles and details of basic access. The Visit-ability movement is reflected in the introduction of a national basic access law before the United States congress.[45]

Another factor in being able to get out and visit others, particularly at night, relates to lighting in the community. Balfour and Kaplan found that the health of older adults is also influenced by neighborhood characteristics. Inadequate lighting at night can impact safety and self-care tasks, such as shopping at night.[46]

The AdvantAge Initiative   The goal of the AdvantAge initiative is to create livable communities that are prepared to meet the needs and aspirations of older individuals to age in place. By using a survey to determine how seniors are living in their communities, local groups were able to develop community-wide planning in the not-for-profit, public, and private sectors. The AdvantAge Initiative survey focused on four key areas: (1) accessing basic needs for housing and security; (2) promoting social and civic engagement; (3) optimizing physical and mental health; and (4) maximizing independence for frail and disabled. More information on this initiative can be found at http://www.vnsny.org/advantage/index.html.

AgrAbility   The AgrAbility Project is funded by the U.S. Department of Agriculture to provide information and technical assistance to ranchers, farmers, and farm workers with disabilities, including information on home modifications. Providing home modification services in rural areas is expensive because households are widely scattered and not typically located close to those who can provide the modifications. While the AgrAbility Project does not pay for individual home modifications, AgrAbility staff find state and local funding sources for those who cannot afford to make the home modifications.[47]

9.4   OTHER ENVIRONMENTAL CONSIDERATIONS

Multigenerational Living: Design for Aging

People are living longer, and the opportunities for three or more generations (grandparents, parents, children) to live together is increasing. In multigenerational dwellings, two major themes must be addressed: to encourage harmony and discourage conflict. Parker proposed five factors that affect conflict: crowding, personal independence, level of privacy, territorial issues, and personal and private spaces. In a crowded environment, undesired interactions are more likely to happen, and interactive activities between family members may be reduced.[48] There are two types of crowding: objective crowding and subjective crowding. Objective crowding can be described as the number of people per unit area, while subjective crowding is the perception of crowding, which can be minimized by using good lightening design, color, and texture. Personal independence is another important component for reducing conflict. If an older person is living with their children, they do not want to be a burden. In order for them to act as independently as possible, it is necessary to design an environment that can accommodate their needs and also provide safety. Privacy can be achieved through the use of private spaces. Territoriality is related to social organization. One "territory" can be affected by various stimuli coming from "territories" nearby. One example is a washroom/toilet that is used during the day and at night. If the toilet is close to a children's bedroom, the adult may feel resistance in using that room at night because they do not want to waken the children.

9.5   LONG-TERM CARE FACILITIES ENVIRONMENT

It is the goal of this book to advance applications of technology and related approaches to allow older people to remain in their own homes, independently, throughout their later years. Yet, it will be necessary for some individuals to move into an environment that offers more personal care, such as an assisted living facility or a nursing home. In this section we discuss some issues and approaches for these residential facilities—some of which can also be applied to individual homes.

As people grow older, they face several losses in their life. In addition to health-related declines and losses in their social life, a relocation from home can be stressful. Long-term care facilities should have a home-like atmosphere. A well-planned environment can reduce agitation, wandering, and incontinence and can positively impact the most significant challenges of Alzheimer's disease. A poorly designed environment can contribute to disorientation, confusion, and precipitate agitation.[49]

Residents with dementia require a more holistic approach that considers the complex relationships that occur in a dementia care facility. Safety, security, awareness, orientation, and positive stimulation must be considered. For example, strategies for managing wandering: "become less concerned with the circularity of the path, and more focused on the quality of the experience while someone is walking thorough the space" (p. 75). The use of cues to help residents to find certain locations is important. Creating a "home-like" atmosphere in facilities might include changing the furnishing and enhancing opportunities for the residents' control and privacy. Four distinct dimensions of a special care unit environment include people with dementia, social context, physical settings, and organizational contexts.[50]

Dementia is a major reason for people moving from their own homes to assisted living facilities or nursing homes. Approximately 6–10% of people over age 65 have some type of dementia. However, prevalence rates may be doubled if milder cases are also considered.[51] Dementia is a broad term to describe a decline in intellectual functioning that is not a normal aspect of the aging process.[52,53] Alzheimer's disease is the leading cause of dementia in persons over 65,[54] and strokes are the second most frequently occurring cause of dementia.[55] Between 20% and 25% of stroke patients are demented after a stroke.[56]

The major characteristic of Alzheimer's disease is a progressive decline in cognitive function.[57] Cognitive skills include orientation, insight, attention, memory, abstract thinking, calculating, problem solving, and organization.[58] With impaired cognitive function, a person may experience confusion, disorientation, limited attention, memory impairment, and decreased ability for learning.[59] Other common symptoms of Alzheimer's disease include language disorders, apraxia, visuoconstructive difficulty, and difficulty with abstract thinking.[60] As Alzheimer's disease progresses, it impacts a person's independent function. A person with Alzheimer's disease will decline in ability to meet safety, self-care, household, leisure, social interaction, and vocational needs.[61] Eventually, the person will lose the ability to perform basic activities of daily living.[62]

Cognitive impairment impacts judgments and decision-making. It is necessary for care providers to create a simple, safe, and familiar environment.[63] Suggestions and guidelines for environmental interventions in the homes of persons with cognitive impairments are common in the literature.[62–66]

The world is experienced through our five senses: sight, hearing, smell, taste, and touch. Sensory deficits are common with aging and can have an impact on the way individuals interact with the environment. This section discusses the environmental interventions to compensate for the sensory decline among residents of a dementia care unit.

Vision[67] Adequate lighting can eliminate confusing or frightening shadows. Brighter lighting not only helps residents with dementia to see better but also helps them to concentrate on a task. It is also important to eliminate glare. Glare may reduce attention span, add to confusion and agitation, and increase the risk of a fall. Shiny floors also can be a source of glare. Windows should have some means to filter or block light. At night, windows should be covered completely because they can act like a mirror and disturb residents.

Hearing[68] The physical environment should maximize the use of residents' remaining hearing. Background noise greatly affects residents with hearing loss, possibly causing agitation and restlessness. Acoustical treatment for hard surfaces can help minimize noise. In rooms where a large number of people gather such as a dinning room, the best solution is to provide sound absorption on walls, ceiling, and floors. Window treatment can also help minimize poor acoustic conditions in rooms. Full drapery treatments have better acoustical benefits than just a valance or vinyl blinds. Furniture or other movable items that are porous, as well as carpets, can also help to reduce sound.

Smell and Taste Odors should be reduced by selecting materials and finishes that are easy to clean. This includes odor-resistant carpets. Fresh air should be used in indoor environments.[69]

Touch Tactile sensation is very important for patients with low vision. Residents with reduced touch sensitivity may not respond quickly to dangerous conditions such as water temperature. Anti-scald devices should be installed at all plumbing fixtures where residents may be at risk.[70]

Other Considerations for Long-Term Care Facilities

Orientation[71] Steps can be taken to make a facility less distracting, such as reducing the number of areas that residents have in view. Reducing the visual impact of a doorway where residents are not supposed to enter can be accomplished by painting the door the same color as the surrounding areas.

Corridors Double-loaded corridors, in which rooms are located on both sides, are common in long-term care facilities. People with dementia may have difficulty navigating this type of corridor because most doors look similar. They can become disoriented. If they have poor vision, this problem may be increased. Furthermore, they may forget where they were going and may become tired and frustrated. Some simple steps can be taken to assist residents in this type of corridor: (1) To attract the attention of the residents, the important doorways should be distinct from one another. For example, a three-dimensional canopy that can be seen from down the hall can be placed over the bathroom door. (2) Create small resting areas along the hallway. (3) Place interesting objects in the hallway. (4) Differentiate hallways using distinct colors, furniture, and light fixtures: (5) Install small cabinets with shelves in the walls outside each resident's bedroom and give them the opportunity to display personal objects. Hanging their own pictures on the wall may also be helpful.[71] Use handrails designed to support and assist mobility and balance.[72] There should be a clear distinction between men's and women's bathroom doors. The toilet should be more visible, which can be accomplished by replacing doors with curtains that can be pulled back. The toilet seat should be a contrasting color from the tank and the bowl.[71]

Cueing   Residents functional abilities can also be increased by the use of cues such as (1) ensuring that the destination is visible all along the path, (2) providing landmarks along the path, (3) providing clear signs, and (4) providing sensory cues such as music and food cooking.[71]

Color   Color serves two purposes in a facility: (1) It helps residents in finding their way, and (2) it can assist residents with low vision to better understand the environment.[71] Light colors make areas seem more spacious; they reflect more light and can compensate for low light levels. White color reflects more light than any other colors. Small rooms, corridors, and spaces with few or no windows benefit from using light colors. Dark colors can make rooms appear smaller. Bright colors complement basic wall colors and can be used as accent colors for doors and columns.[72] The best color contrast for a person experiencing difficulty with depth perceptions is black against white; however, the environment should be carefully planned because a black and white environment can be boring.[72]

Signage   Although the use of signs can help residents to find their way in the facility, too many signs can be confusing. Signs should be large, easy to read, well placed, designed with realistic graphics, and evidence good color contrast. Signs should be placed where residents will easily see them.[71]

Locating Outdoor Spaces   There should be unrestricted access to outdoor space. If residents can see the outdoor spaces from inside, they are more likely to go outside. Large windows also help residents in locating the outside area, as well as in orienting them for both time of day and season.[73] Outdoor spaces can provide numerous benefits for residents. Exposure to natural sunlight can greatly influence feelings of well being. An outdoor environment can provide opportunities for activities such as gardening. Yet, many activities that are performed inside the facility can be accommodated in a well-designed outdoor space. It can also offer a quiet place, which may be difficult to find inside.

Continence   The management of incontinence too often includes putting residents in diapers and mopping up. Although the causes of incontinence can vary among residents, often residents are incontinent because they cannot find their way to the bathroom.[49] Residents may need assistance in finding the bathroom by using appropriate cues. They may also need help in finding the toilet, removing their clothes, and transferring to the toilet.

Dressing   If the closet has two doors, a divider can be incorporated in the center, so most of the clothes are kept behind a locked door, thus reducing the number of choices for the resident and making clothing selection easier, but still possible. A light in the closet will also help with making selections.[71]

Wandering[74]   Residents may wander because they cannot find their way. Providing cues may help. Residents may want to go outside, and it is important to provide them with easy access. It is also helpful if doors they are not supposed to use are painted with the same color as the walls. Other solutions include placing a strip of fabric across a door at the height of the handle or placing a dark floor mat in the front of the door, which can look like a hole in the floor, which may dissuade residents from exiting from that door. Adding a second doorknob that must be turned at the same time as the main knob may also discourage some residents. Using alarms or monitoring systems is yet another strategy.

Rummaging and Hoarding[75]   Creating special "workplaces" where residents can feel productive and have something to do, can help to minimize this behavior.

Combative Behaviors[76]   These behaviors often occur when a person is being assisted in bathing. Use of hand-held showers helps reduce what would be frightening—having no control of water spraying on them. Creating pleasant bathing areas by adding a few plants or artwork can make this environment more relaxing.

Creating a Home-like Atmosphere   It is important to let the individual personalize their space in the facility.[77] Residents should choose what is in the bedroom including appropriate furniture from home. Creating places for ornaments where residents can bring their own objects from home, along with and hanging their pictures, is important in creating a home-like atmosphere. Windows can be personalized by placing ornaments or plants on windowsills that are visible from the outside. The facility should also have spaces where residents can perform familiar roles and activities. One example is a therapeutic kitchen with small worktables. Interior spaces designed for group activity should be divided into smaller spaces, providing residents with fewer distractions. Replicating within the facility, familiar places in the community can help with orientation. Privacy is another important consideration for a long-term care facility. To enhance sense of autonomy and control, the facility should have private areas for meetings with family members and friends. The perception of control can also be enhanced by good design. Residents should be able to monitor the temperature and lighting in their rooms.

The Dining Environment in Nursing Homes   Although the negative effect of a poor dining room environment may not be as evident as a missed medication, the dining environment of nursing home residents affects the amount of calories and nutrient intake. An attractive environment that minimizes distractions, permits leisurely eating, and encourages socialization can contribute to better nutrition intake. Light background colors, simple fabric and carpet patterns, and adequate, low-glare lighting can contribute to a better dining environment in nursing homes.[78] Braun found that arranging the environment by decreasing the frequency of interrupted feeding due to excessive environmental stimuli can improve feeding in elderly with dementia living in special care units.[79] Lighting enhancement and noise reduction may promote improved nutritional status of Alzheimer's residents.[80]

9.6   CONCLUSION

As we develop new applications of technology to support people in living independently as they age, we must also consider the environment where that technology will be used. Even the best technology in a home that is not accessible will not promote independence. Applying the principles of universal design to our homes, our communities, and our products is an essential component of our work in advancing technologies to promote independence. And for homes and other spaces that are already built, we can modify them to meet the needs of their residents and visitors.

REFERENCES

1. Novelli, W. D. (2002). Helping aging boomers to age in place. Paper presented at 2002 Seniors Housing Symposium, Orlando, Florida. Retrieved October 24, 2004, from: http://www.aarp.org/leadership/Articles/a2003-01-03-ageinplace.html.
2. Swenson, M. M. (1998). The meaning of home to five elderly women. *Health Care for Women International* **19**, 381–393.
3. Percival, J. (2002). Domestic spaces: Uses and meanings in the daily lives of older people. *Ageing and Society* **22**, 729–749.
4. Pynoos, J., and Sanford, J. (2002). New tools for better home modification. *Case Manager* **January/February**.
5. Allen, S., and Resnik, L. (2003). Promoting independence for wheelchair users who live alone: Can home accommodations substitute for human help [Abstract]? *Proceedings of the International Conference on Aging Disability and Independence*, Washington, D.C.
6. Duncan, R., Pynoos, J., and Sabata, D. (2003). Common ground: What do we mean by home modification [Abstract]? *Proceedings of the International Conference on Aging Disability and Independence*, Washington, D.C.
7. Hutchings, L., and Olsen, R. (2003). Aging in place with a developmental disability: An environmental intervention study [Abstract]. *Proceedings of the International Conference on Aging Disability and Independence*, Washington, D.C.
8. Pynoos, J., Cohen, E., Davis, L., and Bernhardt, S. (1987). Home Modifications: Improvements that extend independence. In: *Housing for the aged: Design directives and policy considerations*, Regnier, V., and Pynoos, J. eds. New York: Elsevier, pp. 227–303.
9. Gitlin, L. N. (1999). Testing home modification interventions: Issues of theory, measurement, design, and implementation. In: *Focus on Interventions Research with Older Adults*, Schulz, R., Maddox, G., and Lawton, M. P. eds. New York: Springer, pp. 190–246.

10. Steinfeld, E., and Shea, S. (1993). Enabling home environment: Identifying barriers to independence. *Technology and Disability* **2**, 69–79.

11. Mann, W. C., Hurren, D., and Tomita, M. (1993). Comparison of assistive device use and needs of home-based older persons with different impairments. *American Journal of Occupational Therapy* **47**, 980–987.

12. Messecar, D. C., Archbold, P. G., Stewart, B. J., and Kirschling, J. (2002). Home environmental modification strategies used by caregivers of elders. *Research in Nursing and Health* **25**(5), 357–370.

13. Bayer, A., and Harper, L. (2000). Fixing to stay. A National Survey of housing and home modification issues. AARP. Washington, D.C. Retrieved October 24, 2004, from http://research.aarp.org/il/home_mod.pdf

14. Pynoos, J. (2001). Meeting the needs of older persons to age in place: Findings and recommendations for action. Andrus Gerontology Center, University of Southern California. November, 7. Retrieved October from http://www.homemods.org/library/pages/Commission11%20on%20Elderly%20Housing%202001.htm

15. Allen, S., and Resnik, L. (2003). Promoting independence for wheelchair users who live alone: Can home accommodations substitute for human help [Abstract]? *Proceedings of the International Conference on Aging Disability and Independence*, Washington, D.C.

16. Overton, J., Pynoos, J., and Sabata, D. (2003). Caregiver adaptation to reduce environmental stress: The role of home modification and assistive device [Abstract]. *Proceedings of the International Conference on Aging Disability and Independence*, Washington, D.C.

17. Mann, W. C., Ottenbacher, K. J., Fraas, L., Tomita, M., and Granger, C. (1999). Effectiveness of assistive technology and environmental interventions in maintaining independence and reducing home care costs for the frail elderly. *Archives of Family Medicine* **8**, 210–217.

18. Mann, W., Hurren, D., Tomita, M., Bengali., and Steinfeld, E. (1994). Environmental problems in homes of elders with disabilities. *The Occupational Therapy Journal of Research* **14**(3), 191–211.

19. Steinfeld, E., Shea, S., and Levine, D. (1996). Technical report: Home modifications and the fair housing law. *IDEA. University of Buffalo.* Retrieved October 23, 2004, from http://www.ap.buffalo.edu/idea/pubpdf/homodscov.pdf

20. Bice, A., George, E., Patterson, P., and Yearns, M. (2003). A quest for better kitchen for older women: The universal design kitchen project [Abstract]. *Proceedings of the International Conference on Aging Disability and Independence*, Washington, D.C.

21. Gitlin, L. N., Miller, K. S., and Boyce, A. (1999). Bathroom modification for frail elderly renters: Outcome of a community based program. *Technology and Disability* **10**, 141–149.

22. Steinfeld, E., Shea, S., and Levine, D. (1996). Technical report: Home modifications and the fair housing law. IDEA, University of Buffalo. Retrieved October 2004 from http://www.ap.buffalo.edu/idea/pubpdf/homodscov.pdf

23. Salmen, J. P. S. (2004). The challenge of safe stairs. *Universal Design Newsletter*. Retrieved October 23, 2004, from http://www.universaldesign.com/pdfs/udnjan04pdf.pdf

24. Fielo, S. B., and Warren, S. A. (2001). Home adaptation: Helping older people age in place. *Geriatric Nursing* **22**(5), 239–247.

25. Gitlin, L. N., Mann, W., Tomita, M., and Marcus, S. M. (2001). Factors associated with home environmental problems among community-living older people. *Disability and Rehabilitation* **23**(17), 777–787.

26. Reid, D. (2004). Accessibility and usability of the physical housing environment of seniors with stroke. *International Journal of Rehabilitation Research* **27**(3), 203–208.

27. The Center for Universal Design (1997). Definition of Universal Design, Raleigh, NC: North Carolina State University.

28. Story, M. F. (1998). Maximizing usability: The principles of Universal Design. *Assistive Technology* **10**, 4–12.

29. Sandhu, J. (2000). Citizenship and Universal Design. *Ageing International* **spring**, 80–89.

30. Steinfled, E. (1994). The concept of universal design. Retrieved October 23, 2004 from Center for Inclusive Design & Environment Access Web site: http://www.ap.buffalo.edu/idea/publications/free_pubs/pubs_cud.html

31. The Center for Universal Design (1997). *History of Universal Design*, Raleigh, NC: North Carolina State University.

32. Peterson, W. (1998). Public Policy Affecting Universal Design. *Assistive Technology* **10**, 13–20.
33. Follette, S. M. (1998). Maximizing usability: The principles of universal design. *Assistive Technology* **10**, 4–12.
34. Mace, R. (1998). Universal Design in Housing. *Assistive Technology* **10**, 21–28.
35. Makigami, K., and Pynoos, J. (2002). The evolution of home modification in Japan. *Ageing International* **27**(3), 95–112.
36. Demirbilek, O., and Quinn, J. (2003). Universal Design in housing: Is it the answer for home design for the aging population? In: *ICADI Proceedings*.
37. Nielsen, C. W., and Ambrose, I. (1999). Lifetime adaptable housing in Europe. *Technology and Disability* **10**(1), 11–19.
38. Noell-Waggoner, E. (2003). Lighting: A key element for independence and safety [Abstract]. In: *Proceedings of the International Conference on Aging Disability and Independence*, Washington, D.C.
39. Figueiro, M., and Rea, M. (2003). Lighting for older adults: Home modifications that help older adults maintain their independence [Abstract]. In: *Proceedings of the International Conference on Aging Disability and Independence*, Washington, D.C.
40. Pynoos, J., Sanford, J., and Rosenfelt, T. (2002). A team approach for home modification. *OT Practice* **8**, 15–19.
41. Tanner, E. T. (2003). Assessing home safety in homebound older adults. *Geriatric Nursing* **24**(4), 250–256.
42. Gitlin, L., Schinfeld, S., Winter, L., Corcoran, M., Boyce, A., and Hauck, W. (2002). Evaluating home environments of persons with dementia: Interrater reliability and validity of the Home Environmental Assessment Protocol (HEAP). *Disability and Rehabilitation* **24**(1/2/3), 59–71.
43. Truesdale, S., and Steinfeld, E. (n.d.) Visit-ability: An approach to Universal Design in housing. Retrieved September 28, 2004, from Rehabilitation Engineering Research Center on Universal Design at Buffalo. Web site: http://www.ap.buffalo.edu/rercud/visitabilitybook.htm
44. Spegal, K., and Liebig, P. (2003). Visitability: Trends, approaches, and outcomes. Retrieved September 28, 2004, from The National Resource Center on Supportive Housing and Home Modification, University of Southern California. Web site: http://www.usc.edu/dept/gero/nrcshhm/research/pages/VA%20PAPER.pdf
45. Smith, E., and Tenenbaum, L. (2003). Make love not war? Advocated partner with builders [Abstract]. In: *Proceedings of the International Conference on Aging Disability and Independence*, Washington, D.C.
46. Balfour, J. L., and Kaplan, G. A. (2002). Neighborhood environment and loss of physical function in older adults: Evidence from the Alameda County Study. *American Journal of Epidemiology* **155**(6), 507–515.
47. Maus, C., and Yearns, M. (2003). Home modification challenges and solutions for rural service providers: Lessons from the AgrAbility project [Abstract]. In: *Proceedings of the International Conference on Aging Disability and Independence*, Washington, D.C.
48. Parker, K. J. (2000). Multigenerational Living: Design for ageing. *Ageing International* **spring**, 90–100.
49. Brawley, E. C. (1997). Criteria for designing Alzheimer's special care settings. In: *Designing for Alzheimer's Disease. Strategies for Creating Better Care Environments*, Brawley, E. ed. New York: Wiley, pp. 41–62.
50. Calkins, M. P. (2001). The physical and social environment of the person with Alzheimer's disease. *Aging and Mental Health* **5**(Suppl 1), 74–78.
51. Hendrie, H. (1998). Epidemiology of dementia and Alzheimer's disease. *The American Journal of Geriatric Psychiatry* **6**(2, Suppl 1), S3–18.
52. Cummings, J. (1984). Dementia: Definition, classification, and differential diagnosis. *Psychiatric Annals* **14**, 85–89.
53. Glickstein, J. (1997). *Therapeutic Intervention in Alzheimer's Disease: A Program of Functional Skills for Activities of daily living and communication*. Gaithersburg, MD: Aspen Publishers.
54. 2000 Progress report on Alzheimer's disease: Taking the next steps (n.d.). Retrieved May 11, 2004, from National Institute on Aging. Web site: http://www.alzheimers.org/pubs/pr2000.pdf
55. Butin, D. N. (1991). Helping those with dementia to live at home: An educational series for caregivers. *Physical and Occupational Therapy in Geriatrics*, 69–82.

56. Van Kooten, F., and Koudstaal, P. J. (1998). Epidemiology of post-stroke dementia. *Haemostasis* **28**(3–4), 124–133.

57. Understanding and caring for the person with Alzheimer's disease. (1985). Atlanta Area ADRDA Chapter.

58. Abreu, B. C., and Toglia, J. P. (1987). Cognitive rehabilitation: A model for occupational therapy. *American Journal of Occupational Therapy* **41**(7), 439–448.

59. Poole, J., Dunn, W., Schell, B., and Barnhart, J. M. (1991). Statement: Occupational therapy services management of persons with cognitive impairments. *American Journal of Occupational Therapy* **45**(12), 1067–1068.

60. Pynoos, J., and Ohta, R. J. (1991). In-home interventions for persons with Alzheimer's disease and their caregivers. *Physical and Occupational Therapy in Geriatrics* **5**, 83–92.

61. Zarit, S. H., Todd, P. A., and Zarit, J. M. (1986). Subjective burden of husbands and wives as caregivers: A longitudinal study. *Gerontologist* **26**(3), 260–266.

62. Pynoos, J., and Ohta, R. J. (1991). In-home interventions for persons with Alzheimer's disease and their caregivers. *Physical and Occupational Therapy in Geriatrics* **5**, 83–92.

63. Understanding and caring for the person with Alzheimer's disease. (1985). Atlanta Area ADRDA Chapter.

64. Butin, D. N. (1991). Helping those with dementia to live at home: An educational series for caregivers. *Physical and Occupational Therapy in Geriatrics*, 69–82.

65. Corcoran, M., and Gitlin, L. N. (1991). Environmental influences on behavior of the elderly with dementia: Principles for intervention in the home. *Physical and Occupational Therapy in Geriatrics* **5**, 5–22.

66. Olsen, R. V., Ehrenkrantz, E., and Hutchings, B. (1993). Creating supportive environments for people with dementia and their caregivers through home modifications. *Technology and Disability* **24**, 47–57.

67. Briller, S. H., Proffitt, M. A., Perez, K., and Calkins, M. P. (2001). Vision. In: *Creating Successful Dementia Care Settings*, Vol. 1: *Understanding the Environment Through the Aging Senses*, Calkins, M. P. ed. Baltimore, pp. 5–24.

68. Briller, S. H., Proffitt, M. A., Perez, K., and Calkins, M. P. (2001). Hearing. In: *Creating Successful Dementia Care Settings*, Vol. 1: *Understanding the environment through the Aging Senses*, Calkins, M. P. ed. Baltimore, pp. 25–32.

69. Briller, S. H., Proffitt, M. A., Perez, K., and Calkins, M. P. (2001). Smell and Taste. In: *Creating a Successful Dementia Care Settings*, Vol. 1: *Understanding the Environment Through the Aging Senses*, Calkins, M. P. ed. Baltimore, pp. 33–40.

70. Briller, S. H., Proffit, M. A., Perez, K., and Calkins, M. P. (2001). Touch. In: *Creating Successful Dementia Care Settings*, Vol. 1: *Understanding the Environment Through the Aging Senses*, Calkins, M. P. ed. Baltimore, pp. 41–48.

71. Briller, S. H., Proffitt, M. A., Perez, K., Calkins, M. P., and Marsden, J. P. (2001). Orientation. In: *Creating Successful Dementia Care Settings*, Vol. 2: *Maximizing Cognitive and Functional Abilities*, Calkins, M. P. ed. Baltimore, pp. 11–42.

72. Brawley, E. C. (1997). The impact of color in environmental design. In: *Designing for Alzheimer's Disease. Strategies for Creating Better Care Environments*, Brawley, E. ed. New York: Wiley, pp. 107–124.

73. Briller, S. H., Proffitt, M. A., Perez, K., Calkins, M. P., and Marsden, J. P. (2001). Continence. In: *Creating Successful Dementia Care Settings*, Vol. 2: *Maximizing Cognitive and Functional Abilities*, Calkins, M. P. ed. Baltimore, pp. 91–102.

74. Perez, K., Proffitt, M. A., and Calkins, M. P. (2001). Wandering. In: *Creating Successful Dementia Care Settings*, Vol. 3: *Minimizing Disruptive Behaviors*, Calkins, M. P. ed. Baltimore, pp. 9–29.

75. Perez, K., Proffitt, M. A., and Calkins, M. P. (2001). Rummaging and Hoarding. In: *Creating Successful Dementia Care Settings*, Vol. 3: *Minimizing Disruptive Behaviors*, Calkins, M. P. ed. Baltimore, pp. 65–71.

76. Perez, K., Proffitt, M. A., and Calkins, M. P. (2001). Combative behaviors. In: *Creating Successful Dementia Care Settings*, Vol. 3: *Minimizing Disruptive Behaviors*, Calkins, M. P. ed. Baltimore, pp. 75–104.

77. Marsden, J. P., Briller, S. H., Calkins, M. P., and Proffitt, M. A. (2001). Autonomy and Control. In: *Creating Successful Dementia Care Settings*, Vol. 4: *Enhancing Identity and Sense of Home*, Calkins, M. P. ed. Baltimore.

78. Yen, P. K. (2003). Impact of the eating environment. *Geriatric Nursing* **24**(4), 255–256.

79. Braun, J. V. (2004). Environmental arrangement for enhancing self-feeding in the elderly with dementia. *Geriatric Nursing* **25**(1), 52–53.

80. McDaniel, J. H., Hunt, A., Hackes, B., and Pope, J. F. (2001). Impact of dining room environment on nutritional intake of Alzheimer's residents: A case study. *American Journal of Alzheimer's Disease and Other Dementia* **16**(5), 297–302.

CHAPTER *10*

INJURY PREVENTION AND HEALTH PROMOTION

Megan Witte

10.1 INTRODUCTION

Unintentional injuries cause 39,000 deaths annually in the United States for adults over age 65. Worldwide, this number expands to 949,000 older adults. In the United States the top three causes of death due to injury in adults over age 65 are falls, motor-vehicle crashes, and suicide.[1] Injuries such as falls can be prevented: several injury prevention programs have proven their effectiveness. Motor-vehicle crashes and suicide are more complex, and exploration of injury prevention strategies to curb mortality and injury in these areas is needed.[2]

The challenge of injury prevention and health promotion involves the individual, caregivers, family members, community members, and society as a whole. In the United States, an estimated $224 billion is spent each year to cover medical care, rehabilitation, lost wages, and lost productivity due to injuries. Fall-related injuries alone are estimated to cost $32.4 billion in the United States.[1]

Using data from the National Hospital Discharge Survey, the Harvard Injury Control Research Center studied hospitalization trends following injury from 1979 to 2000. While the number of hospital admissions due to injury has decreased among young males, it has increased among older females. In fact, older females have the highest hospital admission rate. While hospital admissions have declined in all age groups, they declined less in the older population and have shown an increase for serious injury admissions in older age groups. In addition, the frequency of discharge to long care institutions has increased in patients over age 65. Hospitalization rates for serious injury (excluding isolated hip fractures) are decreasing for the young and increasing in older age groups.[3]

Injuries among older adults, especially falls, are also becoming a major socioeconomic concern in Europe.[4] There are approximately 1.2 million people over age 85 in the United Kingdom. Five hundred thousand have difficulty walking and 200,000 have dementia.[5] These statistics are a definite concern when considering the possibility of injury and the potential costs involved with injuries.

A recent article described injuries among adults over 60 in Brazil. The data obtained from the Mortality System Information and Hospitalization Information

---

Smart Technology for Aging, Disability, and Independence, Edited by William C. Mann

System of the Federal Health Department of Brazil from the year 2000 (last available year) reported that the mortality rate due to injury for older Brazilians was much higher than that of the overall population, especially among older women. Of these mortality rates due to injury, most were due to traffic accidents (48.2% are pedestrian) or falls. Fifty-six percent of nonfatal injuries were due to falls.[6]

Injury prevention must also consider those injuries that occur on the road. This includes injuries relating to older drivers and older pedestrians. Pedestrian injuries and driving is covered in more depth in Chapters 6 and 7.

Most injuries are avoidable and include extrinsic and intrinsic factors. Extrinsic risk factors relate to the home or living environment, while intrinsic factors exist "within" the person and are mainly physiological. The effects of extrinsic factors can be reduced or even removed by adapting the physical environment, such as installing automatic illumination for nighttime bathroom use. The impact of extrinsic factors can also be reduced by increasing awareness and use of telecare or making an individual more aware of what they can do to be safe in their own home. Intrinsic factors are those that affect a person's cognitive state, vision, balance, posture, gait, or sensory abilities as well as the effects of medications that could negatively impact one's abilities.[7]

Close ties between human and environment contribute to likelihood of injury. Manipulation of the physical environment potentially plays a key role in injury prevention.[8] Falls and other injuries frequently occur due to poor design of homes and communities and poor maintenance of these areas. Weather conditions also play a role in injury. Cold weather accompanied by snow and ice can increase falls. Increased use of heating systems during the winter increases the chances of fire and carbon monoxide poisoning.

While extrinsic factors such as the environment and physical factors such as sensory loss play key roles in the rate of injury, psychological factors also contribute to the risk of falls and injury. When a person falls, he or she will likely experience decreased confidence and begin a cycle of fear leading to decreased participation in daily activities. This can lead to further decrease in physical capacities, which increases the likelihood of falls.

People with sensory deficits have an increased risk for injuries. Low vision decreases ability to see at night and impedes appropriate detection of ground surfaces. Hearing impairment decreases auditory awareness of potential hazards and/or decreases the ability to hear alarms when they are sounding. Results from an analysis completed by Lighthouse International suggest that hearing and vision impairments increase the likelihood of falls significantly and that having dual impairments increases this risk even more than if a person had just a visual or just a hearing impairment.[9]

10.2 FALLS

Each year approximately 10,000 Americans age 65 and older die as a result of a fall. Someone this age dies from a fall approximately every hour.[1] Falls are the leading cause of death due to injury for people in this age group.[1] Men in this age group are

22% more likely than women to die as a result of falling. However, women are hospitalized three times as often as men after sustaining a hip fracture from a fall.[1] According the Centers for Disease Control and Prevention, one in three people over age 65 fall each year.[1] Of those who fall and fracture their hip (both men and women), 23% die within 3 months post injury.[1] These rates continue to rise especially after age 80.[10] With approximately 300,000 adults age 65 and older suffering hip fractures each year, costs for fall-related injuries could reach $32.4 billion by the year 2020.[1]

Elders who have fallen comprise 40% of nursing home admissions.[11] In Australia in 1998, 1754 people over age 65 were hospitalized for fall-related injuries. Eighty-nine percent of those admissions were due to fractures and half were hip fractures. Women were more likely to sustain a fracture to their upper or lower limbs, while men were more likely to have fractured their skull, face, and ribs. There were no significant gender differences for fracturing the hip. Men were more likely to sustain a head injury from a fall, which increased burden of care and mortality relative to those who fractured a hip.[12]

Why do Elders Fall?   Falls are perhaps the most common of injuries among the elderly, and are due to several factors which include, but are not limited to muscle weakness and impaired balance.[13] Risk factors contributing to likelihood of falls include age, neurological conditions, musculoskeletal condition, decreased physical strength, foot disorders, medication use, and alcohol use.[10,14] Little and Batson suggest that basic anthropometrics contribute to fall risk. Their research has shown that those with shorter femoral bones and tibias were more likely to exhibit reaching patterns that put them at risk of falls independent of age. Those with shorter trunk and arm lengths were at risk as well.[15]

Low-Technology Prevention   One form of simple technology to prevent injury from falls is the hip protector. A common form of hip protector is a padded plastic shell. In Norway these were tested in a nursing home with subjects at high risk of a fall. Use of hip protectors over the intervention period demonstrated a 69% reduction of fractures.[16] However, compliance is an issue in residential care facilities. A British study found that 16% of the 153 people in residential care who agreed to wear hip protectors never wore the protectors issued to them. The 24-hour compliance rate for those who wore them at least once was 29%, with 37% of those participants being compliant during the day and only 3% at night. Forty-seven percent were compliant during the day the first month, but this rate dropped to 30% by the end of the intervention.[17]

More recently, a soft hip protector has been placed on the market. These protectors utilize air pads for hip protection in a fall. The pads are made from open-cell viscoelastic foam encased in a waterproof, airtight urethane pouch. When a person falls, the shock is absorbed in the foam, which leads to air displacement in the open cell structure of the foam. The displaced air travels within the airtight pouch and inflates it. The pouch inflates similar to that of an automobile airbag; however, it does not explode like an automobile airbag. Rather, it returns to its pre-fall form and can perform the protective action again during possible subsequent falls. The inflation of the protector also displaces the force from impact away from the trochanter to soft tissue and muscle to lessen the impact of the fall on the trochanter.[18]

Walking Aids There are many devices to aid in fall prevention. Some devices are well known and have existed for years, such as canes and walkers. New devices to aid in walking continue to be developed. A team at the University of Texas and Innovative Health Solutions in Texas developed the WalkAbout. It is designed to completely encircle the user and relies on body contact to move with users as they walk. The user does not need upper-body strength to properly use this aid. To enter the device, there is a simple gate/latch system. The base at the feet is larger than the waist-high circumference at the top. Four legs connect the base and waist level rails to ensure stability. The legs have caster wheels. The top (waist level) rail is padded for comfort when the person chooses to rest their arms. A safety seat called the Walk-Abelt prevents falls if users lose their balance. The WalkAbelt is made of strong nylon webbing and is attached to the top rail. It can be adjusted to fit the anthropo-metric measurements of the client so that it does not interfere with the user's natural walking pattern. The WalkAbout was tested at the Acute Care of the Elderly unit of the University of Texas Medical Branch, Galveston, Texas and the nursing home at Manor Park, Inc., Midland, Texas. Of the 65 participants, all were at high risk of falls and had varying diagnoses including Alzheimer's, Parkinson's, stroke, and head trauma. No falls occurred during the trial period. Of those who participated, the WalkAbout was the only way 17 of them could walk. Ninety-seven percent of the users could walk further than they could using the device they usually used. Ninety-five percent said that they felt safe using the WalkAbout, and 92% found the seat comfortable.[19]

Environmental Modifications Several options are available for increasing structural and environmental independence and safety in the home. These options are discussed in Chapter 9. Some simple fall prevention strategies dealing with the environment will be discussed briefly here. Furniture is a major potential hazard for falls. The safest place to position furniture is either in corners or low-traffic sections of the room, thereby providing a clear path of travel. Furniture should be sturdy and stable without sharp corners. Other home furnishings to be considered are throw or scatter rugs. Use of scatter rugs should be avoided if at all possible. If rugs need to be placed, it is necessary to ensure that they are securely placed via the use of a rubber mat underneath or some other means of anchoring. For elders with demen-tia, using barriers and gates may also be another option in preventing hazards within the home. Barriers or gates can prevent injury, especially near stairs, which is espe-cially important if stability issues are involved.[20]

High-Technology Fall Detection/Prevention Several major means of fall detection that include video, acoustic or vibrational analysis, intelligent telecare systems, and worn devices, have been and continue to be explored. Sensor technol-ogy is an important component in many of the previous mentioned systems and will be discussed separately.

Video   This type of monitoring is both the most expensive and most intrusive form of fall detection. Wiring and equipping a home as well as monitoring the video take time and money. This form of monitoring is also not always very appealing to the potential user because it limits or even takes away privacy. Video monitoring devices are commercially available and can be purchased from security companies.

Acoustic or Vibrational Analysis   This type of analysis detects falls through vibration in the floor from thuds or other impacts using frequency analysis. This method assumes that a differentiation can be made between an impact from a fall and an impact from another source. Also, variations in flooring materials can affect this type of detection.

Intelligent Telecare Systems   Time-use analysis is used to monitor levels of activity in the home. For example, a lack of activity could be tracked via the system, which would then send a warning to an outside source such as a caregiver. Telecare systems will be described in greater depth in Chapter 5.

Worn Devices   Worn devices have the capability to detect a fall immediately. Those with intelligence and telemetry built into the device also have the capability to determine if help is needed. A recent Veteran's Administration Merit Review Project utilizes a wearable analog sensor/accelerometric system. Accelerometers are mounted on eyeglass frames in both front corners. They are also mounted on both sides of a waist belt. The eyeglass mounts measure linear acceleration of the head, while the waist belt mounts measure acceleration of the trunk. Data are collected and transferred to an embedded computer system. The data are then calibrated and stored for analysis. A wireless, wrist-mounted controller controls the system. A desktop version of this system was successfully tested, and the wearable digital version is still being developed. Potential uses include both vibrational analysis on wheelchairs and athletic and occupational injury prevention. This could extend to fall prevention and/or detection in the home.[21]

At Virginia Tech the e-Textile team is exploring clothing that monitors daily activity and gait patterns. The current prototype will eventually have the capability to monitor vital signs and motion to prevent falls. They are developing pants made from a material that feels like soft burlap that can monitor a person's gait pattern, which could help reduce falls. The team also hopes that eventually the suit could also measure diseases that cause gait disturbances such as Parkinson's disease. Currently, gait analysis is conducted using video in a laboratory. Setup for the analysis takes about an hour for each participant. The video is checked frame by frame. The goal is to make a pair of pants that can mimic the lab equipment. To achieve this goal, accelerometers, piezoelectric films, and microcontrollers have been utilized to detect the foot changing direction or to calculate stride length when using the pants. Currently the team is conducting trials doing side-by-side comparisons of the pants and video lab equipment (Figure 10.1). Eventually the Virginia tech team hopes that the pants will not only be able to perform a gait analysis and monitor symptoms of abnormal gait, but also detect the current activity of the wearer.[22]

Figure 10.1   Comparing the Hokie suit's ability to measure a person's stride to a video gait measurement system at the Virginia Tech Locomotion Laboratory.

Sensors   Fall detectors are continually being developed and improved upon. A system proposed in 2000 included the use of a worn alarm the size of a small radio pager that was connected to a community alarm system. The final design of the system had the capability to reliably detect falls in 180 different scenarios, which greatly enhances early intervention in case of fall.[7]

Over the last 15 years, sensor technologies have become less expensive and more readily available. Sensor technologies can combine intelligent software and device hardware to respond to a variety of physical environmental stimuli, such as thermal energy, electromagnetic energy, acoustic energy, pressure, magnetism, or motion, by producing a signal, usually electrical. Inexpensive sensors that detect opening and motion could, for example, monitor activity patterns. If a pattern changed (i.e., a person failed to enter the bathroom or open the refrigerator within an expected timeframe), the sensors, linked to a computer, could alert care providers. Socially isolated older and disabled persons within the general community are already aware of and are utilizing pendant alarms and or/burglar systems incorporating these technologies.

To date these systems have been considered separately. To call for assistance users typically have a radio activated pendant that can be worn on the body or placed in fixed positions in the house. A number of limitations exist with these systems. They require the active intervention of the user. An unconscious person cannot activate this type of emergency response system. Research also shows that on many occasions people do not wear their pendant.[23] Active systems like pendant alarms could be complimented by a passive sensor system that calls for assistance without the need for the person to initiate the action.

A number of studies address the benefits of sensor technologies to advance independent living of older persons. The Kaiser Permanente tele-health research project is one of the largest but was restricted to video linkup in conjunction with physiological monitoring.[24]

In the United Kingdom (UK), extensive research has been conducted on the use of infrared sensors in at-risk older persons' homes. Results from these studies demonstrate satisfaction among caregivers as well as among care recipients.[25] The UK Telecare study investigated the use of using sensor technologies to aid independence for older persons in social housing.[26] Recommendations from this study support the notion that improvements to housing such as the installation of nonintrusive sensor devices could help maintain persons at home longer and is cost effective in reducing hospitalization and/or premature institutionalization. Both studies confirmed that the majority of older persons were accepting of sensor devices and believed that they enabled them a higher degree of security and function.

In Australia there is increasing interest in application of sensor technologies in housing. Most notably, work by the Commonwealth Scientific and Industrial Research Organisation (CSIRO) in conjunction with the University of New South Wales has centered on biomedical monitoring falls prevention using accelerometers worn by the occupier in combination with other less intrusive sensors.[27,28]

10.3   MEDICATION ERRORS

Medication errors involve omissions or commissions of a drug that do not treat the patient as therapeutically intended.[29] Medication errors are preventable in most instances and can occur in the ordering and administration stage. This section will focus mainly on how errors in administration can be avoided.

A study using data from the national Toxic Exposure Surveillance System provided a retrospective review of all cases reported to the American Association of Poison Control Centers Certified Regional Poison Information Center in 1998 and 1999 ($N = 6365$). Goals of the review were to determine the main issues of people over age 50 who called in to report a poisoning. Poisoning in females was usually due to therapeutic error, adverse drug reactions, and ingestion. The study also discovered an inverse relationship between older age and acute class, suspected suicide, food poisoning, and inhalation and dermal exposures.[30] This section focuses on poisonings from medications.

To understand medicinal issues other than polypharmacy with older adults, it is necessary to understand how aging affects the body. Basic physiologic changes impact how a drug affects the body, including (1) decreased lean body mass, (2) increased body fat, (3) decreased intracellular water and decreased total body water, and (4) decline of albumin production. These factors all have the ability to change drug concentration in the blood, which can enhance drug effects in many instances. These physiologic changes can have great influence on drug absorption, distribution, metabolism, and excretion. Some elders may experience exaggerated or blunted effects of these drugs due to the aforementioned physiological changes.[31]

With increasing age, drug metabolism generally declines due to decreased hepatic blood flow and decreased liver mass. This increases the chance of drug toxicity with some drugs by prolonging the time it takes them to undergo biotransformation. This includes many drugs in the benzodiazepine class such as Valium.[31] Drug excretion also declines with age due to decreased kidney function and cardiac output.[31]

Older adults consume twice as many prescription drugs compared to younger adults.[32] Drugs prescribed most often for people over age 55 include diuretics, cardiovascular drugs, and analgesics.[33] Approximately one-third of drugs utilized by this age group are prescription, while the remaining two-thirds are over the counter.[34] Problems arise when drug dosages are of the wrong amount, taken at the wrong time, or omitted altogether. Alcohol intake also causes major difficulties because it has adverse reactions with over 50% of the most prescribed drugs.[34] Medication errors also involve informal (care given on an in-kind, nonpaid basis) caregivers. In a study of participants providing care for older adults, 67% expressed problems with at least one activity involving medications for their care recipient. The study reported four themes, including (1) maintaining continuous supplies of medication in the home, (2) assisting with administration, (3) making clinical judgments, and (4) communicating with care recipients and health professionals.[35]

Potential Side Effects Varying side effects of certain drugs can increase the likelihood of injurious behaviors. Table 10.1 describes these side effects.

Nutritional Consequences Drug effects can also cause nutritional deficits in older adults as a result of decreased nutrient absorption, reactions between drugs and substances in food, changes in rates of food absorption, and changes in the way nutrients are used.[37] Special care is required when reading directions about what a particular drug can or cannot be paired with (edema and congestive heart failure are possible side effects of combining Alka Seltzer with low-sodium diets) and how it should be taken (with food or on an empty stomach).[38]

Polypharmacy Polypharmacy is inappropriate or excessive use of medication. Polypharmacy occurs when someone is using medications unnecessarily or inappropriately and/or using duplicate medications. The person may be seeing more than

TABLE 10.1 Drugs and Their Potential Side Effects[36]

Drug	Potential side effect
Amphetamines	Hallucinations, paranoia, other abnormal behavior
Phenobarbital	Visual hallucinations, depression, excitability
Levodopa	Hallucinations (both visual and auditory), delirium, paranoia, nightmares, night terrors, depression
Digitalis, glycoside (Digoxin/Lanoxin, etc.)	Amnesia, visual hallucinations, paranoia, nightmares, confusion, delusions, belligerent behavior
Desipramine (and other antidepressants)	Anticholinergic induced psychosis
Diazepam (Valium)	Depression, suicidal thoughts, excitement hallucinations, rage

one physician or using more than one pharmacy to have prescriptions filled. Polypharmacy issues can also result from the patient having sensory or physical problems that affect reading about or handling their medications. A person may also need supervision to properly manage their pharmaceutical regimen. This could be due to memory loss, feeling too tired or ill to take their medications, or not taking medications because they are wary of the side effects. Some patients may not take their medication because they do not feel it is necessary.[39]

Low-Tech Prevention   Elders and their caregivers can take several basic steps to prevent incorrect dosage. One is keeping a running record of all medications, including over-the-counter drugs and herbal remedies. This list should include the drug name, dosage, times of day it is taken, and the physician who prescribed it. This list should be kept with medicines and with the elder in their purse or wallet.[40] To prevent polypharmacy, open dialogue must exist between the physician and patient. Patients are encouraged to bring their list of medicines along to each visit for review. There may be better medicines available or other patient information that could affect the patient's typical pharmaceutical regimen.[40]

Difficulty in reading labeling on the bottle is common among older persons. If not readable, a person will have difficulty following directions properly and may not notice important information such as expiration dates. They could even choose the wrong drug when reaching in the cabinet. One way to avoid this is to make sure the lights are always on when taking medications.[40,42] Another way to avoid mistakes is to use a magnifier.

Combining medicines with alcohol can have significant impact on both the drug and person's performance and can even be lethal. Another common mistake is to stop using a prescription drug when one feels better. Prescription drugs should continue to be taken as directed unless the physician gives instructions to stop. Taking more or less of the recommended dose is also not advised. It is very unsafe to take prescription drugs that are prescribed for someone else.[40]

A patient should be mindful of what foods they are combining with their medications and should plan meals around medication schedules. They may also find it helpful to have someone assist them with meal planning and grocery shopping to keep nutritional needs met while taking medications.[41] Fluctuations in weight while taking medications should be monitored because change in weight can influence drug interactions within the body.

Making a medication schedule, subsequently checking off medications as they are taken, can decrease dosage errors significantly. This not only serves as a good written reminder for patient and caregiver as to what medications were taken and when, it can also serve as valuable tool when visiting the doctor. In addition to the schedule, the patient can add any symptoms or side effects he or she experiences while taking the medication. Color-coding medications can be helpful in avoiding medication mix-ups. This can be done using colored markers or stickers and should correspond to the color-coded schedule.

Pillboxes can be valuable memory aids. The patient or caregiver can prepare the dosages for the week. If a person has multiple doses throughout the day, they can be separated into a paper cup or similar item marked with the appropriate time for the drug to be taken. Using egg cartons to sort medications is not advised due to a slight risk of salmonella.[40] Electric alarms and buzzers are also available to cue people to take their medications. Devices that vibrate or have flashing lights are available for people with sensory impairments.[42]

High-Tech Prevention In addition to having buzzers and alarms providing medication cues, future technologies may involve a smart phone. These are cellular phones that can be programmed to provide reminders and prompts. The phones can also cue a person to when their prescriptions run out and need to be reordered. These technologies are discussed in greater depth in Chapter 2. Other means of providing medication reminders may involve a television or computer interface. Systems are being developed that utilize magnetic sensors to tell if a person has accessed their medication. The sensor can then communicate with a computer system that monitors the access of the medication and even communicate that information back to the patient or caregiver.[43]

Medications are prescribed to aid users, but using several different medications at the same time without monitoring concurrent effects may greatly increase potential for injury.[44] New technology developed by the American Society of Consultant Pharmacists (ASCP) Research and Education Foundation identifies medical hazards, which can contribute to or aggravate disabling conditions such as depression or delirium. This program is known as the Geriatric Risk Assessment Med Guide (GRAM®) that can be used by pharmacists and other medical professionals to help detect and prevent possible medication related problems.[45]

10.4 FIRE

Adults between age 65 and 75 have a death rate from fire that is twice the national average. Those between 75 and 85 are three times the national average, and for those over 85 the risk is four times the national average. Over 1200 Americans over 65 die due to fires each year. Twenty-five percent of total fire deaths in the United States are older adults. Thirty percent of fire deaths occur in the home. In the United States, residential fires cause injury and death to people over age 60 more than any other age group, and approximately 3000 older adults are injured in residential fires each year.[46,47] Sensory impairments, limited mobility, low socioeconomic status, and location of the home are all factors in elder fire deaths.[46] Additionally, approximately 30% of elders live at home alone, which increases their risk of injury from fire.[46] These statistics strongly indicate the need to address fire prevention for elders.

The increased risk of death by fire with increasing age is also due to (1) decreased physical and cognitive capabilities, (2) increased medication usage, and (3) psychosocial issues such as depression. These factors make it more likely that a person will both start a fire accidentally and take much longer to escape a fire. In addition, sensory impairments can decrease a person's ability to detect a fire or hear a smoke alarm. Low socioeconomic status contributes to increased fire risk mainly due to housing conditions. Twenty percent of elders live at or below the poverty line, which increases their risk of death or injury from fire.[46] Many elders live in substandard housing, including older homes and manufactured homes. Routine maintenance of heating or electrical systems may be overlooked. These homes may also lack smoke alarms.[46] Space heaters, stoves, and fireplaces may serve as a substitute for inadequate heating systems, which increases risk of fire. Substandard housing in some urban areas may also have bars on doors or windows that keep criminals out, but may also prevent a resident's escape during a fire.[46]

Those in rural areas are also increasingly at risk. Someone living in a rural area is twice as likely to die from a fire as those living in an urban area. Fire departments in rural areas have much larger fire districts than more populated areas, which increases emergency response time.[47] Compared to a large town or small city, the likelihood of death from fire in a rural area triples.[48]

Fire safety awareness of older adults was studied by visiting homes of older adults. Two-thirds of study participants had physical impairments that could decrease their likelihood of successfully escaping a fire. Three-fourths of participants were not worried about injury from fire, but all had at least one factor that would contribute to injury from fire. Less than one-third of subjects complied with recommendations given to increase fire safety.[49]

Smoking is the leading cause of fire deaths in older adults, with fires due to cooking the leading cause of fire-related injury. Seventy-five percent of fire deaths are the result of carbon monoxide poisoning.[50] A person can quickly be affected by carbon monoxide and/or smoke inhalation because it can spread in a manner of seconds.[51] Burns cause the remaining 25% of fire deaths.[50] Those who do survive a burn require extended hospitalization involving therapy and skin grafts. The costs of these treatments are high.

Time of day and time of year also have a relationship with incidence of fires. Most residential fires occur between December and February. In the United States, heating malfunction is the second leading cause of residential fires. Fires are less likely in apartments or nursing facilities than in single-family residences because those heating systems are usually professionally maintained.[47] House fires usually happen between 6 and 7 P.M., thereby increasing risk of fire injury at that time. People are also more likely to be indoors at this time, which increases risk.[48] However, fire deaths at home usually occur during the night.[52] Many deaths and injuries result from alcohol consumption or combining activities such as smoking or cooking with drinking or taking medications that cause drowsiness.[47]

Many frail older adults living at home are on oxygen therapy. One study completed a retrospective review of 3673 consecutive patients treated at an adult burn center between 1992 and 2001. Twenty-seven of those reviewed had burns that were due to the use of oxygen therapy. The average age of these patients was 68.1 ± 9.2 years. Twenty-three of the incidents occurred at home, and the remaining four incidents occurred in long-term or acute care institutions. Twenty-four of these patients were smoking while using oxygen, two were lighting pilot lights, and one was lighting someone else's cigarettes. Thirteen of these patients required hospitalization for treatment. The average cost of each hospitalization was $8055. Four patients did not survive. Their deaths were directly correlated with the extent of the injuries.[53]

Low-Tech Prevention

A major factor in fire prevention is to have a functional smoke alarm in the home. Having smoke alarms and properly educating those most at risk provides the best injury prevention. The Centers for Disease Control and Prevention (CDC) has programs that distribute smoke alarms. A system that does not require an annual battery change is most effective.[54] Properly installing and maintaining a smoke detector can double the chance of survival since they provide early warning. Three-fifths of deaths from residential fires could be prevented annually if people had fire alarms in their homes.[47] The key factors to remember when using a detector are to install one near the bedroom and to install one on each floor. Installation must not be in corners or other areas of dead air space. Batteries should be tested monthly and changed twice a year. If mobility is limited and a person is unable to reach their fire alarm safely to test it, a dowel rod or aluminum rod are both lightweight devices that can be used to reach the battery test button.[55]

It is also important to have an escape route plan and to practice it. While many people have a route planned, without practice a person will be unable to ensure they are physically capable of managing the escape, especially if the person uses a walker or a wheelchair. The person also must ensure that windows or other means of exit are not blocked or painted shut. Elevators should never be used during fires, and residents should try to close doors behind them as they go. A person should also have a backup escape route planned in case this is needed. Another way to ensure quick escape and avoid injury is to have three main items by the bed, including eyeglasses (if used), a phone (cordless or cellular), and a whistle. The eyeglasses will aid vision during escape. The phone is necessary to call for help *once safely outside or if having difficulty during escape.* The whistle serves to both warn others and provide a way for rescue workers or others to locate you in case the person has difficulty escaping the home. It is also a good idea to notify friends and family, building managers, or the fire department if an older resident has an impairment that would make escape difficult.[56]

Another way to prevent injury from fire is to conduct an audit of all extension cords and wires throughout the house to make sure that there are no exposed wires. UL-approved units that have built-in circuit breakers are also better to use than simple extension cords when a person needs to plug in an extra device. Clutter should also be removed around outlets, heaters, smoking materials, and the stove.[47] If a fireplace is used often, the chimney should be cleaned after using two cords of wood.[20]

Smoking materials must be monitored closely. Cigarettes and pipes should never be left unattended. Ashtrays should have wide lips to prevent the cigarettes or cigars from rolling out of the ashtray. This will also prevent ashes from blowing out of the ashtray. Never place ashtrays on arms of furniture because they can be easily toppled.[56] Properly disposing of smoking materials is also important. These should be disposed of in a metal waste container or in the toilet. Smoking materials can also be set in water overnight and then disposed of in a nonmetal waste container if this is the only option.[56]

Attending to the stove and oven while cooking also decreases likelihood of a kitchen fire. Items in an oven should be checked every 15 minutes. The type of clothing worn while cooking is also important. For example, a person should not wear dangling sleeves because they could catch on a pan, causing a burn; also, the sleeves could catch on fire. Careful placement of shelves and curtains is also necessary in the kitchen to avoid the chance of these items catching fire. If some type of window treatment is necessary near a stove, the best choices are Venetian blinds or mini blinds.[20]

High-Tech Prevention   Technology for new, more precise fire alarms is available. There are three main types of fire alarms: photoelectric, ionization, and thermal. Photoelectric detectors best identify slow, smoldering fires. Ionization detectors best react to gases and fast-flaming fires. Thermal detectors detect fires through heat. Newer detectors available on the market incorporate all three of these elements with other advantages well. These other advances include the ability to reduce false alarms through environmental compensations such as adjusting for humidity, air pressure and velocity, temperature, and dirt. These devices can also track their own alarm history, number and type of internal trouble, date manufactured, and date cleaned. These devices will increase in reliability and cost-efficiency while being a discrete element of the home.[57]

Other fire detector technology available includes fire alarms for people with hearing impairments. These detectors utilize strobe lights as a means of alert to a fire or smoke rather than an auditory alarm.

10.5   POISONING

Poisons can be solid, liquid, or gas. Examples of solid poisons (other than improper use of medications) include fertilizers and powdered household cleaning products. Plants are also potential solid poisons. Liquid poisons include items like liquid household cleaning products, lighter fluid, or sprays like paint or aerosol products. Gas poisons are usually invisible and include carbon monoxide or radon that come from sources such as automobiles, heaters, furnaces, or old stoves.[58]

U.S. poison control centers handle and average of one poison exposure every 15 seconds. In 2000, these centers reported approximately 2.2 million poison exposures, with more than 90% of these exposures occurring at home.[59] Approximately 475,000 of these poison exposures resulted in treatment at a healthcare facility with 100,000 resulting in hospitilization.[59] In 2000, 920 poisoning deaths were reported to poison control centers; 19,741 poisoning deaths were reported to national vital statistics in 1999.[59] The most common poisoning incidents in adults were from pain relievers, sedatives, cleaning substances, antidepressants, and bites/stings.[59]

Prevention Strategies   There are several ways to decrease the risks of poisoning. Many of these involve proper storage and labeling, preferably in a locked cabinet. All potential poisons should be kept in their original container. Former food containers should never be used to store chemicals, and sniffing containers to determine the contents should never occur. These substances should not be kept near food.

Because poisonous gas may be created when mixing chemicals, household products should not be combined. Directions and cautions on labels of poisons should always be read and followed carefully. Special attention should also be paid to expiration dates and should be discarded according to the label at the appropriate time.[60]

Taking some basic personal precautions can also decrease poisoning risk. When chemicals and other household products are used indoors, windows should be open and fans used to ensure proper ventilation. When using spray chemicals, users also need to make sure the nozzle is not directed at their own face or other people. Protective clothing (gloves, long pants, long sleeves, socks, shoes) should also be worn to avoid contact between the chemicals and the skin.[59]

A physician or poison control center should be notified immediately should an accidental exposure to household or chemical items occur. If a person has collapsed or is not breathing, call 911. The caller should (1) remain calm, (2) have the name of the product nearby (and its ingredients if possible), (3) know the person's age and be able to approximate their weight, (4) know the phone number they are calling from, and (5) follow the directions given to them by the emergency operator.[60-62]

Carbon Monoxide Poisoning

In the United States, most fatalities from unintentional poisonings are due to carbon monoxide exposures. These poisonings are more frequent in the winter months due to increased use of heating systems.[63] Symptoms of carbon monoxide exposure include headaches, dizziness, fatigue, irregular breathing, and sleepiness. If exposure continues, these feelings can extend to feeling nausea, vomiting, and heart palpitations. If these symptoms dissipate after a person goes outside but then they return upon home re-entry, then the person may have carbon monoxide poisoning.[64] If the levels of carbon monoxide are high and a person is exposed for a prolonged period of time, then he or she could become unconscious or could die.[64]

Carbon monoxide is an odorless gas and cannot be detected by humans. Burning any fuel produces carbon monoxide. Therefore, any fuel-burning appliance in a home is a potential carbon monoxide source. When appliances are kept in good working condition, they produce little carbon monoxide. Improperly operating appliances can produce fatal carbon monoxide concentrations in your home. Likewise, using charcoal indoors or running a car in a garage can cause carbon monoxide poisoning.[64] Sources of carbon monoxide include, but are not limited to, automobiles in a closed garage, charcoal grills, fireplaces, furnaces, ranges, room heaters, and water heaters.[64]

Carbon Monoxide Detection When a fire develops slowly, carbon monoxide may be in the atmosphere long before any other means of detection. Today multisensor devices (smoke and carbon monoxide detectors combined) are available. Carbon monoxide detectors can provide a warning of a fire in such areas as bathrooms or other places where steam could interfere with other means of fire detection and produce false alarms (i.e., thermal detection systems). Carbon monoxide detectors also work well for fire detection in dusty areas (dust can simulate smoky conditions in regular fire alarms). Another good place for a carbon monoxide detector is outside storage areas or other enclosed areas where the carbon monoxide may be detected before fire or smoke spreads outside the enclosed space.[65]

Carbon monoxide detectors are important for homes with fossil fuel appliances such as natural gas furnaces, natural gas water heaters, wood burning stoves, fireplace inserts, or fuel oil furnaces. It is suggested that two be placed in the home: one at the highest level in the home (e.g., top of the stairs or the hallway near the bedroom areas) and one near the appliance itself. Carbon monoxide detectors may be purchased at most hardware and department stores.[66]

Presence of potential carbon monoxide hazards is both visible and invisible to the average consumer. Visible signs of a carbon monoxide hazard include: (1) rusting or streaking on a vent or chimney, (2) a loose or missing furnace panel, (3) sooting, (4) loose or disconnected vent or chimney connections, (5) debris or soot falling from the chimney, fireplace, or appliances, (6) loose masonry on the chimney, and (7) moisture inside of windows. Nonvisible signs that require trained service technicians for identification are: (1) internal appliance damage or malfunctioning components, (2) improper burner adjustment, and (3) hidden blockages or damage in the chimney. Only trained technicians should attempt to fix these problems.[66]

Prevention Strategies Several strategies can be employed to prevent carbon monoxide poisoning. One is ensuring proper installation of appliances using professional installation. Once installed, manufacturer's directions should be followed for safer operation. Appliance operation malfunctions can be observed through (1) decreasing hot water supply, (2) a furnace running constantly or being unable to heat the house, (3) sooting, and (4) unfamiliar burning odors.[66]

To avoid carbon monoxide poisoning, charcoal or gasoline-powered engines should never be used in enclosed, confined spaces like garages, tents, or rooms with poor ventilation.[64] In addition, carbon monoxide detectors should be placed in the house, especially near bedrooms. All chimneys, vents, and any other part of a heating system in the home should be checked annually for improper connections, rust, or other stains. A trained professional should complete any servicing required. Additionally, any fuel burning appliances other than those listed previously should be installed by a professional and inspected annually.[67]

Food Poisoning

Food also has the potential to cause injury. This can occur through either someone receiving a food that they have a reaction or an allergy to or a food that is served at the wrong consistency or texture. Food poisoning can occur when food is stored or prepared in a way that makes elements in the food unsafe. Refrigerators should be set at 41°F or lower to prevent multiplication of bacteria. Freezing at 0°F stops bacterial growth but will not kill all existing bacteria.[68]

Leftovers can be a source of poisoning. Leftovers, especially if hot, should be refrigerated immediately. If left out for more than 2 hours, the food should be thrown away since it could be contaminated. Leftovers should also always be dated and should not be eaten after more than 3–5 days. If the safety of the contents of the leftovers is questionable, they should be thrown out. Even taste testing a small amount of a questionable item can make a person very sick.[68]

Proper food preparation is also essential to prevent poisoning. First and foremost, hands should be washed with soap and hot water for at least 20 seconds to prevent the spread of bacteria both before and after food preparation. This is especially important when handling raw meats, poultry, and fish. Extra precautions, such as wearing rubber or plastic gloves, should be taken if a person has cuts or other forms of infection on their hands. Gloved hands should also be washed since they come in direct contact with the food and the preparer only needs to wash the gloves rather than the gloves and the hands.[68]

Raw meat should be thawed in the refrigerator or the microwave and never out on the counter. If items are thawed on the counter, they are being thawed at room temperature, which is ideal for bacterial growth and makes the food dangerous to consume. When using the microwave, it is important to follow the directions on the package. Food experts suggest leaving about two inches between the food and the inside of the microwave to ensure heat circulation. If food is thawed in the microwave, it should be cooked immediately. Raw meat and poultry should never touch other foods during the preparation process.[68] Another option when thawing meat is to put the meat in a water-tight plastic bag and submerge it in cold water. When using this technique, the water should be changed every 30 minutes to keep the food cold, thereby slowing bacterial growth that could be taking place in the outer thawed portions of the meat while waiting for the inner portions to thaw.[68]

Precautions also need to be taken to ensure proper cooking of meat. Hamburgers should be cooked until they no longer have a red center and the juices run clear. To be safe, cooked meat should be tested with a meat thermometer. Foodborne illnesses can be prevented when the internal temperature of cooked meats is at least 160°F.

Preventative measures should be taken when microwaving food as well. Directions, including standing time, should be followed to make sure the food is safe to eat. When a microwave cooks food, it creates heat pockets in the food, but allowing the food to stand in the microwave when it is finished allows the heat to spread throughout the food.[68]

Special attention should also be paid to food that is made with eggs. Shell eggs can have a bacterium called *Salmonella enteritidis*. By cooking eggs at 140°F, this bacterium can be killed. However, consumers should be wary of homemade foods that contain raw eggs, such as cookie dough or homemade ice cream. Commercial products made with pasteurized eggs do not pose this problem. Pasteurized eggs have been heated sufficiently to kill bacteria and may also contain an acidifying agent that kills bacteria. Salmonella poisoning from products like commercial preparations of cookie dough is unlikely. Using pasteurized eggs for homemade goods instead of raw eggs will also help prevent salmonella poisoning. These eggs are usually available in the dairy section of the grocery store.[68]

Food poisoning can also be decreased when proper cleaning procedures are followed in the kitchen. If dishes must be washed by hand, they should be washed within 2 hours of their use. If left sitting for long periods of time, the food and water in the dishes in the sink provide "food" for bacteria to feed on, and they will multiply.[68] The rest of the kitchen also needs to be properly sanitized on a regular basis. Counters, sink drains, and disposals should be cleaned with either bleach solutions (1 teaspoon bleach per 1 quart water) or commercial kitchen cleaning agents. Soap and hot water work as well, but are not as good at killing all strains of bacteria. Using just water will remove dirt but will not kill bacteria. Wet dishcloths and sponges are also places that harbor bacteria and should be cleaned and changed on a regular basis.[68]

Technology to Prevent Food Poisoning   The University of Florida has developed a prototype microwave oven for the Gator-Tech Smart House. It reads RFID tags on a food product, automatically sets up the correct cooking protocol, and speaks to the user about the food product. When this device is commercialized, it could identify foods with ingredients to which the user has allergies and then alert the user. Proper cooking would ensure that the user does not consume undercooked food. While still in prototype stage, high-tech devices such as this will be available in the future.

Basic Safety Prevention Programs   The Florida Injury Prevention Program for Seniors (FLIPS) is a good example of a consumer education program. It includes modules dealing with fall prevention, fire safety, and poison, food, and medication safety, with each module including an instructor's guide, learning objectives, pre-test, post-test, answer keys, educational strategies, appendix of references, resources, handouts, and activities to be provided to clients seeking education in these areas. FLIPS also distributes brochures statewide which focus on similar topics as previously stated.[69]

10.6   NUTRITIONAL HEALTH

Nutritional Needs for People Over Age 65   As people age, caloric needs are reduced, but the need for protein, vitamins, and minerals is the same or even higher. Chronic conditions have the potential to influence diet and/or nutritional status. A doctor, dietician, and/or pharmacist should be consulted to ensure that nutritional issues from chronic illness are addressed effectively.[70]

Use of Alcohol   Use of alcohol is not recommended. Alcohol is high in calories and takes nutrients away from a healthy diet. Use of alcohol can also potentially damage vital organs, including the brain, heart, and liver. Memory impairment from alcohol can further affect nutritional status by causing a person to miss a meal or a dose of medication. Furthermore, alcohol should not be mixed with medicine. Safe consumption of alcohol for people over 65 is no more than two drinks per day for men and no more than one drink per day for women (this depends on medical status and personal factors).[70]

Monitoring Weight Changes   Monitoring weight is vital to ensure a healthy lifestyle. If significant weight changes are noted, a doctor should be consulted. The doctor can suggest safe ways to stabilize weight. Avoiding "fad" diets is also important because these diets often may not meet nutritional needs or be safe for those with certain conditions. Lifestyle changes with suggestions from health professionals are preferable to drastic changes.[70] Local Area Agencies on Aging can also provide tips to monitor weight changes and provide tips for a healthy lifestyle. Smart houses that monitor a person's weight and offer guidance on diet will assist in maintaining a healthy weight.

Meal Planning and Preparation Tips The inability to eat large meals is a common issue for many elders. One way to remedy this is to eat six small meals rather than three large meals. Frozen dinners or a restaurant salad bar are also options if eating a larger meal does not suit. Remembering to eat may also be a problem. In this case, an alarm can be set as a reminder.

If meal preparation is difficult, many options exist. One is to keep ready-to-eat foods available such as fruit, yogurt, cheese, crackers, peanut butter, whole wheat bread, hearty soups, and milk. Another option is to add medical nutritional products to foods for extra nutrition. Cooking large quantities of food ahead of time and freezing in serving-sized portions can also help. There are also many mixes available where only water needs to be added before eating, cooking, or baking. Most food can also be prepared in a microwave, making meal preparation easier and faster.

Meals on wheels or home health services are other options to ensure that a good meal is received. Local Area Agencies on Aging can help locate these programs. If a person does not like eating alone, several senior citizens' centers have meal programs that also provide the opportunity to socialize while eating.

Shopping Tips When shopping, reading labels is especially important to ensure that what is bought meets nutritional needs. A nutritious diet should be low in fat and high in calcium and should include vegetables. When reading labels, salt, fat, and sugar content should be considered due to food restrictions that often involve these ingredients. In the future, we may see food with RF ID labels that could be used with readers that speak to shoppers about the nutritional value of the product.

10.7 CONCLUSION

Preventing injuries and promoting health through education and technology can have great impact on the chances of a person maintaining their independence in the home for a longer period of time. Technologies and education can ease the stresses of older age and caregiver burden when applied appropriately. These tools also have the potential to reduce health-care costs. Through continued exploration into these areas, health promotion, independence, and quality of life can be enhanced.

REFERENCES

1. National Center for Injury Prevention and Control. (2001). *Injury Fact Book 2001–2002*. Atlanta, GA: Centers for Disease Control and Prevention.

2. Binder, S. (2002). Injuries among older adults; the challenge of optimizing safety and minimizing unintended consequences. *Injury Prevention* **8**(4), iv2–iv4.

3. Shinoda-Tagawa, T., and Clark, D. E. (2003). Trends in hospitalization after injury; older women are displacing young men. *Injury Prevention* **9**(3), 214–219.

4. European Commission DG5 (1996). Proposal for adopting a programme of community action on injury prevention in the context of the framework for action in the field of public health. Luxembourg.

5. Sixsmith, A., Hollock, S., Courtney, P., and Garner, P. (2004). SIMBAD: Smart inactivity monitor using array based detectors. Retrieved September 8, 2004 from http://www.lancs.ac.uk/fss/ihr/hrdn/2004conferencepresentations/andrew%20sixsmith/simbad_presentation.ppt.

6. Gawryszewski, V. P., de Mello Jorge, M. H., and Koizumi, M. S. (2004). Injury among the elderly: The challenge to integrate preventive activities in public and individual levels. *Revista da Associacas Medica Brasileira*, **50**(1), 97–103.

7. Doughty, K., Lewis, R., and McIntosh, A. (2000). The design of a practical and reliable fall detector for community and institutional telecare. *Journal of Telemedicine and Telecare* **6** (Suppl 1).

8. Peek-Asa, C., Zwerling, C. (2003). Role of environmental interventions in injury control and prevention. *American Journal of Epidemiology*, **158**(3), 77–89.

9. Brennan, M., Horowitz, A., and Su, Y. (2003). Sensory impairment and risk of falling among older adults: The special case of dual impairment of vision and Hearing. International Conference on Aging, Disability, and Independence. Washington, D.C.

10. Stevens, J. A. (2003). Falls among older adults: public health impact and prevention strategies. *Generations* **26**(4), 7–14.

11. American Geriatrics Society. (2001). Guideline for the prevention of falls in older persons. *Journal of the American Geriatric Society*, **49**, 664–672.

12. Peel, N. M., Kassulke, D. J., and McClure, R. J. (2002). Population based study of hospitalized fall related injuries in older people. *Injury Prevention* **8**(4), 280–283.

13. Tinetti, M. E., Doucette, J., Claus, E., and Marottoli, R. A. (1995). Risk factors fro serious injury during falls by older persons in the community. *Journal of the American Geriatric Society* **43**, 1214–1221.

14. Edelberg, J. (2001). Falls and function: How to prevent falls and injuries in patients with impaired mobility. *Geriatrics* **56**(3), 41–45.

15. Little, C. D., and Batson, G. (2003). Reaching patterns, anthropomorphic measurements and falls among older populations: a pilot study. International Conference on Aging, Disability, and Independence. Washington, D.C.

16. Forsen, L., Sogaard, A. J., Sandvig, S., Schuller, A., Roed, U., and Arstad, C. (2004). Risk of hip fracture in protected and unprotected falls in nursing homes in Norway. *Injury Prevention* **10**(1), 16–20.

17. Cryer, C. Knox, A. Martin, D., and Barlow, J. (2002). Hip protector compliance among older people living in residential care homes. *Injury Prevention* **8**(3), 202–206.

18. Win Health, Ltd. (n.d.). *HipSavers Hip Protectors.* Retrieved August 25, 2004, from http://www.winhealth.co.uk/HipSavers.htm

19. Wolfe, R. R., Jordan, D., and Wolfe, M. (2004). The WalkAbout: A new solution for falls in the elderly and disabled. International Conference on Aging, Disability, and Independence. Washington, D.C.

20. New York State Office for the Aging. (n.d.). Home safety tips. Retrieved September, 8, 2004, from http://agingwell.state.ny.us/safety/articles/tip.htm.

21. Nakahara, A. K., Jaffe, D. L., and Sabelman, E. E. (n.d.). Development of a second generation wearable accelerometric motion analysis system. Retrieved September 8, 2004, from Stanford University Web site: http://guide.stanford.edu/2ndVA/nakahara.pdf

22. Virginia Tech Department of Electrical and Computer Engineering (2004, June 8). When style and comfort are not enough. Retrieved August 25, 2004, from Virginia Tech Department of Electrical and Computer Engineering Web site: http://www.ecpe.vt.edu/news/ar04/hokie.html

23. Breen, T. (1992). Community alarms systems. In Dibner, A. S., *Personal Response Systems: An International Report of a New Home Care Service*, ed. New York: Haworth.

24. Johnston, B. et al., (2000). Outcomes of the Kaiser Permente tele-home health research project. *Archives of Family Medicine,* **9**, 40–45.
25. Sixsmith, A. J. (2000). An evaluation of an intelligent home monitoring system. *Journal of Telemedicine and Telecare* **6**, 63–72.
26. Porteus, J., and Brownsell, S. (2000). *Using Telecare: Exploring Technologies for Independent Living for Older People.* The Housing Corporation and Anchor Trust: Kidlinton, Oxon.
27. Wilson, L. S., et al. (2000). Communication: Building the hospital without walls—A CSIRO home telcare initiative. *Telemedicine Journal and e-Health* **6**(2), 275–281.
28. Wilson, L., (2001). The caring computer: the role of informatics and telecommunication technologies in aged care. *Australasian Journal on Ageing* **20**(4), 164–165.
29. Booth, B. (1994). Management of drug errors. *Nursing Times* **90**(15), 27–30.
30. Skarupski, K. A., Mrvos, R., and Krenzelok, E. P. (2004). A profile of calls to a poison information center regarding older adults. *Journal on Aging Health* **16**(2), 228–247.
31. Gerbino, P. P. (1985). Considerations in prescribing for the elderly. University of Pennsylvania *Center for the Study of Aging Newsletter* **7**(1), 5.
32. Bennett, W. I. (1987, December 13). Monitoring drugs for the aged. *The New York Times Magazine: Body and Mind,* 73–74.
33. Health Statistics on Older Persons United States, 1986: Analytical and Epidemiological Studies Series 3, No. 25, DHHS Publication No. (PHS) 87–1409. Hyattsville, MD: U.S. Department of Health and Human Services, National Center for Health Statistics, U.S. Government Printing Office, Washington, D.C. June 1987.
34. Salerno, E. (1986). Psychopharmacology and the Elderly. *Topics in Geriatric Rehabilitation,* **1**(2), 35–44.
35. Smith, F., Francis, S. A., Gray, N., Denham, M., and Graffy, J. (2003). A multi-centre survey among informal careers who manage medication for older care recipients: Problems experienced and development of services. *Health Soc Care Community* **11**(2), 138–145.
36. Lewis, S. C. (1989). *Elder Care in Occupational Therapy.* Thorofare, NJ: Slack.
37. Finley, T. (1983). Food interaction with drugs. *Generations* **6**(6), 51–54.
38. Furukawa, C., and Shomaker, D. (1982). Community *Health Services for the Aged.* Rockville, MD: Aspen Systems Corp.
39. Simonson, W. (1983). Methods to insure proper medication use by older adults. *Generations* **6**(6), 42–45.
40. New York State Office for the Aging. (n.d.). Using your medications wisely. Retrieved September 8, 2004, from http://agingwell.state.ny.us/pharmacy/articles/media01.htm
41. Davis, L. J. (1986). Nutrition and pharmacy. In: *The Role of Occupational Therapy with the Elderly,* Davis, L. J., Kirkland, M., eds. Rockville, MD: The American Occupational Therapy Association, Inc., pp. 79–91.
42. Centers for Disease Control and Prevention (CDC) (1986). Perspectives in Disease Prevention and Health Promotion National Poison Prevention Week: 25th Anniversary Observance. MMWR **35**(10), 149–152.
43. Justiss, Mann, Helal, Dasler, and Richardson (2003, June). Partnerships with industry: Development of an intelligent home automation system. RESNA 26th International Conference, Atlanta, GA.
44. American Society of Health Systems Pharmacists. (2000). Snapshot of medication use in the U.S. ASHP Research Report, December 2000.
45. Cameron, K. A., and Allsworth, J. (2003, December). Assessing medication effects to prevent functional decline. International Conference on Aging, Disability, and Independence. Washington, D.C.
46. Cornell University, Joan and Sanford I. Weill Medical College. (n.d.). The fire risk series: Fire risks for older adults. Retrieved August, 11, 2004, from Cornell University, Gerontologic Environmental Modification (GEM) Web site: http://www.cornellaging.com/gem/injury_fire_risk.html
47. Worth, A. (n.d.) Fire alarm: seniors face high death rate to blazes. *Good Age Newspaper.* Amherst H. Wilder Foundation. Retrieved August 11, 2004, from http://www.wilder.org/goodage/Features/fire1011.html
48. Hall J. R. (1998b). The US fire problem overview report—leading causes and other patterns and trends. Quincy, MA: NFPA publications.

49. Stiles, N. J., Bratcher, D., Ramsbottom-Lucier, M., and Hunter, G. (2001). Evaluating fire safety in older persons through home visits. *Journal of the Kentucky Medical Association* **99**(3), 105–110.

50. Brigham, J. R., and McLoughlin, E. (1996). Burn incidence and medical care use in the United States: Estimates, trends and data sources. *Journal of Burn Care and Rehabilitation* **17**, 95–107.

51. National Fire Protection Association. (1986). Firepower video [on-line]. Available: http://www.nfpa.org.

52. Hall, J. R. (1998a). *Patterns of fire casualties in home fires by age and sex, 1991–1995.* Quincy, MA: NFPA publications.

53. Robb, B. W., Hungness, E. S., Hershko, D. D., Warden, G. D., and Kagan, R. J. (2003). Home oxygen therapy: Adjunct or risk factor? *Journal of Burn Care Rehabilitation*, **24**(6), 403–406.

54. Centers for Disease Control and Prevention, Office of the Director. (2000). CDC performance plan: Revised final FY 1999 performance plan and FY 2000 performance plan. Retrieved September 8, 2004, from http://www.cdc.gov/od/perfplan/2000/2000xfire.htm

55. Worth, A. (n.d.) Fire alarm: Seniors face high death rate to blazes. *Good Age Newspaper.* Amherst H. Wilder Foundation. Retrieved August 11, 2004, from http://www.wilder.org/goodage/Features/fire1011.html

56. Cornell University, Joan, and Sanford I. Weill Medical College. (n.d.). Fire safety tips for seniors. Retrieved August, 11, 2004, from Cornell University, Gerontologic Environmental Modification (GEM) Web site: http://www.cornellaging.org/gem/injury_fir_tips.html

57. Mezenberg, T. (1999). Smoke detection: getting the big picture. Retrieved on August 25, 2004, from the Canadian Fire Alarm Association Website: http://www.cfaa.ca/journal-99-december-2.html

58. New York State, Office for the Aging. (n.d.) Poison prevention tips. Retrieved September 8, 2004, from http://agingwell.state.ny.us/safety/articles/poison_prevention.htm

59. Litovitz, T. L., Lein-Schwartz, W., White, S., Cobaugh, D., Youniss, J., Omslaer, J., Drab, A., and Benson, B. (2001). Annual Report of the American Association of Posion Control Centers Toxic Exposures Surveillance System. *American Journal of Emergency Medicine* **19**(5): 337–396.

60. National Center for Injury Prevention and Control. (n.d.) Poisoning prevention: Prevention tips. Retrieved September 8, 2004, from http://www.cdc.gov/ncipc/factsheets/poisonprevention.htm

61. Centers for Disease Control and Prevention (CDC) (1986). Perspectives in Disease Prevention and Health Promotion National Poison Prevention Week: 25th Anniversary Observance. *MMWR* **35**(10): 149–152.

62. Centers for Disease Control and Prevention (CDC) (1982). Persectives in Disease Prevention and Health Promotion Carbon Monoxide Intoxication—A Preventable Environmental Health hazard. *MMWR* **31**(39), 529–531.

63. Centers for Disease Control and Prevention (CDC) (1999). Carbon monoxide poisoning deaths associated with camping—Georgia, March 1999. *MMWR* **48**(32), 705–706.

64. Centers for Disease Control and Prevention (CDC) (1982). Perspectives in disease prevention and health promotion carbon monoxide intoxication—A preventable environmental health hazard. *MMWR* **31**(39), 529–531.

65. British Fire Protection Systems Association. (2001). BFPSA application guidelines for carbon monoxide (CO) fire detectors. Retrieved August 25, 2004, from http://www.bfpsa.org.wk/html/publ_fra.htm

66. New York State, Office for the Aging (n.d.). The "senseless" killer. Retrieved September 8, 2004, from http://agingwell.state.ny.us/safety/articles.sense.htm

67. Centers for Disease Control and Prevention (CDC) (1995). Unintentional carbon monoxide poisonings in residential settings—Connecticut, November 1993–March 1994. *MMWR* **44**(41), 765–767.

68. U.S. Food and Drug Administration. (2003). Can your kitchen pass the safety test? Retrieved on August 8, 2004 from www.cfsan.fda.gov/~dms/fdkitchn.html

69. Elfenbein, P., and Lehman, J. (2003, December). Florida injury prevention program for seniors (FLIPS). International Conference on Aging, Disability, and Independence. Washington, D.C.

70. New York State Office for the Aging. (n.d.). Strong and healthy: Your guide for better nutritional health. Retrieved September 8, 2004, from http://agingwell.state.ny.us/eatwell/strong.htm

INDEX

A

Activities of daily living, 2
Acoustic analysis, 355
AdvantAge Initiative, the, 340
Aerotel, 176, 198
  heart monitor, 176, 198
  medical parameters monitoring devices
    blood pressure monitor, 191, 198
    glucometer, 191
    spirometer, 191
Age in Place,
  preference for, 307
  enhance, approaches to, 316–317
Aging, 2
  vision, 285–286, 289, 291, 303
  medical conditions, 286
  cognition, 294
  Older Americans Act (OAA), 295
AgrAbility, 340
AIBO, 85–86, 101
Ambient intelligence, 47
AMD Telemedicine, Inc., 183, 197, 200
  dermascope, 183, 200
  video phone, 197, 200
American's with Disabilities Act (ADA),
    295, 297–298
ASIMO, 89–90, 101
Assistive listening devices (ALDs)
  assistive listening system (ALS),
    130–131
    FM, 130
    infrared (IR), 131
    inductive loop, 131
    personal, 130
Assistive technology
  high-tech
  for cognitive impairment, 147–155
  for hearing impairment, 125–134

  for mobility and movement impairments,
    134–147
  for vision impairment, 111–125
  others, 153–155
Automatic teller machines, 154
Automobile, 247, 248
  crashes, 250–276
  safety equipment, 254, 273
  design, 263, 272–273

B

Banryu, 90, 101
Bathing products, 19
Biotronik Home Monitoring System, 172,
    200
  CardioMessenger, 172, 200
BLEEX, 71, 79–80, 101
Bluetooth, 45, 167
  ECG Shirt, 166
Brunnel Active Balance Saddle, 98–99, 101

C

Cable modems, 165
Canes, 222–223
Carbon monoxide, 364–365. *See also*
    Poisoning
  detection, 364–65
  poisoning, 364
  poisoning prevention, 365
Cardea, 92, 101
Cardiobeat
  Cardiolert, 174–175, 200
Cardiocom, 179, 192
  Carestar, 192, 200
  TeleScale, 179, 200
CardioNet
  Mobile Cardiac Outpatient Telemetry
    (MCOT), 173, 200

Cardionics, 177–178, 200
 SimulScope, 177–178, 200
Care-O-bot, 92–94, 101
Caregiver Adaptation to Reduce
  Environmental Stress (CARES),
  309
Caregiver issues, 202–204
 AlzOnline.net, 202–203
 Assisting Carers using Telematics
  Intervention to meet Older Person's
  Needs (ACTION), 203
 Resources to Enhance Alzheimer's
  Caregiver Health for Telephone-
  Linked Care (REACH for TLC),
  202
Carewatch, 55
Chronic Obstructive Pulmonary Disease
  (COPD), 180
Closed circuit television (CCTV), see
  Electronic reading aids
Cognitive Prostheses, 147–148, see also
  Memory; device for
Communication, mobile phone, 34
Conferences, 24–27
Congestive Heart Failure, 170–180
 MindMy Heart, 180
 Telescale, 179, 200
Consumer
 assessment study, 16
 communication, 25–26
 participation, 24
 perspective, 13, 16, 23
 roles, 25
Controls on electronic devices, 20
Cooking memory aid, 54
CUSTODIAN, 56

D
Daihen Corp. Patient Transfer System, 95,
  101
DARPA grand challenge, 71
Dermatology, 180–182
Devices
 and Arthritis, 235–237
 low-technology, 221–237
  for bathing, 229
  for hearing, 233–235
  and mobility impairment, 221–226
  and self-care, 226–230
  types, 229

 for vision, 231–233
 and Stroke, 237
Digital ID, 47
Digital Subscriber Lines (DSL), 165
Disability, 2
Disability Discrimination ACT (DDA), 295,
  see also legislation
Driver(s)
 Rehabilitation programs, 262, 265–267
 Number of, 248
 Caregivers, 249, 255
Driving
 ability and health, 250–254, 285
 alternatives, 248, 254, 255, 256–258
 assessment/screening, 259–262, 266
 cessation, 248, 253, 254, 255–256,
  285–286, 289
 conceptual framework, 249–50
 crashes, 285
 disability, 286
 disparity, 286
 educational programs, 262, 263–265
 interventions, 259, 262–269
 self-restriction, 262–263
 simulators 262, 267–268
 technology, 258, 259, 262, 268–72,
  273–27
Drugs, see Medications

E
E2Home, 56
Electronic reading aids, 111–114
Electronic travel aids, 117
 Accessible pedestrian signals (APS),
  120–122
 GPS add-on to a PDA, 119
 LaserCane, 118
 Miniguide, 118
Environmental interventions, 2
Environmental interventions in long-term
  care facilities
 behaviors, combative, 344
 color, 343
 continence, 344
 corridors, 342–343
 cueing, 343
 dinning environment, 345
 dressing, 344
 home-like atmosphere, creating a, 344
 outdoor spaces, locating, 343

orientation, 342
rummaging and hoarding, 344
signage, 343
wandering, 344
Emergency Medical Services, 189–190
Life Support for Trauma and Transport
(LSTAT), 189–190
Integrated Emergency Medicine
Network, 190
Enhanced Data GSM Environment (EDGE),
167
Environmental modification, 354
Exoskeletons, 79–82

F
Fall(s), 352–357
detection, 354–357
prevention, 353–357
risks, 353
Fire(s), 360–363
alarms, 363
causes of, 361
prevention of, 362–363
risk(s), 360–361
Fatigue, 12

G
General Packet radio Service (GPRS), 167
Global Positioning System (GPS), 47
for preventing wondering, 152–153
for vision impairment, 116, 119–120
transportation 289, 294
Global Systems for mobile Communication
(GSM), 167
Guido, 78, 101

H
HAL-3, 79, 101
Hearing aid(s), 125
implantable hearing devices, 128
auditory brainstem implants (ABIs),
129–130
bone-anchored, 128–129
cochlear implants (CIs), 129
middle ear implants (MEIs), 129
styles of
behind-the-ear (BTE), 126
body-worn (BW), 126
bone-conduction, 127
in-the-ear (ITE), 126

technology, types of
analog programmable, 127
conventional analog, 127
digital programmable, 127–128
HelpMate II, 96, 101
High-technology devices, 23
Hip protectors, 353–354
HIRB, 95, 101
Home (s),
assessment instruments, 328–338
"Peter Pan", 307
single level, 309
Home automation, 33
Home environmental problems
bathroom, 310, 312–313
bedroom, 314
fire and shock, 314
interventions, model for, 316
kitchen, 310–311
other rooms and spaces, 314
outdoor spaces, 314
stairs, 314
Home modification
barriers to implement, 315
benefits, 309
caregiver burden, see Caregiver
Adaptation to Reduce
Environmental Stress (CARES)
common, 308
definition, 308
independence through, strategies to
promote, 308
not undertaken, reasons for, 309
schemes, classification, 308
Home Care, 190–197
AMD Telemedicine, Inc., 195
Aerotel's Medical Parameters Monitoring
devices, 191, 198
Automatic Message Routing System, 197
Cardiocom's Carestar, 192
Consortium for Health Outcomes,
Innovation, and Cost-Effectiveness
Studies (CHOICES), 196–197
I-Trax Health Management Solutions, 194
Low ADL Monitoring Program, 196
QRS Diagnostic, 191–192
TERVA, 195
Well@home Telemanagement System,
193
HRP-2, 91–92, 101

I

iBOT, 82–83, 101
Intelligent telecare systems, 355
Impairment
  cognitive, 231
  vision, 231–233
  hearing, 233
Implants, *see* Hearing aids; implantable
      hearing devices
Incontinence, 17
Independence, 2, 33
Infrared, 168
In-home robot, 99–100, 101
Inkha, 74–75, 101
InMotion, 99, 101
Instrumental activities of daily living, 2
Integrated Services Digital Network
      (ISDN), 167
Intelligent Transportation Systems (ITS),
      289, 294
I-Trax Health Management Solutions, 194
  CarePrime, 194, 199
  Health-e-Coordinator, 194, 199
  I-Talk, 194, 199
  MyFamilyMD, 194, 199
  MyNurseLine, 194, 199

K

KARES II, 85, 101
Koolio, 78–79, 101

L

Legal issues, 204–208
  Center for Telemedicine Law, 205
  Health Insurance Portability and Privacy
      Act (HIPPA), 206–208
  Privacy Enhancement in Data
      Management in e-Health (PRIDEH),
      208
  state licensure, 204–206
Lighting
  importance of, 327
  principles and guidelines, 328
Lighting Research Center, 327
Low-technology devices, 16

M

MADMEN, 70, 101
Medic4All, 174, 201
Medication(s), 357–360

nutritional consequences of use, 358
  side effects, 358
Medication errors, 357–360
  prevention of, 359–360
Medtronic Carelink Network, 173, 201
Memory
  device for 148–152
Microsoft Light Control, 55
Microsoft Vision, 56
MindMy Heart, 180
Mobile phones
  as device for memory, 150
  as personal organizer, 115–117
  smart phone, 117
  text-messaging, 134
Mobility, 247–8, 250, 255, 257–8, 260, 263,
      265, 267, 273, 274, 275, 276
  community, 285–305
  devices, 19, 77–79, 301–303
    pushrim-activated power assist
      wheelchairs (PAPAWs), 141–142
    manual wheelchair add-on, 142–144
  elderly, 285, 289, 291, 297–298,
      303–304
  ifrared, 300
  infrastructure, 299–301, 304
  microwave, 300
  safety, 289, 300–301, 303–304
  walkable communities, 298, 304
  technology, 289, 291–294, 302, 303–304
Multigenerational dwellings, 340

N

NASA, *see* Robots, space
NeCoRo, 87, 101
Needs and barriers, 23
Note taker, *see also* Personal organizers,
      PDAs
  as personal organizer, 115–116
  GPS add-on, 119
Nutritional health, 367–368
  alcohol use, 367
  meal planning and preparation, 368
  shopping tips, 368
  weight monitoring, 367–68

O

Opthamology, 184
Other countries, Home Modification and
      Universal Design in, 326

P
PackBot, 71–72, 101
PAM-AID, 77–78
Paro, 86–87, 101
Patient Care Technologies, Inc., 193, 203
  Well@home Telemanagement System,
    193, 201
PDA, *see also* Personal organizer(s)
  as device for memory, 151
  for visual impairment, 115–117,
  add-on GPS, 119–120
  software
    medicine reminder software, 149–150
    PEAT, 151
Pearl, 92–93, 101
PeolpleBot, 94–95, 101
Personal assistance, 12
Personal Emergency Response Systems
    (PERS), 154
Personal organizer(s), *see also* PDA
  for visual impairment, people with,
    115–117,
  add-on GPS, 119–120
  as device for memory, 150, 151
Philips WWICE, 55
Plain Old Telephone Service (POTS),
    165
Poisoning, 363–367. *See also* Carbon
    monoxide
  food, 365–67
  prevention strategies, 236–64
  technology for prevention, 367
Polypharmacy, 357–360
Power Suit, 81–82, 101
Power wheelchair(s), *see also* Mobility,
    82–84
  control method, 144–145
  features, 145–147
  robotic wheelchair(s), 146–147
Predator, 72

Q
QRIO, 87–89, 101
QRS Diagnostic, 191–193, 201

R
Raptor, 83–84, 101
Reachers, 226
Remote Monitor, Control, and Identify
    Input Suit (REMCIIS), 211

Resources to Enhance Alzheimer's
    Caregivers Health for Telephone
    Linked Care (REACH for TLC),
    202
RFID tags, 367
Risk factors, 352
  extrinsic, 352
  intrinsic, 352
Robo Nurse, 96, 101
Robobear, 98, 101
Roboceptionist, 73–74, 101
Robonaut, 69–70, 101
Robot(s)
  appearance, 102–103
  assistive, 75–100
  definition, 68
  entertainment, *see* Robots, monitoring
  future of, 103–105
  human interaction, 100, 102
  industrial, 68, 75–76
  military, 70–72
  monitoring, 85–100
  neuroprosthetic, 104–105
  office, 73–75
  personal, *see* Robots, assistive
  rescue, 73
  space, 68–70
  surgical, 72–73
Robotics, 67–68
  robotic wheelchair(s), 146–147
RP-6, 96–98, 101

S
Safety prevention programs, 367
Satellite, 167
Self-care
  device for mobility and movement
    impairments
  bathing/showing, 138–139
  food preparation, 135
  house chores, 135–136
  toileting, 137–139
  device for vision impairment 122–125
  color identifier, 124
  money identifier, 125
  talking prescription reader, 123
  voice activated universal remote controls,
    122
Sensor technology, 42, 356
  environmental, 43

passive, 43
fiber optic vibration, 43
kinematic, 43
piezoelectric, 43
Sensory deficits, 352
Smart appliances, 46
Smart card(s), 156
Smart house, 33–65
  commercial ventures, 48
  computer, 43
  construction, 56
  design, 55
  Gator-Tech, 61
  hardware, 44
  sensors, 42–43
  software, 43–44
  wireless technology, 44–45
Spacelabs, 177, 201

T
T-52 Enryu HyperRescueRobot, 73, 101
Tama, 98, 101
Technology wireless, 44
Technology, 1, 42
  basic assistive, 221
  driving, 258, 259, 262, 268–72, 273–27
  funding for assistive, 238–240
  resources for assistive, 240–244
Teddy, 98, 101
Telecardiology, 170–179
  Aerotel, 176
  Ambulatory Blood Pressure Systems,
    177
  Biotronik Home Monitoring System,
    172
  Cardiolert, 174
  CardioNet's Mobile Cardiac Outpatient
    Telemetry (MCOT), 173
  Cardionics, 177
  Medic4All, 174
  Medtronic Carelink Network, 173
  TeleCardio-FBC—Brazil, 178
  Telecare's ProTime Microcoagulation
    System, 176, 200
  Visual Telecommunications Networks,
    Inc., ViTel Net, 175
Telecare's ProTime Microcoagulation
  System, 176, 200
Telecommunication, for hearing impairment
  telephone and mobile phone,

talking on, 131–134
  visual system for, 134
  video, 134
Teledermatology, 181–182
  Apollo telemedicine system, 182
  University of Pennsylvania, 181
Telediabetes, 188–189
  MyDiabetes Team, 188–189
Telehealth
  cardiology, 170–180
  chronic obstructive pulmonary disease,
    180
  components, 163
  congestive heart failure, 180–
  dermatology, 180–182
  diabetes, 188–189
  emergency medical services, 189
  future use of, 211–212
  homecare, 190–197
  legal issues, 204–210
  limitations, 210–211
  radiology, 183
  rehabilitation, 183
  reimbursement, 208–209
  standards, 209–210
  surgery, 187–189
  technology, definition, 161
  technologies, description, 200–203
  transmission methods, 166
Telemedicine
  definition, 161
  Department of Defense, 162
  Department of Health and Human
    Services, 162
  Department of Veterans Affairs, 162
  history, 168–170
  National Aeronautics and Space
    Administration (NASA), 168
  Office for the Advancement of
    Telehealth, 162, 163
  purposes, 161
  Telemedicine and Advanced
    Technologies Research Center, 162
  United States Army Medical Research &
    Materiel Command, 162
  U.S. Department of Agriculture's Rural
    Utility Service, 162, 163
Telepsychiatry, 184–187
  equipment guidelines, 186
  functional outcomes, 186

reliability of, 185
satisfaction with, 186
Telerehabilitation, 183–184
Definition, 183
Virtual reality, 183
Telesurgery, 187–188
Transfer
bed and chair, device for, 140–141
liftchair, 141–142
Transportation, 247, 248, 249, 256, 257,
285–305
access, 289, 296–298, 303
alternative, 285–287, 295, 297–299
Global Positioning System (GPS), 289,
294
legislation, 295–296
options, 286, 296–299, 304
paratransit, 286, 287,
personal, 286
Personal Digital Assistant (PDA),
292–294, 303
preferences, 287
public, 286–287, 289, 292
radio frequency ID, 290, 293
safety, 289, 303
smart technology, 289, 291–294,
303–304
Supplemental Transportation Programs
(STPs), 296–299, 304
technology, 289, 291, 300

U
Unimate, 68
Universal Design
definition, 318
history, 318–319
principles, 319–321
Universal Design guidelines
bathrooms, 324
decks, 326
entrances, 321
garage and carports, 326
hardware, 323
home automation, 323
interior circulation, 322
kitchens, 325
laundry area, 325

light and color, 323
plumbing fixtures controls, 324
storage, 326
switches and controls, 323
vertical circulation, 323
windows, 326
Universal Mobile Telephone System
(UMTS), 167

V
Vehicle
accessibility, 289, 297
buses, 289, 291–292, 301, 303
maintenance, 285
modification, 289, 301, 303
Vibrational analysis, 355
Video, 355
Virtual reality, 183
head mounted display, 184, 213
Visit-ability, 338–340
Visual Telecommunications Networks, Inc.,
175, 201

W
Wakamaru, 90–91, 101
Walkers, 222–223
Walking aids, 354
Wandering,
prevention, device for, 152–153
Washing devices, 19
Wearable Walking Helper, 80–81, 101
Weston, 84, 101
Wheelchairs, 223–226
pushrim-activated power assist
wheelchairs (PAPAWs),
141–142
manual wheelchair add-on, 142–144
Wired connections, 167–168
Wireless
application protocol (WAP), 45
connections, 44–45, 168–170
local area network (LAN), 169
Worn devices, 355
WL-16, 83, 101

X
X10 system, 58